Lady Georgiana Fullerton

Lady-bird

A Tale

Lady Georgiana Fullerton

Lady-bird
A Tale

ISBN/EAN: 9783337074425

Printed in Europe, USA, Canada, Australia, Japan

Cover: Foto ©ninafisch / pixelio.de

More available books at **www.hansebooks.com**

LADY-BIRD.

A Tale.

BY

LADY GEORGIANA FULLERTON,
Author of "Grantley Manor," "Ellen Middleton," &c.

"With caution judge of possibility;
Things thought unlikely, e'en impossible,
Experience often shows us to be true."
                              SHAKESPEARE.

BALTIMORE:
PUBLISHED BY JOHN MURPHY & CO.
No. 182 BALTIMORE STREET.
1868.

Preface.

LADY-BIRD is almost universally conceded to be the best, as it certainly has been the most successful, of Lady Georgiana Fullerton's novels. It does not, perhaps, display as much power as Ellen Middleton; but it is not in any way inferior to Grantley Manor in this point, and far surpasses that work in truthful delineation of character, and especially of the supernatural influence of religion in moulding it. Every prominent person in the work shows its action, and we nowhere find in this work, as in too many works of fiction, any pretended substitute for faith and grace: for in much of our lighter literature the natural is elevated above the supernatural, and a kind of approbation is given to those who seek a pretext for endorsing the indifference of our day,—a day whose great disease is its belief in the unnecessariness of a church as the channel of essential grace to man.

Lady-Bird is the heroine of the tale,—a girl of an unloving, aristocratic father, who married for pride when disappointed in love, and who for his wife and daughter has naught but reserve, coldness, and arbitrary manifestation of power, tempered towards his Spanish wife only by her state of sickness,—for her life was one of suffering. Gertrude Lifford, our Lady-Bird, had grown up in seclusion, her active inquiring mind developed by her own undirected reading, with no companions except Maurice Redmond and

Mary Grey, the child and foster-child of a widow near Lifford Grange, who were allowed to become her playmates in childhood. Accident brings her into society, and Mr. d'Arberg wins her affection; but they are not destined to marry. In this affection,—in its thwarting by her father,—in the train of circumstances that lead to her union with Maurice Redmond,—lies the interest of the volume; and the self-reliance of Gertrude, its fatal effects to her peace, her hour of trial with no consoler—no adviser at hand, are depicted with a sweetness of style, an elevation of sentiment, a beauty of expression, which few of our writers have attained.

In all will be found the most perfect naturalness: nothing is exaggerated, nothing improbable; events as they occur show their effects on the various personages of the tale, making the lesson conveyed to the mind so marked that the most careless reader cannot but be impressed with it. There is a total absence of all that can feed in the young those silly romantic feelings which have been the bane of so many, and tended in the tale to unfit the heroine herself for the stern realities of life.

We thus honestly commend to the reader a tale, which little needed any preface to those who know the earnest piety, the wide benevolence, and singular talent of the noble authoress.

BALTIMORE, April, 1857.

Lady-Bird.

CHAPTER I.

> "Gloom is upon thy silent hearth
> O silent house! . . . .
> Sorrow is in the breezy sound
> Of thy tall beeches whisp'ring round;
> The shadow of long mournful hours
> Hangs dim upon thy early flowers,
> Even in thy sunshine seems to brood
> Something more deep than Solitude."
> Mrs. HEMANS.

> "Come to the woods in whose mossy dells
> A light all made for the poet dwells;
> There is light, there is youth, there is tameless mirth
> Where the streams and the lilies they wear have birth.
> Joyous and free shall your wanderings be
> As the flight of birds o'er the glittering sea.
> Come forth, O ye children of gladness, come,
> Where the violets lie may be now your home—
> Away from the chamber and the sullen hearth
> The young winds are dancing in breezy mirth,
> Their light stems thrill to the wild wood strains.
>   *   *   *   *   *
> Bring the lyre and the wreath and the joyous lay,
> Come forth to the sunshine." . . . .
> Ibid.

THE old manorial residence of Lifford Grange was one of those habitations which have remained in the same family for many centuries, which have been two or three times rebuilt in the course of a thousand years, and each time have retained some portion of the old mansion; the new one, as it was called, being—at the period of which we speak—about as deserving of that appellation as the Pont-Neuf at Paris, which happens to be the oldest of all the bridges that span the Seine. An avenue of yews led up to the house; on each side of these sepulchral-looking trees was a row of fine beeches, whose light foliage contrasted with the hue and mitigated the gloom of the more solemn evergreens. "La parure de l'hiver et le deuil de l'été."

The immediate approach to the house was through a square court equally divided by the carriage-road, on each side of which were two patches of grass, one of them adorned by a sun-dial on which the sun never shone, and the other by the dry basin of a fountain into which four hideous Tritons peeped, as if in the vain hope of discovering water in its recesses. On the other side of the house there were broad gravel walks, and an extensive garden—if anything so flowerless could deserve the name. A river that looked like a canal divided it from the flat extent beyond. Deeply and sullenly flowed this stream, which had not the beauty of clearness although the rank weeds in its bed were easily discerned. There was neither life nor spirit in its rapidity: sullenly and silently it hurried along, as if in haste to exchange the open space it had to traverse for the shade of a dark thicket which lay between the park and the river into which it was about to flow.

The most ardent admirer of old-fashioned places must have owned that there was something melancholy in the aspect of Lifford Grange, with its massive walls, its heavy portals, its projecting windows, all unadorned by the smallest sprig of jessamine, the least invasion of ivy, the slightest familiar touch of daring tendril or aspiring creeper. The interior of the house corresponded with the exterior. It had large drawing-rooms, and furniture which it would have required a giant's strength to move, light-excluding windows and unapproachable fire-places. Heavy red woollen curtains descended to the floor in cumbrous folds. A regiment abreast might have marched up the stair-case, and moderate-sized houses have been built within the bed-rooms. There was a certain kind of grandeur about the old Grange, and none of the usual appendages of such a place were absolutely wanting, but there was a total absence of comfort in its arrangements, and of charm in its aspect both within and without.

The character of the owner seemed stamped upon its walls, and inscribed on its portal. Mr. Lifford's family was as ancient as his house, and his pride as lofty as his rooms. He was the last descendant of a race which had clung to the Catholic church, through the ages of persecution, with a fidelity which had given him an hereditary attachment to a religion, the precepts of which he did not observe, the spirit of which he certainly did not exhibit. He had not enemies, for he kept too much aloof from others to interfere with them, or to be interfered with himself. There was a kind of dignity and smooth coldness about him which repelled without rudeness, and chilled without offending. It would have been equally difficult to affront or to flatter him; his heart (if he had one) was a sealed book which his few associates had never read; none knew if its pages were inscribed with fair or foul characters, or were as blank as the handsome immoveable face that formed, as it were, its title page.

During a journey that he made into Spain soon after coming of age, he had married a Spanish girl of a family as ancient as his own. She was an orphan, and her guardians readily bestowed her hand on the young Englishman; whose quarterings, wealth, and religious profession answered the conditions they deemed indispensable to a union with a daughter of their house. Angustia was her name; on the day of her marriage it sounded in strange contrast with the beauty of her face and the brilliancy of her prospects;—a very few years later, when a pale, suffering, and hopelessly infirm woman took possession of an apartment on the ground-floor at Lifford Grange, from which she never emerged but to take a few turns in a garden-chair on the sunny side of the house, it seemed more in accordance with her destiny.

The first years of her marriage had been spent in Spain, and during that time she had two children, a girl called Gertrude and a boy two years younger. Soon after the birth of this last child, she and her husband came to England; and at about the same period a paralytic stroke deprived her of the use of her limbs, while a complication of diseases reduced her to a state of almost continual suffering, and withdrew her entirely from society. Her husband shut himself up more and more in a proud retirement from the world, unsolaced, as it appeared, in that haughty seclusion by any engrossing pursuit or the performance of any active duties. The only inmate of his house was his uncle, who had been educated in Spain, had there received holy orders, and since his nephew's return to England had inhabited the Grange and fulfilled there the office of domestic chaplain, occasionally assisting the priest of the neigbouring village of Stonehousecleigh. His nature might have originally been cast in the same mould as his nephew's; his manner indeed was rougher and more abrupt— but in his case the rock had been smitten, the rugged bark had been softened, the ice had been melted by that light which never shines in vain on the human heart, by that fire against which no adamant is proof, and which no natural bias can resist. That he *had* a heart no one could have doubted who had witnessed his solicitude, his almost paternal kindness for the pale invalid, who seldom conversed with any one but him, and who had no other comforter or friend.

Her apartment was the least gloomy in the house, but at the same time its aspect was of the gravest character. A few valuable Spanish pictures hung on its walls, a large crucifix in carved ivory stood opposite to her couch, and some books of devotion, with heavy clasps and rich bindings, were always lying within her reach. A bed of mignonette sent its sweet sober smell into this room, where, during the brief hours of winter sunshine, or the long afternoons of summer, wrapped in Indian shawls and propped up by cushions, she would sit at the window, her eyes fixed with an earnest and singular expression on the dull landscape, or the pale northern sky. The illness which had brought her to a premature old age had also slightly impaired her speech and affected her memory, and hence she had not learned to speak English fluently.

This and the continual sufferings she endured had isolated her more and more from her children. She sent for them now and then, and silently pressed them to her heart, or for hours watched them at play on the terraces near her window; but there was little intercourse between them and herself. They bounded by her in all the recklessness of youth and health. They sometimes stopped to kiss her in that half-fond half-impatient manner with which children return caresses which detain them from their sports. She had nothing wherewith to attract them but a love which was almost too timid to show itself. A barrier seemed to rise between her and those impetuous young spirits which were rushing into all the fulness of that life which was decaying within her; but who could count the prayers which rose from that lonely heart for those she scarcely dared to love as other mothers love?—who can tell what mysterious deliverances from danger—what sudden arrests on the border of an abyss—what softenings of the heart when maddened by passion—what strange reactions from evil and aspirations towards heaven—may have been, in after life, the result of those prayers poured forth on a bed of pain by one who hardly counted in her children's existence, and the pressure of whose feeble hand was often the only token she could give them of her love?

Once a day her husband came to see her, and sat by her

for a few minutes. His presence seemed to impart a chill to the very atmosphere. Mrs. Lifford mechanically drew her shawl tighter on her breast during these visits, and her face became paler than at other times. Sealed were the secrets of those two hearts; how little or how much they had cared for each other none of those about them seemed to know, "*rien ne se ressemble comme le néant et la profondeur.*" The smooth surface of that monotonous existence might have covered a volcano, or concealed an abyss.

The children of this marriage were strangely unlike each other. Born under the same roof, growing up amongst the same influences, they early exhibited the most striking dissimilarity of character and of manners. Edgar was a fair and gentle boy, whose placid gaiety no grave faces could subdue, and no dull mode of life affect. Docile and pliable, he readily received every impression, and adopted all the opinions which his father put forward. If Mr. Lifford cared for anything in the world, it was for his son. He talked to him of his ancestors, of his possessions, of the various honours which had been conferred on his family in past times, the alliances they had made, the historical records in which their names were emblazoned, the rank they held in the estimation of all who valued the real nobility of an ancient descent above the paltry distinction of a modern title; and the child's large blue eyes expanded with wonder and admiration at the greatness of all the Liffords that had been, that were now, and that would be hereafter. He felt an innocent surprise at belonging himself to that favoured race, and a sincere compassion for those whose ancestors had not been Crusaders, whose quarterings were defective, and whose genealogy was imperfect. There was truth and goodness in the nature of that child; and if, in his father's teachings, there had been something akin to it—a touch of feeling or a spark of enthusiasm—they might have kindled a noble ambition, and if in some respects visionary, would yet have taught a lesson which has redeemed from contempt many an illusion, and exalted many a delusion. '*Noblesse oblige!*'—that old French motto—would have been the source of generous sentiments, the spur to high achievements; but pride in its coldest and hardest form, and in its most miserable proportions, was learnt as a lesson and adopted as a theory by a mind which it served to narrow, though it did not pervert it.

But there was another mind and another heart of a far

different stamp than that of Edgar, which was impressed, indeed, but never moulded by these teachings. It would have been difficult to determine whether the tacit antagonism which had established itself between Gertrude and her father was the result or the cause of the dislike he seemed to have taken to her. Was it because he did not love the foreign-looking girl whose beauty might have gratified the most fastidious paternal vanity, that she never, from her earliest childhood, adopted his views, imbibed his prejudices, or seemed impressed by his stateliness?—or did he not love her because she was proud, though with a different kind of pride than his own: daring and untractable in spite of her slender form and delicate organisation; and because her self-cultivated intellect exercised itself in independent thought, and even in disguised sarcasm? If for a moment he unbended in conversation with his son, his rigidity returned the instant she entered the room, or that the sound of her voice reached his ear. Was it accidental, or from a strange instinct of revenge for his coldness, that, when scarcely old enough to appreciate the meaning of her words, she seemed to take pleasure in holding cheap all distinctions of rank, all ancestral pride, all the order of ideas with which her brother's ductile mind had been so easily impressed? Almost before she could speak plainly, she had sung about the house—as if in defiance of the old family pictures, which seemed to frown upon her—the old rhyme which had marvellously taken her fancy:

"When Adam delved, and Eve span,
Where was then the gentleman?"

As she grew older, she sneered at heraldry, irreverently laughed at coats-of-arms, put embarrassing questions to Father Lifford, as to the real value of such distinctions in a religious point of view,—wondered if the apostles could have proved sixteen quarterings; and, in reading history, it was always the interest of the people, the cause of Liberty—whether in the just acceptation of the word, or in the perverted sense in which it has too often been misapplied—that aroused her sympathy, and awoke her enthusiasm. The misfortunes of kings, the heroism of loyalty, the prestige of great names, had not the same power to move her; and her brother—not in malice, but in the simplicity of his indignation—often repeated to his father and to his uncle what appeared to him her enormities in these respects; and the cold contempt of the former, the dogmatic manner in which the latter condemned them, without giving an explanation or permitting an appeal, only confirmed impressions which a more condescending treatment might have effaced.

Obliged to be silent at home on such topics, Gertrude often gave vent to her feelings when in the society of the only companions which chance had placed within her reach. At an early age a severe illness endangered her life, and during her convalescence the doctor had insisted on her associating more with other children, as the only means of checking the premature development of her mind, and diverting her from the incessant reading which was rapidly exhausting her mental and physical strength. Father Lifford, to whom the question was referred, suggested that Mary Grey, a little girl a year or two older than herself, and the daughter of a widow who lived in the village of Stonehouseleigh with whom he had been acquainted several years, would be the fittest resource in such an emergency. He was aware how carefully Mrs. Redmond had brought up her child, and also the one which her second husband had bequeathed to her care, when—after a few months marriage—he had died, leaving her poorer than before, and with two children to support instead of one.

Indeed, it was supposed by those who knew most of Mrs. Grey, that, when she consented to marry Maurice Redmond, a poor artist, whose face bore the impress of consumption, whose heart had been nearly broken by the loss of a beautiful young wife—an Italian singer—and whose last days were embittered by anxiety about his little son, it was not in ignorance or in recklessness that she did so; but that if her heart had been touched and her feelings interested, it had been more through that pity which is akin to love, than from any more romantic motive; that she well knew how few were the days of happiness that awaited her—if, indeed, with that knowledge a thought of happiness could exist—but that she also knew that she thus gained the right of soothing those few days of lingering life, and of seeing a smile on the pale lips of the dying man when he heard his little boy call her mother.

Everybody said it was like Mrs. Grey to make such a marriage, and this was true. It was very like her, whether those who said it shrugged their shoulders as they spoke, or had a tear in their eye. She made many sacrifices, and worked hard in different ways to make the ends of her small income meet. Maurice always called her his mother, and when they were children it was almost impossible to make him and Mary understand that they were not brother and sister. The large village or small town of Stonehouseleigh, where they lived, was about a mile and a half distant from Lifford Grange. It consisted of one long street, on one side of which flowed the same stream that passed through the gardens of the Grange, now widened into a river, and on the other side rose some hills, to whose breezy heights and sunny nooks an abundance of gorse, of heath, of sweet-smelling thyme, and of shining blackberries attracted the steps of little wanderers from the town.

Mrs. Redmond's cottage was on the outskirts of the High Street. Every inch of the small garden that separated it from the road was encumbered with flowers; lilacs and laburnums, Guelder roses and seringa, dahlias and hollyhocks succeeded each other in endless variety. Convolvulus and heartsease struggled together, sweetbriar and jessamine hustled each other. They overran the paths and climbed to the windows. Roses, also, in all their rich and common variety, not the pale, hectic-tea-rose, or the triumph of horticultural art and Nature's degradation, the black rose, but the glorious blooming cabbage rose, the beautiful moss rose, the lovely blush rose, lent their perfume to the air, and their bright colours to the aspect of the little garden.

Mrs. Redmond had lived in Normandy at the time of her first marriage, and had imported thence a number of rose-cuttings, and a great respect for tisanes, those simple medicines of the French peasantry. There were few of her poor neighbours who had not applied to her for remedies against their various ailments, and, if her skill was not always successful, her tender charity and sympathy were seldom unavailing. Gertrude Lifford's acquaintance with Mary Grey, when once it had begun, soon ripened into intimacy. For some weeks they played together every day in the gardens of the Grange; and, when she was quite recovered, she often walked to the cottage, and persuaded her maid to leave her there, while she visited her own friends in the village. Maurice Redmond, as well as Mary Grey, looked forward to these visits with the delight which children feel in companions whose society is an unexpected pleasure, an unlooked for event. Edgar sometimes came with his sister, and they met in their walks on the hillocks of the downs and the green alleys of the Chase. Some of the village children were occasionally called upon to join in their sports, which were at once of an active and of an imaginative character. Gertrude was the chief object, actor, and ruler in these childish pastimes. Her beauty, intelligence and waywardness, exacted a sort of homage which they all instinctively paid her. The high-spirited Maurice, the gentle Mary, the shy daughters of the tenant of Leigh House Farm, and the sturdy boys of the game-keeper at the Lodge owned her sway, and submitted to all her caprices. If there was a dispute about the distance between the pink thorn and the acacia-tree—which was to be the starting-point and the goal of a race—it was her verdict that settled the question. If they played at holding a mimic court, she was always the Queen, and thrones of moss were erected, and crowns of wild flowers woven for her girlish majesty.

They called her " Lady-Bird,"—a name which Maurice had given her one day, when, after a quarrel, he sought to appease her. She had been bent on some rash experiment, against which Mary had remonstrated; provoked at her interference, the impatient little beauty had pointed to a sober-looking insect on an ivy-leaf, exclaiming at the same time, " You are like that dull moth, Mary!" At that moment a gorgeous butterfly, with gold and purple wings, had dived in the bosom of a red rose in her hand, and Mary rejoined. " And you are like that gay butterfly; " but Maurice cried out. " No. Mary is a humble bee, and you a stinging wasp!" Upon which the offended beauty burst into tears, and, to make his peace with her, he had called her " Lady-Bird." There was something appropriate in this name.

She was, in a restricted sense, the only little lady amongst them. In her looks and in her manner, there was a mixture of reserve and vivacity, of impetuosity and timidity, which answered to it singularly. She looked so proudly and so gracefully shy if a stranger addressed her; she was so passionate and easily ruffled, so pretty in her anger and eloquent in her wrath. wild in her mirth and restless in her movements. All the children in the neighbourhood soon knew her by that name, even though they were not—like Mary and Maurice—her associates and play-fellows. The urchins at the cottage-doors used to call out as she passed, " There goes the Lady-Bird." As time went on, the intercourse between Gertrude Lifford and Mrs. Redmond's children became more habitual. It was far more so than any one was aware of, except the maid who accompanied her in her walks. Her father knew nothing of it, and her uncle had no idea of its extent, or that Maurice was as often her playmate as Mary.

He was one of those boys who show early the gifts with which Nature has endowed them, whose genius is apparent to the most common observer, to whom everything seems easy, and nothing unattainable. With few facilities for education, he had managed to learn a great deal. He had read all the books within his reach, and, at the age of thirteen, had made himself acquainted with most of the principal English writers, especially the poets; had learned some Latin and some French, and made such progress in music—which had been his father's and his mother's art—that many of those who heard him play the organ and the pianoforte augured for him the distinctions, the advantages and sufferings of an artist's life. He met with great kindness in the neighbourhood. Books were lent him; opportunities of hearing good music afforded him. An organist in a neighbouring town gave him gratuitous instruction.

But from the first moment that he became acquainted with the little girl from Lifford Grange, the beautiful Lady-Bird of his childhood, a new impetus was given to his imagination. She entered with delight into all the schemes of childish amusement which his fancy could suggest. He entertained her, her little brother, and Mary with stories which he remembered or invented about Knights and Princesses, Fairies and Enchanters; with verses which—though rude and incorrect—were not without a vein of poetic genius. He taught them to sing old ballads, to recite poetry, to act historical scenes. All this was particularly congenial to Gertrude's lively imagination. She liked to enact Queen Margaret meeting the Robber in the forest, or Amy Robsart disappearing through the trap-door of the castle; scenes from the "Midsummer Night's Dream," or passages from the life of Robin Hood. But their grandest and favourite performance, reserved for the long summer evenings and the prospect of an uninterrupted holiday, was Campbell's ballad, "O'Connor's Child," dramatized by Maurice to suit their exigencies.

With a bunch of shamrock in his cap and a wooden sword in his belt, he knelt on the greensward to ask of Edgar the hand of his sister, while the little boy was taught to stammer out in answer—

"Away, and choose a meaner bride
Than from O'Connor's house of pride;

> Our name, our tribe, our high degree,
> Are hung in Tara's Psaltery.
> Witness to Eath's victorious brand,
> And Cathal of the bloody hand.
> Glory, I say, and power, and honour,
> Are in the mansion of O'Connor,
> But thou dost bear in hall and field
> A meaner crest upon thy shield."

In what they called the second act, Gertrude, with a veil tied round her head and a cloak loosely thrown on her shoulders leant her head on her hand and her elbow on a stile, while Maurice sang the lines in which Connocht Moran tempts his mistress to fly with him.

> "Come far from Castle Connor's clans,
> Come with thy belted forester,
> And I, beside the Lake of Swans,
> Will hunt for thee the fallow-deer,
> And build thy hut, and bring thee home
> The wild fowl and the honey-comb."

In the third act of this childish drama they flew together through the green alleys of the Chase, her feet scarcely touching the grass as she ran, repeating—

> "And I pursue by moonless skies
> The light of Connocht Moran's eyes."

Then they stopped under some hazel trees, and built themselves a cabin with the boughs; and he went out to search the game with knife and spear, and she " his evening food to dress would sing to him in happiness,"

> "Sweet is to us the hermitage
> Of this untried untrodden shore,
> Like birds all joyous from the cage,
> For man's neglect we love it more."

Then came the fourth act with its death-scene. How tragic they all thought it! In an old hollow tree they sat, Gertrude with her finger on her lips and her glancing eyes looking timidly about her. Then, with her mouth close to Maurice's ear, she whispered. "I hear the baying of their beagle," and he answered in the same key, "'Tis but the screaming of the eagle." Then a great effort was made to stir up an old dog who had been pressed into the service to enact the "Couchant Hound" that starts up and listens, but this generally failed, and Edgar and Mary with hats on and with sticks, personifying the murderous brothers, rushed upon Maurice, who always fought too long and would not let himself be killed, which, as Mary observed, was very unreasonable, as it was part of the play, and Gertrude screamed,

"O spare him Brazil, Desmond fierce!"

till she grew tired and hoarse, and fainted away before her lover was fairly killed.

The last act, however, was Gertrude's delight. She recited wonderfully well the spirited lines in which the daughter of O'Connor, in the madness of her passion and the delirium of her anguish, presents to her assassin brothers "the standard of O'Connor's sway," and pronounces a curse, which is to be fatally fulfilled on that battle day, and which dooms their whole race to destruction. Her eyes flashed, her cheeks glowed, her slender childish form trembled as she cried—

"Go then, away to Athunree,
High lift the banner of your pride,
But know that where its sheet unrolls,
The weight of blood is on your souls.
Go, where the havoc of your kerne
Shall float as high as mountain fern;
Men shall no more your mansion know,
The nettles on your hearth shall grow,
Dead as the green oblivious flood
That mantles by your walls shall be
The glory of O'Connor's blood.
Away, away to Athunree."

Many a famous actress might have won applause for the look and tone of wild inspiration with which she swore

"That sooner guilt the ordeal brand
Should grasp unhurt than they should hold
The banner with victorious hand,
Beneath a sister's curse unrolled."

Such were the amusements of these children during about two years, and to Gertrude they were the happiest she had known. Then Edgar went to school, and soon after Maurice went to a school in London, and seldom came to Stonehouseleigh. Everything changed.—Gertrude and Mary were still friends, but there was no excitement to the former in their intercourse, and the latter took life very much in earnest, and had a great deal to do in her own home, and many cares and thoughts and occupations which Lady-Bird did not understand, and in which she had no sympathy. And though they were fond of each other, there was no great intimacy between them: still, enough to become at any moment closer, as it did when a subject of common interest arose.

The link that connected them was an odd one; some may think it unnatural, but people are very different, and young girls, especially, have strange grounds of sympathy. Certain it is, that the circumstances which will be related in another chapter served to bring them together, and to give an interest to their intercourse which it had gradually been losing during the last few years. Perhaps it grew out of the fulness of one heart, and the emptiness of the other—something that required a vent in the one, a void to be filled in the other. This will be better understood as the story proceeds.

CHAPTER II.

"Sweet recreation barred what does ensue,
But restless, dull, and moody melancholy,
Sister to grim and comfortless despair,
And at her heels a huge infectious troop
Of pale distemperatures, and foes to life."
SHAKESPEARE.

ON the prostrate stem of an old beech-tree towards the end of the month of May, about six years after Maurice had left Stonehousleigh for London, Gertrude and Mary were sitting in a spot, which exhibits in all its varieties the peculiar beauties of English forest scenery. The first tinge of spring was colouring with its delicate green the thorns, the aspens, and the briars, which in innumerable natural avenues and picturesque intricacies formed a labyrinth, out of which sturdy oaks rose in grim majesty, their gnarled and twisted branches still exhibiting all the barrenness of winter, save where here or there the young moss or the misletoe clung to their rugged arms, and disguised their leaflessness. Daisies, cowslips, and primroses, the blue hyacinth and the frail anemone, were scattered about in abundance, here in rich clusters, there in brilliant carpets, everywhere in graceful beauty and confusion. It was exactly the moment when spring shows as great a variety of colours as autumn, when it is as gorgeous in its greetings as the latter season in its adieus. As short-lived as it is beautiful, this hour of Nature's promise is no sooner arrived than it disappears, and deepens into the monotony of summer.

Often in their childhood these two girls had met to play where now they came to converse. Their bonnets were lying on the grass, and served as receptacles for the flowers which they gathered by handfuls without moving from their places. "So you are expecting Maurice to day!" Gertrude exclaimed, after a pause in the conversation. She was answered by a smile and a faint blush of pleasure, not of embarrassment.

"How this spot puts me in mind of old times!" (at that age the lapse of a few years constitutes a remote antiquity) "of our games and our spoutings under this very tree, upon which we are now sitting. Is Maurice much altered since he last went away? Should I know him again?"

"He is a great deal taller, but his features are not changed, at least I think not, but as I have seen him every year in my winter visits to my aunt, perhaps I can hardly judge. His large dark eyes and pale complexion are just what they always were."

"And is he as fond of poetry as ever? Music has not made him neglect it?"

"O no! he thinks, like Shakespeare, that 'music and sweet poetry agree, as well they may—the sister and the brother;' the more he studies the one, the more he delights in the other. When I was in London he brought something or other of that kind to read to me almost every evening. It was pleasant there to hear of fields, and woods, and streams. Only it would have made me long to come home again, if only he could have got away too."

"Then you know what it is to be so weary of a place as to hate the very sight of it?"

"No, not quite that either; I did not hate London, only I like the country much better."

"Whereas I would give anything to go to London. It is too bad really never to have seen it."

"You can hardly imagine how different it is from Stonehousleigh, or even from Lancaster, Chester, or any of the towns in our neighbourhood."

"The more unlike it is to this part of the world, the better it would please me. The thickest of the London fogs, of which people talk so much, would be brighter to me than the finest day at Lifford Grange."

"It makes me sad to hear you speak in that way of your home."

"My home!" (O! 'the world of dreary gloom that rose in the shadowy depths of those deep-set eyes,' as the word was re-echoed with emphatic meaning.) "You who have had change in your life, Mary, and that before you cared or wished for it, can hardly understand the pining desire I feel for it. It is becoming quite a passion with me. The world must be such a beautiful, such an exciting thing!"

"Do you mean the world that God has made, or the one man makes, according to Cowper's definition?"

"I mean the world as God has made it, as man has adorned it, as genius describes, and as imagination paints it. I mean London, not as you saw it, Mary, from a small house in an out-of-the-way street, and in its work-day dress of business and routine, but London with its luxury, its wealth, its court, its parliament, and what Charles Lamb—a greater poet perhaps than your favourite, Cowper—calls its poetry. And I mean Paris with all its brilliancy; Italy with its bright skies, its paintings, its music, its ruins, and its churches. I mean the Alps with their eternal snows. I mean the sea with its restless waves. I mean politics, and literature, and theatres, and society, and everything that has change, and life, and spirit, and movement about it. That is what I read of, long for, pine for, and never shall enjoy."

"You look like a child, Lady-Bird, but you do not talk like one; no, nor like the very young girl that you are. How do you come to know and to wish for all these things? I have seen more of the world than you have, but they have scarcely entered into my thoughts."

"Books, Mary, books tell me a great deal, and give me strange feelings of pain and of pleasure. You do not know how much I read—sometimes for hours together; and when I do not read, I dream. Do you know the pleasure of that?"

"Well, I rather like it at times; but as I sleep very soundly, it does not happen to me often."

Gertrude smiled, and said: "I do not mean sleeping, but waking dreams.—sitting with folded hands, and eyes fixed on some object that amuses without engrossing the mind; and letting yourself drift, as it were at random, down the stream of your impressions, borne here and there by the current of your thoughts; motionless as if nothing was stirring in your soul, and weaving the while the thread of your own destiny into a web which a sound or a word can dissolve, as the wing of an insect breaks the light gossamer, or a breath melts the fanciful landscapes that frost prints on the windows. Have you never dreamed in *this* way, Mary?"

Mary answered with a faint blush and a smile, "Yes, but when my thoughts stray away, I endeavour to catch and bring them back again."

"Yours always run in the same direction, I suspect, so you always know where to find them."

Mary's head was turned away, and Gertrude continued, "The last book I have read is 'Corinne.' I found it in the library, hidden under a heap of pamphlets, and have *lived* in it for the last three days. It has redoubled my wish to see, to hear, to *live* in short, for life is not life without interest and excitement, I am sure of that. You read French, Mary—do let me lend you 'Corinne;' it will show you what I mean so much better than I can express it."

"I had rather not, dear Lady-Bird; it may be right for you to read such books—it would not answer for me."

"I believe you never read any but religious books," Gertrude scornfully exclaimed.

"O, when Maurice is at home he reads all sorts of things out loud, while I work—novels, and plays, and poetry; but I have not much leisure for it at other times. Then, you know, our positions in life will be so different, that what may be good for you might be useless, or worse than useless to me."

"My position in life? What do you suppose it will be—to live and die an old maid at Lifford Grange, or retire to some nunnery, perhaps? Sometimes I have so longed for something new, that I have been almost thinking of that last alternative. I wish with all my heart they had sent me to a convent-school; I would have worked day and night to distinguish myself, and to gain prizes. A stimulant is everything, and emulation would have been a powerful one. Does not your heart beat, and your cheek flush when you read something very eloquent?—one of those passages that raise you half-way between earth and heaven? You smile, Mary, and I know what you would say. It is not through such ecstacies as these that we can rise to heaven. But better rise in any way than grovel on the earth; give me the wings of a butterfly, if I cannot have those of an angel. *You* never get absorbed in anything but your prayers; you never pore over a book, or meditate on a poem; once on'y I have seen you read with your soul in your eyes; but it was the life of St. Francis Xavier, and in that—"

"Oh, in that there was enough to make a heart less cold and hard than mine burn within itself as it read, and even mine, dull as it is, could not but warm at such a flame."

"I thought I should elicit a spark of latent enthusiasm by hat allusion. But, tell me, does not Maurice care about the things I was speaking of?"

A slight cloud passed over Mary's face, and she answered, "Only too much."

"Why *too much*, if they are not wrong?"

"I can hardly explain myself; but it seems to me difficult to care so much about beauty of every sort, and to be at the same time always contented with the state of life allotted to us."

"But Maurice is, or, at least, means to be an artist, and I have read, and I think I can understand that an artist lives on beauty of every kind, and that variety and excitement can alone keep alive the fire that inspires him; that genius dies away in an atmosphere of monotony and dulness."

"But a quiet life is not necessarily a dull one," expostulated Mary. "I should have thought that genius, and art, and all those things you speak of, ought to make a man busy and happy in himself, and in his home, especially if—"

"If what, Mary?"

Mary bent down her head, and twisted together the blades of the long grass that grew at her feet, and then looking up into Gertrude's face, she said with simplicity:

"Especially if he loved, and was beloved."

"Love!" Gertrude repeated. "Love must be a very strange, a very strong thing. It may be the deepest of all joys, or the acutest of all miseries, but a quiet calm feeling, I do not think it can be. I have read that it stirs up the heart and moves the inmost soul, as a storm does the sea, or a hurricane the forest."

"If so, we ought to fear it, but I do not believe that it is a right sort of love that you speak of. What is right should be calm."

"Can that be calm of which people die?"

"Do people die of love?"

"Don't you think they do?"

"I don't know, but would it not even then be possible to suffer and to die calmly?"

Calmly were her eyes raised to the soft blue sky over her head—but Gertrude's were fixed on a rapid stream that murmured along the bottom of the valley where they sat.

"Now that brook," she exclaimed, "I like it better than all the other beauties of Nature put together. It never remains in the same place, it hurries on, it is chafed with the stones that stop its onward course, and I like it for its anger; I love to see it foam and struggle, and long to help it on, and send it faster and faster where it is going—"

"And where is that?" Mary asked.

"Why to the wide sea, I suppose."

"And then—when it gets there?"

"Then it is lost amongst the waves, and the eye sees it no more."

"O! does not that make you think of life and eternity, and would you not rather be like the silent stream that glides through green pastures and gives freshness to the fields and beauty to the flowers, than resemble that restless, useless, brawling rivulet that often swells into a torrent, and does mischief in its course?"

"Your thoughts, Mary, are all tuned to one key."

"Is not that the true secret of harmony?"

"A discord now and then has a good effect."

"You are too fond of them, dear Lady-Bird."

"Harmony can be very dull, and dulness harmonious. Since Edgar's departure nobody quarrels at Lifford Grange, and we are gradually dying of ennui. At least, I am. Everything goes on '*comme un papier de musique,*' and I have almost wished that the house would catch fire, or I the measles."

"Oh, that is so wrong, dear Lady-Bird. Do unsay it immediately."

"I did not say the small-pox. I should not like to be ugly."

"Is that all you care about? I cannot bear to hear you speak in that reckless manner."

"Why, to tell you the truth, I am not happy, and I like to joke better than to complain. Sir Thomas More joked on the scaffold."

"*He* might well smile at the idea of death, but you—"

"O; I have no wish to die, though I sometimes talk nonsense about it. I can be at times more serious than you would suppose."

Mary took Gertrude's hand, and kissed it affectionately. Both remained silent a few instants, and then the latter exclaimed,

"It is so trying to be thwarted and teased about every trifle. You know how long I have wished to have a dog. and a short time ago the coachman gave me one—a little spaniel, one of the breed they have at Woodlands. It was my constant companion, and the greatest amusement to me. I kept it out of everybody's way. Jane took care of it when I was in the drawing-room, and it was so fond of me that I loved it foolishly in return. Well, last Monday it escaped from her, ran into the dining-room, and jumped on my knees. My father asked whose dog it was, and when he heard it was mine he ordered it to be sent away; I begged him very earnestly to let me keep it; he peremptorily refused. I told him that it was fond of me, and he sneered. The blood rushed to my face, and I said some passionate words. He rang the bell, and desired that a groom should instantly carry my dog back to Woodlands, and that if it made its way again here it should be shot. O ! Mary, I am very foolish; but I can hardly speak without a choking sensation in my throat, and my cheek burns like a hot coal. God forgive me for what I said, or rather felt at the time. I thought of Pélisson and his spider."

"Was Father Lifford there—what did he say?"

"He never looked up from the newspaper, but I think he frowned and bit his lip when my father spoke of their shooting the little animal."

"He has not been shot?" Mary anxiously asked.

"No—he was given to a lady who was just leaving Woodlands, and she took him away with her. I went to my room and cried for some hours, more with anger than with sorrow. In some ways my father treats me like a child, and in others as a servant or a slave, and I am too like him to endure it patiently."

"But you have a great deal of personal liberty; is not that some compensation?"

"Liberty to wander alone about an extensive prison, that is all; and even that is the result of neglect—not of kindness."

"Dearest Lady, are not your mother and Father Lifford kind to you?"

"Mamma, you know is always ill—always suffering. She can seldom bear the sound of a voice above a whisper. She tells me not to shut myself up in her sick room: she has hardly strength enough to talk to me. I some times wish to be more attentive to her, but I do not know how to set about it. As to Father Lifford, I don't think he likes me much; Edgar is his favourite, because he is such a good boy. He is always finding fault with me, and I like his scoldings better than papa's silence. In confession he is sometimes very kind, but that is quite another thing, you know. He would be kind, perhaps, at other times also if I behaved differently, and did not read books that he disapproves, or *would* learn Spanish, or *not* laugh at the divine rights of kings, or think Napoleon a great man, or not talk of things *he* says I do not understand, but which I am sure I know more about than he does."

"O Lady-Bird, how can you think so? He must be much wiser than you, at his age—and a priest too."

"I am not talking of theology, or morality, or history, or geography, but of other things which I have read, thought, and made up my mind about, and which he will not even discuss, or allow that they admit of argument. I *dare* not speak of them before papa. There is something *under* his silence that frightens me. But I am not afraid of provoking Father Lifford, because I know the worst he will say."

"That is not generous."

"O yes, it is, because he says all sorts of severe things to me, and can order me to be silent if he chooses. Then I console myself with thinking that I had the best of the argument."

"Come, come, Lady-Bird, I will not listen to any more of your iniquities. The sun is just about to set and we must be going home."

"Another day over! another sun setting! another to-morrow coming!" Gertrude murmured to herself, as with her bonnet in her hand and her back against the stem of a tree, she fixed her eyes on the gold and crimson clouds that were blazing in the west. "How beautiful they are, those sunset clouds! How like another world, and a brighter one than this. I sometimes think that the land of my birth may have some of the dazzling beauty which shines in that western sky. I am haunted by a vague recollection of that country where I was born and where I spent the first years of my life. Perhaps the air of the south breathed into my veins a fire which will not let me rest contented as you all do, in this dull corner of the wide world. Come, let us go home."

"Let us go home!" Words that in some cases are as sweet music to the ear, and the deepest joy of the heart. To others, a sound full of sad meaning, a thought that weighs heavily on the soul, and clouds the brow with the remembrance of suffering, and the anticipations of trial. Home! Home! Beautiful English word; shelter, refuge—happiness, or consolation. Would that you were always the heaven you sometimes are; binding up the bruised heart, or gladdening the young spirit!—not the sanctuary of tyranny, and the mockery of domestic bliss.

"I must go home," Gertrude Lifford said; and Mary Grey repeated, "Yes, we must go home." But a different tone was in the voices, and a different picture in the minds of each of these young girls.

"I know" (the one began as they walked along the alley of hazel wood that led to the common), "I know you think it strange that I am not more attentive, as it is called, to my mother, but what can one do when people do not like attentions, if they ask one not to put oneself out of the way on their account?"

"Perhaps, show them that it is love, and not a mere sense of duty that prompts one. Few people like attentions which do not seem the result of affection."

"Love and affection are strange words to me. I thought that duty, not feeling, was to be the rule of our actions. I should be much worse than I am, if once I began to act from impulse. There rises up at times in me a spirit of defiance which takes possession of my whole being, and steels my heart against all gentle feelings. I rebel against the common-place things that people say about loving others, as if love was to be called up and laid aside at pleasure! It is possible to be a slave, and it may be a duty to remain one (that is, by the way, one of the points about which I argue with Father Lifford), but to make oneself love people, simply because it is right to do so, is an impossibility, an absurdity. You looked vexed, Mary, do not suppose that I do not love mamma. Heaven forbid—poor patient suffering mamma. I do love her, and if I did not I should not say so, for I hate every description of lying, and canting lies worse than any others. But I wish you to understand that your way of considering the subject would be no security against evil in a nature like mine."

"But when I speak of *love* I do not mean a mere human feeling, though even that" (Mary's voice faltered a little as she said this) "might teach us something of the nature of true devotion; but I mean that principle of charity which has all the force of duty, the vivacity of impulse, and the tenderness of affection."

"Was it charity that used to make you so attentive to Maurice?"

A deep flush suffused the pale little girl's face, but she answered steadily:

"He was always delicate; it came naturally to me to care for him and to watch him, and it was too great a happiness to be like a duty."

"He was very captivating, certainly, and clever, also, as far as I recollect, but then we are like Miranda in her island, we have no opportunities for making comparisons. Do not be angry. I am sure he was charming. Mamma used to call him 'El Chico,' and Father Lifford liked him too. How old is he now?"

"About twenty-one."

"Of age, then?"

"O yes, we sent him a large nosegay by the coach, or his birthday would have past unnoticed."

"He is organist at one of the London chapels, is not he?"

"Yes, and he practises and composes a great deal, and reads also many books, and writes verses. I think it is a good thing for him to have those tastes—it keeps him out of mischief."

"I see that your fears for those you love are greater than your ambition, Mary. Do you value his genius only because it may keep him out of mischief?"

"It is my way of saying more than I well know how to say, dear Lady-Bird. But it is not little I mean."

"I believe you often *do* mean much more than you say, you little quiet mouse, and that if one went deep enough into your thoughts, one would find in them——"

"O nothing, I assure you, that would reward the trouble of diving. But, tell me, who was it who rode just now across the lane to the common?"

"Mr. Mark Apley, the son of Mr. Apley of Woodlands. Had you never seen him before? He rides so well, and has such beautiful horses! I have often met him when I have been walking with Jane. One day that I was gathering some honeysuckles, and was trying to reach a branch that was too high for me, he caught it with his stick, and held it close to my hand."

"Did you thank him?"

"Only by a low curtsey, and I have not bowed to him since. But it would be very amusing to know a few people. Even such a little thing as that gives one something to think about."

If Gertrude had at that moment dived into the thoughts of the little mouse by her side, she would have seen her innocent astonishment that her dear Lady-Bird, whose mind was as active as her spirit was restless, whose love of reading was a passion, whose conversation—young as she was—was full of originality, should want "something to think about," but she was not right to be astonished. A tendency to ennui, joined to a craving for excitement even of the most trivial description, is the disease of certain minds, and there is but one cure for it. Call it what you will; self-education, not for this world but for the next; the work of life understood; perfection conceived and resolutely aimed at; the dream of human happiness resigned, and in the same hour its substance regained; the capital paid into the next world, and the daily unlooked-for interest received in this;—such is the strange alchymy in which God deals, and the secret of so many destinies which the world wonders over, and never learns to understand.

"Oh, how beautiful the view is at this moment!" Mary exclaimed, as they came in sight of the common, which shone like burnished gold in the rays of the setting sun, while the peculiar perfume of the gorse in full flower was wafted to them by the evening breeze. Clumps of dark fir-trees rose out of that sea of yellow blossoms, and views of distant country and masses of forest trees were visible in the distance.

"You have wings to your feet," Gertrude cried out as her companion preceded her, while she stopped to gather the feathery balls of a full-blown dandelion.

"What are you about, Lady-Bird?—what a strange nosegay you are making!"

She was breathing upon the downy globe, and the light stamens were flying away in every direction.

"I am telling myself my own fortune. Wait a minute,—I see them still."

"What do you see?"

"My airy messengers."

"Oh, baby of sixteen, to play at such nonsense!"

"Have you never read about the Indian women on the banks of the Ganges?"

"What, the widows who burn themselves?"

"No, the babies of sixteen who kneel by the broad river, and send their leafy lamps floating down the stream; and if the light they carry is still burning when it vanishes from their sight, then they think that their hearts' desire will be accomplished. Cannot you fancy how they must bend over the brink of those deep waters, with their hearts beating, and their eyes straining after the little fiery bark that follows the current?—how they must tremble when it gets entangled in the leaves of the lotus; how they must shout for joy when it turns with the bend of the river?"

"It is a fanciful notion and a pretty one, I own: but what made you think of it just now?"

"I have my superstition, too; but I am a votary of the air—not of the water. I send my messengers aloft. They carry my thoughts with them on the wings of the wind, they tell my secrets to the clouds and my hopes to the breeze. There, fly where I send you!" and another downy ball was launched into the air, and the wind bore away the light atoms. Once a sudden gust blew them back into her face; she brushed them away and said, "That means disappointment." A slight cloud gathered on her brow, and she walked on in silence to the gate of her own home, the old Manor House of Lifford Grange. There she parted with Mary, and sauntered up the avenue.

CHAPTER III.

"O absence! what a torment would'st thou prove,
Wer't not that thy sour leisure gives sweet leave
To entertain the time with thoughts of love."
SHAKESPEARE.

MARY hurried home with a quicker step than usual, and hastily mounting the narrow stairs of the cottage, she looked into the room where Maurice was to sleep that night. She smelt the violets which she had put there an hour before, and fancied they had lost something of their sweetness. The books he had left in her care were neatly arranged on the shelves. A little picture of St. Maurice, and a black profile of herself—a birthday present of a few years back—hung on each side of the chimney. She wiped some grains of dust off the deal table where he used to write when a boy, and in her heart there was a joy that made it flutter a little, and in her eyes a shade of unwonted excitement.

For a few minutes she stood at the open window, gazing on the London road as far as her eye could reach. Then it rested on the one tree of their garden, the old thorn "just flushing into green," on the narrow gravel walk and the gate beyond it, on each familiar object and then on the sky above them, so familiar also with its fleecy clouds and sunset colouring, and yet so full of novelty, in its ever varying combinations of beauty. Now the bright hues were fading away, and the twilight hour was arrived, that charm of northern climes, that lingering adieu of the parting day, which is so sad or soothing, according to the temper of our minds.

Every noise gradually hushed into silence, the faint rustle of the leaves as the night wind stirs them, the low twitter of the birds amongst the branches that conceal them, the occasional distant bark of a dog, the fall of a footstep, or the rumbling of a carriage far away on the high road, all is in harmony—all is subdued, as in the quiet landscapes of Paul Potter, or in the poetry of Cowper. The mind that appreciates the beauty of an English twilight hour must be at once calm and imaginative. It is neither vivid enough to excite nor powerful enough to captivate, where the mental faculties are stagnant or the action of the soul precipitate. It came home to Mary's feelings with peculiar force, and had she ever dreamed life's moments away, she would have done so then; but she had quite a morbid horror of idleness, and turned away from the indulgence of a few minutes reverie, as others less scrupulous might have done from a sin. When she went down to the sitting-room her mother was at the tea-table.

"I have been thinking and thinking, Mary dear, what we had better do about a fire. He might like one after his journey, though certainly it is not cold to-day."

"O yes, mother! one of your French wood-fires. We will light it with the cones that we picked up in the Chase. We can make it burn directly."

In a moment she was on her knees before the grate, and a bright flame threw a glow on her cheeks which the night air had bleached. Then she turned round while still on her knees to her mother, who took her head between her hands and looked fondly into her eyes.

"O, mother, how foolish it is of people to surprise their friends. It takes away so many happy hours of expectation." Then starting up, she exclaimed, "There are the wheels! O, listen. it is the coach!"

There was a moment's silence, the sound grew more distinct, and then the coach itself stopped at the gate, the maid opened the door, and Mary rushed into the passage, and held in her breath, not to lose the first sound of a step—the first accent of a voice that had been music to her ears ever since she could remember.

"It is a letter, Miss Mary, not Mr. Maurice."

Numerous were the thoughts that had time to shoot across her mind during the seconds that intervened between the utterance of these words by the maid, and her return to the fireside. There was room for the recollection of Gertrude's exclaiming. "That means disappointment!"—her heart inwardly re-echoed the ejaculation, but added, as if to re-assure herself, "He must be coming to-morrow." Sitting down at her mother's side, she opened the letter, and made a sign to her to read at the same time as herself, but she had got to the end before Mrs. Redmond had found her spectacles. "Take it, mother," she said in a faint voice, "I think we ought to be very glad;" and she went to the window and leant her forehead against the glass and squeezed her hands together, trying very hard to feel glad.

When her mother had finished reading and called to her to say so, the struggle was over, and in answer to the anxious look with which Mrs. Redmond was awaiting her comments, ready to grieve or to rejoice as she led the way, she was able to say: "It is all right, dearest mother. We must rejoice at his good fortune, we must prefer it to the selfish pleasure of seeing him here; but perhaps I understand now why people *should* come as a surprise." She tried to smile, but the attempt was a failure; one little sob escaped her, but after that she went about her business as if nothing was the matter. On her way to her own room, she walked softly into the one she had that morning prepared with such care, and carried back the books and pictures to her own: there she read again the letter which she had so rapidly perused at first. It was as follows:—

"My dearest Mary, I had hoped as you know to have been with you to-night, to have been sitting this evening between you and dear mother, to have heard your loved voices, and looked on your dear faces, and can hardly believe that it is not to be so, that these summer months which we had so reckoned on spending together will see us further apart than we have ever yet been, and that by my own doing. But when I tell you what has occurred, I am sure you will think I was right in taking advantage of an offer at once so unexpected and so advantageous to my future career, and to the destiny which you are to share with me.

"You know, my Mary, that you have made up your mind long ago to be an artist's true wife, and to allow me to love my art with a passion which you have promised never to be jealous of. If some post of profit alone had been offered to me, some means of making money which would have separated me from you for some years, I should have either rejected it, or at least not accepted it without consulting you; but in the present instance what is proposed to me is an extraordinary opportunity for the cultivation of talents which may one day make me eminent, for the development of a gift which, if it exists, I must answer for to the Giver, not let it lie dormant in the mere exercise of an almost mechanical employment.

"I believe I possess it, that precious gift of genius, because my sufferings and my enjoyments are of a peculiar nature, and ally themselves with a high wrought enthusiasm or an unaccountable depression, which are both unknown to those in whom that electric spark has never vibrated

"Once it seemed to me, dearest Mary, that to go to Italy, to that land of art, of music, and of inspiration, was a dream that never could be realised. I have heard others talk of what Nature is in those southern climes, of the harmony it breathes into the soul, of the influence of its skies on the imagination, of its very air on the spirits, and I have longed with a vain and ardent longing to carry there my dreamy conceptions, my imperfect but as I fondly hope not worthless imaginings. Now all is offered to me: sunshine and leisure, variety and stimulus, emotions to experience and liberty to enjoy them. In accepting it I feel that you will accompany me in spirit to the bright scenes I am about to visit, that the image of your sweet face and the sound of your gentle voice, which has cheered me so often amidst the drudgery of many years, will accompany me henceforward amidst all the wonders of Nature and art.

"As usual, I have allowed my thoughts and my pen to run away with me, and have not yet told you the simple state of the case. It is this—a few weeks ago young Dee, the painter in whose studio I was lingering in admiration of a fine painting that he was copying, introduced me to its possessor, who happened to enter the room at that moment. His name is M. D'Arberg. He is half French and half German by birth, though his mother was English. He speaks exactly like an Englishman. He seemed pleased with my enthusiasm about his picture, entered into conversation with me, and I often met him afterwards at Dee's. He is one of the most peculiar persons you can conceive, and at the same time you cannot point out any peculiarities in him. He is handsomer than any one I have ever seen, and yet if you ask me what is most remarkable in his appearance, I should say it was the look of repose, and that the most striking charm of his manner is that he has no manner at all. I never saw such perfect simplicity. He does all sorts of kind and extraordinary things as if they were the commonest in the world, and in such an unpretending manner, that you forget to thing them strange, till you think over them afterwards.

"He was speaking yesterday to Dee about me, and what they were both pleased to call my genius; and Dee happened to say how ardently I longed to go to Italy, and what an advantage it would be to me, but that I was too poor to afford it. He pulled his memorandum book out of his pocket, made a few calculations with a pencil, and then told him that he was going to Rome for two years, and that if I could arrange to set off with him at once, he would take me there to assist him in some literary pursuits he was engaged in, and at the same time, that he would allow me leisure and afford me opportunities for prosecuting my musical studies. Dee said he spoke of it as simply as if he had been proposing to take me for the day to Richmond or Brighton. You can easily imagine my agitation when the offer was made, and what a mixture of pain and pleasure was involved in it. I felt I could not hesitate, and yet to go without seeing you, without hearing from you! but I knew what you would say, what you and dearest mother would feel, and I accepted—and rapidly achieved the necessary preparations.

"They were very kind to me at the Chapel about resigning my post so suddenly. I feel shy at the idea of such long tête-à-tête hours with M. D'Arberg. I hope he will not weary of my society. I have so little to say for myself, except to those with whom I think aloud, like you and Dee. This eve ning, when you will be expecting me at the green gate, I shall be on my way to Italy. O, Mary, that thought makes me wretched! I hope you will not think me unkind. You would not think me indifferent, if you were to see the kisses I imprint on this paper, and the tears that fall upon it. I shall always wear round my neck what you gave me when we last parted. Give mother one of your gentle kisses for me. O that I could clasp you both to my heart!

"Does Lady-Bird ever embrace you now? She was no proud when we used to act together. But now, if we were to meet, I should have to call her Miss Lifford, and to kiss even her hand would be too much boldness. Will you tell Father Lifford how much I regret not to have had his blessing before my departure. Write to me often—pray for me, think of me, love me, and believe me, your ever affectionate and devoted

"MAURICE."

Was it very unreasonable of Mary not to feel satisfied with this letter?—to have wished that there had not been so many fine words in it?—to be as jealous of Italy as if it were an enemy?—to go to sleep with an aching at her heart deeper than the pain of separation, and which re-produced itself in a variety of dreams, all relating to Maurice? She was always going to him, and getting near him without being able to overtake him, or to make him listen to her. Sometimes the form of a woman, whose features she could not discern, was hovering round him and keeping her at a distance. When she disappeared, another took her place and sang a beautiful song, in which Maurice joined while she could not, and the spot where she was standing—and where she felt herself rooted—was growing darker and darker, while he and the bright vision were disappearing along a road of light such as the sunbeams form on the flashing foam of the billows. She made a great effort to follow them, and awoke with her pillow wet with tears, and his letter in her hand. He the while was crossing the sea with a fair wind and a careless heart, over which thoughts of tenderness and of regret careered swiftly and lightly as the fleecy clouds which scud before the breeze, and throw no shade on the glad waves of the ocean.

"Come now, Mary, tell me the truth—Maurice is your lover—I am sure of it."

"He loves me very much, and I love him dearly."

"But I mean that you are engaged to marry him."

"O, no!"

"No! but in this letter he says as much?"

"We are both perfectly free."

"He does not seem to have any doubt of your affection."

"No. He never could doubt of that."

"I am not talking of sisterly affection. What I mean is that he reckons on your sharing his fate, whatever it may be."

"We have always been accustomed to talk and to think in that way. But it does not mean all you suppose. We have never made any promises."

The interest that Gertrude had shown in Mary's disappointment, the numerous questions she had asked on the subject, her evident desire to see the letter he had written, and which Mary readily enough had yielded to, had occasioned the foregoing conversation. Perhaps she was not sorry to see what impression it would make on one not keenly interested like herself in its contents. Gertrude's curiosity was roused by the little romance it disclosed, and Maurice's way of writing, his account of M. D'Arberg, his longings after change and novelty, with which she could so entirely sympathise, formed a glimpse into the world which captivated her fancy. She entered into the subject with a zest and an intelligence which became irresistibly agreeable to Mary. However well regulated the mind may be—however disciplined the feelings—it is scarcely possible that a girl of her age should keep locked up in her own breast the one thought that fills her existence; and the more matter-of-fact are her habits of life and of mind, the less acquaintance she has with novels and poems and the romantic experience of others, the more perhaps is felt the need of such sympathy. Not that Mary abandoned her accustomed reserve, and made what is called a confidante of Gertrude. On the contrary, she never admitted that she was engaged to Maurice, or that she considered any of his affectionate expressions as assurances that e loved her more than he had always done since earliest childhood, or than she would and might love him to her dying day, even should they never be more to each other than in the past or the present time. It was an odd instinct that made her at once so reserved and so communicative. She had her secret, with which no one was to intermeddle; but to talk of him to somebody besides her mother (who was a sort of second self) was an unspeakable satisfaction.

And Gertrude had also a singular power of extorting more than winning confidence. She questioned with a sagacity—investigated a subject with a perseverance which it was almost impossible to evade. She was unconsciously artful with all her playful brusquerie, and always on the watch where her interest was excited. Maurice's allusion to herself and the sort of homage it implied had amused her imagination. It reminded her of their former intimacy, and she did not dislike the thought that he preserved a sort of respectful remembrance of it, tinged with a shade of romance that did not in the least interfere with what appeared to be his attachment to the companion of his childhood. It became an established thing that she should read his letters—and to become acquainted with a person in that manner had a peculiarity in it which amused her fancy. Her comments upon them furnished Mary with more *piquant* materials for her answers than she would otherwise have found. But, always scrupulous, she carefully prefaced such remarks with " Lady-Bird thinks" or " Lady-Bird says." It seemed to her as if thus she could keep more on a level with his present state of mind, and as if the intelligent comments on his descriptions of Italy and of society—which Gertrude dictated—kept up between them a more animated intercourse than she could otherwise have sustained, and it was strange how these two girls during that time lived in thought amidst the scenes, the persons, and the objects which the young artist described; but it was in a totally different way. His presence amongst them—his image ever present before her mental sight was what gave *them* interest in Mary's eyes; whereas in Gertrude's it was his connection with a world which she pined to be acquainted with which gave *him* importance.

He wrote well; he lived with artists and literary men. He spoke of Italy with an enthusiasm that kindled hers. The very names of the places which he mentioned were music to her ears: it was like the sound of the trumpet to the war-horse, or the cry of the hounds to the hunter, for the self-taught but deeply read and excitable girl, to hear of poetry in real life, of history in visible monuments, of religion in its grandest and most majestic symbols. The wild Italian dreams of liberty and independence which were stirring many hearts at that period were reflected in his eloquent words, and added another element to the fervour of his effusions. He had become intimate with artists of all sorts, and several eminent persons had shown him great kindness. His efforts, his studies, his occasional successes, his hopes and his fears, his friendships, his gratitude, his hatreds, his sympathies were all uncertain, ardent, wayward and fanciful, as also were the compositions which from time to time he put forth, and which were applauded by some and criticised by others.

There was genius in everything he composed, but not enough unity of purpose, or concentration of mind for excellence; but he was perhaps too young yet to excel, and his good looks, his intelligence, his admiration for Italy, and passion for his art won him favour with all his associates.

Mary always showed Gertrude his letters; whether they contained expressions of affection for herself, or projects for the future, or allusions to his childish recollections of her whom he always called "Lady-Bird." But, as was said before, into the secrets of her own heart she did not admit her. With all her ingenuity and penetration, Gertrude could not satisfy herself as to the precise nature of Mary's feelings for Maurice, or as to the seriousness of his attachment to her, and this doubt was a perpetual stimulus to her curiosity. The passages about herself in his letters pleased her imagination, and she felt slightly disappointed if in two or three successively there was no allusion of the sort.

Once he wrote from Florence: " I was sitting this morning on one of the benches of the Cascino, enjoying the fresh air after a night of intense study, listening to the murmurs of the Arno, and the distant sounds of the gay city. A flower girl passed me, and threw into my lap a hyacinth and a sprig of jessamine. She laughed and told me they would help me to dream of my absent mistress. The gift and the smile were both charming, and, strange to say, both flowers were associated in my mind with recollections of home and of the past:—you, my Mary, with the pure white little flower that you were always so fond of, and our Lady-Bird with the sweet perfume and glorious colour of hyacinth. It was the sceptre she always chose when she acted Titania. The Italian girl had indeed thrown a spell over my dreams, and I remained long in that spot, treading again in fancy the alleys of the Chase, and living over in imagination the happy days of our childhood."

After a long interval he wrote thus from Rome:

" Have you ever been pursued by a consciousness that certain objects, certain faces, certain appearances, have a relation to your fate, a deeper meaning, a different sense for you than for the rest of the world—an influence over you which you feel without being able to analyse it? Some eyes have had that effect upon me. Whenever I have seen the peculiar expression I mean, it has always caused me an unaccountable emotion; and I have an intimate conviction that such eyes as those must have, at some time or other of my life, some strange connection with my destiny—whether for good or for evil I know not. It is not often that I have met with the eyes I mean, and when I have done so, it has been in faces as different as possible in every other respect; in the old and in the young, in men and in women. Other eyes look *at* you, these look *into* you. I can only compare the glance I mean to a ray of light shining through the darkest leaf of a purple heartsease. Before I left England I never met with it but in one person. Look well at Lady-Bird the next time you see her, and then tell me if you perceive what I mean. Since I have been abroad I have observed it once in an old monk who was praying in one of the side chapels of the Cathedral of Padua, another time in an actress I saw performing the part of Francesca di Rimini at Naples, and once again very lately in one of the handsome boys who were begging on the steps of the Pincio. Was there a likeness in the soul that spoke through these eyes—else why that strange resemblance, when all else was dissimilar? I have mused upon this for hours, and almost lost myself in thought. But what I cannot lose is the habit of talking aloud to you, dear Mary; though I can fancy that *your* eyes, which have never looked anything but peace into my soul, are now gently smiling at my fanciful folly."

Again, some months later, he wrote thus from Naples.

"Countries, like names, like flowers, like sounds, have a likeness to particular people, independently, I think, of all association. That the calm beauty of an English landscape should always put me in mind of you is not extraordinary—for we have lived and grown up together amidst its quiet scenery; but why does this country so often bring to my recollection the image of Lady-Bird, as I remember her in our days of forest games and fireside stories? The other day at Sorrento one of my Italian friends was repeating to me, as we sat by the sea-shore, almost intoxicated by the perfume of the orange-blossoms, Filicaja's well-known address to Italy. When he pronounced the words, ' Fatal gift of beauty,' I instantly saw before me *her* face, with that eager, wistful, and sorrowfully-indignant expression it always had when listening to some tale of pity or of crime. O God forbid that to her the gift of beauty should be fatal! Let her resemble Italy in its charm, but never in its woe!"

At another time he reminded them of some rude verses he had addressed as a boy to Gertrude, and which ran thus:—

'Come, Lady-Bird; come, rest you here; O do not fly away,
See, we have made a throne for you; come, fold your wings and stay.
We do not love the dragon-fly that darts about the lea,
We care not for gay butterflies, all gorgeous though they be;
We do not love the birds that soar so freely up on high,
We do not care for those that sing their matins in the sky;
We do not love the red rose wild, all bright with early dew,
But we love you, the 'Lady-Bird,' and weave a crown for you.
We read of humming-birds whose wings like living jewels glow,
We ween the Lady-Bird has eyes that still more brightly show;
We see the fire-flies shine at night, in countries far away,
We care not for their light if she will fold her wings and stay."

And he said that he had translated, or rather imitated it in French, and set it to music; that it had had great success, and was sung at all the concerts during that winter. "C'est la fille des cieux, c'est l'oiseau du bon Dieu" was the favourite romance of the season. Once he had heard a peasant girl on the shore at Amalfi warble a few notes in a voice that reminded him of hers, or in a picture gallery he had seen a face that was like her, or some famous actress had, by a look or a gesture, made him think of "O'Connor's child" in the green bowers of Oakland Chase.

In the course of the time that he remained in Italy Mary was once very ill, and Mrs. Redmond, who was wholly employed in nursing her, asked Gertrude to write to him and explain the reason of their silence. The task was not unpleasing, and she called him "dear Maurice," as she had done when they were children. And when Mary was recovering, she wrote under her dictation, and mingled playful comments of her own with the more grave communications she was charged to make, and in this way a sort of correspondence was established which amused them all. Nobody knew of it at the Grange, and no one thought it odd at the cottage. Time went on, and no events marked its course. In gloom and in sunshine, through the winter and the summer, it sped its onward way, unmarked by any vicissitudes, unenlivened by any change, except those modifications which it wrought in the character of one who was passing from girlhood into woman hood in constant struggles with herself, in warfare with her own thoughts and feelings, but with hardly any contact with the world without.

CHAPTER IV.

> " Now bank and brae are clothed in green,
> An' scattered cowslips sweetly spring,
> An' birdies flit on wanton wing.
> There wi' my Mary let me flee,
> There catch her ilka glance o' love,
> The bonny blink o' Mary's ee ! '
> Burns.

> " With goddess-like demeanour forth she went,
> Not unattended, for on her as queen
> A pomp of winning graces waited still;
> And from about her shot darts of desire
> Into all eyes, to wish her still in sight."
> Spenser.

THREE years had elapsed since the time when this story began, and Maurice Redmond had returned from Italy with stronger health, keen aspirations after success and distinction, a mind stored with images of beauty and dreams of harmony, and to all appearance a heart unchanged in its warm affection for the mother and the companion of his childhood. On a sultry evening in August, not many days after his arrival, he sauntered with Mary Grey towards an old stone bridge over the Leigh, about a mile from the village. The river at that spot was bright and clear; the alders, with their dark foliage, were reflected in its waters as in a mirror; water-cresses and forget-me-nots floated near its shores; the stately mullein grew on its banks; the king-fisher dipped his beak in the stream, and the dragon-fly darted to and fro on its surface. On the mossy stones of the bridge they sat down together— Maurice with his foreign-looking straw hat in his hand, a ribbon tied loosely round his neck instead of a cravat, and his dark eyes looking as if they were almost too large for his pale and thin face; and Mary with her neat brown dress, her white shawl carefully pinned, her bonnet tied under her chin with the most English precision, and projecting over a face that happiness was making almost beautiful.

So *he* seemed to think; for he untied the strings and pushed back that close bonnet, and gazed upon her with a smile that brought a blush into her cheek, which, though no longer sallow as in her childhood, had scarcely more colour than a white cornelian. That gentle Mary Grey had a most loving nature, but a timid one also, that is, in all that concerned her affections, for otherwise there was in her a store

> "Of hardy virtues, which like spirits start
> From some unknown abyss within the heart."

But she had no confidence in her own powers of pleasing; her qualities were of the sort that every one else could appreciate better than their possessor. Maurice's affection, or rather her own love for him, was part and parcel of her being. He had returned from Italy essentially improved in health, and far handsomer—at least in her eyes—than she had expected. His was certainly not the idéal of manly beauty, but there was something ideal in it. His complexion was transparent; there was a pensive expression in his face when he was grave, and a joyousness when he was pleased, that were very attractive. His forehead was like marble, except when a sudden flush suffused his temples. His figure was slight, his voice low and gentle; but now and then a sudden transport of anger or of emotion would convulse the almost feminine beauty of his features. It was like a storm on the Mediterranean.—rising in an instant and subsiding again with inconceivable rapidity.

Mary's presence was singularly soothing to this nervous irritability, which might be the effect of his passion for music, or more probably its cause. In her society he felt a repose, a "bien-être," which he hailed with rapture, and expressed—as he did whatever he felt—with enthusiasm. It came as a surprise to her, this apparently unchanged affection of his, for during the years of his absence she had taught herself not to expect it, had never thought of the possibility of loving him less, but always of the probability that he might be changed, and had schooled herself into the belief that if it were so she would have nothing to complain of, although much to suffer. When first she saw him again, her heart involuntarily sank within her; he was too handsome—as she thought—too clever, and too happy for her to influence his destiny, or to have any hold on his affections. She mentally exclaimed,

> "I am not fair like thee,
> The very glance of whose clear eye
> Throws round a light of glee."

But when she discerned the germs of suffering in his highly wrought imagination, in his febrile organisation, and perceived that he was often tormented by anxiety and nervous depression of spirits, then she saw in his life her place, in his destiny her part, and putting her hand to the plough, counted the cost that day, and never looked back.

That evening hour! How soothing it was to both! How full of sweet memories, and pleasant thoughts of the future! Maurice had been at home for some days, but they had not yet taken a walk alone together—Mary, the most industrious of bees, had not much time for strolling; she had considered it her first duty on his return to look over his wardrobe as she used to do, and mend whatever was amiss in it. He tried to laugh or tease her out of her housewifely ways, but without success—she was much too notable a little person to be influenced by his reckless remarks on the subject, and often assured him that, though he was a great deal more famous, he was not much richer than when he went away, and that he should always remember that one stitch in time saves nine, with various other proverbial aphorisms and apposite sayings besides; so he was obliged to content himself with walking about the miniature garden, gathering now one flower, now another, while she sat under the thorn tree, working and singing, and now and then giving utterance to certain little indignant comments on the iniquities of foreign laundresses and sempstresses.

But Sunday was come, and after vespers they walked (an old habit of theirs) to the bridge over the Leigh. She gathered a wall-flower that grew in the crevices of the arch, and fastened it in his hat. He smiled and said: "How sweet it smells! An Italian lady would faint with its perfume. What compensation for us in our chilly climes, though not flowerless fields, as Cowper unjustly calls them, that we need not be afraid of the breath of these

'Sweet nurslings of the vernal skies,
Bathed in soft airs and fed with dew.

And what a blessing it is that home is all it is to us in spite of drawbacks in it, and of attractions elsewhere; that those rude voices that were singing just now the litany we were so fond of as children, have a charm for me which the most sublime strains of the Sistine Chapel cannot match; that these alders speak more to my heart than the chestnut groves of

Subiaco, or the pines of Vallombrosa; and that my English Mary has more beauty in my eyes than the proudest Roman lady, or the prettiest girl of Albano. But you must see those sunny climes, my Mary; you must stand with me one day, and look from the deserted gardens of the Villa Mattei at the dream-like Campagna—you must kneel with me in St. Peter's and feel the Miserere wringing your soul with unearthly melody—you must receive on that gentle little head of yours the wonderful blessing which on the day of the Resurrection falls on Rome and on the world. Oh, you must come with me to that land of poetry and of religion, and learn to love it with the twofold love of the Christian and the artist."

"Maurice, I have never, even as a child, heard the name of Rome without emotion, and to go there with you, to visit the tombs of the Apostles and the relics of martyrs, to receive the blessing you speak of by your side, kneeling in some corner of that great prostrate city, to see what you admire, to feel what you have felt, would be indeed a dream of happiness; but would it not be like digging up this daisy here, and planting it in the middle of the camellias and the cactuses of the Woodlands conservatory, to take *me* amongst the people and to the places where you have been lately living?"

"I know *one* person who would appreciate you, Mary. Guess who?"

"Somebody who would like me, Maurice? Not Emilia Orlandini?"

"O, you spiteful little girl. I did not think you had as much malice in your composition—so to take advantage of my confessions. I hope you did not show *that* letter to Lady-Bird?"

"No, I contrived not to do so, but it was difficult. It is always difficult not to do what *she* wishes."

"So I remember of old—how she used to govern us by her smiles and her tears; but I, at least, am made of sterner stuff now-a-days."

"Do not boast," said Mary, gaily.

"But to return to what I was saying," he continued, 'it is M. d'Arberg who would like you."

"Indeed! I thought he was such a superior person—so clever and literary, and all that sort of thing."

"Yes, he is that, but what he is most particularly, is a man of one purpose, and he likes simplicity and earnestness better than anything else in life. I cannot explain it exactly, but there is a likeness between you: I suppose you are both very religious. But I have seen other people who were so too. but not just in the same way."

"Maurice, I liked so much what you said just now about loving Rome. 'As a *Christian* and an artist.'"

He coloured deeply, and with his eyes turned away from Mary's and fixed on a leaf which was floating down the stream, he hurriedly exclaimed:

"You must not think me better than I am, Mary, my faith has, thank God, never wavered; I admire goodness and truth and piety as much as ever, and my soul—with all its powers of reason, intelligence and imagination—worships in our divine religion the union of whatever is beautiful to the eye and exalting to the mind; and in Overbeck's studio to-day—as in the treasures of the Vatican of yore—the close connexion of the Catholic religion with the highest development of man's genius is so clear, that he who runs may read. But to feel all this," he paused and she added—

"Is something, but not all."

"The requirements of our religion," he continued. "are as stern as her forms are attractive. Oh! if enthusiasm might be accepted instead of sacrifice—if homage and sentiment sufficed—if the bowed knee and the enraptured heart were enough—who with the soul of an artist would not be at the same time the most religious of men? But to bow the knee, not in rapture, but in humiliation—in penance, not in ecstacy—to turn away from the cup of pleasure——But I shall be making my confession to you, Mary, if I go on."

He took her hand and drew her to himself, then, pointing to the river, he earnestly said: "Unstable as water, I cannot excel. It is the same in every respect. Wishes, hopes, resolutions, projects, written in fair characters enough on the sand, but the first wave washes them away, and no token is left on the shore."

"O, but there is a token left, though you know it not yourself. To try and to fail, to fall and to rise again, is not like the stagnant depth of an immoveable indifference. Maurice, there is one thing I am firmly convinced of, and I bless God for it. you will be good, or you will be miserable."

"Then, indeed you must take care of my happiness, my stern little prophet, or I shall hardly thank you for your prediction."

At that moment, there was a splash of oars in the distance

and in a short time a small boat came in sight, which Gertrude and her brother often used when he was at home, but in which, for the first time, she had ventured alone. Her straw hat had fallen back on her shoulders, and the dark blue ribbons with which it was tied hung loosely round her neck. The exercise had flushed her cheeks with the brightest crimson, and as she looked up towards the bridge, a smile illumined her face, like a ray of sunshine on a damask rose. Ceasing to row, she allowed the boat to float at pleasure, and it soon got entangled amongst the weeds and the water-cresses.

She bowed graciously and gaily to Maurice; and throwing to Mary, a handful of forget-me-nots, cried out: "There, you shall have them all, except this white lotus, which I must keep to astonish Father Lifford with it this evening. But how am I ever to get out of this boat? I feel like the man in Molière's play —' *Que diable suis-je venue faire dans cette galère.*'" In an instant Maurice was on the edge of the bank, and swinging himself forward by the help of a branch, he stepped into the boat, and seizing the oars, soon disentangled it from the weeds and set it afloat again. Then with a smile he said,

"Where does the Lady of the Lake, or the river rather, please to be taken?"

"By all means to the shore. I have collected treasures enough for to-day, and will not dare my fate any longer."

He pushed to the shore and threw the rope to Mary, who had come down to meet them; and jumping out of the boat, held his hand out to Gertrude, who, touching it lightly, with one bound sprang on to the bank. She stood there in the shade of the dark alder trees with her red Indian shawl carelessly thrown round her shoulders, and in her hand the broad leaves of the lotus, which she used as a fan. Her attitude and her figure were as graceful as possible. There was something so free and yet so reserved in each gesture and in each glance. She had a way that was peculiar to herself, of drawing back her head while she raised her eyes, and of looking as it were from under her long eye-lashes; and the modulations of her voice, her distinct and musical articulation, were equally uncommon.

"I wish you joy of your return, Maurice, and I hope you are as happy to find yourself in this country again as I should be to leave it. Mary and I have often talked about you."

"And you once had the kindness to write to me; I shall never forget it."

"Shall you stay here some time?"

"Yes. I hope so."

"Then we may often meet again—good bye, dear Mary—good bye, Maurice!"

She drew her shawl over her breast, hastily tied the ribbons of her hat, and disappeared along one of the green alleys that led straight to the Grange. Maurice drew Mary's arm in his, and they turned towards the village.

"Well, now you have seen Lady-Bird again, what do you think of her?"

"I don't know exactly,—she does not seem proud"

"O, no! not at all in some ways."

"She is like a picture I once saw."

"In Italy?"

"Yes, in Venice. It had that same eager wistful look that she has. Is she happy, Mary?"

"I think not; her home is rather a gloomy one for a young girl, and she is painfully anxious to leave it."

"I suppose she is very clever?"

"She is very amusing—very droll at times, and strangely eloquent at others. She reads an immense deal, I believe."

"Does she care for music?"

"She has a most beautiful voice,—quite a wonderful voice; but never having been taught, I don't suppose she sings well —what *you* would call well."

"She must be dreadfully bored in that old house. I remember how stiff her father used to look, and her mother always ill, and the dear old priest so absent, and a little cross, too, sometimes."

"Not really cross, I think, but Lady-Bird tries him by the odd things she says and does; and he does not perhaps quite understand how bored she is, and that even to make any one angry with her is a sort of relief to the dulness of her life."

"Does she come to see you often?"

"Yes, pretty often; by fits and starts. Sometimes she comes every day, and then perhaps we are weeks without seeing her."

"Does she never go out into society, I mean?"

"No. I do not believe she has made a single acquaintance in the neighbourhood. Nobody ever dines at Lifford Grange, I hear, except the agent or the doctor, and that very seldom."

"Then she has no admirers, I suppose."

"O dear no, I should think not, unless ―— "

"Unless what?"

"Unless Mr. Mark Apley was one. He is often riding about here, and going backwards and forwards on the road between the Grange and Stonehouseleigh, that is, when he is at home, which is only at one time of the year. When we meet him he looks at her as if he thought her very pretty, but he has never been introduced to her."

"And how does she look on those occasions?"

"Half proudly and half shyly, as if not sorry to be admired, and yet impatient at being watched."

"Here are her flowers," Maurice said, as they entered the little sitting-room of the cottage, "shall I put them into this vase?" and without waiting for an answer, he arranged them in such a graceful way that Mary stopped to admire it.

"Here is your pianoforte arrived at last," she said. "Now I shall hear some of the things that fine ladies and great musicians have admired."

"The fine ladies more than the great musicians, I am afraid. I was the fashion amongst them, and they made much of me and of my songs, but even in my art—which I love with passion—I am too unstable to excel."

He ran his hand over the keys, and hummed a tune which had something of the wildness of a Neapolitan air, with the tenderness of a German melody.

"How pretty that is!" Mary exclaimed.

"It is my 'Lady-bird,'" he said, "the song I wrote to you about, which I composed last year at Naples. They used to encore it every night."

"No wonder, for it is gay, and yet there is something that touches one in it, something of sadness, which I suppose must be the perfection of music."

"Mary," he said in a moment, as they still sat together at the pianoforte, "I have thought of a plan which, if I can carry it into effect, will enable me to remain here several months without being a burthen on dear mother, and which may also be of use to me when I settle in London. I think I might give lessons in the neighbourhood. Don't you think it would answer? I did so at Florence one year." Mary smiled her assent, and Mrs. Redmond was consulted. She produced a bit of paper, and had soon written in pencil the names of several young ladies and gentlemen whom she sanguinely supposed would be sure to take lessons. The fact was, that there was no music master in that part of the country, and the deficiency had often been regretted by Miss Apley, who was on all occasions Mrs. Redmond's oracle.

"Don't you think, mother, that you might call on Miss Apley to-morrow, and tell her that Maurice means to give lessons? She wished particularly to see you, I know, about the work at the school, and you know you don't dislike paying her a visit."

"Yes, Mary darling, but I am a little foolish about asking a favour."

Maurice coloured, and Mary with her quick perception keenly felt that he was annoyed at the expression her mother had used, and instantly exclaimed,

"But, dearest mother, do you know that I can hardly consider it as a favour. Maurice's talent is not a common one, and the advantage of taking lessons from him in this out-of-the-way place, is a benefit received more than a favour conferred."

"But perhaps she does not know that he has so much talent, dear, and if I say so she will think it is all my partiality."

"O for Heaven's sake, mother," Maurice impatiently exclaimed, "say nothing at all about me. I will speak myself to Father Lifford. But whatever you do, don't puff me; I can't endure that."

He played a noisy bravura, which put a stop to further conversation; and thoughts of Italy, of the women who had flattered him, of the friends who had applauded him, of the way in which genius was considered there as superior to any other distinctions, and the footing of intimacy on which he had been with persons of the highest rank rose to his mind, and made him silent and abstracted during the rest of the evening.

He compared these recollections with the aspect of the little room in which they were sitting, and for the first time disadvantageously; for, whether from the love of change and contrast, which have great charms for persons of his disposition, or from affection for Mary, the very soberness and thoroughly English character of his childhood's home had been agreeable to him. But now he thought again of the palaces, the villas, the ilex avenues, the orange-gardens of Italy; and, as he looked at Mary quietly working at the table by the light of a single tallow candle, she did not seem to him less pleasing than before, but he said to himself, "Yes, I shall transplant you, my English daisy, to that bright land. Its fervid sunshine will animate that somewhat too calm expression. Its influences will call forth all the feeling and the intelligence which this passionless existence would end by stifling. When I produce my first opera at the Scala or the Fenice, how that pale face will flush with excitement, how that breast—which is now breathing so calmly—will throb with emotion, when she will have to witness the failure or hail the success of what costs me almost more than my life's blood!—and those eyes, that always seem to turn more readily to Heaven than to earth, will they not flash with triumph and sparkle with delight, if the enthusiastic cries and the wild applause of an Italian audience call on the successful maestro to come and receive the meed of praise which they so well know how to bestow? O, my quiet, gentle Mary, you must drink with me of that bewildering cup—even though you should have to share my sufferings too."

Ten o'clock struck, and Mrs. Redmond and Mary folded up their work and prepared to go to bed. As Maurice followed them into the passage, he called Mary to the garden door, and putting his hand on her arm, he said in a whisper, "Which had you rather be, intensely happy at times, and very miserable at others, or never know the extremes of human bliss and woe?" She looked surprised and almost pained at the question, but after an instant's hesitation answered, timidly raising her eyes to his, "I suppose that I have already been too happy not to have to suffer in proportion; but come what may—a higher joy or a deeper grief, I care not if the last reach me alone, and the first is shared with you."

"Angel of goodness!" he fervently exclaimed, "and I, on the contrary, was wishing just now to force thee to partake the torments of my feverish existence. Keep thy divine peace of heart, my Mary, and Heaven forbid that in my wayward folly I should ever seek to disturb it." "Why should you, indeed?" she ejaculated with unaffected surprise. He smiled but felt a little disappointed. Why, he could scarcely tell. She did not guess his thoughts; how could she? But others had done so, and life becomes flat and stale when everything has to be explained, and he could not always explain himself even to himself; and a cloud was on his brow as he shut himself up in his room, and—flinging open the window—he threw himself on his bed, and snatching up a pencil and paper he began to compose, but not music. His mind was not tuned to harmony just then, but he wrote rambling verses, and went to sleep with some unfinished lines in his hand.

CHAPTER V

"Noble et légère elle folâtre,
Et l'herbe que foulent ses pas,
Sous le poids de son pied d'albâtre,
Se courbe et ne se brise pas.
Sur ses traits, dont le doux ovale
Borne l'ensemble gracieux,
Les couleurs que la nue étale
Se fondent pour charmer les yeux.
A la pourpre qui teint sa joue,
On dirait que l'aube s'y joue;
Son front léger s'élève et plane
Sur un cou flexible, élancé,
Comme sur le flot diaphane
Un cygne mollement bercé."
LAMARTINE.

"Music is the food of love."
SHAKESPEARE.

How strange it is that people think it worth while to make the best of themselves to themselves, to equivocate with their own hearts, while all the time they know it is of no use—that it is the shallowest of deceptions—that even a Queen's speech, or a ministerial harangue are not more devoid of any pretensions to sincerity, than their special pleadings at the bar of their own understandings. But still the inward and intimate *sham* is carried on, and doubtless, the thief and the assassin have an internal advocate who presses for an acquittal, even while the dagger is sharpening and the booty secured. There are some, indeed, who never appear to commune with themselves, whose minds are like railway travelling, never stopping but at certain stations, never looking beyond a certain terminus.

Mr. Lifford might have been of this number, and if so, his mental line of road must have lain through the dullest and dreariest of intellectual regions. It had gone on its way crushing and extinguishing in himself and in others everything that gives light and joy to existence. Whether, in the language of St. Paul, his thoughts ever accused and excused one another was doubtful. Perhaps he was too essentially despotic to allow even of inward remonstrance, and the rebellion of his own conscience, if it ever broke out, was put down by the iron rigidity of his will.

But in his daughter's character there were other elements at work besides that same *will*, which she had inherited from him. Some of the tenderness of her mother's character was mixed with it. This had seldom been called forth, but a gleam of it was now and then visible which took by surprise those who were accustomed to her reckless moods, and her stubborn resolution. She had one of those natures that could not be governed by ordinary means, and—like the Spartan boy—she would have suffered a thousand tortures before she yielded to threats or submitted to violence. Two or three times, between the age of childhood and that at which she had now arrived, she had come into open collision with her father. Once, in a paroxysm of passion, an imprecation escaped her lips, which the instant it was uttered terrified her to that degree, that she gave a scream of horror, and fell on her knees before him. If he had opened his arms, she would probably have loved him from that moment with all the energy of her strange character. Had he been moved to anger or to indignation, she would have continued to sue for pardon and reconciliation; but he left her with a sneer, and she remained alone with her remorse and her anger, and neither could master the other, till some days afterwards in confession—that secret arena where so many fierce battles with self are fought—the proud spirit yielded; and, after shedding torrents of tears, pale with emotion, she went straight from the chapel to her father's room, implored a forgiveness which was coldly granted, returned to the feet of one who as his Lord's representative was always kind though at other times stern, and who, after absolving and blessing her, dismissed her in peace.

Good was it for Gertrude that she should have known what such a conquest effects, what such a moment is. She never forgot it. There are seeds sometimes sown that lie for long years under a hardened surface, but the rain may some day fall, the sun may one day shine, and the harvest may be reaped.

There was one element in Gertrude's character which resembled neither father nor mother, and that was a wild gaiety —which was particularly attractive in one as beautiful, as naturally clever, and as original as she was. It was almost impossible for any one to resist its fascination. Even Father Lifford—who thought it bordered on levity, and conceived it to be rather a point of duty to snub her—could not help at times feeling its influence, and when she succeeded in making him smile it put her in good humour for the rest of the day, as she used to tell Mary Grey.

It would have been impossible in so dull an existence, and with such a craving for change and amusement of any sort, that the return of an old playfellow who formerly contributed so much to her enjoyment should have been indifferent to her, or that she should not have been ready to renew an acquaintance which had once given her so much pleasure. His letters to Mary had interested her imagination; she felt curious to see how far he was in love with her quiet friend, and whether her feelings for him had any tinge of romance, or partook of what Gertrude considered the common-place nature of her character, for thus she estimated one of the most *un*common-place persons in the world, one of those rare self-forgetting natures that have more feeling than passion, more heroism than courage, and more tenderness than sensibility.

A day or two after the meeting at the bridge she sent her maid to tell Mary that she meant to sketch that afternoon in Oakland Chase, and that if she had nothing else to do it would be very kind of her to meet her there, as it was some time since they had seen each other in comfort. The message was delivered, and the expected assent given, and at the same spot where, about three years before, this story opened, Gertrude and Mary were again sitting—the first drawing with untaught skill the old trees which had been the favourite haunts of their childhood, and the other busy with some plain work which she had brought with her.

The summer was far advanced—there were no flowers on the grass around them, and the birds had ceased their songs, but the rich foliage and deep shade of the forests were in all the glory of maturity. Gertrude had expected that Maurice would join them; but he did not do so, and she felt disappointed. Mary's conversation seemed to her more uninteresting than usual, and at last she abruptly asked,

"Where is Maurice? What does he do with himself during these long summer days?"

"He is reading out there by the stile," Mary said. "He walked with me as far, and then said he should be in our way, and that he would amuse himself with his book till I came back."

4

"But what nonsense that was to think he should be in our way. I hope he does not mean to avoid me, Mary. Does he remember what good friends we used to be?"

"I believe, dear Lady-Bird, that is one of the reasons that he feels shy with you now. He says he cannot expect that you will consider him as an old friend."

"And why not—I should like to know? Have I so many friends that I am likely to be ungracious to the only ones I have known in childhood? I have observed, Mary, that you are sometimes inclined to be formal and ceremonious with me, and it bores me to death. O yes, to death," she repeated, with her pencil on her lips, and peeping into Mary's bonnet, who was shaking her head and smiling. "What a pity it is," she exclaimed, " that we cannot make an exchange!"

"What exchange, Lady-Bird?"

"Of our homes, I mean—I should have been very happy at the cottage, and you would have been a sort of model young lady at Lifford Grange. You would never have said or done a foolish thing, and have looked as steady and demure as any of the family pictures. As it is, my uncle says that you are a pattern of perfection, and then sighs and shrugs his shoulders as he looks at me. Don't you wish that you were Miss Lifford? Is it not a very enviable destiny to spend one's life at Lifford Grange—a sort of secular cloister, of the Carthusian order, for we never talk without necessity."

"You are not following the rule *now*, I suppose," Mary said. "But, dear Lady-Bird, I am not sure that you would find my life very gay, though *I* feel it to be happy."

"Why, it must be a *little* amusing to have a lover, which will never happen to me. *You* would never have thought of it, if it had not come in your way, but be candid—is it not amusing?"

"Mary coloured, and shook her head again—" Now, mind your drawing, Lady-Bird, and do not talk in that manner."

"Well, I will not, if you will go and tell Maurice that he is not to keep out of my way, and fancy that we are not to be friends as we used to be."

"I will go, if you will promise not to talk as you did just now, especially before him."

"O no, I won't—go your ways, Mary Grey. Is it not a '*douce violence*,' to send you on such an errand? In the meantime I will finish this old oak, and you shall have it as a reward."

Mary walked quietly away down one of the avenues of the Chase, and Gertrude, watching her as she disappeared amongst the trees, said to herself—"She is like the 'Bonny Kilmeny who ga'ed up the glen,' pure as pure could be. There is no one so good as Mary, I do believe. She does not seem to care much about Maurice, but I shall know more of that when I have seen them together." And this last word putting her in mind of a pretty song that she had once learnt, and that began—" We have been friends together, in sunshine and in shade,"—she warbled it at intervals, when not too much engrossed by her drawing.

When Mary returned, and Maurice with her, she greeted him with a playful kindness that made him at once feel at his ease; and sitting down on the stump of a tree opposite to the one she occupied, his heightened colour subsided, and his manner, which had been a little stiff at first, became natural and animated. She asked him questions which drew from him some lively descriptions of places and of persons abroad, and the bright smile with which she responded to anything that amused her, carried him back to the days when to relate a story that would make Lady-Bird laugh or cry was the height of his ambition. He was surprised to find how much she knew about pictures and statues, poets and musicians,—how well acquainted she was with the history and the literature of Italy, and with what rapid changes of manner she seemed transformed in an instant from a wayward child into an eloquent woman; and then again, when apparently most in earnest, would break suddenly off into some strain of fun and nonsense.

The sort of conversation that established itself between them was entirely new to Mary; it interested but puzzled her. Maurice had been living a great deal in society abroad, and had acquired a readiness and fluency of language which nothing but the habit of conversation can give, except in one as naturally gifted as Gertrude was. Her singular intelligence made her instinctively guess what others learnt by degrees. She would have made a speech in Parliament, or preached a sermon, or acted a play, or harangued a mob if called upon to do so; nothing came amiss to her, but solitude and constraint. She was very quick also in discerning the characters of others, except when baffled by one of such extraordinary simplicity as Mary's. Maurice she judged at once. "More talent than ability; more ardour than vigour; more imagination than sense, and sensibility than feeling: an abundance of words at his command, and a sufficient amount of thought to turn that abundance to account." This view of the young artist was rapidly sketched in her mind, as she sat conversing with him, with all the *laisser-aller* that was habitual to her, and the animation which a new amusement called forth.

The drawing was not finished till the sun was setting, and Jane had appeared to escort Gertrude home. She gave it to Mary, as she had promised. It was the old hollow tree in which they used to act "O'Connor's child." That evening Mary spoke twice to Maurice without attracting his notice. His eyes were fixed on the sketch.

"I do not think M. d'Arberg would like her as much as you," he said at last, as if he were answering a question.

She laughed, and said "Who?"

"Lady-Bird. She would not suit him, I think. She is too like Undine."

"Who is Undine—an Italian you know?"

"O no, dear Mary; she only lives in Fairy-land. Lady-Bird knows all about her, I am sure."

"She knows a great deal," Mary said with a sigh. Her gravity made Maurice laugh.

"Not how to make a home as happy as you would, my darling Mary."

"She might if she *loved* her home. It is so easy to make those we love happy—that is, if they love us," she timidly added. He pushed aside the oak-tree, and drew his chair close to hers, and told her the story of his opera—the great work he was meditating; and she listened to it for the tenth time, as if it had been the first.

When that evening the clock struck ten, and with a Cinderella-like punctuality she got up and folded her work, he said to her, gaily, "You are worth a hundred Lady-Birds, Mary!" She put her hand on his mouth; he kissed it, and whispered, "You will not mind, will you, if I play for an hour or two longer? Dear mother does not, I know; she is too deaf to hear it upstairs."

"I do mind,—you ought to go to bed and *rest;* you will wake like a ghost to-morrow. Like the ghost in the last scene of the opera."

The opera had now become a conspicuous point in her thoughts. He did not rehearse it oftener in imagination than she did. Never having been in her life in a theatre, she had a very vague idea of a dramatic performance; but it was -

enough for her that it was his dream his work, his object; the story was founded on their favourite ballad of " O'Connor's child," and she could fancy, she said, how beautiful it would be to see it all acted, as they used to act it, and at the same time to hear his music telling in another way all they used to feel about it.

As she lay awake in her room that night, listening to the sounds of his playing below, and watching the light clouds quickly passing over the heavens, she felt angry with herself that the words, "You are worth a hundred Lady-Birds," seemed to mix with the music, and to be written in the skies.

In about a fortnight's time, Maurice had obtained two or three pupils in the neighbourhood, and by degrees he became known; his reputation established itself, and he grew to be somewhat of a lion in Lancashire. He was sometimes invited to some of the country-houses where he gave lessons. His perfectly gentleman-like manners, his good looks, his knowledge of French and Italian, and his really beautiful playing, made him a general favourite wherever he went. On Sunday he always played the organ at the Catholic chapel at Stonehouseleigh; and strangers used often to come there to hear the exquisite music with which he accompanied the different parts, and filled up the pauses of the service. To Mary it sounded like the strains of Heaven itself, and her heart and her love were both so pure, that there was nothing unworthy of the place or of the hour in the joy that overflowed that heart, as, with her face buried in her hands, she felt as if he were translating into melody the speechless adoration which was rising from her own soul.

Gertrude always came there for vespers,—sometimes with Father Lifford, or else with her maid; and at the conclusion of the service, as the congregation dispersed, she usually waited in the churchyard while he was in the sacristy, or Jane was lingering with her friends from the village. Her seat was a tombstone near the gate, and the simple inscription upon it, "Requiescat in pace," contrasted with the expression of her face. Strangers sometimes remarked how beautiful, but how restless it was. They would have wished to say to her, "Rest in peace," but that time was not come. Whatever power religion exerted over her tended to a struggle, and interior strife was the result of salutary impressions. Better for her that it was so; the best of of such characters and intellects as hers is the difficulty they find in self-deception. They err, they offend, the will is stubborn, and the heart undisciplined—but they were gone too deep into themselves, and too far beyond themselves to act the part of the false prophet to their own souls, and to cry out " Peace where there is no peace."

One day as they were walking back from the chapel, Gertrude asked Mary with a look of great interest, if it was true that Maurice had been giving lessons in the neighbourhood, and on Mary's answering in the affirmative exclaimed, " Then I shall take some, that is,"—turning to him, for he just overtook them at that moment.—" that is, if you will be kind enough to undertake a beginner who has never had any regular instruction, whose fingers are as stiff as her voice is unmanageable. I shall try your patience dreadfully, but will you?"

He coloured, bowed, but did not look pleased. She remarked it, and with her usual impetuosity, turned to Mary and said—

" Why is he so cross about it? Don't you like to teach me, Maurice?"

" Yes." he answered, colouring still more deeply, " but I cannot bear——" He broke off suddenly, and added, " I mean that I do not know if I have an hour to spare that will suit you. When would you wish me to come?"

" When could you?"

" At five o'clock."

" Yes—at five o'clock—three times a week—that will be delightful! That hour is just the one that will suit mamma. Do you know, Mary, that music is, I find, one of the few things that mamma cares about. When I asked her about taking lessons, and told her that Maurice was giving them, she seemed quite pleased, and said that the pianoforte should be put in the room next to hers; and that when she was well enough, the folding-doors should be opened, and she would like to listen. She thinks it will do her good to hear a little music. She has never heard any since she left Spain—except the little songs you used to come sometimes and sing to her when you were a boy," she added, turning to him.

Maurice smiled in a constrained manner, and asked which day he should come. It was settled for the next Tuesday, and he took his leave with a cloud on his brow.

When Mary asked him afterwards—with an unconscious uneasiness which she could hardly define, and which she would not perhaps have felt had he gladly accepted Gertrude as a pupil—whether it annoyed him to give lessons at the Grange, he answered impatiently: "You do not suppose, do you, that it is pleasant to be treated as a friend, and to be considered and paid as a music-master?" She felt depressed, but said it gave her much pleasure to think that his playing might be an enjoyment to Mrs. Lifford who had so few pleasant moments in her life, and that it would bring Gertrude into frequent companionship with her mother, which might prove an inestimable comfort to both. He assented, but remained restless and disturbed during the remainder of the day.

But after the first lesson had been given, his annoyance seemed to have passed away, and he told Mrs. Redmond and Mary, how strange it had seemed to him to find Mrs. Lifford again on that same couch where he used to see her when a boy—only still paler and thinner than he remembered her then. "There she lies wrapped up in shawls, and propped up by pillows—her face so white and wan that it looks as if one could see through it, and her eyes appearing unnaturally large and bright. After I had given Lady-Bird some instructions, she asked me to play something very gently, as she thought her mother would like it. I thought, at that minute, of Mozart's Agnus Dei, and I played it very softly, but with a great deal of expression. I never in my life tried so much to play well—not when I was most anxious to make an effect at a concert as I did then to please that pale woman who had not heard any music for sixteen years. When I had gone on for about twenty minutes, varying the air with a few simple chords, I left off, and looking through the door towards her couch I saw that she had covered her face with her thin transparent hands, and that large tears were rolling through her fingers. She called Lady-Bird in a faint voice, and told her to go on with the lesson—that she had heard enough of the soul of music for one day. This was said in broken English, but I liked the expression so much. There is something very quiet and solemn about those two rooms. Hers is so full of pictures and silk hangings, and all sorts of foreign looking things, it looks quite like a chapel; and the next is a library, and opens on the garden. Lady-Bird has a beautiful voice, but it bores her to practise much, and what bores her I suspect she never does; as to playing she will not even attempt it. But she is coming here to-morrow at three o'clock to look over the music I brought you, and to choose the songs she will learn."

"O then, it is singing lessons you give her, Maurice dear?" Mrs. Redmond asked, as he began to turn over a heap of books by the pianoforte.

"I suppose so, mother," he answered with a smile. "Anything she chooses to learn; but one might as well try to teach the lark to sit still on a bush, and practise her trills, as make Lady-Bird apply herself to anything but what she fancies at the moment."

"She will try your patience very much, dear Maurice."

"O I shall play and sing to her, she will learn in that way; she has so much genius."

CHAPTER VI.

> "'Tis amazement more than love,
> Which her radiant eyes do move;
> If less splendour wait on thine,
> Yet they so benignly shine,
> I would turn my dazzled sight
> To behold their milder light.
> But as hard 'tis to destroy
> That high flame as to enjoy;
> Which how eas'ly I may do,
> Heav'n (as eas'ly scaled) does know."
> WALLER.

THE next day Gertrude was true to her appointment. She was in high spirits,—sung a roulade as she arrived at the green gate, better than any she had accomplished the day before; told Jane to call again in an hour; and, asking leave to gather some of the honeysuckles and jasmine on the wall which felt hot with the sun, she stood some time outside the house, playing with Mrs. Redmond's cat who was purring on the window-seat. She kept gently pinching its paw, and then kissing it to make up for it.

"I am sure Mary never teased anything in her life; did she, Mrs. Redmond? But it is a bad plan to make people too happy, Mary.—they say it never answers; and though 'they say' is a very spiteful, odious, and tiresome imp, I believe he is right sometimes. Puss will be much more glad to see me the next time I come, because I have plagued her a little, and then been very kind. *Does* Mary ever tease you, Maurice?"

"Only I believe by never giving me an opportunity of

finding fault with her," he answered from within the room, where he was writing out some music.

"O, but that is a very great fault, indeed,—perhaps the most provoking one a woman can have. Won't you reform, Mary? It is very hard on poor Maurice. Men do so like to scold and lecture, one should not deprive them of their little amusements. It is selfish to be always so good. Father Lifford, for instance, how bored he would be if I was as good as you and mamma. Othello's occupation would be gone."

After going on for some time in this way, she came into the room and began to examine the music. Opening a volume of manuscript songs, her attention was arrested by one, entitled, "The Blind Man to his Mistress."

"Is this your own composition?" she asked of Maurice, as sitting down at the pianoforte she tried the notes.

"Yes," he answered; "I wrote both the words and the music after seeing, at a ball, a blind man who was engaged to be married to a young girl,—he seemed to listen to the sound of her footsteps while she was dancing with others."

The poetry ran thus :—

"Yes, others say they love, but is the love of those who see
The same deep undivided love my blindness gives to thee?
O do those who can gaze each day on the fair earth and sky,—
Do they watch as *I* do for each faint whispered word or sigh?
And do they count it joy to hear thy footstep and thy voice,
And in thy slightest touch, as in the greatest bliss, rejoice?
And do they breathe more freely when the free and blessed air
That fans their aching brow has played through thy long floating hair?
And does a sense of gloom oppress their heavy heart with weight
Unspeakable if e'er in vain thy coming they await?
O, if they love and *see*, can they e'er gaze on aught but thee?
If so, their love is not such love as my blind dreams of thee!"

Gertrude read these lines, and seemed thoughtful for a moment.

"I envy," she exclaimed, "the power of rendering into verse the passing impressions of the hour,—of fixing, as it were, into shape that floating poetry which haunts the mind, and makes us what wise people call romantic. I imagine that poets are much less so than those who do not spend their capital of imagination upon paper; and, judging from the lives of poets and persons of genius, it seems to me that in general they have less deep feeling than silent people,—I do not mean people who are not talkative, but those who canno' tell themselves their own story."

"But, my dear, everybody must know their own story,' Mrs. Redmond put in, "and if so, they can tell it I suppose though not, I dare say, pleasantly for other people to hear indeed. I forget a great many things that have happened to me, and I suppose that is what you mean."

"I believe," Maurice said, "that imagination makes people suffer with tenfold power from all the afflictions that com in their way. It awakens presentiments of evil, recalls past sufferings, multiplies causes of annoyance, and wears out the spirits almost as much by the stimulus of fictitious and feverish enjoyment, as by its fanciful miseries."

"And yet you would not be without it, would you?" she said, turning suddenly round, and fixing her eyes upon him. He looked at her for a second, and then hastily said, "No; we sometimes cherish the cause of our sufferings;" and then, snatching up another heap of music, he carried it to the pianoforte, and turned it over in a hurried manner.

She repeated his last words. "'Cherish the cause of our sufferings!'—difficult, I should think, if not impossible. But, if so, it confirms what I was saying just now. You see, Mary, one must make people suffer sometimes, that they may appreciate their happiness on the whole."

Mary's colour rose, and she looked graver than the occasion required. There was some emotion in her voice as she answered, "A worthless happiness it would be, given by such means, and bought at such a price."

A serious reply to a gay remark always throws a degree of embarrassment into the conversation where it occurs; and it was the case in this instance. The impression was not dissipated till after Maurice had played two or three things, out of which Gertrude chose what she wished to learn. She then put on her bonnet and shawl, and stood a few minutes talking to Mrs. Redmond, and admiring her knitting. As she was preparing to go she said to Maurice,

"Then to-morrow, at five?"

"Yes," he answered; "but perhaps I may not be quite exact, as it is a long way from here to Woodlands, and my horse is not over brisk. Perhaps you will not mind if I am a few minutes late."

"No; I shall practise this song in the meantime. You give lessons at Woodlands then?"

"Yes, to Miss Harriet and Miss Fanny."

"Are they promising pupils?"

"Diligent ones," he said with a smile. "They asked me a great deal about you the other day."

"Did they? I hope you will not give me a bad character the next time they do so. Is Harriet Apley the one with a plump figure and rosy cheeks?"

"Just so; and Fanny has dark eyes and a pale complexion."

"Is there a governess in the house?"

"Yes, for the youngest daughter. She must be about your brother's age."

"By the way, Mary," Gertrude exclaimed, "I had a letter from Edgar the other day. He is growing so priggish, poor dear boy, it is quite ridiculous. He talks of quarterings, and heraldry, and old families, and of all that sort of trash to papa's heart's content, and my particular *discontent*. I shall have no patience with him if he bores me with any of that nonsense when he comes home."

"But is it not rather nice of him to care about what interests his father so much?"

Gertrude sat down again at the table opposite Mary and said—"Now that is the sort of thing about which we shall never agree. I think your notions about always trying to please people, and making oneself agreeable to them, and accommodating oneself to all their fancies, are next door to hypocrisy. If I was to sit smiling benignantly for instance. and looking all delight when papa and Father Lifford talk politics, whereas I feel ready to bite my lips through with vexation at having to be silent and not argue against what seems to me such absurd prejudice, I should really feel ashamed of myself."

"But does it never occur to you that they may be right and you may be wrong? There is so much to be said on both sides of every question which does not involve points of faith and morality, and should you not give those to whom you owe so much deference at least the benefit of a doubt?"

"To hear a *mésalliance* spoken of as a crime! It makes me so indignant; and that Father Lifford especially should talk in that way! It is so against the spirit of religion."

"I am not so sure of that," Mary exclaimed with some warmth. "We cannot judge these points, or estimate the evil of such things. I cannot but think, Lady-Bird, that you are too positive in your opinion."

"I am astonished, Mary," Maurice rejoined, "that *you* should object to that. I do not know any one so obstinately resolved as you are on certain points."

"Is not she, Maurice?" Gertrude cried with exultation. "I know so well the expression of her face when anybody approaches one of her strongholds. Half defying, half deprecating, she guards her opinions like an angry dove her nest."

Maurice laughed and looked fondly at Mary, who, with a little reluctant smile, gently said—

"Principles—not opinions."

"O come, Mary, that won't do. And why can't I have my political opinions?"

"Nonsense, Lady-Bird, you know very well that you have no such thing. It is all from the spirit of contradiction that you dislike kings and heraldry and all that sort of thing. I dare say that if you had had to sit without speaking and to hear republics and radicals and democracy praised, you would have been by this time a determined aristocrat."

"Heaven forbid!" Maurice ejaculated. Mrs. Redmond looked up from her work with alarm.

"Why, you are not a Radical, Maurice, I hope!"

"No," he answered, "but I hate all distinctions of class and artificial divisions. What I do like is a spirit above prejudice, and the disposition to estimate things according to what they are, not according to what they are *called*."

This lucid explanation satisfied Mrs. Redmond, and she finished putting up a small parcel of dried violets, which Gertrude had promised to employ that evening as a remedy against a slight cough which she complained of. It so happened that the sheet of paper which she used for the purpose, was one on the inside of which Maurice had been scribbling the day before, and had forgotten to destroy, so that when Gertrude undid the packet that evening, her attention was attracted by the writing within the sheet, which had escaped Mrs. Redmond's observation, and the following lines met her eyes—

"Do I not love thee? No, I feel for earth and sky and sea
And all things beautiful in life, all that I feel for thee.
Do I not love thee? No, I gaze on rose or lily bright
With the same look I fix on thee, of wonder and delight.
Do I not love thee? No, my ears in the spring-time rejoice
As much in the birds' songs as in the music of thy voice.
Do I not love thee? No, the stars, the whispering winds, the flowers,
The murmur of the waves at night, and the sweet citron bowers,

Have breathed into my soul a sense of beauty and of love
As keen as thy bewitching eyes have ever made me prove."

"Are these Maurice's own writing, I wonder?" Gertrude said to herself, as she put down the paper. "And are the bewitching eyes he alludes to mine?" She was sitting at her dressing-table, and looked into the glass, as the doubt—if doubt it was—suggested itself. What she saw there did not tend to do away with the supposition—and it was not an unpleasant one, especially as it was an expression of intense admiration, and not of love that the verses contained. For Maurice to have been in love with her would have been exceedingly inconvenient and tiresome. It would have raised all sorts of questions and discussions between herself and her conscience, and interfered with an intercourse which was beginning to amuse her; but to be worshipped as a star, a bird, a wave, or a flower, was perfectly safe, right, entertaining and agreeable, and with this conviction she retired to rest, and the next day looked forward with pleasure to her music lesson.

These music lessons became quite a new, strange enjoyment to Mrs. Lifford. When she was well enough, the doors between her rooms were opened, and Jane was released from her post of chaperon. During that whole hour her eyes were fixed on her daughter. She gazed on her as at a living picture—each lovely contour of feature, each dimple, each glance she learnt as it were by heart, and the full tones of her deep, sweet voice vibrated in her soul with almost painful power. In her mind, so long accustomed to silence and meditation, every impression took that form, each pleasurable feeling became an aspiration, and every emotion turned into a prayer. Quite different was the way in which that hour was spent by the pupil and the master. It was one of much enjoyment to both, nor did either of them think that enjoyment wrong. The love of music, the desire of improvement on the one hand, the interest of imparting instruction to one as highly endowed as his scholar on the other, were legitimate sources of pleasure and excitement. Sometimes there were pauses in the lesson, occasioned by questions and answers, suggested by the music they studied, or the recollections it called up. Gertrude liked to hear of Italy, and when tired of practising, she asked for descriptions, which Maurice was ready enough to give. He often talked of his friend and patron, M. d'Arberg, for whom he had an enthusiastic admiration, and quoted his thoughts and his sayings. The glimpses of the world which she thus obtained greatly piqued her curiosity. No one else had ever talked to her of what she was only acquainted with through books, and though she was and felt herself to be much cleverer than Maurice, still he had wherewith to amuse and to interest her exceedingly.

It would have been impossible for him not to delight in giving her pleasure, and the pauses between the songs were sometimes so long that Mrs. Lifford would inquire if the lesson was finished—which reminded them that it was a lesson and not a conversation which they had to carry on. At the end of the hour Gertrude often desired him to play or to sing some of her favourite airs, some of Shubert's melodies, or a Spanish Guerilla song, or a symphony of Beethoven; and then, sitting by her mother's couch—with her hand locked in hers—she dreamed of scenes and of places which her fancy conjured up. It was quite a new feeling to the mother and the daughter to enjoy anything together, and Mrs. Lifford never perceived that there was anything objectionable in these lessons. She knew nothing of the world, or of any heart but her own—so pure a one that it had never taught her to suspect evil or danger, and indeed in this instance there was no evil to be discerned, and if there was danger it was remote. Had she been more experienced and keen sighted, she might have observed both admiration and—at times—emotion in Maurice's countenance, and in Gertrude's a consciousness of that admiration, and a certain pleasure in it, albeit not the slightest approach to anything beyond a momentary gratification at its existence. She might, indeed, have felt, when they practised together the beautiful music of Anna Bolena, and sang with great expression, the air, "*Fin dell età piú tenera,*" like Madame de Maintenon when she wrote to Racine after the pupils of St. Cyr had acted Andromaque. "*Nos petites filles ont si bien joué votre tragédie qu'elles ne la rejoueront de leur vie;*" she might have said, "*Ils l'ont si bien chanté qu'ils ne le rechanteront de leur vie.*" But gentle, kind, and pure-hearted as she was—and intelligent, too, in some ways—very eloquent in her native tongue, to a degree that would have surprised those who never heard her speak but in broken English, she was not endowed with Madame de Maintenon's talent for government, and would never have ruled St. Cyr, or swayed the heart of the Grand Monarque.

And so these lessons went on for several weeks. Maurice

framed his engagements so as not to omit them. He was very busy and in good spirits, his health improved daily, and he was as fond of Mary as ever. He always talked to her a great deal of Gertrude. He explained to her that he admired her as a master-piece of creation, as a type of loveliness, an artist in soul, an ideal of beauty and of genius; but that it would be as unreasonable to suppose that his admiration of her had anything to do with *love*, as to have accused him of being in love with Titian's Flora, or the portrait of the Cenci, because he had spent hours in contemplation before them, or because he worshipped intellect, talent, and beauty in art and in Nature.

Mary listened rather gravely to all this, and said she thought he worshipped beauty a great deal too much in everything—that it was a sort of idolatry. "What did it signify," he answered, "if he loved her better than anything else in the world?" There was no answering that, but her brow had often now an anxious expression, and the thought of "deep violet eyes with a light shining in them, like a ray of sunshine through a dark heart's-ease," was apt to "come painfully often between her and the midnight skies."

One is rather prone—especially in a novel—to be unjust towards those who do right things in a disagreeable manner, and to blame the conduct of disagreeable people without sufficiently considering their actions in themselves. Some very sensible proceeding may meet with general condemnation if it is the act of the author's *bête noire*, and if he has been fortunate enough to inspire his reader with a sympathetic aversion. Mrs. Lifford was amiable and interesting both from her character and her sufferings, and scarcely to blame for an ignorance which in her position was very natural, but her blindness and her imprudence were undeniable; and an event soon took place which roused painful feelings in more hearts than one, and deepened Gertrude's resentment against her father. Yet in this instance, though his mode of acting was neither kind nor judicious, he was undoubtedly perfectly right in the main.

He came one day into the library next to his wife's room, at an unusual hour, and whilst Gertrude was taking her music lesson. He stood at the door for five minutes like the statue of the Commendatore. His cold glassy eyes fixed on the flushed and animated countenance of his daughter, who was singing with considerable animation an Italian bravura; he then turned them on the pale but not less excited face of the young musician, who seemed to watch her lips as if "the airs of heaven were playing on her tongue," and thrilling through his soul, and then on the maid busily absorbed in her work at some distance, and without saying a word, he turned on his heel and left the room unobserved by any of the three.

That evening, when Mrs. Redmond, Mary, and Maurice were at tea, the maid came in and gave him a letter which had just been brought from Lifford Grange. He supposed it to be a message about some music which he was to have written for to London, and hastily opened it. Mary—who was watching him—started at the expression which suddenly overspread his face. It was the paleness of anger that blenched his cheek, and made his mouth quiver.

"What is it?" she asked in an almost inaudible whisper.

"There!" he said, "take and read that. This is the sort of treatment one is exposed to in England—the only country where it would be tolerated. Oh, the vulgar pride of rank, the insolence of fancied superiority!"

He dashed the note on the ground, and walked up and down the room with a scowl on his brow, and a burning spot on his cheek. Mary picked up the paper which he had crumpled and torn, and smoothing it again, read its contents, which were as follows:—

"Mr. Lifford presents his compliments to Mr. Redmond, and begs to inform him that Miss Lifford will not continue her music lessons, and at the same time he requests him to have the goodness to send his account."

Maurice stopped opposite to Mary, and with an impatient "Well!" awaited her comments on this note. She felt embarrassed, for it did not appear to her insolent, as he called it, though ungracious it certainly was, and there was an instinct in her woman's heart which whispered the cause of this abrupt dismissal. She kept her eyes fixed on the paper for some seconds, and then said in a hesitating manner,

"It is annoying, but—"

"It is insulting!" he rejoined. "I shall send him neither answer nor account."

"Maurice, if you are so proud, how will you ever make your fortune, and how shall we realize our hopes, and provide for mother in her old age?"

He clenched his hand and cried, "I would rather die than touch his money."

She sighed and said nothing more, and two hours passed

gloomily away. Then a knock was heard at the door, and the maid announced Miss Lifford. Maurice and Mary both gave a start. Mrs. Redmond, who had been dozing in her arm-chair, rubbed her eyes and said, "Dear me, how d'ye do, my dear young lady." Gertrude shook hands with her, and she thought her hand cold and nervous, but before there was time to remark upon it, she had turned away, and was standing before Maurice. "I am come," she said, "to thank you for the lessons you have given me, and the trouble you have taken with me. You must not be shocked or annoyed at the letter that I hear my father has sent you. There is nothing offensive to *you* in this proceeding. It is only that anything that gives me pleasure, anything that relieves the monotony of my life, and affords me interest or occupation is immediately forbidden. I suppose that my books will soon be taken away from me, and if I could be commanded not to *think*, it would doubtless be done, and my mind would become as stagnant as my existence, as dull as that hateful canal that flows under our windows. But, thank God, *that* is impossible—and I will neither be an idiot out of obedience, or ungrateful out of submission; and so I once more thank you for the instruction you have given me, for the first enjoyment I have shared with my mother, for the happy moments I have had while you played to me and talked to me of other lands which it will never be my fate to see. That is all I had to say: it is late and Jane is in a hurry. Good bye, I am glad that I was able to say this to you all."

She was gone in an instant, and Mrs. Redmond asked what it all meant. Mary explained it to her in a few words, and then turning to Maurice with some emotion said: "Now, Maurice, you cannot feel proud or angry any more—she is a dear beautiful Lady-Bird, and I wish she was not shut up in such a dull cage; it would be better for her" (and for us too, she inwardly added).

"True, my little dove," he answered, "and what would you do with her if you could?"

"Open her prison-door, and let her fly away to a happy home of her own."

He smiled, and putting a sheet of paper before her said, "Come now, make out an account for me for this Blue-Beard at Lifford Grange."

She laughed and began casting up figures, while—leaning on his hands—he sat looking at her, feeling the repose of that sweet face, and glad to find how very dear she was to him.

"Twenty guineas I make it out to be!" she triumphantly exclaimed. "Indeed! What a fortune!" he answered gaily, imitating her manner; and they talked nonsense, and built castles in the air, and were as happy and as merry as possible during all the rest of the evening.

A few weeks elapsed, during which Gertrude called two or three times on Mary, once to lend her a book she had wished to read, then to return some music which Maurice had left at the Grange, and began to beg for some of Mrs. Redmond's *Pot-pourri*. It was natural enough that she should find pleasure in these visits. That cottage was, in every way, a pleasant spot. Its garden was bright with autumnal flowers; there was a perfume of domestic happiness within and about it. Mrs. Redmond's gentle manner, Mary's affectionate welcome, Maurice's respectful homage were as soothing to her feelings as the fragrance of the flowers was agreeable to her senses. Then she had also an odd kind of curiosity in watching Mary and Maurice together. She had read as many novels as she could possibly lay her hand upon, and had studied them till she knew them almost by heart, but of love in real life she had never seen anything, and, concluding that these two young persons were engaged to one another, it amused her to observe how far they realised the notions she had formed of lovers.

"I believe," she said to herself one day, "that she would follow him to the end of the world, to prison and to death also, and give her life for him or burn her right hand and not wince as she did so, if it could be of use to him; but, somehow or other, her love seems to be more a religion than a passion, more of devotion in it than of fervour, rather drawn from the depths of her own heart, and freely bestowed upon him, than irresistibly attracted towards him. As to Maurice, I do not know if he is capable of loving deeply—I think he has more dependence upon her, more selfish attachment to the happiness she creates for him than any more devoted feeling." While she was thus musing, her eyes had unconsciously fixed themselves on Maurice, and—abstracted in her own thoughts—she was not aware of it.

Mary, in a somewhat constrained voice, said to her: "You are very silent, Lady-Bird; what are you thinking of?" And Gertrude, turning to her with a smile, answered, "I believe that instead of buying my thoughts you would rather buy my silence, for I was thinking of something you always forbid me to speak about." Mary coloured, and said: "Then, indeed, Miss Lifford, I will not repeat my question." Gertrude shrugged her shoulders impatiently.

"Why will you call me Miss Lifford, when I call you Mary? It is so stiff and nonsensical."

"I think your father would be surprised if he was to hear Mary call you Gertrude," Mrs. Redmond said.

"I don't care what he thinks—his notions about *rank* are absurd. If people have been equally well educated, surely they are equals to all intents and purposes."

"No! not in every sense, dear Lady-Bird."

"That is one of those convenient answers that sound well," Gertrude rejoined, "and in reality mean nothing. In what sense are *you* not my equal, I should like to know?"

"I am not in the same worldly position as you are; I do not live in the same society."

Maurice's brow clouded over, and, hastily snatching up a newspaper, he sat down with his back to the table.

"What society *do* I live in?" Gertrude impetuously exclaimed. "I never see any one beyond the walls of Lifford Grange, except here, and at home I sometimes make the maids my companions from sheer ennui at being so much alone."

"That is a peculiarity in your case," Mary answered; "but if your father did not shun all society, you would live with people whom we should not associate with."

"Yes, my fate *is* a very peculiar one. I begin to be fully aware of that, and therefore if I should ever act in a very peculiar manner, who is to blame me? Not my father, surely?"

"You are accountable to One of still higher authority."

"Aye! but He is no respecter of persons, Mary! He does not care for quarterings and old parchments."

"But He has bid us honour our parents, and not set up our own judgment against theirs."

"Well, but answer me truly. In the sight of God are we not all," and she glanced round the room, "perfectly equal?"

"I should think not," Mary said with a smile, as she glanced at her deaf patient mother, intently busy over Maurice's shirt, which she was mending.

"Ah! you may be right there," Gertrude quickly rejoined, "but then grant at least that if there is superiority amongst us, it is not with me it lies. Your mother is my superior; so are you!—Do not dispute it. Let it be for argument's sake, and my point is established."

"The blacksmith may be your superior in one sense, for aught you know; and yet I suppose you will hardly consider him as altogether your equal?"

"Indeed I should, if instead of being coarse, vulgar and ignorant, he was good-looking, clever, and better informed than myself. If I saw him employ every moment not engaged by his labours in cultivating his mind, and improving the talents that Heaven had bestowed upon him, if his sentiments were refined, and his character elevated, can you imagine for a moment that I should not think that man my equal—nay, my superior, and feel humbled to the dust in comparing his greatness and my littleness?"

Her features were glowing with enthusiasm, and she spoke so loud, that Mrs. Redmond looked up from her work with an inquiring smile, and seemed a little anxious when she saw Gertrude's flushed cheek and Mary's grave countenance. The latter answered calmly:—

"You would be quite right in admiring such a man, and in considering him as your superior in all essential respects; but all this would not make him your equal in a social point of view, or break down the barrier which a difference of rank would place between you."

"I hate and despise conventionalities," Gertrude replied, "and especially cant, which is the worse form of conventionality. I am tired of hearing what should be, and want to hear of what *is*."

"I will tell you, dear Lady-Bird, what invariably *is* the case when women begin to talk of hating and despising what others respect. The love of independence is the first step towards evil—" "Or towards virtue and happiness," Maurice murmured in a low voice, "and *not* the virtue of mere habit —not a common-place happiness."

The colour in Mary's cheek now rivalled that in Gertrude's, and she fixed her calm clear eyes steadily upon her, which seemed to make her uneasy; but proudly throwing back her head, she exclaimed:—

"I am not ashamed of anything I say!"

"And not of anything you *do?*" Mary said in a very low whisper—so low that no one else heard it but her to whom it was addressed—and then bent her eyes on the work she was employed upon. Gertrude moved hastily away, and sitting down by Mrs. Redmond, she took up a faded Cape jessamine that was lying on the table, and said to her,

"I am sure this comes from Woodlands! Does it not?"

"Yes. Miss Apley gave it me yesterday, when I went to her about the geranium cuttings she wanted from our little garden. She was speaking of you, Miss Lifford!"

"Was she?" Gertrude exclaimed with sudden animation; "what did she say about me?"

"It was in talking of this great breakfast that is going to take place there; a ball, I believe, and a concert, all in one, for Mr. Apley's coming of age. Maurice is going to play there, at least they want him to do so; all sorts of great London performers and singers are to be there, and company from a great distance." (Maurice at this moment left the room, and threw himself on the bench in the garden.) "Miss Apley was saying how much she admired you: that it was quite a pleasure to them all to meet you in their drives, and that they had so long been wishing to make your acquaintance. She asked me if you were out. I said that you were grown up, but had not yet been presented, I thought."

"No, indeed; and if I do not some day present myself to the world, I do not suppose that any one else will do it for me!"

"Miss Apley said that they had sent an invitation to the Grange, and they did so hope you would be allowed to come, but were sadly afraid it would be refused."

"It will be refused." Gertrude gloomily ejaculated; and her eyes—so bright a moment before—were suddenly overcast like a summer sky by a thunder-cloud.

"She said that if you had any friends in the neighbourhood you would like to go with, they would ask them directly."

"I have no friends," Gertrude said in the same gloomy manner. "I know nobody—nobody but you."

Maurice came and leant against the window, and hastily gathering a nosegay of jessamine and roses, he held it out to her. She took it, and smelt at it in an absent listless manner, and soon went away. As she walked through the garden with her maid, who had been waiting for her at the gate, she unconsciously dropped it. He picked it up and pulled it to pieces. Mrs. Redmond said to her daughter, "There is an orphan-like look about that young creature, though she has a father and mother." Maurice came in and practised some difficult passages, playing with great brilliancy and effect.

"You must play that at Woodlands," Mary said, when he had finished some variations on a beautiful air of Mendelssohn's

"Oh, I can play in that way to you, my little Mary, but there———"

"What! Has the English air turned you shy, Maurice— you who have been so used to public performances—who have played in Italy before artists and fine ladies?"

"I suppose it is English air, and English coldness that makes me faint-hearted. It is so seldom that an English audience show any pleasure or feeling, especially at a private concert; and weak applause paralyzes the spirit and the fingers."

"But you will win fame, Maurice dear!" the widow ejaculated.

"Fame is a big word, mother," he answered, with a half smile.

"Praise." Mary said, "the forerunner of Fame."

"Cleverly said, little Mary! but I will own to you that there is one sort of praise than which hisses would be more acceptable. You are conscious, perhaps, of having played very ill, and these people come up to you with a smile on their faces, and exclaim, 'Oh, how beautiful that was! What a charming thing! You never played so well in your life!' and you wax sick, or wroth with their nonsense. And worse still than that, perhaps you have played well, and *that* you also know—by the throbbing head, the aching nerves, the icy hands which bear witness to it,—you have poured out your soul in an improvisation, and then somebody asks you for that pretty thing over again! They might as well encore a flash of lightning, or cry 'Bis' at the fall of an avalanche."

"You must forget these troublesome people, and think only of those whose hearts beat in unison with yours," and she laid her head on the pianoforte, in an attitude that pleased his eye and amused his fancy.

He stroked her fair hair and said, "You are my good genius—no, that is not the word, my good angel rather. How is it that you always understand me?"

"I have an echo *here*," she said, with her hand on her heart, "which responds to what you feel. Do you remember how fond we were as children of the echo in the ruins of the abbey, and how we used to make it repeat, word after word, our favourite verses?"

"Yes, I do; but how vexed we were, also, when noisy chil-aren or fine ladies came there, and made our dear echo repeat harsh sounds or silly words. So in the world, the folly and the heartlessness of others disturb the harmony you speak of."

"I should have thought it would only have deepened it," she said.

"The truth is, Mary, that you do not quite know what an artist is, and on what kind of stimulus he lives. You are always talking of genius as of something very holy, very exalted, very pure, and you seem to forget in what a rank soil it often thrives, and how little of a religious spirit has accompanied some of its highest manifestations. It is a fire, but not always from Heaven."

"Oh, yes! from Heaven!" she exclaimed with fervour, 'surely from Heaven it comes, pure, bright and undefiled; like all that God creates, it is good; and, like all that man misuses, dangerous. The flame that burns amidst foulness and corruption does not lose its purity, and genius, inhabiting a mean and vicious soul, is a spark of heavenly fire shining through the mist of human depravity."

"Then genius may atone for moral perversity?"

"Oh, no! for what sin, what disgrace can be greater than to use for vile purposes so glorious a gift of God—to drag through the mire what was meant to raise us to Heaven!"

"Why, Mary, you surprise me! Have you, after all, a poet's spirit within you?"

"No, indeed," she answered, "it is only the echo I was speaking of just now. I cannot say things of this sort out of my own head, but I remember what you say and what you read to me, and, like the bird in the fable, make myself smart with borrowed feathers."

"No, indeed, Mary darling," her mother called out, "I am sure you are not like a bird in a fable. You always were a good child—is it not true, Maurice?"

"She is, indeed," he answered; "and the only bird she is like is a true dove, a messenger of peace, the type of heaven's love. And now let us think of this fête at Woodlands. You are to go there with me, Mary—Miss Apley said so. How shall you be dressed?"

"I have not thought of that yet. I suppose that I shall put on my white muslin gown, and the blue and white chain that you brought me from Venice, and I am afraid I must buy a new ribbon for my bonnet, and perhaps a new shawl. It is very expensive indeed, to be an artist's——" She hesitated, and he said, "An artist's bride?" She shook her head and laughed.

"How will Lady-Bird be dressed?" he asked.

"I don't know, indeed, but I am afraid she will not go '

"O but I hope she will—it will make a great difference to you if she does."

"I hope so, too; for it would be a very good thing for her to become acquainted with persons in her own rank of life."

"She does not care for all that—she has no mean prejudices, and never uses cant phrases. She is as guileless as a child—"

"O Maurice, do you think she is so perfectly artless as that?"

"*You* do not, I see. Ah, Mary, what woman was ever a true friend to another? I should have thought you might have been an exception to the rule, but it is always the same, I suppose; a woman never likes to hear her best friend praised."

Mary had a little struggle with herself, and then said: "I think she has very fine qualities, and it is impossible not to admire, to pity——"

"And to love her," he quickly added, "and the fewer friends she has, the more we ought to cling to her. To love her only next to what we love best. You will love her next to me, and I will love her next to you."

"Indeed, Maurice, we must not look forward to that, or expect that our intimacy will continue; we cannot be of use to *her*, and she may do us harm."

"What nonsense that is, and how selfish, too! I never should have suspected you of such narrow-minded folly."

He turned away with an expression of deep annoyance, and did not recover his tranquillity for some time. It was the first time since his return that he had spoken harshly to Mary. Perhaps she had been unwise in what she had said, and she reproached herself for it as for a fault; but she had seen a rising cloud in the horizon, which threatened his peace as well as her own, and for one instant had betrayed what it would have been more prudent to conceal. She did penance for it with secret tears and aching reviewals of every word that she had uttered. He did no penance, he shed no tears, he questioned not his heart; but when she received him with a smile and made his breakfast for him as usual the next morning and showed no consciousness of offence, he was perfectly satisfied, and thought how comfortable it would be to have such a sweet-tempered wife.

CHAPTER VII.

> "Et de ma vie obscure, hélas! qu'aurais-je à dire?
> Elle fut—ce qu'elle est pour tout ce qui respire——
> Sur les mers de ce monde il n'est jamais de port,
> Et le naufrage seul nous jette sur le bord!
> Jeune encore j'ai sondé ces ténèbres profondes,
> La vie est un degré de l'échelle des mondes,
> Que nous devons franchir pour arriver ailleurs."
> LAMARTINE.

> "But what are these grave thoughts to thee?
> For restlessly, impatiently
> Thou strivest, strugglest to be free.
> The only dream is liberty,
> Thou carest little how or where."
> LONGFELLOW.

GERTRUDE stood at her window on one of those drizzling melancholy mornings that impart a degree of gloom even to the most cheerful landscape; and never had the scene she looked upon appeared so utterly uninviting to her eyes. An English park—beautiful as it often is—does not always present a very exhilarating appearance. The large solitary trees with their sweeping branches and wide-spread shade, the green secluded glades, the absence of any token of human life, the timid herds of deer gliding about amongst the fern and through the distant vistas like graceful and noiseless apparitions, have a peculiar charm of their own, but it is more akin to a pleasing melancholy than to anything like gaiety.

The musing philosophy of Jaques would seem the natural frame of mind which the sylvan and majestic scenery of an English park would inspire; but there was neither beauty nor dignity attached to the flat stateliness of such a park as that of Lifford Grange. Avenues of *not* fine trees, clumps of small ugly ones, the flat unbroken extent on every side, the canal-looking river creeping sullenly through it, stamped the whole scene with indescribable gloom, and, seen through the medium of fog and rain, would have presented a cheerless aspect to eyes more favourably inclined towards it than Gertrude's.

If the view had seemed to her ugly from her bedroom

window it seemed uglier still from the breakfast room, where she waited for the appearance of her father and of his uncle—her usual companions at that meal. She looked at the tall windows with a sort of aversion, at the family pictures with resentment, at the two sofas facing one another on each side of the chimney as if they had been her enemies, and at the huge clock which recorded the passage of so many uninteresting hours as if it had done her an injury. "I had much rather go into a convent at once." she mentally exclaimed, "than spend my life in this way. I wish Father Lifford would not laugh at me when I talk of it. La Trappe itself would be gay compared to this place."

At that moment the said Father came into the room with his snuff-box in his hand, his stiff hair—half black and half grey—bristling fiercely round his head, and the lines in his forehead more indented than ever. His slouching gait, his heavy figure, and ill-made cassock made him appear older than he really was. The keen expression of his eyes and the strength of his frame often surprised those who would have deemed him at first sight a feeble old man. There was not apparently any love lost (to use a common expression) between him and Gertrude. If there was any reciprocal affection it certainly did not appear on the surface of their intercourse. He was devotedly attached to her mother, whom he had known in Spain from the days of her childhood. To her he was always perfectly kind and gentle; but towards others his temper—without being bad—was stiff, and his modes of judging and of dealing with people naturally severe. Between him and his nephew there was a strange mutual forbearance, and an odd kind of regard. That he must have secretly disapproved and lamented his indifference to religion, his want of practical charity to the poor, his omission of many duties and merely decent observance of others, none could have doubted who were acquainted with his own fervent piety, his untiring devotion to the spiritual and temporal welfare of his neighbours, and—under a rough exterior—the real kindness of his heart; but, however much or little he might at any time have remonstrated with him in private, he never showed his disapprobation at other times, or spoke of him and of his faults to others. On his children he inculcated a profound respect for their father, and as his notions of passive obedience were strict, he was always much annoyed at Gertrude's independent turn of mind, and at her untameable determination to have her own opinion, at least—if she could not have her own way—on every subject.

He did not attempt to exercise any direct authority over her; "he was neither her father nor her tutor," he said, and did not wish to interfere with what was the business of her parents. As her confessor and spiritual guide, his province was distinct; and though his natural austerity inclined him, perhaps, to exhibit to her more of the stern than of the attractive aspect of religion—its restraints rather than its joys,—there was greater kindness and indulgence on his part, and respect and submission on hers than would have been easily imagined by those who witnessed the general tenor of their intercourse at other times, when he freely and sarcastically commented on her conduct, and she was barely restrained by a sense of duty from returning flippant answers to his remarks. It belonged to her character to be in awe of him there where he was always just and gentle, whereas she set him at defiance when he was, or appeared to her, harsh and despotic.

On the morning in question he stood before the chimney, warming his hands at the fire, and turning round occasionally to look at Gertrude, who was impatiently knocking two spoons together, and now and then pushing back her chair an inch or two from the table, and then back again towards it with a brusquerie that made the cups rattle and the urn tremble. "How late my father is this morning!" she exclaimed at last; it makes one lose half the day, to be kept waiting in this manner."

"What a loss to the world one of your half days must be!" remarked Father Lifford, looking at her full in the face from under his bushy grey eyebrows.

"Not to the world, perhaps, but to myself," she answered, in a voice of suppressed indignation.

"Why now, how would you have employed the last half our had you breakfasted at the usual time?"

"In reading, I suppose."

"Hum—in reading! Oh, very good. In reading what?"

"My French books," she quickly replied.

It happened that Father Lifford had an inveterate dislike to French literature, and the sight of Molière's plays, which Gertrude was everlastingly poring over, tried his patience sorely.

"Your French books!—ay, it is a pity, indeed, that you have not had time to study this morning 'Les Fourberies de

Scapin,' the last thing I saw you reading. Excellent moral lessons you must draw from your studies, and great profit you derive from them, doubtless."

Gertrude coloured, bit her lip, and looked as if she would have liked to make a violent answer; but she only abruptly got up and walked to the window, where she rapidly played with her fingers on the glass, as if beating time to her agitated thoughts.

"What weather!" she ejaculated, after a few moments silence; "what torrents of rain! It looks more like the end of November than the beginning of September. How *can* mamma keep up her spirits on such a day as this?—always nailed to her couch,—always looking on that one view. I wonder she does not turn to stone."

"Do you, indeed? Much you understand about that. Take care you do not get hardened quite in another way."

"O, as to being hardened, I feel myself stiffening every day. I shall soon be a sort of moving statue. Are *you* not sometimes afraid of being petrified here?"

He shrugged his shoulders, and betook himself to the newspaper. Mr. Lifford walked into the room a few minutes afterwards, and Gertrude poured out tea and interchanged a few words with him, such as pass between people who must speak to one another for form's sake, but who have not a single thought or interest in common. When breakfast was finished, Mr. Lifford got up, and assembling together the letters and newspapers which lay on the table, took a large card from among them, and pointing to it, said, "You must write an excuse in answer to that, Gertrude. I told you what to say the last time they sent one; you have only to repeat the same thing now."

Gertrude looked at the card and saw it was the invitation that Mrs. Redmond had spoken of. She took it up, and her strong wish on the subject overcoming not so much her timidity as her reluctance to express such a wish to her father, she looked him in the face and said, "I should like very much to go to this breakfast, I wish very much to accept this invitation—pray let me go." He seemed surprised, and hardly prepared for such a request. Not that he had the least thought of granting it, but he had never thought of a *reason* to give on the subject, and he only said, "Are you joking?" There was so little that looked like a joke in Gertrude's face or in his, that the question seemed unnecessary. "No, I am asking you a favour," she replied, but there was not anything supplicating in her manner. "Did you think of going *alone?*" he coldly inquired. She made no answer, and he added, "You must know that it is out of the question," and he left the room. She remained for a moment standing near the chimney with the card in her hand. As if speaking to herself she said,

"I will ask mamma about it."

"Your mother is very suffering to-day," Father Lifford observed, "you had better not trouble her about such a thing."

"Very well, I will not, but will *you* do so when she is better?"

"I!—why should I? What is this all about?"

"It is about my going to this breakfast at Woodlands, and I assure you that it would be a good work, if you could help me about it."

"A good work to get you to a ball! Is the child mad?"

"No, she is not mad—but she may go mad, if people don't take care. She is tired to death of —— "

"Of herself, I suppose," he interrupted, "and no wonder."

"Do you think my life amusing?"

"Were you sent into the world on purpose to amuse yourself?"

"Certainly not, as far as I can see. Don't be angry with me, Father Lifford, do you know that for once I do not want to quarrel with you?"

"That is extraordinary. What has caused this change?"

"Why, sometimes I get a little frightened about myself. I am afraid of getting to hate everybody."

"It is on your knees you should get rid of that feeling, my child."

"I think I had better be a nun, Father."

"What? *you* a nun! Alas for the convent that received you!"

"What is that other card there near the sugar-basin?"

"This? It is the same piece of nonsense as the other. These good foolish people have invited *me*."

"How civil they are; O how I wish we were all more like other people."

"Like what people?"

"I will not tell you, you would be shocked."

"You are not generally afraid of shocking me."

"But what I mean to say is this. Mamma is so good that she is not like other people."

"Do you wish she were less good?"

"No, but I wish she were not always ill and in pain." He sighed and said in a low voice, "It is God's will."

"But it is not His will that papa should be so proud, and so harsh."

"How dare you speak in that way of your father? You deserve to be treated harshly, you are a rebellious and undutiful child."

"There is an end of it! Always met with that. Always told that I am wrong and others right. Well—this cannot last for ever. Some day or other I must take my own fate in my own hands, and then—" This was said to herself, but even mentally she did not finish her sentence, but hurried away to her usual refuge, a large deserted library, which she called her den.

It was a lofty room, in bad repair; cobwebs lay undisturbed against the angles of the ceiling, and the panels of the door; dead flies and torpid butterflies were strewn on the broad window-seats, two immense globes stood between the windows, and books covered with dust lined the shelves of the tarnished gold and white bookcases; a gigantic map of the country hung over the chimney. It was a dull, desolate-looking room, but yet Gertrude liked it, and had spent in it some of the pleasantest hours of her life. There were neither chairs nor tables in it, but plenty of space and light. She could walk there with that rapid pace which relieves the mind when over-excited. She could take down a volume from the aforesaid bookcase, and sit for hours on one of the window-seats, alternately reading and gazing on the sky and the careering clouds; or watching with interest the struggles of a fly in some spider's web, or the resuscitation of a paralysed moth, on which a ray of sunshine might have accidentally fallen.

They are strange things—those long solitary hours in early youth—nothing like them exists later in life. There is such ceaseless thought about self, with such small self-knowledge; such intense thinking, with so little reflection; such abstraction of mind, with such sensibility to outward impressions; such worldliness in the visions which the mind frames for itself, such utter disinterestedness in the sacrifices it contemplates. Time is wasted with spendthrift prodigality; hopes erected on the most flimsy foundations; and in the magic glass in which these imaginary shapes are reflected, everything assumes a form and a colouring widely differing from reality.

There was a store of unemployed energy in Gertrude's character which should have spent itself in action. Unfortunately, her present duties were all of a passive nature. No labour or exertions were called forth, only the silent endurance of privation. Father Lifford had once attempted to make her visit the poor, and teach in the school which he had established, and she had entered on these occupations with eagerness and delight. They were beginning to tell beneficially on her character, when, suddenly, on some frivolous pretext of a fever in the neighbourhood, but really from a wayward and inconsistent exercise of power, her father interfered, and desired that she should no more visit the school and the cottages, though he neither knew nor cared that she wandered about the lanes, and in and out of Stonehousecleigh, only accompanied by her maid. Father Lifford told her, indeed, that there was more merit in obedience than in exertion,—in sacrifice than in labour; but the vent which would have been afforded for the flame which was smouldering under a heavy load of ennui was thus at once stopped up, and Gertrude fell back on her own thoughts, her desultory reading, and her dangerous habit of dreaming life away. She spent it in repinings at her fate, and murmurs against her father. These feelings fermented, as it were, in her heart during long solitary hours, and when she appeared at meals, there was a dark, resentful expression in her eyes, and a heavy cloud on her brow. The next day her mother sent for her. She was better than usual. The weather had changed, a south-westerly wind was breathing its sweet influence over the face of Nature, and through the open window there came a smell of flowers. The couch of the invalid had been moved near to that window, and—propped up by pillows—she lay with closed eyes, and hands joined together, enjoying the perfumed air that played on her pale cheek. She did not hear her daughter come in, and remained motionless and abstracted, while Gertrude took a low stool, and, placing it between the couch and the window, sat down, with her face buried in her hands, and feeling the singular repose of that scene operating strangely on her mind. Not that it soothed her: on the contrary, she felt excited; but for the first time began to wonder over her mother's fate, and to ask herself if she had ever had any of the thoughts that worked in her own brain,—any of the feelings that stirred her own heart so often.

She raised her head and gazed on that mother's face, and for the first time saw that it was beautiful, and like her own. And she knew her own was so—too well she knew it. She thought, as if it were for the first time, that she was that mother's child.—that the same blood ran in their veins—that their features were formed in the same mould. Were their hearts so unlike?—were their minds so dissimilar?—had the iron hand of suffering crushed the power of emotion where once it might have existed?—or were other hearts unlike her own? —had her mother never felt a wish beyond that couch, to which since she could first remember her she had been nailed? —had her eyes never sparkled with anger or with joy, or her lips never uttered any but the short broken sentences that fell from them now? "O mother, mother, were you ever young, ever thoughtless, ever rebellious like me?—had you ever longings for earth's happiness as you now have for Heaven's bliss?"

These words were uttered in the faintest whisper, but the last words reached Mrs. Lifford's ear, and she opened her eyes and smiled, which was a rare thing for her to do. "Heaven!" she said slowly, "Heaven is a long time coming." Then rousing herself as from a dream, she put out her hand, and made Gertrude a sign to come nearer to her. She gazed on her face, and it seemed as if she also was reading new things in her child's countenance and was startled at what she saw there, for she looked at her with a kind of anxious questioning expression. Gertrude turned away and said, "You are much better to-day, mamma; I never saw you look so well,— you have quite a colour." Her mother smiled mournfully; she felt the red spots glowing in her cheek, and knew that they were burning with disease, not with health. But increasing fever gave her more strength than usual, and for once she seemed inclined to speak, but was so unused to hold any conversation with her daughter beyond a few words of endearment, that she did nothing but press her hand and call her names of fondness in Spanish.—till, suddenly rousing herself, and leaning on her elbow, she said, "Gertrude, you are very happy, I hope?"

Gertrude grew crimson, hid her face in her hands, and hot tears came struggling through her fingers. Now was the moment to speak and enlist her mother on her side, but there was that in her nature which made her prone to resist and slow to complain. However, after an instant's struggle with herself she said, "Mamma, I remember that twelve years ago I had such a wish for a wax-doll, that I lay awake at nights thinking of it, and cried whenever I passed the shop where it stood. But I would not ask to have it, from a proud angry feeling that no one had ever thought of making me a present of a doll. I told Father Lifford of this feeling of anger, and he bade me go directly to you and ask for the doll. I did not like to do so, but was obliged to obey. Just now I felt vexed that you could ask if I was happy, and I could not bear to speak and say that I am not. But I will speak the truth—I am not at all happy."

"No!" ejaculated the mother, "not happy with youth and health, and life before thee? O my child, that I could teach thee to be happy!" After a pause she added with touching earnestness, and with her hand on her forehead, "But there is so much confusion there—here in my heart I feel it all. God knows what I would say—O my God, teach my child what is happiness." Again she paused, and then with a faint smile said, "What would make thee happy, Gertrude?—not a wax doll now?" Gertrude put her mouth close to her mother's ear, as if afraid of being overheard, and whispered, "To go to the breakfast at Woodlands would make me happy; I have set my heart upon it, as much as ever I did as a child on a wax-doll." Mrs. Lifford looked surprised and puzzled; she held her temples in her hands as if collecting her thoughts.

"A breakfast, darling! But who could take thee there? My Gertrude, it is impossible."

"Mamma, they have asked Father Lifford—persuade *him* to go and to take me." The boldness of this scheme struck her mother silent with astonishment: she shook her head, but Gertrude went on.

"Mamma, I *must* have some change—some amusement. I cannot bear the life I lead any longer; I am sure that papa hates me."

"O child, child, down upon thy knees, and ask to be forgiven for such a thought! *Pray, pray*, there is no safety against such thoughts except in prayer But what has thy father done to thee? How dreadful!" She made the sign of the cross on her daughter's forehead, and sighed deeply.

"Do not look so frightened, mamma. I did not say I hated him. O Heaven forbid! and perhaps I am wrong, and he does not hate me; but that he does not care for me is certain—nobody does but you, mamma—you do, perhaps. I have not always thought so, but somehow or other I have felt to-day as if you did."

"Hast thou then really supposed that thy mother? . . . . O my long and bitter sufferings, my palsied limbs, my dim and confused memory, my faltering tongue, have you indeed done this? It was just,—it was right; but now I thank thee, O my God, that the veil has been lifted,—that she has had a glimpse into the heart that beats under the load that it must bear, aye, and loves to bear!" she exclaimed with increasing energy, and talking in Spanish, which she always did when strongly excited. She fell back exhausted, and a paroxysm of pain ensuing, Gertrude was obliged to call the maid who usually attended her mother, and to leave her to her care.

The next day Mrs. Lifford was somewhat better again, but she did not send for her daughter. She employed that interval of ease in two conversations, the first of which was with Father Lifford. When he sat down by her couch, and was preparing as usual to read to her out of a Spanish book of devotion, she put her hand on his arm and said, "I have something to say to you, Father." He removed his spectacles, took a pinch of snuff, and put himself in a listening attitude. "There is something I have to ask you, that I have some hope that you will do for me, even though you may dislike it very much." He looked up quickly, and she continued, "I am anxious about Gertrude."

"So am I," he gruffly ejaculated.

"She is not happy. The life she leads is a dull one for a young girl—you know it is, Father," she added earnestly, as he knit his brows and shrugged his shoulders.

"I don't say it is gay, but what's the use of talking? There is nothing to be done. It will be better, I suppose, when Edgar comes home."

"'She has set her heart upon going to this fête, this breakfast at Woodlands. That young heart of hers will overflow with bitterness, if she is always refused every amusement, every pleasure which her imagination paints to her in glowing colours, and mine aches, dear Father, when I think of my helpless state,—my utter incapacity——"

"Come, come; don't complain. You have borne your sufferings well hitherto. Do not let this foolish girl's fancies make you repine at God's will."

"Heaven forbid that I should murmur! But when I am able to think,—when an interval in my sufferings gives me time for reflection, then I become anxious about the future character, and the probable fate of my child, and I tremble as I muse on it. Authority will do nothing with her; coldness and indifference still less; her heart must be softened—worked upon—and won,—and *you* must do this."

"I must do it!—A right proper instrument you have fixed upon, indeed, for the purpose; a cross and crabbed old man like me!"

"O Father, Father, belie not your own heart."

"Don't talk to me of my heart. I have a conscience, I hope, and a soul to save,—but a heart that is to win hearts, phoo, phoo, that is all nonsense! Send for the child yourself—give her now and then a mother's kiss, and leave me to teach her her duty,—that is my business, and I *will* attend to it."

"Are you going to refuse me the first favour I have ever asked of you?"

"But in the name of patience what is it?"

"Something that you will at first protest you will never do; that you will think ridiculous, and even wrong perhaps——"

"You are going to ask me to do something wrong! What has come over you?"

"It may *seem* wrong at first sight; but depend upon it, dear Father, there may be more merit in it than in your noblest actions,—in your greatest austerities."

"I don't know what you mean by austerities—I never do noble actions. I don't know what you are talking about. I never knew you so foolish before!"

"Listen to me, I entreat you, and do not be too much startled. You must go to this breakfast at Woodlands, and take Gertrude there."

"O now I must send for the doctor. You had better ring for a composing draught, my dear child. You are not yourself."

"I never was so much myself; my thoughts and my mind are clearer than usual. I have reflected deeply; something must be done to change the current of that child's feelings,—to soften her heart,—to make her see that we understand her."

"It is very easy to understand her. She is a headstrong girl, who has set her foolish heart on a piece of worldly dissipation and vanity, and you are a foolish mother, bent on indulging her."

"Father, you *know* me,—you know where, with all its faults, its weakness, its past infidelities, its present unfaithfulness to grace,—you know where my heart, and its hopes and its affections are set. *He* whom I should have loved alone,—He who had claimed me from my infancy, and whose consecrated spouse I should have been,—He whom I forsook in an instant of infatuation, but who mercifully appointed me a fate which has been a continual safeguard from the world I had rashly sought, and a school in which to learn the lesson he assigns me,—*He* knows that could I place my child in His everlasting arms at once and forever, safe upon earth and on her way to heaven, my soul would be at peace. Or if that high vocation was denied, could I see her useful and contented in a home of her own, no worldly pleasures or advantages would I covet for her. I care not that the eyes of men should look on her rare beauty, that jewels should gleam on her brow, or her eyes win the love and admiration of crowds. I want no riches for her—no greatness—no splendour, but peace of heart and gentleness of spirit,—the love of God, and of man."

"And is this—what do you call this thing?—this breakfast at Woodlands to bring her to this blessed state of mind?"

"You must think me absurd; but *have* patience with me, bear with me, I am so helpless—so weak; but I have thought much about this,—I have asked myself if to send her for once into a new and exciting scene, which might make her home appear to her even more dull than before, and increase her desire to visit such again, was either wise or prudent, and the answer my conscience has given me is this:—'Did she not long for the pleasures which have hitherto been denied her? Did not she picture to herself in glowing colours the enjoyments she is debarred from? Heaven forbid that I should thrust them upon her! But I know that she *does* long for them, and that her spirit rebels against the forced seclusion of her life. The light of worldly amusements cannot be so injurious to a young mind, as the exaggerated pictures which it dreams of them. We *cannot* make her existence agreeable at home, you know it but too well. Sickness and suffering are bad companions for a child, and though God in his boundless mercy has opened to me sources of bliss which make me sometimes exclaim in the words of a French writer, "*Je souffre à en mourir, et cependant ma vie est un Paradis anticipé,*" I cannot expect that young heart at once to understand what the experience of life—and a life of singular trials—has by slow degrees led me to feel."

Mrs Lifford threw herself back on her pillow exhausted, but soon rousing herself again, continued : "If I obtain for Gertrude the fulfilment of her wish, she will see a mark of affection in this effort; but she does not know what it costs me, for I must obtain it from one—— O Father, not yet entirely subdued is this proud heart of mine. It is so painful to ask *him* anything !"

"Like mother, like child,' the old man gravely said.

"O do not say that—do not say that !" she cried. "Let me not think that she too will have to pass through a fiery trial on her way to peace and joy. That grace must force its way into *her* heart through the breach anguish opens, and over the scattered ruins of every earthly affection. But you will grant my prayer—you will go to Woodlands."

Father Lifford moved uneasily in his chair, again took snuff, and then—like a man who brings out his words under the influence of the rack or the thum-screw—he said, "My dear child, I am not come to my present age, or have read good books all my life, without learning that to do what one hates is better than to please oneself. I also know that a good sort of woman like you may better understand foolish young girls than an old man like me; so that, for aught I know, you may be right and I may be wrong. I also hope that I have no fear of ridicule, and if you like to expose yourself to it by sending a young lady into the world in the charge of an old priest, it may be a wholesome mortification for the young lady and for the old priest: so you may please yourself about it. If her father gives his permission, I will drive to this place with your daughter. I will sit like an old bear in a corner of the grounds; and when she has derived from the entertainment all the benefits you anticipate, or when it comes to a natural end—which I presume such things do—I will bring her home again ; but only be prepared for the impression it will create that the girl's parents are fools, and the old man a greater fool than them: but, as I said before. I don't care—it will be as good a mortification as any other."

"I know that it will be a mortification to you; but as to its being ridiculous I cannot agree with you. You are Mr. Lifford's uncle—Gertrude's nearest relation There is nothing unbecoming in an ecclesiastic going occasionally into society, and who would watch over my child with so paternal an eye ?'

"Tush, tush! Don't talk to me of paternal eyes, or any of that nonsense. I shall not watch her at all. I will see she gets there—and if I can, that she comes back; but nothing else will I undertake—and this, remember, I will only do once."

"She will make acquaintances, and may have hereafter opportunities of going out with others."

"Much good it will do her," he murmured between his teeth.

"You *do* see something true in what I have said?"

"I see you mean well, and I am not sure enough that you are wrong to oppose you; it may be for the best, and so let nothing more be said about it. It's of no use to hold under a man's nose the physic he is to take."

Late that day, when Mr. Lifford paid his accustomed visit to his wife, instead of the few common-place sentences which were habitually exchanged between them, a scene took place such as had not occurred for years. The pent-up sufferings of a woman's heart found vent in that hour. Strange, that the question of a girl's going to a breakfast or not should have called up the expression of a sorrow, of a passionate emotion, of something bordering on resentment, which had remained silent for years. Mrs. Lifford, soon after her marriage, had understood her fate, and quietly accepted it—at times almost rejoiced in it. She had done violence to her conscience by marrying. Her will had first been over-ruled by that of her relations. The heart, which had clearly recognised its vocation to a different and higher destiny, had—half in weakness, half under a transient impression wrought on her fancy—surrendered itself to an earthly love; and when, after a few months of something which she supposed must be happiness—but scarcely felt to be so—she suddenly awoke to the conviction of her husband's utter indifference, and accidentally discovered that the little affection his nature was susceptible of had been previously expended on another, that it was out of vanity alone that he had married her, that the memory of his first love occupied the only spot in his heart which was open to anything like feeling, and that indifference to herself was gradually changing into aversion—she experienced a strange sensation, in which something like satisfaction was combined with grief and shame. Perhaps it had a kind of affinity with the sort of relief which a criminal feels when his guilt is discovered, and the necessity for concealment is at an end. She had not gained the earthly happiness she had sought by doing violence to her convictions, and it was a kind of relief to her to find the hand of God upon her still. even in the form of chastisement. When its weight grew heavier, and pain and solitude became her portion, still more distinctly did this feeling rise in her mind. Hers was no common destiny, and no common love had ordained it. Deep, fervent, intense expressions of gratitude had been poured forth from that lonely couch during long vigils of pain, and days of incessant suffering. for a fate which had in some sense restored to her the vocation she had lost ; but in a woman's heart—although grace may master, sway, rule, and direct it, though it opens to her a world of bliss which throws human happiness at an immeasurable distance—there remains (except in the case of saints) something of infirmity, something of self-pity, something which is neither a wish nor regret. but which looks like them at moments, and would appear so to those who do not readily comprehend the mysteries of the human heart.

And so it was in that hour; that pale dying woman (for dying she was. although months and even years might yet elapse before her death) could look upon the cold, handsome, unexpressive face of her husband. and think how he had slighted, neglected and injured her, and not feel one touch of resentment or of regret—day after day she had done so. It was her daily meditation, after his short, formal visits to her, how wonderful God's ways had been with her, how, by His divine art, He had turned the transient joys she had snatched at into pangs, which had proved so many stepping-stones from the earth which they obscured, to the Heaven which they disclosed. But this day, when she endeavoured to find the way to his heart in behalf of her daughter, and found its avenues impenetrably closed—when, in answer to her pleadings for a permission, which was all she wanted, that Gertrude should occasionally have some little change and variety in her life, and, in particular, that he would allow the carriage to take her and Father Lifford to Woodlands on the day of the breakfast, he returned a short negative, and even sneered at the consent which his uncle had given to the mother's request, then that mother did not look at him calmly. There was no anger in her face, but an intense feeling of some kind. With her hands clasped and her cheek burning with excitement, she reiterated her request. When he turned away as if weary of the subject, and prepared to leave the room, she spoke to him with a voice and in a manner that obliged him to turn back and to listen. What she *said* cannot easily be written; what she *felt* not many could understand. That she gained her point some might wonder at, who do not know what an unexpected burst of passionate emotion can effect on the coldest and hardest hearts, when it takes them by surprise. Her sentences were broken, her words strange and abrupt, her countenance somewhat wild; for such excitement was too powerful for so feeble a frame. When her husband—half afraid, perhaps, of making her dangerously ill by opposition, disturbed, if not touched by her allusions to the past, with not enough affection for his daughter to make him consider the subject as it concerned her welfare—gave the desired permission as he would have ungraciously granted a holiday to his groom—she sighed deeply, and when the door was shut upon him, turned her face towards the wall and wept bitterly.

How little persons know, and especially young persons, of the trials of others! How they will exact, and then not appreciate what has, perhaps, been effected at an amount of anxiety and of pain which they do not dream of. Balzac, in his powerful tale "Eugenie Grandet," shows one the struggles, the anxieties, the art, the passionate solicitude with which the miser's daughter procures the few little common place comforts with which she supplies the orphan cousin, who has come to reside under her father's roof—the spoilt and now forsaken child of fortune, who uses without noticing. or squanders without enjoying what she has purchased or begged in fear and trembling, what she has obtained at the price of scenes which have made her heart quail and her cheek blanch. And the picture is true to the life; every day it is exemplified in domestic life. Secret acts of heroism are performed, which look so easy and common-place, that no one would guess the secret prayers, the previous struggles, the amount of resolution they have required; and they pass by without comment and without praise.

When Mrs. Lifford told her daughter that she was to go to the Woodlands' breakfast, the girl's eyes sparkled with delight, and she fondly kissed her mother; but if she had guessed what that mother had suffered the day before to open to her that prospect of amusement, there would doubtless have been something more gentle in her voice and more tender in her kiss; but, to know it, she must have learnt what it was better for her not to learn, and have understood what she will one **day,** perhaps, too well understand,—her mother's fate and her father's character.

CHAPTER VIII.

> "And then I met with one
> Who was my fate; he saw me and I knew
> 'Twas love that like swift light'ning darted through
> My spirit; ere I thought, my heart was won
> Spell-bound to his, for ever and for ever."

So many chapters in novels begin with descriptions of beautiful days, that it seems useless to add another to those already written by abler painters in words; but to speak of flowers, of birds, of blue sky, and of sunshine—of fleecy clouds and soft breezes, at certain times and on certain occasions, has its use, however hackneyed these expressions may be. It is to the mind what the recitative in an Italian opera is to the ear, or a frame to a painting. It brings the thoughts into tune; it calls up a variety of pictures, differing according to the imagination of the reader—to the scenes with which his memory is stored—to the impressions of which he is susceptible. "The day was beautiful."—Has not every one at once, before his eyes, some picture that appeals to his feelings or his fancy, that suggests a train of remembrances, that brings tears into his eyes, or a smile on his lips?

The day was beautiful on which Gertrude Lifford opened her window to examine the aspect of the sky, and ascertain that it did not threaten to interfere with what she called her first day of pleasure. No such shade marred the face of the heaven. It was fair and bright, and hazy in the distance—an autumnal English sky—and even the flat extent of the park looked less ugly than usual, as it showed its green surface in the light of the early morning. Gertrude was satisfied, but her excited spirits would not suffer her to sit still. The hours seemed interminably long till she could reasonably begin to dress. Her dress had been a source of great anxiety to her; and as Madame de Staël was heard to say that she would have been willing to barter all her literary successes for the gratification of experiencing for a single day the pleasure of being beautiful, so Gertrude would almost have given up her beauty for the sake of knowing that she would be dressed like other people—for the assurance of not appearing old-fashioned and ridiculous; for, between her mother, who had not been out anywhere for years, and never but in Spain, and the milliner at Stonehouseleigh, whose knowledge of the fashions was limited, she felt great apprehensions as to the result.

But she need not have done so; she was not dressed like other people certainly, but if vanity were the cause of her uneasiness she might have been content. A piece of fine rare Indian muslin delicately embroidered in white—which had made part of her mother's trousseau, and had never been made up—was now turned into a gown for her. A magnificent mantilla of old Spanish lace was her shawl. A Leghorn straw-hat with a wreath of poppies and corn-flowers, which, with the skill in such handiwork acquired in a convent, Mrs. Lifford had made for her, and a chain of elaborately carved coral going twice round her neck, completed her attire. When she went into her mother's room she found her sitting up on her couch, with various cases of antique workmanship smelling of foreign perfumes by her side. From one she took out some diamond rings, from another a pair of bracelets of a curious Moorish shape, which she put on her fingers and her wrists. Then she gave her a fan with highly finished paintings and richly ornamented handle, and showed her how to hold it. Then she bade her go to the foot of the couch that she might look at her; and as she stood there in all her picturesque beauty, with her youth and her brilliant dress, and the exultation in her eyes, she seemed a strange vision in that chapel-like room so full of holy pictures and religious ornaments, so dark for the sake of its suffering inmate, so silent and so still, that those who entered it instinctively lowered their voices, and trod lightly on the soft carpet.

"Gertrude," said her mother, fixing her eyes on her daughter's face. "The world is not happiness."

"Perhaps not, mamma, but it is pleasure."

"I too went to a ball once, and I carried that fan in m hand. It is a long time ago. It was at the time of my sister's marriage. She has died since. Her name was Assunta Strange, was it not? Mine is Angustia. I am glad they did not call you so, Gertrude."

"Yes, dearest mamma; see how well I use my fan. May I dance, mamma?"

"Dearest, you have never learnt; you do not know how."

"I did not know how to do *this* a moment ago," she answered, playing again with the fan in the true Spanish fashion, and then coming round to her mother's side she bent over her fondly, and said, "To-morrow I shall tell you if the world has been pleasure to me. Do be well to-morrow, mamma; you are much better than you were. There was a time when you could not have exerted yourself as much as you have done lately."

"Heaven bless thee!" was her mother's only answer.

"The carriage is at the door," the maid whispered.

"Mamma, must I say good-bye to papa?"

Mrs. Lifford winced, as it were, at the question, looked at her daughter, and seemed to hesitate. "Yes," she said at last. "Yes; come this way first; let me arrange those two curls that are straying on thy neck. Throw thy head a little back, and take these orange-blossoms with thee. That will do; go to him,—he may remember the bull-fight at Seville."

"Shall I ask him if he does?"

"O no, no!" the mother answered, with a shudder, and with another kiss dismissed her child.

Into a room nearly as sombre as the one she had left, but with nothing in it to please the eye or the feelings, that vision of youth and beauty walked. In the attitude her mother had placed her in, with the weapons she had armed her with, into her father's presence she went, with a lighter step and a more confiding spirit than usual. He looked up from the table where he was examining some accounts, and said in a tone of annoyance.

"What do you want?"

"Nothing," she answered, in a faint voice.

"Then why do you come here?"

"I really don't know."

"It would be better, in that case, not to interrupt me."

"I will not do so again," she said, and left the room.

A servant met her at the door, and told her that her uncle was in the carriage. She hastened after him, jumped into the heavy, old-fashioned coach, and slowly and steadily they proceeded to Woodlands.

Father Lifford was making a great effort—a real sacrifice—in thus putting himself out of the way, in going out of all his usual habits, and amongst strangers. It was an act of true kindness; but his nature was too stiff to mould itself easily to such an effort. He could do such a thing because on the whole he thought it right, though at the same time he did not feel quite sure of it. That uncertainty, not as to his good intentions, but as to the wisdom of his unselfishness, gave him a certain degree of uneasiness which added to his intense dislike of the whole affair. He had ensconced himself in the corner of the coach, and fenced himself round with newspapers and books, as if he were about to take a long journey. First he said his office, which lasted a quarter of an hour, and then took up a newspaper, and then another, without turning round or speaking. He did not like a draught, and only one of the windows was let down. Gertrude, who found it hot, changed her place to the one opposite, so as to get the air which blew from the south-west. It fanned her cheek, and disarranged her hair, which did not signify, for it curled of itself; and taking off her bonnet, she drew over her head the hood of her mantilla. Father Lifford accidentally looked up from his newspaper, and the frown on his brow at that moment relaxed a little. For some time she was not conscious that he was looking at her, but was busily employed in twisting her coral chain into twenty different shapes. The old man seemed to dwell on thoughts which her face and her dress had suggested to him; and when she observed that he was watching her, and said gently, "I am so much obliged to you, Father Lifford," and he answered "Poor little fool!" there was in his manner what she felt to be kindness.

When they arrived at the lodge, and drove through the park, the sight of tents decorated with flags and streamers met their eyes, and the sound of a band of music was heard in the distance. Other carriages—less heavy and stately than theirs—rapidly passed them and the whole scene was bright and animated in the extreme. Woodlands was not a very fine place, there was nothing particularly picturesque about its scenery, but on a fine sunny day like the present one, it had enough of the beauty which belongs to most English country places to appear to advantage, especially as art and decoration had been profusely employed to give brilliancy to the aspect of the well laid out gardens, and the large cheerful rooms, which were almost as gay with flowers as the parterre.

Neither Father Lifford nor Gertrude were shy, but both were doubtless uncomfortable when (their names having been shouted from the bottom of the staircase) they entered the drawing-room where Mrs. Apley was receiving her guests— he from an intense aversion to the whole proceeding, and she from a consciousness that their appearance might excite surprise. She did not feel sure that her dress was not very peculiar. She had cast a quick glance at some of the women who had arrived at the same time as herself, and it seemed to her that somehow they looked very different, and so they certainly did. A young antelope turned into the midst of a herd of English cows would not have presented a greater contrast than did the Spanish-looking girl amongst the tribe of fair-haired and pink-cheeked young ladies that filled the room. Father Lifford was too well bred not to be civil, however cross he might feel, and he said a few words to Mrs. Apley in a tone that did not betray how much he wished himself anywhere but where he was, and said something about his niece's ill health, but nothing about her husband's non-appearance; which all did equally well, for Mrs. Apley was rather deaf and very absent, and so replied with a sweet smile that she was truly glad to hear it, and as this was evidently kindly meant it also perfectly answered its purpose.

As soon as she could, Gertrude passed into the next room and stood leaning against the wall, looking about her. The noise as well as the sight of a crowded room was new and strange to her. It surprises people who notice it for the first time to observe what a business talking is. Young people who have never been in society as children, and only heard of the amusements of grown up people, can imagine what is the pleasure of a ball, a concert, or a play, but to stand for hours talking as fast or listening as patiently as possible to persons, many if not most of them neither agreeable nor amusing (for so they hear the great majority of the human race deemed by those who make society the business of their lives) should be either a great pleasure or a great duty strikes them as incomprehensible, or that it should be done at all, if it is neither the one nor the other, still more so. It is even strange to those who have been used to it all their lives, when they begin to analyse the subject; just as when we meditate on the intellectual process through which we read, write, or play on an instrument. We wonder over and could almost admire ourselves for it, if we did not remember in time that a child at a village school can do the same. No, society is sometimes a duty, sometimes a pleasure, but more generally the gratification of an instinct which requires it even when it has ceased to afford enjoyment. It is almost indispensable to those who are not exclusively engrossed by other objects; it takes us out of ourselves, and that is an excursion which we all more or less like, till we have learnt to live on such terms with that odd creature *Self*, as not to require a frequent leave of absence from its tormenting companionship.

Perhaps no one will so soon thoroughly understand as Gertrude the nature of that relief, no one may so soon appreciate as much that artificial means of killing time, but as yet she is only a looker on, and it seems unprofitable enough to watch the civil or rude behaviour, the eager or listless manner, the too light or too heavy talk of the old young people or the young old people who congregate together in what by courtesy is called *the world*. By degrees she distinguished two or three persons whose appearance interested her, and soon Mrs. Apley came into the room where she was standing in patient contemplation of her fellow-creatures, and introduced some of them to her. Amongst others her son, the hero of the day. For several years Gertrude had known him by sight, and had been conscious that he admired her. There had even been a sort of approach to acquaintance between them. He had held a gate open for her, and once picked up something she had dropped and rode after her to restore it. He alluded to this in an agreeable manner, and entered into conversation with her in a way that made her feel herself immediately at her ease with him. She was not the least shy, although her eyes were so, and this contrast was piquant. Young Apley was amused by her remarks, and fascinated by her countenance. He had heard something of the peculiarities of her home, and knew how secluded had been her life. This excited his curiosity, and that—as well as his admiration of her beauty—made him long to know more of her, and when he was called away and obliged to attend to other people, he sent one of his sisters *to make the civil* to that pretty girl with the corn-flowers in her hat. "She is such a duck," he whispered to Harriet Apley, who looked herself much more like that bird (not a popular one in his own character, but who stands in fashionable slang as the synonyme of charm) than the tall slim Gertrude, who would have looked somewhat contemptuous had she overheard this expression of praise from her admirer's lips.

She was a round, pretty, plump little creature, who had been *out* ever since she could speak. When asked at sixteen, if she was soon coming out, she laughed and said she had never been *in*. There was something in her pretty round mouth and her merry round eyes that had gained her the name of Cherry, when she used to appear at dessert as "the picture of a child," and, now that she was grown up, Cherry was still rather attractive, though no longer reckoned the picture or the "beau idéal" of anything. She was as civil as she could be to Gertrude, but soon got tired, for she thought talking to girls was very dull work. She was one of the people who speak of talking to women, or talking to men, quite irrespectively of the merits or peculiarities of the individuals of each sex. The dullest man was (at a party at least) a more agreeable companion than the cleverest woman of her acquaintance, and that not merely from a spirit of coquetry, though perhaps she was a coquette, nor from the wish to be married, though perhaps she did wish it, but simply because—as she often said—one did not go into society to talk to women.

Perhaps, if she had been *into* herself at any time of her life, she would have discovered the reason of this, but she was one of those whose self was always out of doors: not that she disagreed with it at home, but she had never attempted to commune with it there. Cherry had been watching for an opportunity of escaping from her present position, and was making inward comments on the impropriety of girls going out without a regular chaperon, or at least some acquaintances that they could join, when the sound of music from the gallery relieved her from her difficulty.

"I am sure you would like to hear the singing," she eagerly said, and naming the most famous singer of that time—one who joined to a wonderful voice the charm of a beautiful face and of an extraordinary genius—she led the way to a row of chairs not far from the pianoforte, and, after placing Gertrude there, in a few minutes slipped away with an easy conscience; and so she might as far as her new acquaintance was concerned, for the duet in the second act of Semiramide had begun. Both singers were perfect in their way, and Gertrude was soon wholly absorbed in the performance.

Some kinds of music require an experienced ear to enjoy them, and are not appreciated at the first hearing; but, in this instance, it was not so. It had an electric effect on one who had not been used to the magical charm of such singing; her cheeks flushed, her heart beat, and her eyes sparkled. The scene was altogether so novel; the crowd of faces surrounding her,—before her the great singer, in whose countenance and gestures the inspiration of genius and of passion was visible;

whose slight frame quivered under that powerful emotion,—
the words of defiance and of revenge hurled from one proud
spirit to another, distinctly uttered and often reiterated,—the
glorious harmony that embodied and accompanied them, all
combined to work her up into a state of silent but oppressive
excitement, which almost seemed to take away her breath.

While she drank in the sounds that thrilled through her
being, she thought of her own destiny, and asked herself what
it would be. She successively wished to be a Queen or an
Amazon, a singer or an actress, anything but what she was,
anything that would give vent to the longing for power and
for action which that spirited music awoke in her soul. Had
she a voice that could win its way to a thousand hearts? Had
she a mind wherewith to conceive, a pen wherewith to trace
what might sway the impulse of minds without number? No,
her spirit answered, no, it could not be. She was too young
and too ignorant, too rash and too unstable for such hopes,
for such tasks, for such stimulants as these. She must
reign through other means, if reign she ever could. She
must sway hearts in another mode, if to sway them she desired.
How little did those placed at her side on that day guess the
thoughts and the wishes, the projects and the hopes, which
were at work in her mind as she sat there in that concert-room,
looking beautiful and shy, and hiding her mouth with her
enamelled fan.

In the midst of her reverie she looked towards the door,
and her eyes met those of Mark Apley fixed upon her in evident admiration. "Is not beauty *power?*" she inwardly exclaimed; and felt it was, as his blue eyes paid homage to the
shadowy beauty of her own. She felt it when he forced his
way through the rows of chairs that stood between them,
drawn on by the magnetism of her now downcast glance, and
when he put into her hand a rose of great value, the only one
of its kind that the conservatory contained. She felt it once
again when the duet was over, and loud bursts of applause
rose from the audience. "O, how I like that sound," she
exclaimed, "I had never heard it before; why don't you ap-
plaud, you who can?" she added, in a low voice, and with a
smile that made Mark Apley clap his hands with an energy
that the pure love of music had never before prompted.
"Now," she said, "I *must* hear that again. You *must* get it
repeated, that beautiful music which says, 'I will subdue you,'
and which, with the same notes answers, 'I will *not* be subdued.' Go, make them sing it again."

She laid her fan, with a pretty gesture of command, not on but near his hand, and gave him a frown which enchanted him. A frown is a charming thing on a pretty face; it is seldom on any face an awful one. Look at the lines about the mouth: there will the young wife, or the husband who may have often frowned at each other in loving hours and lovers' quarrels, see the first expression of displeasure in the face whose frowns they have smilingly defied. Mark Apley rushed to the pianoforte, and obtained the repetition of the duet. Again Gertrude listened to it with delight, but now there was something perhaps more definite in her thoughts, and as she pulled to pieces the rare flower in her hand, she built up a vision as bright as its petals.

"See, you have destroyed it," he said, gathering up one of the rosy fragments from the floor. She put her little foot on the others, and said with a smile, "Regina e guerriera."

"But you should be queen of flowers, and not war with your subjects."

"I would not if they swore allegiance to me; but this one was rebellious; it would not bend without breaking."

"You are inclined to be a tyrant, I think."

A cloud passed over the beautiful face on which he was gazing, and she answered quickly. "No, I love not tyrants;—but listen to what they are singing now. O what is it?"

But she would not let him answer, her finger was on her lip, and her soul was on the wing. "Suivez moi," the wild appeal to liberty in Guillaume Tell was drawing her on, as it were, into a world she knew not yet. It seemed a summons to something new and free, into which her spirit had not yet soared; and when it ended she murmured. "Oui, que je toi suive;" and Mark, who was very pleasing, but not very wise, asked, "Who?" and she answered, "The inspiration of the moment," which he did not understand, but he thought her very clever as well as very lovely, and never had felt so fascinated by any one before.

At that moment there was a movement amongst the singers and the audience. The principal performers left the immediate vicinity of the pianoforte, and Mrs. Apley went up to them, and said a few words, which were received with a gracious smile, and they placed themselves on a sofa, while through the door behind the pianoforte Maurice Redmond came in. He and Mary had been standing in that door-way ever since the concert had begun, and he had not for a moment taken off his eyes from the spot where Gertrude had been sitting with Mark Apley. All eyes were now turned upon him, and hers amongst the number. She saw that he was very pale, and with a rapid glance, perceived that Mary saw it also, and was looking as white as a sheet. He sat down at the pianoforte—there was an empty space between it and rows of people on every side. They were unusually silent at that moment; nobody was near him—his nervousness increased—he was evidently not well. Drops of sweat were starting on his forehead. Mary's color went and came; she could not go to him, of course, or stir from her place, but she grew paler every second, and pressed her hand tightly on her heart. His nervousness was becoming insurmountable, and the silence of the audience increased with their wonder that he did not begin. Both felt dreadfully alone in that crowd, and when he said in a low husky voice, "It is of no use, I cannot play," she heard it and leant back against the wall with a faint giddy sensation at her heart.

But a light step at that moment crossed the room, and in an instant Gertrude was by his side. She put an open music-book on the desk to stand as it were between him and the audience; she gave him her smelling-bottle, and with a few of her gay words, and with a glance of her beautiful eyes, she revived him more than fresh air or a cordial could have done. It was what he wanted; she had done what she meant, and cared not then a straw that there were looks of astonishment and whispered remarks going on in the room. The colour returned to his cheek; one look of ardent gratitude he turned upon her and said, " I can play now, Lady-Bird." She then went to Mary stood by her in the door-way, and held her cold hand in hers while he sounded a few preluding chords with an uncertain hand. They were both still afraid that he would fail, but the fear was soon dissipated. It had been but a moment's depression—now he was more powerfully stimulated than he had ever been yet, and played far better than usual. He strained every nerve, and his frame now quivered with excitement, as it had done before with agitation. But he did wonders under this influence, and the fastidious artists who were listening to him were astonished at the performance of one, who had never yet appeared in London or in Paris, and whose name was not yet much known, except in the towns of Italy where he had gained some reputation. They warmly applauded, and as they led the way the rest of the society joined in it.

The delicate touch and profound sensibility with which he rung some changes on a German air, completed his success. The beautiful Prima Donna's eyes filled with tears, and she praised him when he had finished, as artists love to be praised. Mark Apley and his sisters and other acquaintances also gathered around him; kind flattering words, and warm expressions of pleasure were buzzed about his ears, and his soul was satisfied. Yes, his soul, not his vanity. There is a joy in praise which has nothing to do with vanity. It is a species of sympathy which those who possess genius in any line almost imperatively require. It is the breeze that fans the flame, the oil that feeds the lamp. Praise, when it is sincerely bestowed, and gratefully received, often produces a kind of timid and humble happiness, as remote from vanity as a mother's exultation at her infant's beauty is different from a haughty consciousness of her own.

"Do you not feel proud of him, Mary?" Gertrude whispered as they too joined the group.

"Too happy to be proud," and she looked at her with grateful eyes. "O that those kind people," she continued, glancing at the Italian artists, "would now sing again. My selfish heart was so tight when they did so befoe, that it could not enjoy what would be now so delightful."

"*Your* selfish heart!" Gertrude exclaimed with a smile.

"Yes, selfish indeed; why think so exclusively of oneself?" and she looked at Maurice as if there was but one self between them.

At that moment Mrs. Apley came up to Gertrude, and gave her a little note hastily written in pencil; it was from Father Lifford. Just after she had been placed in an unapproachable position in the music room, he had received a message to the purport that a dying person had sent for him soon after he had left home, and not a moment's time was to be lost in attending to it. He hastily requested Mrs. Apley kindly to take charge of Gertrude during the remainder of the day,—the only expedient he could think of, as the carriage had not been ordered till some hours later, and he himself went off on foot to the cottage where he was wanted. Nothing could be more agreeable to Gertrude than this incident, as far as regarded her own prospect of amusement; the few hours before her appeared like a whole life of pleasure to be enjoyed ere the moment of departure should arrive.

The concert was at an end, and it was now rumoured that

dancing was soon to begin. Several young men were introduced to Gertrude by Miss Apley. and she was soon surrounded by a number of persons, bent on making themselves agreeable to her. She grew very animated and talked a great deal. Very amusing she was, though many of the things she said would not bear repetition; but they were lively, original, quaint, and withal natural, for there was not a grain of affectation about her. Mark Apley hovered near her, and drank in the sweet poison of love, as if he had been a bee diving into a honeysuckle. How every moment her spirits rose, as she perceived that a glance of her eye could bring him back to her side, if for an instant he made an effort to attend to others! The music struck up. "Will you waltz with me, Miss Lifford?"

The colour rushed into the rich olive tints of the Spanish girl's cheek.

"I cannot waltz. I do not know how."

"What!—have you never tried?"

"No, indeed. Do you think people dance at Lifford Grange?"

"Oh, but you will dance naturally,—I know you will,—just as your hair curls naturally. I see it does, for the wind,—as it blows it about, only makes it curl the more. Those locks at the back of your head that have escaped from the plaits,—they were not meant to curl; confess it."

"O nothing does what it ought with me," she answered; and seizing the two rebellious locks, she straightened them down as if to punish their wilfulness, and then threw them back to wave and curl on her neck. "Go and dance, Mr. Apley; I will look on, and perhaps learn."

"Come with me," he eagerly exclaimed; "there is no one in the gallery. I will teach you; it will be the work of a minute."

He gave her his arm, and they flew, rather than walked, through the rooms into the one where the concert had taken place. On one of the window-seats Maurice was sitting in a lounging attitude. He gave a start when they entered the room, and sprung to his feet. Gertrude let go Mr. Apley's arm, and cried out,

"Ah, there you are,—resting after your successes; enjoying your triumph."

"Do you think he would play us a waltz?" Mark said to her in a low voice. "It would make you learn twice as soon."

"Maurice," she eagerly cried, "do play that German waltz that I used to like so much; Mr. Apley is going to teach me to waltz."

"Is he?" Maurice coldly answered. "I do not know that I can remember what you want."

"O, but anything will do,—only make haste, because we have no time to lose."

If there was anything imperious in her manner of saying this, it was only the wilfulness of a child that would not be contradicted by one who had always yielded to her slightest wishes; but susceptible as he was, it wounded him to the quick. He felt as if the world had already done its work with her, and that she spoke to him in a tone of offensive dictation. He flushed to the very temples as he sat down at the pianoforte, and began playing in a rapid and abrupt manner. It was not a gay tune, or else he played it strangely. She kept calling out to him now and then, "Not so fast,"—or, "You are not playing so well as usual, Maurice!"—and he bit his lips almost through with vexation.

And the truth was, he did not play well. There was an accompaniment that put him out singularly,—the noise of swift steps; the rustle of a muslin dress; the tone of a joyous laugh; the sound of two voices interchanging gay reproofs and instructions. Once an exclamation—"O stop, I am so giddy;" and the answer, "O no, no, don't stop." But the music ceased at once, and the musician darted up from his place, and rushed forward. What business had he to do so? He felt it, and turning back as suddenly, played a wild air of Strauss's with feverish vehemence, and then the waltz in Robert le Diable, which intermingles notes of despairing sweetness with the discords of hell. "That will do, Maurice—I thank you so much. I have learnt all I wanted." And away she went, with her light step, her beautiful figure, her flashing eyes, and her unconsciousness of the pain she left behind her.

"Come, Mary, have you had enough of this *pleasure* for to-day? Shall we steal away by the back door, find the pony chaise, and go home?" "Yes," she said, and put her arm in his, and soon they were driving through fragrant fir woods, in the refreshing coolness of the evening. They did not talk of Woodlands, but he said he should like to go and shut himself up with her in some quiet retreat, where the sounds of the world would never reach them, where only Mary's voice would be heard—only Mary's love would be known.

"Still your Italian plans," she answered with a smile.

"O no, not Italy—some quiet English spot. I am tired of beauty—weary of admiring—sick of efforts and struggles. Let me float down the stream hand in hand with you, Mary."

"No, no! it is up, not down the stream that we must row. What has made you so faint-hearted, Maurice? Do you not remember those lines you used to repeat to me in London, when I pined much for the cottage and the country?"

> "O Time, O life, ye were not made
> For languid dreaming in the shade,
> Nor sinful hearts to moor all day
> By lily isle or grassy bay,
> Nor drink at noontide's balmy hours
> Sweet opiates from the meadow flowers."

"O for a lily isle," he exclaimed, "or grassy bay; if such there are in life's river! Or an opiate that will send one to sleep on its shore!"

"No, no, my dearest child, you must ply your oars with courage, even though it be against the tide; you must not lay them down while there is work to do."

"Why do you call me *child*, Mary?"

"It is my fancy. I think there is something of a mother's love in my affection for you, and then it seems to give me a right to scold you sometimes."

"You are an angel, Mary. How calm and sweet every thing is now! There was something oppressive in the air at Woodlands."

After a pause, he said, "Mary, we must not be ungrateful—she was very kind." She turned to him surprised. Was he speaking of Gertrude? She had not felt ungrateful to her; on the contrary—what did he mean?

"O, nothing, nothing," he answered, and sighed.

The light died away before they reached their home. The moon threw its rays on the quiet waters of the Leigh. The mignonette and the carnation smelt sweetly in the widow's garden, and Mary—as she sat at the window of her little bedroom—felt glad that the day was come to an end, and that not many such were likely to recur in her life.

Gertrude, in the mean time, was in the midst of the ball which had succeeded the other amusements of the day at Woodlands. The carriage came for her at six, but she was persuaded to keep it waiting till twelve. In Miss Apley's room she made such alterations in her dress as could be contrived at a moment's notice; her mantle and straw hat were put aside, some white and red camellias were arranged in her hair. A nosegay of hot-house flowers, which had filled a vase on the dressing-table, was fastened on her breast, and relieved the plainness of her simple muslin corsage. As she stood at the end of the room by the side of Mark Apley, waiting for the music to strike up, and with true Spanish grace playing with her large fan, many eyes were turned upon her, and many inquiries made about her. She *had* learnt to waltz during her brief lesson in the gallery; soon she was flying round the room, her feet—her almost incredibly small feet—scarcely touching the ground, her cheeks flushed with exercise and animation, and her partners every moment increasing, and undisguised admiration raising her spirits to the highest pitch.

If she had been plain or only ordinarily good-looking, it might have been wise to send her for once into that world which she had so longed to be acquainted with. She might have been disenchanted with what she had pictured to herself as so delightful, and mortification might have changed the bias of her excitable temper into some other channel; but her beauty, her originality, and the peculiarity of her manners—which were refined without being conventional and strange, but at the same time graceful—obtained her that kind of success which she but too well appreciated, but too much enjoyed.

In the course of the evening the heat of the ball-room grew intense, and through one of the open windows several persons went into the shrubbery to breathe the fresh air, and walked towards a grotto which stood at the end of one of the alleys. Gertrude had just done waltzing for the third or fourth time, and followed some young girls, whose acquaintance she had made, out of the stifling room into the garden. They loitered near the house, but out of curiosity she went further and arrived at the grotto, which looked invitingly cool. She was just going to step into it, attracted by the refreshing sound of the water which trickled down its walls, when somebody said to her, "Pray forgive me for speaking to you, but you should not go into that place, heated as you are. It is dangerous."

Few and simple as were the words of the speaker, they affected her in a singular manner. She felt touched without knowing why, and turned round to look at the person who had given her this warning. He was unlike any one she had ever seen, except a picture in her mother's room of the Duc de Gandia, by Velasquez, which had been since her childhood her ideal of manly beauty. That face alone had borne any resemblance to the one which was now before her. So perfectly symmetrical, so majestically good, so expressive, and yet so calm. A tall slim figure, a well-shaped head with a most thoughtful brow, a smile of strange beauty, an attitude at once dignified and easy—the head a little thrown back, and the hand resting on the left hip.

She had not felt shy at any time that day, nor was she given to be shy; but now a sensation of that kind stole over her, and she said "Thank you" with an unusual timidity, and bowed her head as she did so, with something of submission as well as of acknowledgment. " I hope you have not thought me impertinent," he said, as she turned back towards the house. This time she smiled as she answered, " O, no !" and hoped he would speak again; but he did not, and she returned to the ball-room, and sat down in a corner, far from any one she knew.

The first sight of the Apollo Belvedere has made a person burst into tears—a beautiful landscape has affected others in the same way—the sight of the Alps or of the sea has awakened strong emotion—eloquence, even when not on a pathetic subject, has stirred the deep well-springs of feeling—and who has not known the impression which a procession, the hurrahs of a crowd, or a sudden burst of music has made upon them? Why should it, then, be strange that the sight of physical and intellectual beauty, of a commanding form, visibly inhabited by a superior spirit, should have had something of the same effect on Gertrude, and that she should have felt her eyes filling with tears—a very rare thing with her.

But there might be something else in this emotion. She had been very happy that day—so she told herself and so she believed—but had she not felt in the very depth of her young heart, that it had been a lonely sort of happiness, that she had been praised and admired and made much of, but no father's or mother's eyes had been upon her, and no one had led her by the hand before all those strangers and said : " She is mine, look at her if you will, love her even if you choose, but your new love is nothing to the love with which we have cherished her in our bosoms, and enshrined her in our heart." No one had watched her success with pleasure—no one as she left the heated ball-room had thrown a shawl over her shoulders, as all the careful mothers were doing to their children—no one had checked or reproved or caressed her that day. Singular waywardness of the human heart—unconscious yearnings after sympathy! A word of kindness from a stranger had touched a spring almost unknown to herself. There she sat watching or seeming to watch the dancers, and new thoughts were in her mind, or rather a new picture in her mind's eye, which was never to leave it again. There it was to remain, perhaps only as a dream that has been dreamt, and haunts us more or less through life, and embodies our imaginings when in romances or in poetry we read of beauty and of love, or when at other times we try to realize the presence of an angel or a hero, of the conquering archangel or the glorious Maccabee. For the first time in her life Gertrude had found it pleasant to submit, and she found pleasure in dwelling on that thought, in rehearsing again in her mind that little act of submission to a perfect stranger, and she made castles in the air about future opportunities of showing the same docility again.

"Do come and dance the cotillon with me, Miss Lifford," Mark Apley exclaimed, as he swiftly crossed the room and stood smiling before her. She sprung eagerly to her feet. She was impatient to fly again over the smooth floor. The music again was resounding, exciting and delighting every sense, and making her heart bound in time with its quick and wild measure. Mark Apley's voice was also pleasant in her ears, for he said he should never lose sight of her again. That he would sit for hours on the bridge of Stonehouseleigh, because she must sometimes drive or walk into the town. That he would go and hear Vespers at the Catholic chapel, for there he should see her—the saint of his devotion. That he was not to be baffled when he had set his heart on anything, and that after spending the happiest day of his life in her society, he should certainly never submit not to see her again.

All this was said in joke, but there was something earnest in it too. She saw perfectly how much he admired her; and music, and admiration, and dancing, and flattery, and nonsense, and liberty were pleasant things enough, but in the midst of them all castle-building went on. "If that voice," she said to herself, "that spoke to me at the grotto were again to address me now,—if it were to say: 'Do not dance so wildly—do not flirt so rashly—it is dangerous!' I should stop at once, like a chidden child, and feel glad to be thus rebuked." But she neither heard that voice again, nor did she see the face which in and out of the ball-room her eyes were ever searching for. She asked Miss Apley, and then Mark, and one or two other persons, who was a tall dark gentleman whom she had seen in the shrubbery. One told her it must have been Mr. Luxmoor, the member for the county, another did not know—could not imagine who she meant, a third thought it might have been one of the Italian singers, but this she knew could not be, because of the good English which the stranger spoke; and nothing else could she learn.

At past twelve o'clock Gertrude's cloak was put on, her hands affectionately pressed by Mrs. Apley and her daughters, with many entreaties not to let their acquaintance drop, but to come and see them as often as she could. Mark took her to the carriage. She saw him watching her from the colonnade, as long as she was in sight, and she drove home with a confusion of ideas in her head, and fatigue and excitement bewildering her thoughts. It seemed to her as if she had lived through a whole life since she left home that morning with Father Lifford. But one thought was uppermost—one image was prominent—one impression supreme, and as she laid her tired, but not sleepy head on the pillow, the idea that passed through her mind was this: "To-morrow I shall look at the Duke of Gandia's picture."

CHAPTER IX.

"The eloquence of goodness
Scatters not words in the ear, but grafteth them
To grow there and to bear."
SHAKESPEARE.

"Love is a great transformer."

On the morrow Mrs. Lifford was too ill to speak. The exertions of the last few days had been too much for her, and the doctor desired that none but her maid should go near her. When Gertrude came down later than usual to the breakfast-room, she found that her two usual companions had left it,—her uncle had gone to the same cottage where he had been summoned the day before, and her father had already shut himself up in his study. She threw the windows wide open, and sat down to her solitary meal, which was quickly finished. Then she took a camp-stool, and Luigi da Porto's romance of Romeo and Giulet, which Maurice had brought with him from Italy. She took them into the shade, underneath one of the largest trees of the park, and there remained for several hours reading and dreaming alternately. She had never felt to dislike Lifford Grange so little. She wanted time for thinking or rather musing, and the profound stillness of that wide solitary park was not irksome then.

It was one of those sultry days in September when not a leaf stirs, when scarcely an insect buzzes in the sunshine; when Nature seems asleep in the plenitude of her power—she has yielded up her harvest, and reposes from her labour. Gertrude had read the words which the enamoured girl addresses to young Montague when he takes her hand in the dance, at that ball which decides her fate. "Benedetta sia la vostra venuta qui presso me, Messer Romeo," and then the book dropped from her hand upon her knee, and she wondered if such a sudden love as that were indeed possible; and on this theme she meditated long. She thought of Jacob and Rachel, of James of Scotland and Madeleine of France, and then again of Romeo and Juliet,—and believed in love at first sight.

Her eyes fixed on the green grass; her head resting on her breast, so motionless that she heard the sound of her own breathing; her hands joined together on the book, she mentally made as it were her profession of that faith,—and seldom as it occurs, who can deny that such love there is? It is not common, perhaps it is undesirable—perhaps unreasonable—but, if it is real, there may be in it as much truth and strength and purity, as in the affections which are excited by a few weeks' flirting, stimulated on the one side by coquetry and on the other by vanity. If at the end of three months' flirtation, and of such conversations as passed the day before between her and Mark Apley, Gertrude had thought herself in love with him, would she or ought she to have stood higher in her own esteem, or in ours, than she does now, when she is conscious of having yielded up her heart at first sight to one whose countenance indeed may be deceitful, whose soul and whose intellect may be unequal to the stamp affixed on his brow, to the promise of his face; but in whom, even if such were the case, she would only have been misled to pay homage to the semblance of all that is admirable in man?

Who he was, whence he came, she knew not; what he was still less: but this very ignorance reassured her, and gave her confidence in the nature of the impression he had made upon her. That he could be anything but exalted in character and intellect she felt to be impossible, and would have staked her life on his excellence, without an instant's hesitation. "Poor little fool," some people will say—ay, it was folly, but not of the meanest sort, and we pity those who have never seen the man on the faith of whose eyes they would have done the same.

While she was thus contemplating, a footstep roused her from her abstraction. It was Father Lifford walking slowly along on his way back to the house. He looked hot and fatigued. Gertrude sprang up from her hiding-place under the spreading boughs, and called to him eagerly:

"Here is a stool, Father Lifford; do come and rest. The air is so sultry."

"Nonsense, child, I am not tired."

"Do sit down a moment," she said in a tone so unusual that he looked surprised, and perhaps something her mother had said to him, in their last long conversation, came into his mind; for his manner changed, and, sitting down as she wished, he wiped his forehead with his handkerchief, and asked her how she felt after a day of such unaccustomed fatigue and excitement.

She had taken her seat opposite to him, on one of the low branches of the elm, her arm twisted round another, and her feet scarcely reaching the ground.

"I am very well, Father Lifford."

"That is more than you look. You have not a bit of colour in your cheeks."

"It is the heat."

"It is sitting up late."

"O no, I never slept better in my life."

"What are you doing here?" She pulled some leaves off the branch and let them fall on the book which was lying on the grass. He pushed them aside with his stick and turned over the pages with it.

"An Italian novel. How very useful! Ah, Gertrude, it is not in this way that you will prepare for yourself such a close to your life as the one I have witnessed to-day."

"To-day—have you seen any one die to-day?"

"Indeed I have, and a girl scarcely older than yourself."

"Was it to her that you were called yesterday?"

"It was; and she died this morning."

"Resigned?"

"Ay, more than resigned—very happy."

"Had she been happy on earth?"

"Yes, nobody in her station could have been more so."

"Did any one love her?"

"Her parents, her brothers and sisters, and she was engaged to be married to a young man who was also very fond of her."

"Then, I am not surprised that she died happy."

"What do you mean by that?"

"I mean that she had had her share of happiness, and it made her good, and so she was fit for death. Do you know, Father, a strange thing? I believe I should be more resigned to die to-day than I could have been a few days ago."

"I am glad to hear it, and pray why so?"

"If you cannot guess, I don't think I can tell you."

"I am not going to guess, but I wish to put to you a question,—do you think you deserve to be happy?"

"I am afraid not," she answered seriously. "I am more afraid not than ever. But let me ask you a question, and do not snub me, dear Father Lifford, because really I want you to answer it,—do not you think I should have been better if I had been happier?"

"I have always told you, child, that you might have been happy if you had chosen it. Why, I have known a poor creature in a hospital, who had never had a moment's ease since her birth, as happy as the day was long. It is your stubbornness that makes you unhappy; and this is an answer to your question."

"No, I do not think it is. Which is the cause and which is the effect? *That* is the question. Tenderness might have made me less stubborn."

"There *is* a tenderness, my child, which should have subdued your heart long ago. I greatly fear that it is sorrow which will have to do that work for you. If small trials, if the sufferings of a wayward spirit are not enough to bring you to His feet, God may in mercy send you some of those strange afflictions which break the heart which would not bend, and destroy the spirit that would not yield."

She joined her hands, and said in a low voice: "Pray for me that it may not be so."

He was pleased at her answer, and looked at her kindly. Then, taking up her book from the ground, and having turned over its pages, he said in a milder tone of expostulation than usual: "Now what teaching is this? Nothing but praise of that poor creature for killing herself on the body of her lover. Can anything be more dreadful. If the story be a true one, as it is said, one may charitably hope that she went mad in that horrible place, and did it in a fit of insanity; but here the author coolly laments that such an example of real love does not occur more frequently, and, I dare say, so besotted was he with this absurd nonsense, that he was not even conscious that he was saying something very wicked."

"I had not thought of that. But do you think Juliet could have helped being in love with Romeo?"

"Of course she could. Why, if Romeo had been a married man—and so he might have been for aught she knew at first—what would she have done? Put him out of her head, of course, or been a great sinner. Nothing is impossible with a good will, and the grace of God."

Strange to say, it had not yet occurred to Gertrude that the stranger who had made so singular an impression upon her, the day before, might be married; and Juliet's words passed through her mind: "If he be married, my grave is like to be my wedding-bed." She smiled at her own folly, for she had formed no definite hopes or ideas connected with that person, but wished to indulge to the uttermost the recollection of that brief interview, and to build upon it certain romantic dreams incompatible with such a possibility. However, making an effort over herself, she recurred to the subject of the girl who had died that day.

"Had she during her illness all the comforts that she could want?" she asked.

"Yes,—she did not care much for anything of the kind, but what was needful she had. What she seemed most anxious about were her funeral expenses, that they should not be a burthen to her parents."

"And what has been done about that?"

"M. d'Arberg pays for them?"

"Who?"

"M. d'Arberg, that foreigner who is staying at Woodland's."

"What M. d'Arberg? Not Maurice Redmond's friend?"

"Yes, the same. Did not you see him yesterday? I just caught sight of him as I was leaving the house. He came to me the other day to speak about the poor Thorns, and I have met him two or three times at their cottage."

"How did he find them out, I wonder?"

"One of Thorn's sons had been his groom, I believe. He is not quite a stranger in this neighbourhood. There is some connection between him and the Apleys."

"Is he tall and dark, and like the picture of St. Francis Borgia in mamma's room?"

"Ay, well perhaps he is. I felt as if I had seen his face before. He is more like a Spaniard than a Frenchman."

"But is he French?"

"Partly so; his father was a German, I believe, naturalised in France; his mother was English or Irish, I don't know which. Have you never heard of his books?—But I forget, you only read this sort of thing," and with his stick he pointed contemptuously at the prostrate novel.

"You know you do not recommend *French* books to me, Father Lifford," Gertrude meekly answered, with a merry look in her eyes, for her heart was bounding with delight.

"That is because you love poison, and French poison is the worst of all. Well, I must go home now; it is getting late."

"O do stop a minute longer, or let me walk back with you;. I don't mind the sun. But tell me about M. d'Arberg and his books."

"Why, most Frenchmen are humbugs, but I believe he is a good man."

"Most Frenchmen humbugs! Now, Father Lifford, that is the sort of thing you say, but I am sure you don't mean, and it vexes me so!"

"Well, put *many* for *most*, and then the phrase will do."

"Strike out *French* also, and it will do still better."

"No, no, I don't assent to that omission. Come, open the umbrella,—the sun will make your silly head ache."

"What has M. d'Arberg written?"

"Philosophical Essays on Christianity. I hate that word Philosophy; but he means well."

"And do you like the book?"

"Very well; as much as I can like any French book. He

has some peculiar notions; but on the whole it is well enough. But nothing of that sort suits *you*, you know. Verse-books, and story-books, and trash are your delight."

"What is M. d'Arberg doing here?"

"Why, visiting his friends, I suppose. Somebody said he had property hereabouts that his mother left him. He is poking about amongst the Irish poor in the manufacturing towns, they say. I hope he has not got a bee in his bonnet."

"Have you that book here, Father Lifford?" Gertrude asked, as they reached the house.

"It belongs to Maurice Redmond; but I believe I have it in my room."

"Will you lend it me?"

"You will not read it."

"Shall I promise to do so?" she asked, with a smile.

"No, but if I let you have it, you must leave off poring over those trashy novels that are always lying on your table."

"Do you call 'Delphine' trash?"

"Ay, and the worst species of it,—all the more mischievous for its cleverness."

"Have you read it, Father Lifford?"

"No, I never read such things; but I know enough of its tendency to warn you against it."

"Then I will bring you all the volumes, though I am dying to know the end of the story, and you shall give me M. d'Arberg's book instead. That will be an exchange that will suit us both."

With these words she left him, and in a moment appeared at the door of his room with the novel in her hand, and carried off, as a miser bears away a load of sterling gold, the books which had now become so full of interest to her.

She went into the library on the first floor, and to her accustomed couch, the window seat.

The huge spider was, as usual, laying in wait in his web, and the dying flies strewed about the floor; her favourite books were in their places, but she passed them with an indifferent eye, for all her interest was absorbed by the volumes in her hand. The name of Adrien d'Arberg was on the title-page, and it was his thoughts that she was going to read. Silently, he would speak to her again, in her solitude, and she would learn to know him, even without meeting him again.

But now that she knew his name, how many recollections of what Maurice had related to her about him, crowded on her memory, and how well they suited with his face, with his voice, and with his attitude! Even then he was no stranger to her, and what would it be when she should have read through those volumes, into which so much of his soul and his mind must have passed?

She began to read; the style was entirely new to her. She was not well acquainted with that species of modern literature to which this book belonged, though well versed in the writings of past times, both in French and in English; she had never before met with a work which employed against vice and impiety all the fascinations of style, the sarcastic ingenuity, and the impassioned sensibility, that are so often displayed in their service. It took her by surprise. Almost every one has known, at least once in their lives, what it is to meet with a book in which, as if for the first time, another mind answers their own mind; and the vague sketches which were lying on the surface of the soul are filled up, as it were, by a master's hand. We then almost worship the spirit that speaks to us through its pages.

There are various magicians of this description — evil spirits and good — ever at work in that line: much is dormant in human hearts which their spells can awaken into existence. Have you ever gazed in a sculptor's studio on the rough block of marble out of which is to come forth the conception of his genius? Perhaps the likeness of some beautiful child of earth, or the fanciful image of a Pagan divinity,— the triumph of form, the dream of sensuality; or else the sublime result of a Christian's meditation, or a poet's inspiration There it lies—ready to appear at the command, and beneath the hand of its master. Has not the author with his pen sometimes the same power as the sculptor with his chisel? May he not call into life, and mould into form those vague and floating tendencies which haunt the human soul? May he not breathe passions yet unknown into its secret recesses, and arouse vices into play which were passively awaiting his foul touch?—or, on the other hand, may he not awaken the love of virtue by the intense homage he pays her; kindle devotion by the flame that flies from his bosom to his pen, and sound the call to perfection by the clarion-cry of his own faith?

These things have been done, and are doing every day.

Life and death are handed down from generation to generation, in the phœnix-like immortality of those works which, in edition after edition, transmit their poison or their balm from one age to another. The hand of Voltaire!—the hand of St. Francis of Sales!—helpless, lifeless, and motionless they lie in the shrine of the Pantheon, and in the humble church of Annecy, till the day of the Resurrection!—their works, in the words of the Bible, " are gone before them," ay, before them in one sense, but have tarried behind them in another.

Gertrude read, and thought, and read again, and the hours flew by unheeded. As certain perfumes have more power when the frame is peculiarly susceptible,—as certain sounds vibrate on the ear with more force at one moment than at another, according to the bodily state, so books impress the mind at certain times in a way which, earlier or later, they might not have done. And it is probable that the strong impression which Adrien had made upon her, during that brief instant when a few words had passed between them, paved the way for the effect which his writings were to have upon her. They did not treat exclusively of religion or of morality;—they were not wholly ascetic or imaginative, argumentative or illustrative. They had been originally written with a limited purpose, but an unlimited scope,—to convince a dear friend of the truth of Religion, not by evidences alone, not by sentiments merely, but by every appeal to reason— every illustration from analogy—every weapon offensive and defensive which Truth and Intellect can furnish, and Faith and Genius can wield.

Gertrude had never had even an intellectual doubt of the truth of her religion, and imperfect as her conduct often was, it would have been often more blamable but for the restraining power which that religion exercised over her: at certain times of her life she had known the joys of devotion, but her intellect had not been sufficiently appealed to. Her understanding had not yet grasped the extraordinary relation that exists between Faith in its full Catholic sense and everything great, good, and beautiful in the domain of reason and of feeling—of science and of art. Adrien's writings seemed to open before her new vistas in every direction, and to display the whole marvellous connection between the highest intellectual aspirations of the human mind, and the smallest point of revealed doctrine. Religion no longer appeared as something true and sacred indeed, but as concerned only with one portion of man's heart—one region of his soul—one aspect of his life; but as the point on which his whole existence revolves, on which his public as well as his private actions must turn, the only principle, the ruling power, the absolute master of every impulse, the disposer of every hour.

She saw the visible world not merely moving alongside but encompassed on every side by a supernatural one, the contact of which becomes every day more startlingly plain. It alluded to the modern discoveries of science, so extraordinarily illustrative of the faith of the Church: it spoke of the sublime aspirations through which the old philosophers felt their way after truth, and how Plato dared to guess what the first Catechism teaches. The perfectibility of man in its Christian sense, the mystery of his vocation, the depths to which he falls, the heights to which he rises, were dwelt on each in turn. Through the confessions of sceptics, the admissions of enemies, the homage of antagonists, through history and science, through the mind to the soul, the chain of evidence made its way. The reasoning was close and as calm as truth, but the feeling was intense, and fervent as love. It was as clever as if the intellect alone had been employed upon it; it was as persuasive as if the heart had alone been engaged in it. Was it strange that it absorbed her?—then roused and then strengthened her? That new thoughts, new interests, new resolutions, were formed?—that her studies were changed?—that her hours were spent differently?—that to get a book alluded to in *that* book, and they were many, became one of her greatest pleasures?—that to learn some of its eloquent pages by heart was her recreation?—that stealing to her mother's side whenever her health allowed of it, she read to her those passages which were most calculated to please her, and then kissing away the tears that sometimes stole down her face, she would lay her cheek against hers and whisper, "I knew you would like it!"

This was all well, but it was better still that in many practical ways she, day by day, improved,—that she was more assiduous in her devotions, more patient in little trials, less bitter towards her father, more tender to her mother,—that she appreciated Father Lifford's qualities more, and cared less for his peculiarities. But it was not so well that a strong human feeling was mixed up with all this, though it may be that Heaven's mercy may work good through its means. The sand on which this promising edifice is rising may indeed harden into stone, and the winds blow, and the rain fall, and its fair proportions stand,—for in that case it will be founded on the rock But if it rests on nothing but the shifting ground of passion or of fancy—what then will be its fate?

She is always copying the Duc de Gandia's picture, and she has written under it these lines from her old favourite Metastasio, though she seldom reads him now—

> "E proviamo al mondo
> Che nato in nobil core
> Sol frutti di virtù
> Produce amore."

CHAPTER X.

> "A prince can make a belted knight,
> A marquis, duke, and a' that,
> But an honest man's aboon his might,
> Guid faith! he mauna' fa' that,
> For a' that and a' that,
> Their dignities and a' that.
> The pith o' sense, and pride o' worth
> Are higher ranks than a that"
>
> BURNS

> "Virtue and knowledge are endowments greater
> Than nobleness and riches; careless heirs
> May the two latter darken and expand;
> But immortality attends the former,
> Making man a god."
>
> SHAKESPEARE.

WEEKS and months passed away, and nothing worthy of remark disturbed the even tenor of Gertrude's life. She went once or twice to Woodlands, but the Apleys were often away, and none of them except Mark seemed particularly anxious to keep up the acquaintance. Perhaps they had been alarmed at his evident admiration of her, and did not wish to encourage any further intimacy between them. Whenever he was at home he contrived to meet her in her walks, and to interchange a few words with her. Sometimes, when his manner was particularly eager, it occurred to her how easily, by a little encouragement, she might bring him to propose to her, and what a change would thus be brought about in her destiny; but it was never more than a passing thought. Her romantic admiration for Adrien d'Arberg forbade her entertaining it;

and though she liked these brief interviews, and her manner did not by any means deter Mark from seeking them, yet one of the "fruits of virtue," which grew out of that sentiment was a reserve in encouraging attentions, which doubtless, as far as they went, were by no means disagreeable to her.

But this very reserve increased Mark's admiration. At the breakfast he had been fascinated by her beauty, and amused by her cleverness, which he did not quite understand, though it charmed him like a firework or a French play; but when he met her now, there was something more thoughtful in her face, more gentle in her manner ; and this became her so well, and gave him such an interest about her, that he would sometimes sit on his horse at the gate of Lifford Grange, gazing with a wistful look at her retreating figure, as she walked up the sepulchral avenue of yew trees towards that house into which no strangers ever entered, and which appeared to him almost like an enchanted palace.

Gertrude had amused herself one day by telling him a wonderful ghost-story about it, which made his hair stand on end, but which he liked so much to hear her relate, that almost every time he met her, he used to begin again with, " Now you know I don't believe that story you told me the other day ;" and each time she added some new detail, which made him exclaim, " O now come, that is too bad—you don't expect me to believe that ?" But he went away for a long time that winter, and Gertrude missed him much, for it was impossible not to like to have her path crossed by such a kind smile, and such cheerful words. His good humour was like sunshine, and his merry laugh had grown familiar to her as something that belonged to those lanes and commons where she so often met him—as the smell of the gorse, or the song of the birds.

She still went often to the cottage at Stonehouseleigh, and now had a new and powerful interest in talking to Maurice. She asked him a thousand questions about the places where he had been with M. d'Arberg. During the years that he had spent with him in Rome, he had been engaged in writing that work which had so deeply interested her, and every minute detail concerning it she listened to with avidity.

" We lived at that time," Maurice told her, " in an apartment near the quattre Fontane, and M. d'Arberg used to write in a little garden full of violets, with a trellis of lemon-trees on one side, and a view over Rome on the other. I often looked at him as he sat at work, and thought what a good model he would have afforded a painter for a St. John writing his Gospel, or a St. Thomas Aquinas his Summa: he never looked impatient or anxious, but used to write those eloquent pages so composedly and fluently that I could almost have fancied I saw his guardian angel by his side dictating to him; and if anybody interrupted him—some tiresome acquaintance, or some begging friar—he would put down his pen, and listen to them with a countenance as undisturbed as if he had nothing else in the world to occupy or engross him. When I look back to the time I spent with that man, I can hardly believe in the perfection of his character,—so perfect, just because it had so little pretension."

"He must be, however, a person to be afraid of," Gertrude said; "goodness and cleverness combined would always be somewhat awful, I should think."

"Well, I never felt that with him. He is so very indulgent,—not merely that he will not say severe things, but one feels sure he does not think them."

"Yet in his writings he lashes with merciless severity certain modes of action and of thought."

"Ay, but no one ever made a wider distinction between the sin and the sinner, the error that blinds a man, and the man whom error blinds; he made a brilliant campaign in Algeria some years ago, and was as distinguished by his valour at that time as he has been since by his literary labours."

"And what made him leave the army?"

"He had only entered it for a particular purpose. The first year that he went into society at Paris he happened to defend the character of one of his friends with so much warmth, that the person who had slandered that friend conceived himself insulted, and called him out. He refused to fight, but the very next day proceeded to join the African army, where he established a reputation which raised him above the suspicion of cowardice. A splendid career was open to him, but he had no vocation for a military life, and retired from it as soon as a peace was concluded. He was adored by the troop he commanded—indeed I have never met with any one who has had any intercourse with him, who could resist the influence of his character and of his manners Have you read the life he wrote of Queen Christina, o Sweden?"

"O no; have you got it?"

"I am afraid not. I went with him into the Tyrol, just at the time he was busy with it. He wished to see the Franciscan Church at Inspruck, which is connected with her history. I shall never forget his admiration of the wonderful tomb of the Emperor Maximilian, in that glorious church. Those twenty-eight colossal bronze figures keeping their silent unremitting watch over the monument of the great warrior. How he liked the Tyrol! There was something so congenial to his feelings, so akin to his own character, in the strength and simplicity of its people; in the intimate connection between the highest beauties of nature, the devotional spirit of the inhabitants, and the pervading influence of religion, which seems there to impregnate the very air—to turn every hill into a Calvary, every valley into an oratory, and every church-yard into a garden. We had been staying at Venice, the city of my idolatry, the enchantress of the earth, the goddess of the sea; beauty bewildering every sense, music floating on the breeze, romance hovering over each stone of its palaces, each ripple of its wave, every stroke of the oar, every turn of the lagoons. I still remembered its moonlight nights, its noonday breezes; the Byzantine churches with their eastern cupolas, their mosaic pavements, their marble landing-places; the gentle splash of the water as we neared them in the gondolas; the musical cry of the gondoliers, as we shot swiftly round the corners; the soft sweet accents of the Venetian tongue; the luxurious repose of the body; the dreaming activity of the excited imagination,—it was all vivid in my mind as an Eastern story just perused, as a fairy tale realised; and when M. d'Arberg pointed out to me one night the moon shining coldly and sternly on one of the snowy peaks of the Alps, while the forests of fir beneath were lying in darkness, except where a solitary lamp (an earthly star as he called it) was burning before a way-side sanctuary, half way down the mountain, I could not forbear exclaiming, 'Give me back St. Mark and its piazza, the sky of Italy and the moon of Venice.' He smiled and said, 'I am afraid, Maurice, that you would have preferred the enchantress, Armida, to the lady in Comus.'"

Gertrude's eyes were riveted on Maurice, and she longed for him to talk on. He saw those eyes and their expression; at that moment there flashed across him something that was at once like a fear and a hope. How many ideas the brain can hold in one instant, and what different emotions agitate the heart at the same time! He thought of their childish sports in the forest; he thought of the lessons he had given her—of her appearance at the cottage the day that her father had dismissed him—of the way in which she had come and stood by his side, when he was taken ill at the Woodlands' breakfast; and now how often she took occasion to stop at the cottage, and to linger there in conversation with him: and the expression of her eyes just then! There was a light in them he had never seen before, and which seemed to put him beside himself. Was it possible that she loved him? It was a sensation of rapture mixed with a thousand misgivings and apprehensions.

His safety, his peace, had consisted hitherto in the utter hoplessness of the sentiment, the dream, the passion—whichever it was—that he had conceived; but in the light of that moment's wild hope he saw his own poverty, he saw duty, honour, and Mary arrayed before him in despairing distinctness. He was one of those men who have the love but not the courage of virtue. That he had hitherto felt her to be utterly out of his reach had been almost a satisfaction to him, for he fancied there was neither danger nor guilt in worshipping her at a distance. That could be no injury to her, and no treachery to Mary. But this new hope, this sudden suspicion that she was not indifferent to the homage which his eyes and voice and actions had involuntarily paid her—was it bliss or was it pain? There she was with that fatal beauty which had so long enthralled him. Ay, he had often before compared her to Italy, and applied to her loveliness that startling epithet. There she was, resting her face on her hand, and bidding him tell her more about his travels, more about M. d'Arberg and himself, and their life at Rome and Venice, their walks on the sea-shore, and their communings by the way, and each time there was a pause recurring to the same subject.

Another person in that room was listening and watching also,—

"One who had poured her heart's rich treasure forth,
And been unrepaid for its priceless worth."

Whether Gertrude was consciously or unconsciously stealing away from her the love which had been the sunshine of her life she knew not, and had the virtue not to decide; but the effect was the same. "She is breaking my happiness to pieces," was Mary's feeling; "perhaps only as a child might destroy a flower of great price which had fallen in its way. My *all* can be to her but the plaything of the hour, and yet she uses it as such, and seems not to know what she is doing. O Maurice, my beloved one! You are not made for trials; you are not fitted for conflicts with the world and your own heart. I might have stood between you and many dangers; but this one nothing that I can do may avert. It is as if you were sinking into a gulf or falling over a precipice, and I was forced to stand by and see you perish, with my hands tied and my mouth gagged. Could I but make you feel that if you love her she will break your heart!"

Always after Gertrude's visits Maurice was more affectionate than usual to Mary, and there was a refinement in the pain that this gave her. It seemed as if the very source of her happiness was poisoned, for these mute apologies were more grievous to her than unkindness would have been. Yet her manner never betrayed the least irritation; only there was a grave tenderness in her countenance quite different from the beaming look and playful shake of the head with which she had hitherto received his assurances of affection.

The winter passed by, and the spring also. Maurice went to London for some months, where he gave lessons and played at concerts with considerable success, but the tone of his letters to Mary was restless and dissatisfied. It seemed as if he could neither stay at nor away from Stonehouseleigh with any comfort. He complained sometimes that she did not urge him to come back, that she did not write to him often enough. He spoke of his own health in a tone of depression, and of London with abhorrence. Mary's trial increased, for now she hardly knew what was her duty, what was best for him. Any sacrifice she was ready to make, but feared to take any step either backwards or forwards. It seemed to her best to wait and to watch, and Heaven knows there is often more suffering in this than in any decision, but of that she never thought.

In the course of the summer Edgar Lifford came home; he was a handsome and amiable youth, with a great deal of information and a little pedantry. Gertrude—who was very glad of his return—laughed at him, and he did not resent it, but treated her with great condescension, and explained to her many things which he supposed she did not understand. Great pains had been taken with him, and he had had admirable instructors, but the essential part of the intellect was wanting, although he might have been said to have good parts, according to the strict letter of that phrase, for his memory and his aptitude for learning were remarkable. There was nothing he could not, and I had almost said, *did* not commit to memory. He was almost too young to be prosy, but he promised much in that line, especially if that shocking opinion be correct, that it is not possible to be a thorough-paced bore, without possessing a great deal of information.

Mrs. Lifford loved her son's goodness, his honest face, his civility to every one, and she imagined that his residence at home would be a great advantage and comfort to Gertrude. Mr. Lifford was as fond of his son as he could be of anything; but as he was himself clever in his way—though no one could make less use of his natural gifts—he quickly perceived his son's intellectual deficiencies, and felt an additional irritation at Gertrude's superiority. When, with a few words of lively sarcasm, hitting exactly the nail on the head, she overturned the well-set, ponderous array of her brother's reasonings, or, when he was really in the right, managed to make his arguments appear ridiculous, his brow grew darker still than usual, and there was something painful in the looks he cast upon her.

Now that Edgar was old enough to dine with them, there was a great deal more conversation at Lifford Grange than was usually the case. That it was lively could scarcely be said, for the two, who, in different ways, might have made it so—that is. Gertrude and her uncle—were the most silent, and Mr. Lifford and his son had it a good deal to themselves. One day a little scene occurred, which was animated, at least, if not lively. Mr. Lifford had been pronouncing himself very strongly against all modern innovations, in which he included the diffusion of education amongst the poor, lodging-houses, wash-houses, and emigration, all of which he declared to have a Socialist and revolutionary tendency. "All this fuss made about the poor at this time is only a species of cant which belongs to the age, and has not an atom of real charity in it."

"True charity," Edgar observed, "consists, in my opinion, in individual exertions, not in combined action. Thus gratitude is awakened in the breasts of the poor, and kindness in those of their superiors."

"But, my dear Edgar, you cannot individually wash the poor, nor can you swim with them on your back to Australia, so that *some* combined action may be useful."

"I own to a great dislike to prospectuses, and lists, and——"

"Bills of fare," Gertrude maliciously suggested, having observed that her brother studied *that* prospectus every morning with considerable interest.

Mr. Lifford frowned and said, "Printed papers have as seldom any real connexion with good works as pertness has with wit."

"I met the other day in the railway," Edgar said, "a gentleman with whom I had a great deal of conversation on philanthropical subjects. I should almost have been inclined to think him a Socialist from some things he said, only that it seemed afterwards that he was quite the reverse. As long as he talked of what the higher classes should do, he seemed to stop at nothing in his requirements; but, on the other hand, he held temporal prosperity for all sorts of persons cheaper than I should be inclined to do, though of course I know that there are things of greater importance. He was a Frenchman, I found, though he spoke English extremely well."

"It was not Adrien d'Arberg, by chance?" Father Lifford inquired.

"That was the name on his portmanteau. He was just come from France."

Gertrude's colour had risen at the sound of the name that interested her so much, and she said quickly, "Did he know who you were?"

"I found he did, and that he had heard of my family and knew how ancient it was, and that we counted kings and crusaders amongst our ancestors."

"How you must have purred when he said that," Gertrude murmured, but not loud enough for her father to hear.

"I did not quite approve of his tone on the subject; he liked old recollections of that kind, he said, and the romance attached to them. It was like the armour that we hang upon our walls, of no real value in these days, but having a certain charm from association."

"A manufacturer's son, no doubt, a Jeune-France!" Mr. Lifford ejaculated with unspeakable contempt.

"No, he does not belong to that school, and he is a far better man than you would suppose." Father Lifford answered.

"And why in Heaven's name," Gertrude exclaimed to herself, "should one *not* suppose him to be so? But, patience 'Wisdom is justified of her children.'"

"He has written a clever book enough, which has made a great sensation in France."

"O, an author too! a Frenchman, and an author! From all such Heaven deliver us! I hope, Edgar, that you were not by way of making more than a momentary acquaintance with him. That is the worst of those infernal railways: they expose one to come in contact with all sorts of people."

"O, I took care not to commit myself in any way to his acquaintance, for I could not tell, you know, what his birth or position in society might be. Dear me, Gertrude, how red you are! Are you very hot, dear sister?—Shall I open the window?"

All the open windows in the world would not have cooled Gertrude's cheeks at that moment, or restrained her from breaking forth. "I pity you, brother, if you could not discern in that man's appearance a surer patent of true nobility than lies in parchments and escutcheons, and a greater honour in having had an hour's conversation with him, than in descending from crusaders and Spanish grandees."

There was an awful pause after this sentence. The sneer at the "Grands d'Espagne" had particularly nettled Father Lifford, who was more than half a Spaniard in his feelings. Edgar was exceedingly puzzled—both at the extreme impropriety of his sister's sentiments, and at her warmth on the subject—as well he might be, not knowing that she had ever seen d'Arberg, or that she was acquainted with his works.

"Really, sister," he began, but his father interrupted him. "Pray do not attempt to reason with Gertrude; since her love of contradiction and perversity of feeling is getting to the point of putting herself in a passion, and insulting us all about a perfect stranger in whom she can take no interest, but on account of his probable low birth and his sneers at what we value and respect, the more we leave her to herself the better; only I do not choose to hear such words uttered again before me; and therefore, Miss Lifford, whatever your degrading sentiments may be, take care that you never let *me* hear them again."

Gertrude had been much to blame, she knew and she felt it, and her irritation had vanished; but a dull aching at her heart succeeded it. When they all left the table she went to the window, and laid her forehead against the glass. Her father and her brother had left the room, and her uncle was following them; but when he got near the door he turned round to look at her. She also turned at that moment, and rushing to him with impetuosity, threw herself into his arms. He did not repulse her, but said, "Pshaw, don't make a scene; you are a bad incorrigible girl." But the manner was not harsh as the words.

"O Father Lifford," she exclaimed, "I have been so wrong. I have behaved ill to you,—you who have been so kind to me!"

"Never mind that; you should grieve at having displeased your father."

"I *cannot*. You—*you* I am sorry to have offended, and if you would let me, I would kneel to ask your pardon."

"No, no, Gertrude, not here. It is not *thus* or *here* that you must sue for pardon; remember your father's must be asked, and that not in outward form alone, but with a humbled heart and a penitent spirit. God bless you, my child!" he added, for he saw the resolution was made, and the proud spirit conquered.

CHAPTER XI.

"I looked, and looked, and still with new delight
Such joy my soul, such pleasure filled my sight;
Nor sullen discontent, nor anxious care,
Even though brought hither could inhabit there,
But thence they fled as from their mortal foe,
For this sweet place could only pleasure know."
DRYDEN.

"About me round I saw
Hill, dale, and shady woods, and sunny places,
And liquid lapse of murm'ring streams; by these
Creatures that lived and moved, and walked or flew,
Birds on the branches warbling; all things smiled;
With fragrance and with joy my heart o'erflowed."
FAYRIE QUEEN.

EDGAR observed that his sister was looking somewhat pale and out of spirits, and his good-natured disposition attributing it partly to the scene which had taken place, and of which he had unintentionally been the cause, he set about thinking on some mode of pleasing and amusing her. Having heard her express one day a great wish to ride, he now endeavoured to find out some means of giving her this pleasure.

"Would you not like to ride, Gertrude," he said to her one

morning. "Would not the exercise be beneficial to your health?"

"I don't know what it would do to my health, dear old boy, but I know it would be of use to my temper,—it would shake a great deal of malice out of me."

"Would you be afraid to ride my horse?"

"I would ride anything, a cow, a stag, a crow, or an eagle."

"If so, I will borrow the gamekeeper's pony for myself, and you can ride Conqueror. I must see about the side-saddle, and you must get something of a habit."

"I don't know what I can do about that. Perhaps I might wear mamma's, which has been put by for so many years. Do you think its old-fashioned shape and embroidered facings will signify?"

"O dear no I have no doubt it will look very well, and we will go towards the open country, where we shall probably not meet any one. You will like, perhaps, to see a large encampment of gipseys on Oakley Common?"

"O, of all things; I delight in their picturesque faces. What a dear boy you are, Edgar, to have thought of my riding. I will copy the *tree* for you this evening, and not say anything disrespectful about it."

"I hope you will not for your own sake, Gertrude, and I am much obliged to you for the promise."

Then they parted, and both were successful in their researches.

At five o'clock, for the day had been very warm and they did not start till then, Gertrude appeared on the steps in her picturesque attire, and sprang lightly on the horse, which appeared at first rather uneasy at the flapping of her riding-habit, but went pretty quietly after a few minutes. She was delighted at finding herself on horseback, and when they got into a green valley, a little beyond the park, she set off at a quick canter till the ground grew broken and uneven, and then they proceeded at a foot-pace through a narrow ravine, and by the side of a rapid stream She was silent, for her enjoyment lay in thoughts that it would never have occurred to her to communicate to Edgar; only now and then she said, "How pleasant this is!" or, "How fine it is to-day!" He stopped sometimes to gather branches of honeysuckle or white convolvuluses, and handed them to her, discoursing the while on botany, geology, and various branches of natural history, and telling her the names of every bird and insect they saw on bush or hedgerow. She thanked him for the flowers, and listened with apparent interest to the comments, but her thoughts were often far away.

"There is a lady-bird," he said, as one of those little creatures settled on his horse's mane.

"Ay, a lady-bird," she exclaimed, roused from her abstraction; "my namesake! Do not you remember?—it is the name that Maurice Redmond and Mary Grey have always given me."

"But I hope they don't do so now, Gertrude; it would be very familiar."

"I wonder," she said to herself, "that he does not add—'and familiarity breeds contempt.'" But without answering him, she held out her hand and made the little insect come upon it, and gazed upon it earnestly, while she murmured to herself in a low voice the pretty nursery rhyme—

"O lady-bird, lady-bird, fly away home,
   The squirrel and field-mouse have gone to their rest,
The daisies have shut up their sleepy red eyes,
   The bees and the insects and birds are at rest.
O lady-bird, lady-bird fly away home,
   The glow-worm is lighting his glittering lamp,
The dew's falling fast, and your fine speckled wings
   Will be moistened and wet with the close clinging damp.
O lady-bird, lady-bird, fly away home,
   The sweet little fairy bells tinkle afar;
Make haste, or they'll catch you and harness you fast
   With a gossamer cobweb to Oberon's car."

As she ended her song the little creature, that had been for a while so motionless that it scarce seemed alive, suddenly expanded its hitherto invisible wings, and flew away in an instant.

"Ah, so I too shall fly away some day, to your great surprise," she said, turning to Edgar; "I must see something of the world before I die."

"I hope you will be well married in a year or two, sister, and then I dare say you will persuade your husband to take you a tour abroad."

"Unless I am married by proxy—like some of the great people we descend from—I do not see the individual who is to have the honour of my hand."

"My father will look to that."

"He may look, but he will not see. Besides, it is my business—not his."

"I cannot admit that, Gertrude; nothing concerns a father more than the marriage of his children, and the alliances of his family."

"Of his sons, certainly," she answered, with an affected gravity; "I would not have you, my dear brother, swerve an inch from that conviction or think of choosing a wife for yourself—not even if you were to meet with an angel from Heaven—if she could not prove sixteen quarterings, or had not had well-attested grandfathers on grandfathers. I feel that on you will rest all the responsibility of the family greatness, and I am sure you will not shrink from any choice that will be made for you, be she ever so ugly, if her ancestors are all right."

"I think virtue is the first thing in a wife, but next to that, I own that I attach more importance to family descent than to personal beauty."

"O my dear Edgar, how absurd you are! Do not be angry." But there was no occasion for this appeal, for Edgar had the best of tempers, and the happiest conviction that he was always right; so that nothing ever ruffled or disturbed him.

After a ride of some length, and mounting awhile, they arrived at a wooden eminence near the downs, which commanded a magnificent view. The stream, which had been compressed within its banks in the narrow valley, expanded into a river in the plain; the hills, overhung with wood, threw broad shadows on the waving corn-fields. The declining sun gilded the rich foliage with its evening light, and odours rose in balmy sweetness from the clover on the one side, and the wild thyme on the other. Edgar, who always was more intent on little matters of detail than on the general beauty of a scene, and whose favourite pursuit just then was entomology, espied a singular insect flying under some trees a little way beneath them. He got off his horse, and, tying the bridle to a tree, ran after it amongst the bushes where he had seen it disappear. Gertrude sat negligently on her saddle in delighted contemplation of the scene before her. She let the reins hang on her horse's neck, and allowed him to crop the short grass at his feet.

At that moment a gun went off in a neighbouring field, startling a covey of partridges, and frightening both the horses, which set off at full gallop. Edgar's broke away from the bush where it was loosely fastened, and rushed past the spot where he was still looking for his insect. He ran after it down the hill, and it was some time before he caught it. When he returned to the spot where he had left Gertrude she had disappeared. He called to her as loudly as he could, but no answer came. Then pushing on his horse, he looked about the downs in every direction and could not see her. In serious alarm he rode on, but unfortunately in the opposite direction to that which her horse had taken. It had started off at the same moment as his; she kept her seat and seized the reins, but beginning to pull at its mouth with all her might, it stuck its head down, and got entirely beyond her control. She was soon out of sight of the spot from whence she had started, and began to feel sick and giddy with the pace at which they were going. She felt herself rushing up and down hill, and over some ditches and through some fences, and then across a road, and again for what appeared to her an interminable time along the open downs, and at last through a gate into what seemed to be a park; there the horse came suddenly to a stop: this threw her off her balance and she fell on the grass. It was soft and she would not have been much hurt if her foot had not been under her, and in this way severely sprained her ankle. She felt a little stunned, but endeavoured to get up and to walk a few steps, but pain compelled her to sit down again, with her back against a hay-stack, which she now saw was the obstacle that had checked the speed of her horse.

It was getting late, and the night was waning fast; she could discern nothing but trees, and heard no sounds but the cawing of rooks. All sorts of ideas began to pass through her mind,—if nobody passed that way what would become of her that night? Once more she tried to walk, but now she could not even put her foot to the ground. Then she called out as loud as she could, and the rooks seemed to caw louder in answer, but nothing else responded. Then something rattled in the hedge behind her, and she held in her breath with affright. Her foot began to swell very much, and she grew faint with the pain. By degrees her thoughts became less clear, and almost assumed the character of dreams; but still they turned upon her present position, and the vague fears it inspired.

Would she die if she remained there all the night? It was a summer evening, and the sky over her head was clear, and the stars beginning to shine one by one; but the air felt very cold, and the grass was damp. If she should have a dangerous illness, would her father grieve for her, and would her mother have strength to come to her bedside, and give her a kiss as she used to do when she was a little child? Would Father Lifford weep if her life were despaired of, or was he a man who never shed tears? She kept asking herself these questions over and over again, and fancying how everybody would look and what they would say at Lifford Grange, if she *were* brought back *dead.* How strange it would be! The chapel would be hung with black, and candles would be lit on the altar, and the "De profundis" would be sung. Then she mechanically repeated over and over again,

> "Eternal rest give unto her, O Lord,
> And let perpetual light shine upon her,
> May she rest in peace!"

Then she ceased to think, but dreamed that she was in her coffin, and that it was being slowly lifted up and carried along Was she going to Heaven? No, it could not be Heaven, for she was so sensible of suffering great pain. It was purgatory, perhaps. Then everything grew indistinct and confused, and a sense of repose stole over her. But she could not move nor speak.

Then she heard the sound of voices and of footsteps about her, and she felt herself talking at random, and heard some one say that she was light-headed. Then later somebody came in and felt her pulse and her forehead, and a glass was held to her lips. Some hours afterwards she awoke, and looked about her with astonishment. She saw nothing but snowy white muslin curtains, and opposite to her a marble chimney-piece, and upon it a transparent night-lamp, with a kneeling figure of a woman in a church, the light shining through the mimic Gothic windows. Her feverish hands were resting on a pink silk eiderdown quilt, and her flushed cheek on a pillow fringed with lace. She saw all this, but felt too weak to wonder at it, and closed her eyes and went to sleep again. The next time she opened them daylight was shining through the chinks of the shutters. She heard some one talking in the next room, and supposed she was still dreaming; but soon the speaker came in, a pretty, well-dressed person, and bending over her she said, "Do not be frightened, Miss Lifford, at finding yourself in a strange place. This is Mr. and Lady Clara Audley's house. You were brought here last night after your fall from your horse. For some time we did not know who you were; but the doctor, when he came, recognised you immediately. A message was sent to your parents to let them know that you were safe, and Lady Clara is anxious that you should feel yourself quite comfortable. I am her maid, Miss Lifford. I hope you find yourself pretty well this morning."

"Yes, thank you," Gertrude answered, and without quite knowing why, could scarcely keep the tears from rolling down her cheeks. "How came I here?" she asked with a bewildered expression. "What happened to me last night? You said I fell from my horse. Where was I found? I was stunned, I suppose?"

"You were found lying near a haystack in the park, Miss Lifford; you had fainted right away, and one of the gentlemen carried you here; it was some time before you came to yourself."

"I scarcely feel even now, as if I had," she ejaculated. "Everything seems so strange. Will you thank Lady Clara for her kindness? I suppose somebody will soon come from my home."

There was a nervous sensation in her throat as she said those last words. She felt very lonely, and partly from physical weakness, partly from the strangeness of her position, she found it difficult not to give way to her emotion.

When the maid left the room she clasped her hands together, and hiding her face in the pillow, murmured, "Nobody loves me—nobody cares for me—I might have died last night, and nobody would have been sorry except poor mamma." Such were her thoughts, not very logical or reasonable ones, certainly, but springing nevertheless from a sense that she had never been watched over or cherished in her home; and how often it happens that in illness or loneliness the long kept-down emotion, the long standing heart-ache, the sense of an injury long forgiven and all but forgotten, will sometimes start up with all the vehemence of former days, and the trifle as light as air—which at other moments might only have excited a smile—will in those hours of weakness call forth a burst of feeling which shakes to pieces the barrier with which the soul had fenced itself round, and imprisoned till it had subdued its own impetuosity. Sometimes that calmness is the result of heroic virtue, sometimes of the force of habitual endurance, and sometimes again of an odd sort of levity, a recklessness of the same nature as that which will make some children (boys especially) utterly heedless of physical pain, and will let them play and exert themselves as usual with a dislocated limb or a festering wound, in any of these cases momentary reactions may take place, but the effects will often be different. Through them the spirit may descend a step towards evil, or it may but grasp more firmly the hand held out to it from heaven.

The next time that Mrs. Martin, the good-natured ladies' maid, came in, it was to bring Gertrude her breakfast, served in beautiful Sèvres china, on a small silver tray. She opened the shutters, to let light into the room. Gertrude asked her to throw open the window also; and, rising in bed, she looked upon such an enchanting scene as had never yet met her sight. The place was one well known to her by name, for it was famous for its natural beauties, and for all that art had done for it. The house stood in a commanding position on the brow of a hill, backed by a magnificent bank of wood, and from it the eye rested on a succession of terraces, each forming a gorgeous flower-garden, now in all the glory of summer just verging upon autumn. Large, dazzling masses of the scarlet geranium faced the deep blue beds of the salvia or the gentian. The heliotrope and the variegated verbenas, the stately hollyhocks and the graceful fuchsias, the dahlias like court beauties in their pompous array, the tall white lilies, standing alone in their majestic purity, were all there in clusters, or in rows. The passion flower, the jessamine, and the convolvulus covered the walls, which stretched from one end of each terrace to the other. Red roses in marble vases adorned every flight of steps, and in the centre of each division of this flowery mosaic, on every story of this sloping garden, a fountain played, which high and clear into the morning air shot up sheets of pure water, or clouds of glittering spray, through which the sun shed its rays on this scene of enchantment.

The last of these terraces overhung the river Leigh, which, broadening into a lake at this period of its course, reflected on that morning the azure of a cloudless sky, and then immediately narrowed again, as if on purpose to show off its silvery windings through the green valley of Arkleigh. A little skiff was lying at anchor, near the stone steps of the landing-place, its white sail gleaming in the sunlight, and its streamers gently fluttering in the breeze. The banks of wood, which reached to the edge of the water, on the other side of the stream, were just beginning to display their rich autumnal hues. The foliage of the copper beech, the coral berries of the mountain ash, and the red leaves of the Virginian creeper, stood out in contrast with the masses of summer's richest green. There was a brightness, a brilliancy, a gaiety in this view which no description can convey. The statues placed amongst the flowers, or presiding over the fountains, were all in some graceful or joyous attitude. Either they seemed to play with the large leaves of the lotus, or to throw up into the air, in mimic sport, the water that fell back in sparkling showers on their marble shoulders, or they seemed to bow their graceful heads under the rays of the sun, and to inhale sweet odours from the glowing masses of flowers which surrounded them.

A part of the park was also visible from the window:— the deer starting from the midst of the tall fern, the cattle standing contemplatively by the brink of the river, the Gothic towers of an old church appearing in the distance, and the blue hills of Westmoreland forming a back-ground to the picture. It was a view not to be weary of, and the inside of Gertrude's room corresponded with the beauty without. It was furnished with a magnificence that would hardly perhaps have been in good taste, if there had not been something poetical in its smallest details. Each piece of furniture, each picture, each bit of carving, the mirrors, the carpet, the writing-table, the stools, the luxurious arm-chairs, the patterns of the curtains, the mouldings of the cornice, all suggested to the mind something pleasing in Nature or in art. Flowers, birds, children's laughing faces, ivy wreaths and clustering grapes, sunny landscapes and graceful figures, appeared at every turn, and as Gertrude closed her eyes for a moment and thought of Lifford Grange, it seemed to her that she must have dreamed of the scenes just described, or else been transported to one of those fairy abodes which she had so often pictured to herself in her childhood.

At that moment she caught sight of a well-known figure on a rough, stout pony, making its way towards the house, looking ill suited to the brilliant scene around him, but more welcome to her just then, than all its beauties put together. Father Lifford—for it was he—was looking paler than usual; not one glance did he bestow on the fine scenery he was passing through. His black coat was wet with the morning dew, and his hair seemed more grey than the day before. He had suffered very much, from the time when Edgar had returned home without his sister, and alarmed the house for her safety. At first, he did not think so much of an accident, as that the child had done something strange. He loved her more than he was aware of, but had never felt easy about her, and he now shuddered as he remembered her weariness of home—her pining for change—her strange questions and her odd fancies.

When her horse was brought home late at night, having been found in a field by some labourers, his anxiety grew intense, and he had never found it so difficult to be calm. Men were sent to seek for her in every direction, and it was only with his head buried in his hands, in incessant prayer before the altar, that he could command his feelings. When the news of her safety arrived, his only thought was to go to her. There were reasons that made him hate entering the walls of Audley House, but they were all swallowed up in the determination to see the child, and ascertain for himself that she was not seriously hurt; and, leaving orders for her maid to follow him, he never rested till he stood by her bedside.

She held out her hands to him, while the tears chased each other down her cheek. "A pretty business this," he growled out, "a mighty pretty business, to have you laid up here in this new-fangled place, with nothing and nobody that is not strange to us about you;" and he held her hand and stroked it gently, while she could hardly forbear a smile at his entire want of appreciation of the beauty and the comfort which were apparent in the smallest details, as well as in the general aspect of her present abode.

"And what is to happen, child? They tell me that you cannot walk, and that the doctor will not let you be moved. This is sad work indeed!"

"Lady Clara says that I must stay here, and ——"

"And what business has she to say anything about it?"

"I mean that she says I *may* stay here, and indeed my foot hurts me so much at the least motion that I do not think I could stir."

"Then you shall not stir. Why do you move about? Can't you be quiet? So you must stay here, I suppose."

"Is papa angry with me? Was he at all anxious last night?"

"Why, you don't suppose we were any of us very comfortable, do you?"

"Poor mamma! I thought of her, as long as I could think of anything '

"Well, there was some grace in that. But we did not tell her anything till we knew where you were."

"And Edgar?"

"O the boy! He cried, but he ate some supper." Gertrude smiled, and laid her hand on the old man's sleeve.

"Father Lifford, I believe you love me, though you never say so."

"Nonsense I love everybody, it is my duty."

"Well, I don't think you love Lady Clara Audley," she maliciously replied, for with her needle-like penetration she had long ago perceived that the mistress of Audley House for some unknown reason was his favourite aversion. She had not indeed seen them together, but the mere sound of her name was at any time sufficient to discompose him.

"Lady Fiddlestick!" he answered impatiently, "I wish her well, but ——" at that moment there was a gentle knock at the door.

"Here she is, I am sure," Gertrude whispered.

"Ah well, I'll go now, child, and come back again another time. Is there another door?" he ejaculated with a look of real distress, but while he was desperately endeavouring to get out at one door and entangling himself in the embroidered curtains of its portières, the enemy entered through the other, and cut off his retreat.

This enemy was about thirty-eight, but looked younger—at least not many women of thirty-eight retain as much beauty—such a smooth fair skin, such glossy hair, and such youthful delicacy of feature. There was something that reminded one of feudal times in her appearance. Something grave, dignified, and almost majestic, though combined with a particularly feminine grace. Her eyes were hazel and rather prominent, her hair auburn, and her lips somewhat thick, though not too much so for beauty. She was dressed in a black velvet gown with wide hanging sleeves, a guipure shawl hung over her shoulders, and a lace cap was fastened by two diamond pins to the thick tresses of her hair. She bent over Gertrude, rapidly said some kind things to her, and then turning to Father Lifford bowed to him most graciously, and murmured something about not having met for a long time. He bowed in return, gravely and coldly, but with perfect civility; for with all his bluntness he was invariably well bred. She then inquired after Gertrude's parents in a kind of half compassionate half mysterious tone, which seemed to annoy him, and he answered the question briefly and abruptly. To her expressions of delight at having the opportunity of seeing Gertrude in her house, and her hopes that she would remain till perfectly recovered from her accident " that they would not deprive her of the wounded bird that had nestled under her wing," he responded as if poisoned honey had been distilled into his ears, and said that his nephew and Mrs. Lifford would doubtless much regret the trouble which their daughter's accident had occasioned; but though the words were civil, there was something so chilling and formal in the tone which accompanied them, that Lady Clara, who observed it, said:

"Time often perpetuates estrangements between those who once were friends, but I entreat you to tell Mr. Lifford that his daughter cannot be a stranger here, and that if he will trust me with his treasure, I will cherish it as I would my own, had Heaven granted me one."

A still graver and colder bow was the Father's only reply, and he withdrew after giving Gertrude his blessing and promising to send over some things which she wanted from home.

And now the lady of the enchanted castle and her young guest remained alone together. Lady Clara fitted well that abode. She had created it chiefly herself, and it seemed in every part of it to bear the impress of her mind and tastes. She had been, from the day of her birth, "a lady nursed in pomp and pleasure;" but not in vulgar pomp or senseless pleasure. Nature had given her a sweet temper, a love of the beautiful, and a kind and noble spirit. Education had added delicacy, grace, and refinement of manners. Nothing mean or vicious had approached her. She had neither suffered, struggled, nor sinned, as the world considers it, and she was the *chef d'œuvre* of what a happy disposition, the best kind of worldly education, and earthly safeguards from temptation can effect. With a slight alteration she could be well described in the words of a living poet:

> "She floated o'er life like a noontide breeze
>   Or cradled vapour on sunny seas,
>   Or an exquisite cloud in light arrayed,
>   Which sails through the sky, and can throw no shade
>   She cared for no sympathy—living in throngs
>   Of her own sunny thoughts and her mute inward songs.
>   She was chaste as the white lily's dew-beaded cup,
>   Which bold—because stainless—to heaven looks up
>   Her mind was a fair desert temple of beauty,
>   Unshaded by sorrow, unhallowed by duty."

When just passing from early girlhood into womanhood, beautiful as a poet's dream, as a painter's ideal, she had appeared to the young owner of Lifford Grange. He saw her at a county ball; he was invited to meet her at a neighbouring country-house, and then to her father's house; he fell desperately in love with her. It was one of those violent absorbing passions that make wild havoc in a man's heart. He was handsome and clever: she was pleased with him, and without hesitation accepted him when he proposed to her. Her parents, though they disliked the marriage, never thwarted their idol, and all of them went to London together, and Lady Clara was engaged to Henry Lifford. But jealous, tyrannical, and proud—he soon alienated from him the inclination which the beautiful spoilt child had felt for him. The outbreaks of his fierce passion disquieted and alarmed her. Gentle, refined, and pure, caring more for the charm and the sentiment of a mutual affection than for the kind of love which made him at one moment adore and at another reproach her, she broke off her engagement as unhesitatingly as she had entered into it, and without a struggle or a regret—as she would have thrown aside a nosegay in which a thorn had stung her—she dismissed him at once, and went on her way as free, as happy, and as calm as if he had never crossed her path.

He went almost mad with anger and despair; and then the pride which was in him as strong as life itself, enabled him to subdue at once all outward expression of love, or of regret: but, like an extinguished volcano, which has consumed every trace of vegetation, and leaves behind it barren and unsightly ruins, the flame thus suddenly extinguished seemed to have burned out of his heart every trace of gentle feeling and affection. He went almost immediately to Spain, and there married the beautiful Angustia, but no sooner was the ceremony performed than he felt himself undone; and the cold admiration—if even such a term as that be not too strong—or rather the assent he had given to the general opinion of her beauty, changed into a feeling of aversion, which he took little pains to conceal.

When they returned to England, Lady Clara had married Mr. Audley, the owner of a large property about twelve miles distant from Mr. Lifford's place, and they generally stayed there during a part of the year. He neither would see nor appear to avoid her—and a total seclusion from the world was the alternative he chose. He would hardly ride out of his own grounds for fear of meeting her. Once in the course of sixteen years he did so, and then the deadly paleness of his cheek, and the expression of his eyes, left it in doubt by which of the two aforesaid passions his spirit was swayed. She, the while, went along the stream of life with "youth at the prow and pleasure at the helm." The person she had married was young, good-looking and amiable. She loved him enough, and not too much for her happiness—enough to make life agreeable in his society, not too much to give her any of the heartaches which are almost invariably attached to an absorbing affection.

It was impossible to see her and hear her talk, at times, without feeling that there was in her nature a power of loving which had not been called into full exercise. She had never had any children, and had not felt the want of them: to those who surrounded her she stood almost in the light of a child herself, although her disposition was not in reality childish; but she lived in an atmosphere of beauty and luxury, of refinement and amusement, which supplied the place of the graver cares and duties of life. In the love of Nature and of art, in transient but not contemptible attempts at literary composition, in intercourse with men of genius, in the creation of the earthly, intellectual, and poetical paradise which surrounded her—she expended the sensibility and the energy which had not been otherwise called into play. Study reading, and society furnished her with occupation, and a succession of pursuits and of fancies—generally harmless, and discarded as soon as they became wearisome—filled up her time. Such was Lady Clara Audley's existence; it had transcended the ordinary course of human prosperity. That she was a happy person some will not need to be told, while others may remain in doubt, according to the view they may take or the theories they may have on the subject of happiness. It had been a matter of curious speculation to her to wonder over the strange mode of life which had been adopted by her first lover and his Spanish wife. She sometimes reflected—now that it was long past, and had become merely a page in the history of her youth—on the sort of passion he had felt for her; and though she fervently rejoiced at having escaped such a marriage, yet she seldom looked on the gates of Lifford Grange without an odd sensation of curiosity and interest. It was therefore no common excitement to her when chance brought into her house Henry Lifford's daughter, of whose beauty she had often heard from Mark Apley and others.

After a few preliminary sentences of thanks on the one side, and kind answers on the other, Lady Clara looked fixedly at Gertrude, and said: "You are like your father, I think,—but I suppose you have your mother's Spanish eyes."

"You have seen him, then?"

"Years ago, when we were both young."

"Was he ever young? I cannot fancy him different from what I have always known him; but I can well imagine I may be like him: I feel it sometimes."

Lady Clara laughed. "What an odd thing to *feel*." Then, seeing her eyes turned towards the window, she said:

"You seem to like my garden. Have you a passion for flowers, as I have?"

"For some, but I hate others; a tiger-lily, for instance, and every sort of calceolaria."

"I believe you are right, and that it is as foolish to ask that general question as those other ones—do you like children, or do you like dogs? Somebody said one might just as well say: 'Do you like people?' What can be more different than a pæony and a rose?"

"Nothing," Gertrude answered with a slow smile, "except some faces I have seen, and——" she hesitated.

"What were you going to say?"

"Oh, I was thinking of Mrs. Apley's and of yours." Lady Clara laughed, for the comparison was very apposite.

"Yes, you put me in mind the first instant I saw you of the moss-rose, the fairest and most richly-dressed of flowers."

"Ah, you have read the pretty German fable on that subject?"

"Not in German, but Maurice Redmond translated it for me, and set it to music."

"What, my handsome young music-master? Is he a poet also? Can you repeat to me the English lines?"

"I hardly know if I can remember them; but I think they run thus:

> 'Weary of pleasure,
> And laden with treasure,
> The Angel of flowers
> Had wandered for hours,
> When he sunk to his rest
> With his wings on his breast,
> And the rose of the glade
> Lent her beautiful shade
> To guard and to cover
> The flower-king's slumber.

When the angel awoke,
Then in rapture he spoke:
"Thou queen of my bowers,
Thou fairest of flowers
What gift shall be mine,
And what guerdon be thine?"
"In guerdon of duty
Bestow some new beauty,"
She said, and then smiled
Like a mischievous child.
In anger he started,
But ere he departed,
To rebuke the vain flower
In the pride of her power,
He flung some rude moss
Her fair bosom across;
But her new robes of green
So became the fair queen,
That the Angel of flowers
Mistrusted his powers,
And was heard to declare
He had granted her prayer.'"*

"I should like to have a statue made on that subject," Lady Clara observed "The angel of flowers hurling the moss at the vain rose; and then, we might place it in the centre of a bower of pink and white moss roses;--Would it not be charming? I will not ask you if you like statues, for I suppose you have not seen many yet, but I feel sure that you like everything beautiful and poetical, or else your eyes belie you. Tell me, is it true that you are called Lady-Bird in the village of Stonehouseleigh?"

"Yes; I believe I am well known there by that name."

"O then it is so; I was once waiting in the ponychaise, at the door of a cottage, and some little brat called out—'there goes Lady-Bird.' I called him, and asked who he meant; he would only repeat 'Lady-Bird'—then his mother came forward, and said he meant Miss Lifford. I was so provoked at not having seen you, for I had long wished to do so. But that name takes my fancy strangely. There is something old-fashioned in it, and I like everything quaint and original,—old books, old names, old curtains, and old houses. The present is so dull, compared with the past."

Gertrude looked round the room, then pointed to the window and said, "If Audley Park is the *present* and Lifford Grange the *past*, I cannot agree with you, Lady Clara."

* From the German of Krummacher.

The latter smiled at the unconscious allusion contained in Gertrude's words, and said, "I have erected this place myself, schemed, planned it, and seen it rise before my eyes. It has been like writing a poem, but now that it is finished it wearies me to be always reading it over again."

"I should like one day to hold such a pen as that in my hand, but to read your poem is for the present enough pleasure. Speaking to a stranger is an event in my life."

"And yet you to me are not shy, my pretty Lady-Bird."

"I have no idea how to converse. I wonder that I learnt to talk at all."

"I imagine that that talent is intuitive, my love, and that the less art there is in it the better."

"Do you think I am *artless*, Lady Clara?"

"Why I can hardly judge of that yet. The perfection of art is to appear not to have any."

"O then I think you must be very artful."

"A compliment, Lady-Bird!"

"O no; I talk of you just as I would of the flowers in the garden. I say what comes into my head, and if it is flattering, it is more fortunate for me than for you."

"Do you know that you amuse me very much. I hope they will let you stay with me some time. I could not gather anything from Father Lifford's manner; does he always seem so stern?"

"He is not given to the smiling mood, certainly; but I cannot disguise from you, Lady Clara, that he looks less benignantly upon you than on the rest of man or womankind. Did you know *him* in his youth also?"

"My dear child, he must have been near forty when I was born!"

"Then why does he look as black as thunder when you are mentioned? What can you have done to him?"

Lady Clara looked pensive an instant, then said, "If we can but keep you here, your convalescence will be the pleasantest thing in the world. We shall carry you gently down stairs, and make you lie on the sofa in the conservatory, amongst the camellias and orange-trees; then you shall drive slowly through the rosery in a garden-chair, and a little later sail on the river in our little skiff, and everybody here shall pay you their court. There are numbers of people in the house longing to see you: my cousin, Lady Roslyn, all the Apleys, Mr. and Mrs. Crofton, and Adrien d'Arberg,—and Maurice, as you call our young musician, is coming on Thursday."

"Is M. d'Arberg here?" Gertrude asked, with a look of sudden interest, which did not escape Lady Clara's attention "Yes. Are you acquainted with him?"

"I can hardly say I am; and yet, I feel to know him well, for I have read his books"

"'I think you will be as much struck with his appearance as with his writings. I have met with but few men as handsome, and with none who possessed the same charm of countenance and manner."

"I have seen him once," Gertrude quietly remarked, and then changed the conversation by asking some questions about a view of Tivoli, which hung over the chimney.

It was enough for her to hear that she would see him again. She was secreting that happiness in her heart, and did not feel inclined to talk about it then. Lady Clara explained the position of the waterfalls, and said, as she rose to go,

"To-day, the doctor enjoins perfect repose; nothing but short dull visits from me, but to-morrow, I trust, his rigour will be abated; and that my Lady-Bird's receptions will commence. Somebody said that an invalid to visit was an indispensable addition to the enjoyment of a party in a country-house. Imagine what a resource you will be to my guests, who having been here a week, were actually beginning to talk of charades and tableaux, and worst of all, of *jeux d'esprit;*" and with a kiss, Lady Clara took leave of Gertrude for the moment.

She remained with her cheek on the embroidered pillow, her eyes sparkling with excitement, her hands playing with her rings, and only one fear standing between her and the rapture of anticipation that was beating in her heart. She had misgivings that her father would at almost any risk order her home, as soon as she could leave her bed; and had she known his feelings about Audley Park and its mistress, she might have feared it still more. She saw herself carried away from this scene of enchantment, and now of deep interest, restored to the dull room which she had so often wished to leave, and which no agreable associations endeared to her. It was an alternative between so much enjoyment, and so much disappointment that she could hardly remain quiet in that state of suspense, and would have probably grown very feverish in the course of the day, if her maid had not arrived with the things she had sent for, and news from home.

It appeared that by that morning's post there had arrived

some intelligence from Spain which imperatively called for Mr. Lifford's presence there to assert his wife's right to an inheritance which had unexpectedly devolved on her. He had made instant preparations for departure, and was to set off in the evening, and to take Edgar with him.

"And what did he say about me, Jane? Did you hear anything from mamma, or Father Lifford?"

"Only Isabella told me while I was packing up the things, that your mamma was surprised your papa had not said one word on the subject, and that she had not mentioned it to him. But of course, Miss, you are not to move till the doctor says you may, and Father Lifford, no doubt, will send the carriage to fetch you when the time comes: so you need not fret about it."

"I suppose papa will be absent for some time?"

"Two months, I heard it said, at the least." Then Gertrude was silent, and tolerably contented. She should probably stay where she was for a few days at least, and she did not despair of obtaining her mother's permission to pay another visit to Audley Park before her father's return.

In the afternoon Edgar came to see her, and made Mr. Lifford's excuses to Mr. Audley, *not* to Lady Clara, for the trouble that Gertrude occasioned in his house, and his apologies that his own sudden departure for Spain prevented him from calling to acknowledge in person their kindness to her. Mr. Audley, who had taken very little cognizance of the whole affair, was quite puzzled to find himself made so prominent in it, but he was very gracious and civil, and was sure it was a great pleasure to Lady Clara, and hoped Miss Lifford would stay with them as long as possible, and all sorts of kind expressions; and then Edgar met his father at the station, and nothing passed between them beyond a brief question whether Gertrude was going on well, with the affirmative answer.— which was received without comment; and both were that night in London, and embarked the next day for Spain. It was Mr. Lifford's pride that had forced him to a piece of civility which cost him a great deal, but which he was too well-bred to omit; but it seemed to him as if Gertrude was destined to be a perpetual source of annoyance, and that chance had now connected her with the plague spot which had been so long festering in his heart.

Gertrude wrote little gay affectionate notes to her mother, in which she spoke of her enjoyment of the change of scene which her accident had so unexpectedly procured her—of Lady Clara's great kindness, and wish to keep her as long as possible; but she added that as soon as she could, she must go home, and show her that she was well again—and that in the meantime, she would write every day. With something between a smile and a sigh, Mrs. Lifford gave these notes to her uncle, who took snuff, "pshawed," and said, "Foolish people all of you." Whom he exactly included in that general condemnation was not quite apparent, but Mrs. Lifford found safety in the number, and satisfied herself that at all events he did not blame her more severely than the rest, whoever they might be whom he so vaguely designated.

CHAPTER XII.

> "Whence and what are we, to what end ordained?
> What means the drama by this world sustained?
> Business or vain amusements, care or mirth,
> Divide the frail inhabitants of earth.
> Is duty a mere sport, or an employ?
> Life an entrusted talent, or a toy?"
> — COWPER.

On the third day after Gertrude's accident, Lady Clara was sitting writing letters in her morning-room, which opened on one side on a conservatory which formed a kind of drawing-room, and on the other on a library where several of her guests were assembled. The three Miss Apleys were sitting round a table, one of them occupied with some abstruse embroidery, another with a design for a flower-garden, and the third, Harriet, alias Cherry, with a music-book, into which she was copying German waltzes. Mrs. Crofton and Mrs. Apley were reading the newspapers near the window, several men were lounging about the room, and the sound of billiard-balls in the one beyond it indicated that others were killing time in a somewhat more active manner.

"Harriet," said Mrs. Crofton, "have you been to Miss Lifford yet?"

"O yes, I went up to her room last night, after dinner; she is looking prettier than ever."

"O, do you think so, Harriet?" exclaimed Fanny, the

next sister, "I was disappointed with her. Have you never observed that her teeth are not quite even?"

"I never knew any one like you, Fanny, for detecting faults," said Mark Apley, who was picking off the leaves of a tall geranium that was apparently growing out of the middle of an ottoman, on which he was stretched out nearly at full length. "If there is a spot, a blot, a flaw in anything, you are sure to pounce upon it. Now, Cherry likes to admire, and I think she is right."

Fanny put down her pen, for she was the copier of music, and going up to him, said something in a low voice which made him laugh and colour, and say, but not angrily, "Leave me alone, don't spoil the button of my coat. Come and look at them playing at billiards."

"No, I will not! your friend Adrien is conceited enough already, without our going to stare at him."

"O Miss Fanny, it would be lucky for you if you had but half as little conceit in your foolish little head as there is in his wise one."

"You are so *entiché* with him."

"Don't use French words, like Lady Roslyn—it is so affected."

"You do not call her affected, do you?"

"Why no, but then——"

"If she is affected," Mrs. Crofton said, "I think she must have been born so. I have no doubt that in the nursery she cried out for a *tartine* instead of for bread and butter, like other children."

Mr. Latimer, one of the men who had been reading before the fire-place, put down his book and said, "There are some people whom nature has provided with stilts, and they may be very charming in their way, but it never answers to provide them for oneself."

"There, now," Mark said, "don't you attempt to get upon them, little Fanny; you are a great love in your way, but in no other way, and certainly not in Lady Roslyn's, whom you as little resemble as your pretty Fido, Lady Clara's greyhound. Are you angry, little woman?"

"*Tout autre que mon [frère] l'eût éprouvé sur l'heure,*" she answered with a smile. "There is a bit of downright French; you don't object to that, do you? And now," she added, in a low voice, "let us go to the billiard-room, and learn grace from Mr. Crofton, dignity from Mr. Ashton, and every earthly perfection from M. Adrien d'Arberg."

The last person whom she alluded to was standing near the window when they entered the room, absorbed at that minute in his own thoughts, which Fanny somewhat unreasonably always ascribed to conceit. Not to be occupied with her presupposed, in her opinion, too great a preoccupation with self.

Few people would have had a better right to be conceited, if advantages of every kind, of looks, of mind, and of fortune, could justify such a feeling: a regular beauty of features, such as is seldom seen in real life; eyes which without being very large were perfectly shaped, and so shaded by thick eyelashes that they appeared dark, whereas they were blue; so earnest an expression, that it might have been thought almost melancholy, if serenity had not reigned in their inmost depths; a mixture of repose and of mobility was a singular characteristic of that remarkable countenance. He seemed as if his own rapid thoughts were passing before him in luminous array, suggesting every instant some new train of contemplation to an ever eager spirit, and an intellect that seemed almost to spiritualise his face. Many, like Fanny Apley, were apt to misunderstand him, because he was so often absorbed in his own meditations that the remarks of others were unattended to, and their attentions to himself unperceived. His own ideas were sometimes followed up by him in a manner that might look like egotism to superficial observers, who did not understand the deep simplicity of his uncommon character. No one ever forgot himself so completely as Adrien d'Arberg did. He was profoundly religious, and there was in his nature a tendency to mysticism that might have led him to a too intense and metaphysical contemplation of the God he adored, if the strong hand of the Catholic religion had not been over him, restraining every exaggerated tendency or fanciful bias, and saying to a naturally ardent imagination and investigating understanding, "So far shalt thou go and no farther."

He was by descent a German, by birth and also position a Frenchman, and had been partly educated in England. These circumstances seemed all to have contributed more or less to the formation of his character and to the tone of his mind. He would have been perhaps a dreamer, had not his life been from his earliest youth devoted to useful objects, and a passionate wish to serve his fellow-creatures been at once the subject of his dreams, and the incentive to incessant labours towards that end. He had something of the *insouciance* of the French character; but his zeal for the honour of God and the happiness of men had prevented its degenerating into levity,—had given seriousness to his views of life, and importance in his sight to his own actions, as well as to the events that passed around him. It had only left him careless of worldly advantages, which sat so lightly upon him that at times he scarcely seemed conscious of possessing them. His English education had imparted to him that keen sense of honour and that gentlemanlike regard for truth which most even worldly-minded Englishmen possess, or at least appreciate. Even in manner there was something which made English people feel at home with him. He spoke our language with the utmost correctness, and a good accent; it was only by its resembling a little more the English of books than the careless routine of common conversation that he would have been detected as a foreigner, or else by his abruptly changing it into French, if any strong interest or emotion impelled him to the use of his native tongue.

He was distantly connected with the Apleys, and when a boy had sometimes spent his holidays at their house. Mark Apley and he had thus been friends from childhood, and their intimacy continued from habit rather than from any congeniality of minds or of character. On Adrien's side there was an affectionate regard for one whose amiable qualities, but weak understanding, commanded more love than respect; on the other, there was all the reverence and admiration which an inferior intellect yields to a superior one, when, as in this case, the acknowledgment is unmixed with the slightest amount of jealousy or of envy.

"Who is winning?" Mark asked, as he came into the billiard-room with his sister, and joined Lady Roslyn, who was leaning against the corner of the chimney, while Mr. Ashton stood on one leg at the end of the billiard-table, with his body stretched across it, and his face screwed up into a shape of intense and ugly earnestness, which contrasted with Adrien's easy attitude.

"O, d'Arberg is beating me hollow, and it is a great shame, for I practised five hours yesterday, and took lessons all last year in London."

"Well, I am sure that is more than Adrien has done," Mark rejoined, with a loud laugh.

"How do you know," Adrien said, turning suddenly round, with a smile; "how do you know that I do not get up before breakfast to practise?"

"To judge by the books in your room," Mark said, with another burst of laughter, "I should say that you studied canon-law more than such cannons as those."

"You do not suppose that I read all those folios, do you?"

"Then why have them on your table?" Fanny observed.

"To press flowers in," he answered; "or to make people think me wise. There, Mr. Ashton, that is game, I think," and, as the red ball flew into one pocket, and the white one into the other, he put down his cue and left the room.

"By Jove, I'll practise till dinner-time!" exclaimed the defeated man, with the energy of a Haydn determined to learn counterpoint, or an Austrian general returning to the charge after twenty defeats.

Adrien meanwhile had joined Lady Clara in her morning-room. There were some of her guests who had acquired a sort of tacit right to invade it, and he was amongst the number.

"How is your Lady-Bird?" he said, as he sat down by her.

"O, much better; and she is coming down this afternoon, so mind you come in here after luncheon. I am longing to show her to you. It is the very prettiest bird you ever saw; and, now that I have caught her, I mean to make an immense deal of her; and——"

"Spoil her," he suggested.

"No, no; it will improve her to see something of us."

"Who are *us*?"

"You and I, if you will not be affronted at the companionship. She is not at all aware of her own cleverness."

"And we are to open her eyes to it?"

"Certainly; I am always against keeping people in the dark about their own merits, as well as about anything else. Truth, M. d'Arberg, never does any harm."

"Why; is not there an ignorance which may be not only a bliss but a blessing?—and is not the one you speak of such? To destroy it seems like brushing away the bloom of a fruit."

"O, but you must not suppose that this charming Lady Bird is all *naïveté* and humility. She does not know how ever she is, but is not without some notions of her own abilities, and has rather a restless wish to put them to the test. And, for my own part, I believe that people are twenty times more likely to be really modest, who have satisfied themselves and others that they have something to be modest about, than if they remain all their lives beating about the bush, instead of ascertaining once for all the capabilities of their own understandings."

"There is truth in that, perhaps, but not the *whole* truth," Adrien said.

"What is your *arrière-pensée?*" Lady Clara asked. "You always have one, I know, when you are talking to me."

"None about this that I wish to keep back. You have taken a great fancy to this girl, who must be, by all accounts, a very peculiar person; and, if you lavish praises upon her, and turn her head, you will be amusing yourself in a less safe manner than by writing pretty poems or inventing new conservatories."

"Well, I will confess to you that she does interest me as a poem; that she does charm me as a flower. There is an inconventionality about her which is quite refreshing, and a readiness of repartee which amuses me beyond description. Every new idea you put before her, every new subject you start, seems to be immediately laid hold of, and viewed in the light of her fanciful imagination. I long to see her in society, *aux prises* with Mrs. Crofton, cross-questioned by Edward Latimer, made love to by Mark Apley."

"Now I *have* an *arrière-pensée*—will you ask me for it?"

"Yes, if it be not severe."

"Would it be severe to say that you are making a plaything of something too valuable to be played with?"

He looked at her in the earnest, calm way which was peculiar to him, and she said quickly, "You take things too seriously, M. d'Arberg. I have passed through life gathering roses, and have found no thorns, and I will teach my Lady-Bird to do so too. I have often talked to you of her father. She sometimes puts me in mind of him. But if he had been half as charming as she is, I should not be now the happy person that I am."

"Ay," said Adrien, with a smile, "did not you then gather a rose and find a thorn?"

"Ay, but I flung away both the rose and the thorn."

"No, I think you gathered the rose and left the thorn behind. But to return to what we were saying just now. It is from my own experience that I dread even kind interferences in what may vitally influence the destinies of others."

"How so, M. d'Arberg? Are you not the most cautious of men!"

"Not always. For instance, when I took Maurice Redmond to Italy I was giving myself the immense pleasure of an *engoûment* acted upon, of seeing enjoyment and apparently showing kindness; but I have often felt since that it would have been truer kindness not to have forced open a bud which, if destined to blow, would have been more surely developed by a slower process. To resist good impulses is one of the most difficult lessons to learn."

"And one I never intend to learn; I think it quite sufficient to resist bad ones, dear M. d'Arberg, and to make this hitherto imprisoned Lady-Bird try her wings, and enjoy her liberty, is, I am convinced, a good one. So the moral of your story is lost upon me, especially as I like you ten times better for having done an imprudent kind thing than for all the prudent good ones you have ever accomplished. But then you will not help me to turn the pretty head I shall show you after luncheon?"

"No, but I shall come and watch the working of your system."

After luncheon Gertrude was carried down to the drawing-room, and thence conveyed in a garden-chair to the conservatory on the other side of the parterre. It was fitted up also as a drawing-room, and Lady Clara often spent there several hours of the day. She placed her on a couch in the midst of a kind of bower of American shrubs, through which the sun was shining and forming with its rays a fanciful pattern on the tesselated pavement. The smell was sweet but not too powerful, the breeze from without gently shook the blossoms of the pink azalias which now and then fell on the silk coverlet which had been thrown over her feet: on the table by her side were poems, new novels French and English, prints and drawings without end. Lady Clara sat opposite to her, arranging cut flowers in fanciful vases of Venetian glass and Bohemian crystal.

"I have sent everybody out this afternoon in the calèche and the pony-chaise—that is, everybody that I did not want to join us here. I shall only let them see you by degrees, Lady-Bird. My favourites shall be first admitted."

"And who are they, Lady Clara?"

"My cousin, Ellen Roslyn, Adrien d'Arberg, and Mark Apley:—that is my beauty, my hero, and my Newfoundland. Here comes the last." And Mark rushed up to Gertrude with a beaming face, and a thousand expressions of delight at seeing her again. "I hope Harriet told you, Miss Lifford, how overjoyed we were at your accident—I mean how sorry we felt about that, but how glad that it brought you here."

"It has been, indeed, a pleasant accident to me," she said. "Had my horse chosen to deposit me under one of my native oaks I should have been less obliged to him."

"I only wish I had had the luck to find you that night, Miss Lifford. I should have been frightened to death, but still so happy."

"By the way," she said, "who *did* find me! How strange it is that I have not yet asked the name of the person who discovered me that night."

"It was Adrien d'Arberg—lucky fellow, and he carried you to the house. I have done nothing but envy him ever since."

Gertrude remained silent, and opened a book as if in absence. "Did I not dream of Heaven that night?" she inwardly ejaculated.

Then she looked up, and the form and the face which for nearly a whole year had haunted her incessantly were once more before her. It was not exactly emotion that she experienced in seeing them again—her heart did not beat quicker, and no deeper colour rose in her cheek. On the contrary a great calm seemed to come over her, a sensation of indescribable repose; it was like a void filled up, a hope accomplished, a prayer granted. "God be praised!" she said to herself, and then marvelled at the solemnity of that mute thanksgiving.

"M. d'Arberg, let me introduce you to Miss Lifford." That insignificant commonplace sentence, so carelessly pronounced, and yet containing in itself the germ of so many happy and so many miserable destinies!

Adrien bowed and said, "I once impertinently introduced myself to Miss Lifford. I hope she has forgiven it."

Gertrude made some scarcely audible answer, but her eyes looked all that such eyes as hers *can* look. From that instant a new era in her life began. What arose in her mind was neither a hope nor a project nor a design, but a conviction that there was for her but one destiny, one future, one possible fate. It was to love Adrien d'Arberg, and to walk this world with a spell on her soul, a secret in her heart, which might either exalt, transform, or annihilate her, but which would never leave as it had found her, which must be the source or the ruin of her happiness.

This kind of sentiment is either so deep and so intense that from its very excess it commands respect, or else it is degrading. There is no medium. Gertrude instinctively felt this, and it was this consciousness that preserved her self-respect, and gave her face such a beautiful expression at that moment. Mark Apley said to himself, "If I could think that that girl was in love with me I would propose to her directly." Adrien did not seem to think much of anything just then, except of a print from Landseer, which he had taken up and was examining. She felt glad that he did not speak to her at first, that she had time to get accustomed to his presence before he directly addressed himself to her, and she began an insignificant conversation with Mark Apley.

"How well you are working those carnations, Miss Lifford! They seem to grow under your fingers. I wish men could work. Don't you think it would make them much pleasanter?"

"Perhaps it would, but there are only some men who ought to work."

"What sort of men?"

"Awkward clumsy ones. It would never do for a man to work well."

"Then," said Lady Clara, 'they should not work at all, on Dr. Johnson's principle."

"Oh, but I quite disagree with the old Doctor."

"Do you really?" Mark exclaimed with a broad grin.

"A woman, for instance, might shoot, if only she did not know how to load her gun and held it as a parasol, and people may sing and act, but they must take care not to do so as well s professional singers and actors. Then, a woman may know Latin, if she does not know it too well."

"You seem very much afraid of perfection," Adrien said, raising his head with a smile.

"Yes, I am," she answered, turning her eyes slowly upon him.

"And I worship it," Lady Clara exclaimed, "wherever I find it."

"And where do you find it?" Adrien asked.

"There," she answered, as her favourite cousin appeared at the door of the conservatory, and certainly, if not in every respect, in outward appearance at least she seemed quite right.

Lady Roslyn was tall and beautiful, and her manner, which was exceedingly peculiar, was in harmony with her looks. It was pretty to see her and Lady Clara together. They were very fond of each other, and family likeness gave a kind of resemblance to two faces and manners, which were yet essentially very different.

"We were talking of perfection, Ellen, and you appeared at that moment—the living proof of an assertion I have just made."

"What assertion, I wonder?" Lady Roslyn said with a smile, as she sat down by Gertrude, whose hand she had affectionately pressed.

"That I adore it. There is a riddle which your modesty will not guess. But tell us, Ellen, whether you worship perfection as I do, or are as afraid of it as this Lady-Bird is."

"You must first define what you mean by perfection, Clara."

"Ay," Adrien said, looking up from the prints he was examining, "*that* is the question. No two of us would agree, perhaps, on that point. Our heroes, I suspect, would be as various as our notions of heroism." Gertrude thought two might perhaps agree, if *one* would explain his own ideas on the subject.

"Well, I am like Miss Lifford," Mark Apley exclaimed; "I am afraid of heroes."

"What is your ideal of a hero, Lady Clara?" Gertrude asked, somewhat timidly, thus hoping that afterwards Adrien would describe his.

"Oh, mine is a polytheism,—a general hero-worship; I have hundreds of favourites in every age and clime, who would have fought like cat and dog had they met upon earth, as their works or their histories meet on my table. Adrien would consign to perdition some of my idols."

"No, I will hope the best for them all; so do not tell me their names."

"Severely charitable!" she exclaimed: "O Mark Apley, who is your hero?"

"The Duke of Wellington, of course," Gertrude said, for she already knew her admirer well enough to be sure that his imagination would not cross the sea in search of one; but when he re-echoed, " The Duke of Wellington, of course!" she coloured violently, suddenly remembering that Adrien was a Frenchman, and fancying she had shown a want of tact in suggesting to Mark his choice of a hero. Adrien perceived it, and relieved her distress by laughing at her about it. She looked at Lady Clara, and said,

"I often speak without thinking, perhaps because I have so often been obliged to think without speaking."

"That must be very disagreeable," Mark observed, "it never happened to me. Whatever I think, I always say."

"Your thoughts, I am afraid, do not soar very high, dear Mr. Apley," Lady Clara observed in too low a voice for him to hear.

"But perhaps they run very straight, which may be better," Adrien whispered.

Mark was a great favourite with his friends. He was so spirited, generous, and kind, and there was an ingenuousness in his simplicity that made it quite loveable. Whenever he said anything foolish, they did not say "poor Mark," but "dear Mark." He was too good to be pitied.

"Guess who I expect to-day," Lady Clara said, "but not àpropos of heroes; by the way, we have none of us produced ours, except Mr. Apley."

"Let us leave them alone, then," Lady Roslyn said, "and tell us who you expect."

"Sir William Marlow, and my brother Henry."

"Oh, is Egerton coming? I shall be delighted to see him," Adrien exclaimed.

"Shall you really, M. d'Arberg? That pleases but surprises me; of all human beings, I should have thought he would have suited you the least."

"And why so, Lady Clara?"

"You differ so entirely on almost every subject."

"But sympathy and liking are quite separate things."

"And there can be sympathy without agreement."

"Of that I am not so sure, except in the case of a predominant affection, which has struck such profound roots in two hearts originally cast by Nature in the same mould that nothing can ever go deep enough to reach the electric bond of their union; except in such rare cases where love is stronger than death, or life also. I can hardly allow that there can be much sympathy where hopes, fears, wishes, and interests are all dissimilar. Do I make you understand what I mean, Lady Clara? The affection that creates sympathy under such circumstances is of the highest and most intense kind; but short of it, there may be regard and liking, but not sympathy: that is at least my view of the subject."

"Then, do you mean, for instance, that there is no sympathy between us?"

"Not the least, I should say." She laughed, but did not seem quite pleased.

"I should have thought that in our tastes and our feelings, our love of beauty in Nature and in art, our interest in literature, there were sufficient grounds of sympathy."

"No, there is matter for agreeable conversation, for very pleasant intercourse, for great kindness on the one side, and a grateful and admiring regard on the other; but sympathy, dear Lady Clara, does not consist in reading the same books, admiring the same views, liking some of the same occupations."

"What does it consist in then?" she asked somewhat impatiently.

"In what would make you understand at this moment all I dare not say on the subject. In what would make you feel that we might not have one taste in common, and yet the most perfect sympathy. But after all I may be quite wrong: as in the case of heroes, we may apply a different meaning to the same word."

"As different," Gertrude said in a low voice, "as when we speak of admiring the Duke of Wellington or St. Vincent of Paul."

Who could have doubted what sympathy meant who saw their eyes meet at that moment?

"Do you and Henry dispute much, M. d'Arberg?"

"No; I believe we disagree too much to dispute."

"You are afraid of quarrelling?"

"No; your brother has an excellent temper, and I am too phlegmatic to lose mine easily, but to argue one ought to have certain points of agreement to start from, and that is just what we have not. Egerton has no chance of convincing me, or I him, because, like Archimedes, we can find no world to rest our levers on; our point d'appui is not the same, and so we cannot bring our argument to bear."

"For my part," Mark said, "I hate arguing.—it is such provoking work,—and especially with Lady Clara, who always manages to be in the right."

"Or to seem so,' Adrien added, "which, perhaps, she will think as great a compliment."

"It is an equivocal one, but I will take it in the best sense. My quarrel with you, M. d'Arberg, is, that you never will let one penetrate to the bottom of your thoughts."

"What is it you wish to see there?"

"Your opinion of me."

"Then it is yourself and not me, that you wish to get acquainted with?"

"O *you!* I despair of ever finding *you* out. I do not know if you are the deepest of enthusiasts or the calmest of reasoners, the most enlightened philosopher or the most bigoted Papist."

"But what if the calmest reasoning awoke the deepest enthusiasm? If what you call the most bigoted, and I call the most earnest Popery, were to turn out after all to be the most enlightened philosophy—as many of the deep thinkers of our age are beginning to suspect?"

"It would require a miracle to convince me of it, and more than one of your modern miracles."

"That is hard upon him, Clara," Lady Roslyn said. "You insist on a miracle, and will not have a modern one. But the thinkers you were speaking of, M. d'Arberg; they may be *deep*, perhaps, but not *free*."

"And do you like free thinkers, Lady Roslyn?"

"I like freedom of thought."

"And is not that free thinking?"

"You are playing upon words. I do not like the free thinking that ends in infidelity."

"Then the freedom you advocate must walk in leading-strings of your own selecting."

"Not of my selecting. M. d'Arberg."

"Of whose choosing then?"

"Oh, if Ellen once begins an argument, we never shall get out of it again," Lady Clara exclaimed, "and it is not your religion but yourself I want to understand. At times I have supposed you to be a devoted supporter of legitimacy, a chivalrous admirer of the exploded theories of divine right, and at others, almost found you out to be a thorough-going democrat, with a lurking tenderness for Socialist opinions."

Adrien laughed, and said, "If you will not use the *key*, Lady Clara, how can you expect to unlock a door?"

"You have never yet given me the 'Open Sesame' into the secret chambers of *your* opinions."

"Has she ever asked you for it?" Lady Roslyn said, with a smile, " *C'est l'obstacle qu'elle aime—elle ne veut que chercher.*"

"You do not know him yet, Ellen; he has at once the most audacious and the most humble, the most impetuous and the most imperturbable spirit imaginable, and while I am saying all this to him he sits looking at me as if I were neither praising nor insulting him."

"Because I suppose you do not intend to do either."

"I believe you like to be a riddle, and to baffle all my penetration. Is not this trying, Gertrude?"

"To which of you, Lady Clara?"

"To me, you most impertinent child," Lady Clara answered with a smile. "I read his books, and fancy that through them I learn to know him; but when I see him again he puzzles me afresh. He writes pages of the most exciting eloquence; he carries you on by the might of his enthusiasm till you almost lose your footing, and feel, at least, if you do not always think with him; but when you meet him face to face he changes his tactics and draws you out instead of on, listens to you patiently, hopes the best for you, as he said just now of my heroes, but leaves you in doubt what is the sentence passed in the secret tribunal of his thoughts."

"If I thought you in earnest I would defend myself, but you must not misconstrue my silence. I do not plead guilty."

"Gertrude shall judge between us in a few days. If she finds you less impenetrable than I have done, I will give in."

He smiled and said, "But perhaps she will use the key I was speaking of." Again Gertrude's eyes met his, but she hastily turned hers away, for she felt that they might express more than she wished.

"But it is very provoking," Lady Clara continued, "that you should be too modest or too proud to talk up to your books."

He looked at her with an amusingly imploring countenance and said, "Dear Lady Clara, I will call on your favourite phrenologist the next time I go to London, and get him to write my character for you; I will talk like a book if you wish it, and hold forth every evening on any subject you may select, if only you will not discuss me any more."

At that moment the sound of a carriage driving up the avenue was heard, and Lady Clara exclaimed, "That must be Henry!"

"Does Sir William Marlow come with him?" Mark inquired.

"Yes, I believe so; I hope they will tell them we are here."

"I will let them know," Adrien said, "I am going to the house."

As he left the conservatory Gertrude watched his tall figure as it disappeared amongst the trees. Mark observed the direction of her eyes and said, "You had never seen d'Arberg before, had you?"

"Yes, once at your house, the day of the breakfast."

"Did you ever see anybody half so handsome?"

"Half perhaps, but certainly not more than half."

"He is a capital fellow. Fanny says he is conceited, but it is not true, nobody thinks so little of himself. How different he is from Sir William Marlow."

Just then Lady Clara's brother Mr. Egerton, and the identical Sir William Marlow were seen at a distance walking from the house, and in a few minutes they had joined them. Mr. Egerton was good looking without being handsome. He seemed pleasing and intelligent. His companion was short and slight, with delicate features and a remarkable forehead. His dark hair was brought back in a way that gave him a rather wild expression. Mr. Egerton had just sufficient shyness in his manner to make apparent his friend's singular want of it. In his way of standing, sitting, shaking hands, or performing any of the ordinary actions of life, there was the stamp of a most profound conceit. His self-complacency hung about him as a garment, or rather it seemed as much his natural attribute as the strut, the hop, or the twitter of certain birds belongs to them. The very sound of his voice was conceited. His calmness was irritating, the way he crossed his legs and caressed his foot exasperating, and the clearness of his articulation despairing. He united in his own person the active and the passive moods of vanity. Soon after the revolution of February, M. de Lamartine declared that a Frenchman's proper occupation is the contemplation of his own magnanimity, and at the same time an English journalist described England as sitting in unapproachable greatness. Now, Sir William Marlow seemed to unite in himself both the characteristics of these two very different nations. From the height of his unapproachable self-satisfaction, he seemed eternally to contemplate his own perfections. That he had good qualities, that he was clever, and that he had a considerable command of language could not be denied. Lady Clara liked him, and perhaps she was right. It certainly is not right to dislike conceit as much as people in general do. It is better to be conceited than to be vicious or cruel, but the strut of a peacock and the impudence of a sparrow are often more irritating than the fierceness of a vulture or a hawk; it is not easy to be just when we are affronted, and such people as Sir William are a walking affront that our own conceit, however kept in order, can with difficulty endure.

Mr. Egerton was evidently struck with Gertrude's beauty. Sir William was never struck with anything. For a few moments Lady Clara kept up an animated conversation with the new comers, in which Lady Roslyn and Gertrude occasionally joined; and then, looking tired with that kind of fatigue peculiar to those who make society the business of their lives, she said she must lie down for an hour before dinner and proposed to go home. Mark Apley drew Gertrude in the garden-chair across the parterre. Mr. Egerton talked to her as they went along. Sir William gave his arm to Lady Clara, and made clever answers to her brilliant remarks; and the sun went down behind the hills, and the dew was thick upon the grass, the flowers gave out their sweetest odours.— the air blew freshly on Gertrude's cheek, and an animated sense of enjoyment excited her spirits. Life appeared to her under a very different aspect than it had ever presented before; she thought it pleasant to be young and pretty, admired and amused. She felt as if her tastes and inclinations were in harmony with the refined beauty of the objects that surrounded her, while a romantic sentiment of admiration for one well calculated to inspire it, imparted a meditative character to her enjoyment, which increased and exalted it.

When she reached her room, she sat down in a luxurious arm-chair, before a small wood fire that burned brightly in the grate, and opened a volume which she had carried off from the drawing-room table. It was the Life of Christina of Sweden, which Maurice had once mentioned to her. Adrien's name was on the title page. "I understand him," she said to herself, "but will he ever understand me? I dare not give him the key to my inmost thoughts, which he so fearlessly holds out to me of his own;" and taking a pencil she sketched in the faintest manner a key on the blank page of the book before her, and wrote under it these lines:

"Da me posso nullo
Con Dio posso tutto.
A Dio l'onore
A me il disprezzo."

CHAPTER XIII.

"Di gelosia mi moro
E non lo posso dire!
Chi mai provò di questo,
Affanno più funesto
Più barbaro dolor."
                        METASTASIO.

MAURICE REDMOND had been for some time past engaged to spend a few weeks at Audley Park. He had given lessons the year before to Lady Clara, or rather played with her and to her; and she soon perceived that his education and his manners fitted him for any society, and that he was an addition to hers. She had accordingly invited him to spend part of the autumn with them; and as he travelled from London to Stonehouseleigh, on his way to Audley Park, he had often turned over in his mind the probable chances of meeting Gertrude at his mother's house, or in some other chance manner, without dreaming that he should soon find her established under the same roof with himself. It was Mary who announced it to him, soon after his arrival. He had devoted two or three days to his home and to her; and one of the first things he heard was the account of Gertrude's accident, of her residence at Audley Park, and of Mr. Lifford's departure for Spain. He had left London with the firmest resolution of banishing from his mind all vague hopes with regard to Gertrude. He had latterly wondered how such ideas could ever have occurred to him: it had, indeed, been but a transient dream called forth by her presence and her unconscious glances, and dissolved in absence; he had now resolved to press Mary at once to fix a period for their marriage, and this satisfied his conscience. It seemed as if he had given up something, whereas it was only that calmer thoughts had shown him the utter impossibility of another destiny, and what he did not give up was the passion which he still nourished in the secrecy of his heart.

Mary thought him looking ill, and hoped the country would do him good. He had worked hard in London, and made a little money. He smiled as he told her so, and asked her if she could begin housekeeping on such slender means as they could command. She made an evasive answer, and looked at him very earnestly. There was evidently something that disquieted her in his appearance: "Why do you look so wistfully at me, Mary?—Are you trying to read something in my eyes?" She gave a quick suppressed sigh, and shook her head.

"Then, Mary, will you agree to it? Shall we be married next spring?" She was silent, and seemed to be struggling with herself.

"Are you afraid of making me too happy by such a promise?" he said, and putting his arm round her waist, he tried to look in her face.

"Too happy," she slowly repeated. "No, my only wish is to make you happy."

"Then you will consent to become my wife?" She looked as pale as the white roses of the porch where they were sitting, but assented gently to his proposal, and in a few minutes left him and went up to her room.

There kneeling by the bedside she burst into tears. In a few minutes she got up and bathed her eyes with cold water. "*His* eyes must not shed tears," she said to herself. "*They* must not burn with hot drops like these. O my God, let him not weep. Let me stand between him and sorrow—and never in the way of his happiness. But *that* never, never could be happiness, and I will stand, so Heaven help me, between him and her. She shall not break his heart. O these blinding tears!" she exclaimed, "how they burn the eyes." There was a strange anxiety about her as she made these exclamations and walked quickly up and down her room: but when she went down stairs again she was more cheerful than usual, and even encouraged him to talk of future plans and arrangements.

When under the influence of her society, Maurice believed all that he desired to persuade himself. There was something so tender and unobtrusive in her manner, she was so indispensable to him in various ways, he was so accustomed to the perfume of sympathy and of affection with which she surrounded him, that it would have been difficult for him to call what he felt for her by another name than love, or to give that name to the tormenting and wayward emotions which he experienced in Gertrude's presence. He would certainly have been very unhappy that day if Mary had refused to become his wife. He was satisfied with this consciousness, and did not trouble himself to reflect what his feelings would have been if, at the moment she had accepted him, he was suddenly to have heard that Gertrude was about to marry, or that he was never to see her again. He asked himself no such probing questions either then or the next day on his way to Audley Park, but only mentally protested, as if to silence some troublesome self-suggestions, that he loved Mary firmly and truly, and that he looked to her for his future happiness,—that in sorrow or in joy, in health or in sickness, she would be to him a shield, a comfort, a friend and a support,—that together they had begun life, and together they would pass through it, and together end it. What injury was it to her if, as artists place before them beautiful pictures to inspire their conceptions, as others listen to the most exciting music they can procure, or revel in the most romantic scenery they can find, and thus influence their imaginations and kindle their enthusiasm?—why should not Lady-Bird be his picture to gaze upon—the muse from which he should draw his inspirations—the "dame de ses pensées," in the domain of art and of romance? It was his scruples that made him untrue to Mary— Mary his gentle sister in his childhood—now his betrothed, soon to be his wife. That was an earnest tie, a serious affection, beyond the nonsense of romance, the trifling of imagination. Did he, could he ever have thought of Lady-Bird as his wife? O no, she was not made for the common-place cares and duties of life; and Shakespeare's often repeated lines about "a bright particular star" came into his head as he was riding up the avenue.

About ten days had elapsed since Gertrude's first appearance in the drawing-room of Audley Park. During that interval the various ingredients of which its society was composed had been shaken together, and the process of assimilation had begun to take place. People had found out whom they liked, or disliked; who amused and who bored them; who made useful butts; who talked and who listened well; who was always in a good humour, and who could not endure a joke; at what hour the library and the newspapers were unoccupied; when the Miss Apleys got somebody to play and sing, and talked all the time themselves, or Mr. Egerton and Mark Apley argued about Protection and Free-trade, or

General Burnwood gave, "in a few words," the history of his campaigns. Some friendships were dawning, some flirtations budding, some aversions growing up,—silent ones which were the deepest, busy ones which were tiresome, quarrelsome ones which were amusing. Lady Clara was the perfection of an hostess; she paid enough attention to her guests to make them feel quite at home, and not too much to infringe on the charm of complete independence. She left well alone; never insisted on those who seemed happy in one way that they should amuse themselves in another, but if the most insignificant person in the society looked bored or neglected, she found them some occupation or amusement. She adapted herself in turn to every one; not so much out of amiability, though she was amiable, but from a wish to see none but happy faces about her, and a dislike to sad ones. "Life," she said one day, "was too short for gloom." "True," Adrien answered. They agreed, but did not sympathise.

Lady Roslyn showed her Mrs. Hemans' beautiful poem of the Revellers, and said,

"You too, Clara, would banish all but the gay in heart from your festive hall."

"No," she said, "but I would try to force happiness upon them, and only allow them that shade of melancholy—not without something of enjoyment in it—which makes us enter into the feelings of poetry, and the charm of emotion. I would not banish *her*, for instance," pointing to Gertrude, "though in Mrs. Hemans' words, 'Her eyes' quick flash through their troubled shroud' does not always indicate a heart at ease; but I try to teach her not to look at things too seriously, not to '*prendre la vie au tragique*,' and I hope I shall succeed."

Mrs. Crofton, who had been listening, smiled and said, "Example can do much, my dear Lady Clara, but Nature is stronger still, and I do not expect that you will succeed in teaching the soul of fire that shines out of those dark eyes to glide along life's stream in the rose-leaf fashion that becomes you so well."

Mrs. Crofton and Lady Clara did not suit. They were a little too alike, and a great deal too unlike. Both lived in and for society; both were irreproachable in their moral characters; but Mrs. Crofton was as plain as Lady Clara was beautiful, and so she had to work harder in her vocation, though she succeeded nearly as well. She was not as eloquent, as graceful, or as amiable; but she was sharper, cleverer, and droller. No one was ever tired of her, and some fastidious people did think Lady Clara was a little too pictorial in her language, and high-flown in her ideas. She was too much engrossed in her own impressions to watch the effect she made on others; but Mrs. Crofton had a lynx eye which always detected the fluctuating symptoms of interest and *ennui* in those she spoke to. In everything she said there was more power and less charm than in the other, as was once said by a witty Frenchman of two ladies, "*Elle était le mâle de l'espèce, dont l'autre était la femelle.*"

Mr. Latimer was very happy at Audley Park, for he had one ruling passion—the investigation of characters, and there was a fine field for it in the present party. He wrote to a friend:

"It is the most amusing thing in the world to live in this menagerie,—this 'happy family,' in which I feel myself like the owl with whom nobody meddles, and who sleeps with his eyes open. There is our hostess, a lovely bird with the most stainless plumage and the sweetest voice, warbling mellifluously on her golden perch, but keeping at a respectful distance from that clever little mocking-bird, Mrs. Crofton, whose sharp beak pecks rather harder than is always agreeable. There is that stately Bird-of-Paradise, Lady Roslyn, and a family of canary-birds, the Miss Apleys, pleasant enough if they did not chirp so incessantly. Then they have got another young creature whom I hardly know how to describe. It is half foreign and half English, a young eaglet perhaps, born in the Pyrenees, but bred in an old house in this old-fashioned county. Such eyes it has, I have no doubt they could stare at the sun if they tried. You know I am not often in the humour in which it would be safe for a child to play with me, but this young eaglet is not afraid of my snarling. Then we have all sorts of other creatures besides, gentlemanlike young birds like Egerton, cock-sparrow geniuses, and would-be statesmen like Marlow, good-humoured, honest geese like Apley, and a very tall French bird whom I cannot make head or tail of; besides many others, for the cage can hardly hold us all. We have not fought much yet. There is only a little beating of wings and hissing now and then. The cock-sparrow has a violent dislike to the tall French bird, but they have not come to blows yet. The canary-birds look with a jaundiced eye at the eaglet, perhaps because they think it will take their goose for a swan. But I think it would come to my perch sooner—and I almost wish it would. It goes by the name of Lady-Bird. By the way, don't you remember a certain Henry Lifford to whom Lady Clara was engaged some twenty-two years ago, when just emerging from the school-room? This is his daughter by a Spanish wife. I hope I shall not make a fool of myself about her."

Gertrude might have made fools of almost all the men who saw her, had she chosen it; and sometimes a wicked wish crossed her mind, that she had known something of society before Adrien had taken from her all desire for the admiration of others. She tried to shake off the impression he had made upon her, but the effort proved utterly vain; a look, a word, or a smile from him were more to her than the homage or adoration of the whole world besides. His unconscious power over her was unbounded. She did not conceive the possibility of differing with him in opinion, of ever acting again in any way that she might have heard him casually condemn. His slightest word was law, his books her daily meditation, his presence or his absence the regulating cause of her cheerfulness or depression. He was on very friendly terms with her, but nothing more. There was great kindness, but no devotion in his manner, and she never wished to see him at her feet: could she ever inspire him with an interest in her fate, which would justify to herself her ever-increasing regard for him—it seemed that *that* would be the highest bliss earth could offer. When they talked together, she was most innocently hypocritical; for she so identified herself with his thoughts and his feelings that they seemed naturally to become hers, and his convictions and opinions to transfer themselves into her mind by an unconscious process of assimilation. She talked to him of her childhood, of her home, of her mother, but in a different way from that which was usual to her. This was not dissimulation; it was a change wrought by the influence he exercised over her. Hardness melted in the light of his eyes; levity disappeared before his earnestness, and pride vanished in the presence of his perfect simplicity.

She happened to be alone in the drawing-room when Maurice arrived. The day was cold, and everybody taking exercise, which she could not yet do; and with a book in her hand, and her eyes as often fixed on the fire as on its pages, she had spent the hours since luncheon. She was taking a resolution which cost her a great effort, but in which she was swayed by the one ruling influence which now governed all her thoughts and actions. She must return to Lifford Grange the next day. It could not be right to stay away from her mother any longer; and if she could drive in the pony-chaise at Audley Park, she was well enough, it was clear, to go home in a carriage. She was not without hope that Lady Clara would invite, and her mother allow her to come back to the Paradise she was about to leave; but she must go and see her mother. Adrien had said something the day before—had asked a casual question—which had fixed her wavering thoughts on the subject: but it was an immense effort to go without being *sure* of coming back—*sure* of finding him there again. For the first time she thought of the future as connected with him,—recollected that though he had relations and interests in England and in Ireland, his country was France, and the chances of life might never bring them together again. "Was this possible?" she asked herself. "Possible to embark one's all of happiness in a bark that casually floats alongside of ours on the stream of life, and then see it drift away in another direction, without the power of remonstrance or complaint?" It seemed like signing her own death-warrant to propose to go away. "But would I not die if *he* thought it right?" she mentally exclaimed,—smiled at her own extravagance, and then sighed; for her conscience protested against the rank idolatry of her heart.

At that moment the door opened, and Maurice Redmond was ushered in. He started when he saw her, but quickly recovering himself he came up to her, and was received most kindly. She was very glad to see him, and they spent some time together before any one came in. "How strange it seems, Maurice, to meet *here*," she said. "Hitherto when we have conversed, it has always been either in the open air, or on the downs or the woods where we used to play in former times, or in Mrs. Redmond's cottage, or mamma's dark room. It seems to me a whole year since my accident. Don't you think there are weeks in which one lives a life?"

"There are moments," he answered, "in which I suppose the happiness or the misery of a whole life can be concentrated."

"Yes," she thoughtfully answered, "I can imagine that it might be so. What has been the happiest moment of your life, Maurice?"

She was thinking very little of the person she addressed. She had forgotten that it had ever crossed her mind that he admired her even in the distant respectful manner which it had once amused her to observe. It was absently she had asked that question, as she might have inquired what was the most beautiful view he had ever seen, and she did not remark that his face flushed as he answered, "The one when I nearly fainted at the Woodlands' breakfast." She smiled and said, "You like extremes, I see. The pleasure of success, preceded by an instant's suffering to make it keener, is your favourite idea of happiness. Well, again I say it may be so, but I don't quite like the receipt. I feel with regard to happiness as children do about a promised toy. 'Give it me *now*.'—How is Mary?"

"Well, quite well," he answered in a tone of dejection; but rousing himself, added, "you know she is so unselfish that she would never tell us if she was not so; that is, as long as she could exert herself as usual."

"She *is* good," Gertrude exclaimed.

"O she is good," he retorted, "good beyond what any one can know or imagine. There are depths of tenderness and of patience in her heart which cannot be fathomed. Even I—who have known her from childhood, and revered her almost as a saint—I am sometimes astonished at her goodness."

"Do you think her as good as one person whom you used to talk to me about—as M. d'Arberg?"

"Yes, I believe so. They are both as near perfection as I can fancy human beings can be, but Mary has none of the stimulants and rewards which a man's career holds out to virtue. She has no earthly reward."

"Except your affection," Gertrude said, for the first time alluding in speaking to him to the attachment existing between them.

"Ay. I love her," he answered, in a tone of unaccountable emotion and irritation; "God help her, I love her very much."

This sentence seemed strange to Gertrude, and she looked at him inquiringly. He did not notice it, but said—"And you have made acquaintance with Adrien d'Arberg. Had I said too much about him, Lady-Bird,—Miss Lifford, I mean?"

"Never mind, Maurice, everybody here calls me so, and you who gave me the name have a better right than any one to do so."

"O Lady-Bird, thank you," he exclaimed, and seizing her hand, kissed it. "Forgive me; in Italy the very beggars kiss the hand that relieves them. It is only in England that it is thought presumptuous." She felt his manner odd, and abruptly changed the subject. "I am going back to Lifford Grange to-morrow." "To-morrow! for how long?" "O probably for good and all."

At that moment Mr. Latimer came into the room, nodded to Maurice, and sat down between him and Gertrude, opposite to the fire. "Well, Lady-Bird, you have not been out to-day. What have you been doing with yourself? What are your studies? I should like to know how you spend your time when we are all out of the way. You are one of the few women I have ever met with who seems to like to be alone. You think a great deal?"

She put her fingers to her temples, and said, "It is a mill, always at work, but it grinds more chaff than corn."

"I believe it would grind anything you chose to put into it. What has it been busy upon to-day?"

"A point of duty, Mr. Latimer."

"O what a dry bone."

"But with marrow in it, too."

"Who threw it in—yourself, or somebody else?"

"Conscience picked it up, threw it in——"

"And it has been ground into nothing."

"No, into something—and something disagreeable, too."

"What is that?"

"The unpleasant circumstance for myself that I am going away to-morrow."

"O stuff and nonsense; you can't go away"

"I wish I could not; but I can, and shall."

"But you will come back here soon?"

"I don't know: one never knows anything in this world, I find. It is all a living '*au jour la journée.*'"

"O but we won't live without seeing you again. We shall all die."

"I will come at all events to *your* funeral, Mr. Latimer."

"And not to Mark Apley's? Poor fellow! he will die first. *I* shall make a struggle, and pine away by degrees. But what do you do with yourself in that enchanted abode where nobody penetrates? Has anybody ever got in? Have you, Mr. Redmond?"

"O yes, he has," she answered quickly, "often enough. He is '*mon pays,*' as the French peasants say."

" They tell me you read immensely."

" How do *they* know anything about it?"

" Here is Lady Clara, and the about-to-be-annihilated Mark. She says she must go away to-morrow."

" So she told me this morning. but I would not believe her. Besides, she ought not to go before the doctor has given his permission."

" I *must*, dear Lady Clara. I have told mamma to send the carriage for me to-morrow."

" Then you must come back as soon as you can, dear child. We cannot do without you."

" So I told her. She will find us lying about like dead flies, if she stays away too long. Perhaps Sir William Marlow may survive, and wander about the house like the last man."

Mark's usually radiant face was overcast. He was provoked at Mr. Latimer's manner to Gertrude. He felt he had not made any way with her since she had been at Audley Park; he was not quick enough to discover where was the danger he had to fear, and was jealous of the sort of easy footing on which Mr. Latimer was with her, although he was quite old enough to be her father. Maurice was disappointed at her departure, and yet relieved in one sense by the reflection that she was to be replaced in the solitary position where none approached her. He felt frightened at his own agitation when any other man spoke to her; Mr. Latimer's manner, his jokes about Mark, were intolerable to him. If he felt that already, what would it be to live in the same house with her, in the midst of such a society? He should never be able to control his nervous irritation. It was better she should go. He would have wished to hurry her away. Once within those old walls of Lifford Grange, he could think of her, dream of her, get a glimpse of her now and then, and no one else would gaze on her beauty,—no one else would call her Lady-Bird, or talk in joke of dying for her. What business had they to joke with such a thought? Poor Maurice, it was no laughing matter to him. While he was dressing for dinner, he embodied these thoughts in verse, according to his usual practice, and set them to an impassioned German air.

" Return, return where careless eyes may never rest on thee,
Where none, not even once by chance, may see thy face but me.
Go back to those old yew-trees' shade, where often from afar
I've watched thee as the learned watch in the deep sky a star.

Go back where birds and whisp'ring winds alone will haunt thine ears
Go back to those deserted walks, the haunts of former years.
The jests, the smiles of thoughtless men, were never meant for one
Who in those silent solemn halls has lived and bloomed alone :—
Let them not praise thee, hold thy hand, and call thee by a name
Which time has stamped upon my brain in characters of flame.
Go, for the sake of pity, go. Thy every word and look,
Here, amidst those who laugh or sigh, my spirit cannot brook."

There were sincere and insincere regrets uttered for Gertrude's departure, and sincere and insincere wishes for her return. She did not care much for any of them. Lady Clara whom she was really fond of, she knew was sorry to lose her. Though worldly in some respects, or rather of the world, there was an openness in her clear eyes and smooth brow which was unmistakeable. The truth was in her, and her smile was a pledge. Adrien had not approached her that day; and it was rather late in the evening before he did so. He had been engaged in a long conversation with Mrs. Crofton and Sir William Marlow. The latter had treated him "*Du haut de sa petite grandeur*" at first; but, finding what an adversary he had to deal with, had become eager, and put forth all the strength of his understanding, and a close encounter had taken place between them on some of the leading questions of the day. Mrs. Crofton, with that admirable art of listening which she possessed to an eminent degree, had stimulated the sharp encounter, and given an amusing turn to it, when Sir William was growing bitter. Nearly opposite to them sat Gertrude, with one of the Miss Apleys, and several men around them. Maurice was sitting on a chair a little behind her, and she now and then turned round to speak to him.

"I wonder," he said, in a low voice, "if they would think M. d'Arberg quite sane here, if they knew some of the things he does. To me, who know how a great deal of his time is employed and the use he makes of his fortune, it seems so odd to see him in this sort of society making himself agreeable like any ordinary man of the world."

"He is very rich, is not he?"

"Very rich, I believe his mother was an heiress, his father married her when he was an *émigré*. His good works are prodigious, also; but they are done so secretly that few people know anything of them. I am convinced he will end by being a priest." Gertrude turned pale; Maurice saw it and a jealous pang shot through his heart. Thank Heaven, she was going the next day, and d'Arberg would not, probably, stay long in England. They might never meet again. Why had he not dreaded their becoming acquainted? Why, fool that he was, had he talked to her so much about him? He went on in an odd abrupt manner to say that he hurt his fortune by his extravagant charities, that this was probably the reason why he had never married——

"O, no," she said in a quiet manner, "Mr. Audley, who knows him well, says he has large property both in France and in Ireland."

"You have ascertained that he is rich?" he answered in a tone of ill-disguised agitation.

"I have heard it," she said, and then became absent, for the hand of the French clock was travelling fast, and her impatience was becoming almost intolerable. At last the conversation at the opposite side of the table came to an end, and Adrien, as if he had perceived her for the first time that evening, came and sat in the chair opposite to her. Miss Apley was talking eagerly to some one on the other side of the couch. Maurice had seized a newspaper, and seemed engrossed with it, but was still near enough to hear every word that passed. "I hear you are going home to-morrow," Adrien said, and looked at her with an expression of interest. "Yes," she answered, without raising her eyes from the nosegay she held in her hand, "life cannot be spent amongst flowers: not mine at least."

"You have enjoyed yourself here?"

"Almost too much. I wish I had not been thrown on this bed of roses, for I am afraid it has unfitted me for another couch."

"Well, it certainly is not a very bracing atmosphere that we live in here. It is floating down the stream, instead of pulling against it."

"And yet," she said, "what fault can be found with such an existence as Lady Clara's? How innocent it is! how affectionate she is! Loving and beloved, giving pleasure and receiving it. I think it is a delightful sight to see her, so beautiful herself, in the midst of beauty of every kind. By changing a single word one could apply to her that beautiful French line,

'Et rose elle a vécu, comme vivent les roses.'"

"True," he answered, with one of his slow smiles, "but was she sent into the world to live the life of a rose, or to bear her part in the great battle-field of life? Her existence always seems to me too much like Eve's in Paradise—Eve *before* not *after* the Fall."

Gertrude pulled off all the pink petals of one of the flowers in her hand and showed him the green calyx which formed a sort of cross. "Aye!" he exclaimed, "it will be found in the end, but ought it not to have been taken up sooner?"

"I should like the battle-field of life," she said, "but to sit still is what I dread."

"We must each of us fight at our post," he answered. "The order of the day is all that concerns us. Do you go early to-morrow?"

"Not very early," she replied, with a faltering voice.

"I wanted to ask you if on Sunday I might hear mass at the chapel at Lifford Grange,—it is nearer than Stonehouseleigh, and I should be glad to see Father Lifford at the same time." Her eyes flashed with a joy that she could not disguise, and she assented briefly, but in a manner that showed the delight she felt.

"Mamma will see you, perhaps, if she is pretty well."

"Would she? I should be so glad to know her."

"She never receives strangers, but——"

"But you think she would see me?"

"I have read to her your books; and you have been so kind to me."

"Kind!" he said with a smile.

"Yes, you carried me here the day of my accident. I am sure she will wish to thank you. Can you speak Spanish?"

"Yes."

"That will do, it is all right,"—and with a movement of irresistible delight she threw up her nosegay into the air, and caught it back again as it fell. He looked a little thoughtful, and did not talk to her any more that evening, but sat on in the same place. Maurice had been asked to sing a new romance which Mrs. Crofton had just received from Paris, the words by Victor Hugo; it was called the "Fou de Tolède." He complied: when he came to the following stanza his eyes fixed themselves on Gertrude:

> Un jour Sabine a tout donné—
> Sa beauté de Colombe

> Et son amour,
> Pour l'anneau d'or du Compte de Saldagne
> Pour un bijou—
> Le vent qui vient à travers la montagne
> Me rendra fou.

She did not observe his emotion, but the music of this song—which was wild like a dream of passion—seemed to suit her thoughts also.

CHAPTER XIV.

> "Not chance of birth or place has made us friends,
> Being —— of different tongues and nations,
> But the endeavour for the self-same ends,
> With the same hopes, and fears, and aspirations.'
>   SHAKSPEARE.

In her mother's arms—at her mother's feet—Gertrude spent the next few days. That dark room had grown very dear to her. Her feelings were now more in unison with its aspect. The picture of the Duke of Gandia seemed to look approvingly upon her, as by every little exertion in her power she endeavoured to contribute to her mother's comfort. She told her again and again all the particulars of her stay at Audley Park, amused her with descriptions of the people she had seen, made her smile sometimes and sigh at others, and understood her smiles but not her sighs. Then she talked to her of Adrien, gave a minute account of his looks, of his manner, repeated every word he had said to her, and announced that he would come to Lifford Grange on the following Sunday.

"You must tell Father Lifford, love. I wonder what your father would feel about it.'"

"About what, mamma? About M. d'Arberg's coming to church? You know the chapel is open to every one on Sunday."

"Yes, dearest, but if he comes I think you must ask him to have some luncheon."

"Yes, to be sure," Gertrude said, with her brightest smile. "we must not let him starve, and then you must see him."

"O no, my dearest child, I cannot do that."

"Oh, you must, dearest mamma, it will do you a world of good. How I wish I had taken to managing you long ago. You would be so much better by this time. I am beginning to manage Father Lifford too. By going a little lame, I make him do whatever I like now."

"O, but Gertrude, that is very naughty."

"No, no, I don't *pretend* to limp, I only show it off. Oh, we could be so happy here if——" Here she stopped, and a dark cloud passed over her face. In a moment she said, "Lady Clara would come and see you if you liked, mamma."

Mrs. Lifford became agitated. "My child, don't let her come. I could not bear it. I am very, very grateful to her for her kindness to you, but indeed I cannot see her. I can see nobody. I am not fit for it."

"Not Lady Clara, then, not anybody but M. d'Arberg. He will talk Spanish to you, and you will understand each other so well. Dearest, when I talk to him, it gives me such a wish to be good like him."

Mrs. Lifford looked tenderly at her child, and said, "Geltrudina, don't give away that little heart of thine to a Frenchman." She put her hand on her heart with a smile, and said to herself, "I have none left to give away. But he is just as much English as French, or Spanish, or anything else, mamma. He is only like himself."

"Do you think he likes you, Gertrude?"

"He does not dislike me, and sometimes I have thought he appeared a little interested about me. But I am no more worthy of him—than Muff," she said, hiding her face with the little dog's flossy head.

"And then, dearest, you should not think of anything of the sort without knowing more about him."

"I do know all about him; I know that he is the best, the cleverest, the noblest of human beings."

"That may be, dear child. Father Lifford says he is very good; but that is not all that your father would think of."

"But, dearest mamma, M. d'Arberg is not thinking of me in the way you mean; other people paid me attentions at Audley Park. He did not. Maurice Redmond says he will be a priest; so you need have no apprehensions on that subject. If he ever should think of me, I have no fear that his family could be objected to. Mr. Audley said it was very ancient, and he is very rich and everything people care about—but he will never dream of marrying me. To be *his* wife would be too great a blessing."

"O Gertrude, Gertrude."

"You will see him on Sunday, mamma; don't think me too foolish till then. Now I shall go down stairs, and play at chess with Father Lifford. It always puts him in a good humour to beat me, and I want him to be in a very good humour just now."

In spite of her remaining lameness, she walked briskly towards the drawing-room. Her manner was altogether changed—its restless listlessness had disappeared, and her mother was confirmed in the belief that a little change was a good thing for her. She did not yet understand the great change that had almost transformed her into another creature,—the awakening of that deep power of loving which had hitherto lain in her heart "like an unopened flower."

Adrien d'Arberg had been much attached in his early youth to a cousin of his who had died of consumption at the age of eighteen. Her virtues, her ardent piety, and her saintly death, had made an impression upon him which nothing had effaced, and her memory had been associated with every interest and exertion of his life. She was a German,—one of those fair, pale girls, whose eyes have a natural sentimentality bordering on melancholy. Her temper was serene and serious. There had been something at once romantic and religious in her affection for him. She had had a presentiment of her early death, and had never looked forward to earthly happiness. Whenever he talked of the future, and of their marriage, she shook her head without sadness, but with a profound conviction that she should not live to be his wife. There was something holy in her face; she was like one of Francia's or Perugino's saints, or like the picture which old chroniclers draw of "the dear St. Elizabeth of Hungary."

A very short time before her death she called him to her, and told him that this might be the last time she should see him, and that she wished to take leave of him then. She enjoined him to do in the world all the good she would have wished to do, and add daily to the treasure they had begun to lay up together in heaven. "She had made her meditation that morning," she said, "on the history of Martha and Mary, and felt as if he would say that she left him to do all the serving alone; but you will not grudge me, Adrien," she added, "that better part which I indeed have not chosen, but which has been chosen for me." She gave him much advice,—amongst other things asked him to write the long work which he had since accomplished. She had a brother whom she dearly loved, and who had lost his faith. His conversion had been the object of her prayers and of her hopes, and now of her request to Adrien. She told him that she had never prayed for health or for any temporal blessing, but for one thing alone, and that she had even offered up her life to obtain it, that was, that he might lead a perfect life on earth, and do much for God and for the Church. " I know not," she added, " if He has accepted the sacrifice; it is delightful to me to hope it, and do you, Adrien, always act as if it were so accepted. In every temptation—not to sin only, but to faltering in the upward path—think of my early death, and remember that you have double work to do."

Still deeper thoughts and tenderer words she spoke, too solemn to be here repeated, and hitherto he had carried them in his heart, and they had borne fruit in his life. She remained his beau idéal of woman, and it was with almost a religious worship that he honoured her memory. He had not thought of love, or of marriage since. Sometimes he had felt yearnings for the religious life, but had not yet found in himself the vocation to it. He had not lived much in society, and no woman but Ida had ever made any impression upon him. Once, in compliance with the wishes of his family, he had tried to like a young person whom they recommended him to marry. They thought she resembled his early love, and fancied she would captivate him, but she had only Ida's features without her soul, and he shrunk from the likeness as from a deception and a snare. On the night that in the course of a stroll through the park at Audley Place he had found Gertrude insensible and carried her home in his strong arms, he had only just seen that she was beautiful, or would be so when animation returned; when he heard from Lady Clara her name, and her family and home were described to him, he felt interested about her.

There were several reasons for his being so, and though it was as yet but a transient feeling, it was more than he had felt for any woman, except Ida. He remembered how, in Italy, Maurice Redmond used to talk to him about her, and his having once shown him a very odd clever letter she had written to him. When he began talking to her, he was a little startled sometimes, but on the whole attracted. As it was said before, from the first moment of their acquaintance he had so much unconscious influence over her, that her somewhat strange opinions and the peculiarities of her impetuous and yet reserved character were so much softened as only to make her original and amusing. She was as quick as lightning, understood in an instant anything he said to her, and astonished him by the vivacity of her intelligence. Perhaps he thought her rather more *genuine* than she was. Perhaps there was a little more of self-knowledge than appeared on the surface of her captivating *laisser-aller*, but her feelings were genuine even if there was a little art sometimes in her way of conducting herself.

It is difficult to have strong volitions, to be excessively clever, to have great powers of self-command, and yet to be open as the day. Shallow waters are easily transparent—but it is rare to find a very deep and very transparent stream. His own character was such, but in both cases the exception is rare. Lady Clara had often spoken to him of Mr. Lifford, and that man's destiny had always been to him a subject of regret. It was positive pain to a nature like his to see blessings wasted, intellect thrown away, means of usefulness disregarded, and by one who could have done so much for all the objects he had most at heart. When he looked at the beautiful animated girl who seemed so ready to adopt all high views and aims, and to sympathise so warmly in everything great, useful, and noble, he wondered if she could not rouse her father from the torpid indifference in which he was sunk, and stimulate him to adopt another course; and this idea had induced him also to become well acquainted with her, and to endeavour to inspire her with such an ambition. By degrees he perceived or guessed what was the case:—that she had no belief in her father's affection, and that if there had not been bitter passages in her life, at least there were sore corners in her heart. Those who have felt themselves how suffering can be turned, I had almost said into happiness and I will not unsay it, but at all events into a blessing, have a sort of yearning desire to make others and especially young people understand it. Bitterness is the worst sort of suffering, but perhaps when the right remedy is applied it is the most certainly to be cured. And by a few unpretending words, some instances quoted here and there from real life, he conveyed to her his own receipt for happiness; but in mixing up the draught he unconsciously put in an ingredient he had not intended. It was an intoxicating addition, and might nullify what in appearance it seemed to second.

As he was waiting in the drawing-room, on the Sunday morning after her departure, for the post-chaise that was to take him to Lifford Grange, he took up accidentally his own book which was lying on the table, and opened on the page where, in faint pencil-marks, she had drawn a key; and he read the Italian lines underneath it. "True," he said to himself "that is the key to what seems at times such a problem to one's self—one's strength, and one's weakness." As he drove through the sombre avenue of Lifford Grange, and caught sight of the melancholy old mansion at the end of it, which, with the sullen-looking view beyond, formed a striking contrast with the scenery between it and Audley Park, he thought what a strange flower had blossomed in that dull spot. As the post-chaise stopped, a servant came up to the door and showed him the way to the chapel, which was at the end of the wing which contained Mrs. Lifford's apartments. It was very small, but well arranged, and the candles on the altar were lighting at that moment. Gertrude was kneeling by the side of her mother's arm-chair, who, when she was well enough to leave her bed, heard mass from a kind of tribune on one side of the altar. One look she cast at the body of the chapel, and saw, with the emotion which a great joy after a moment's anxiety produces, Adrien kneeling and absorbed in prayer.

There is something more touching in a man's devotion than in a woman's; when it is earnest it is so real, so humble, and so deep. It seemed to her as if the light of heaven played round that noble head bowed down in intense adoration. Though she was looking at him, she knew that he would not look at her. *His* spirit was soaring far above earthly thoughts, and she was glad of it; she had understood at once in knowing him what theologians mean by perfection—a comparative term after all—but a necessary one to describe the angelic life which some of God's creatures are enabled to live on earth; and a glance from him at that moment would have disappointed her. She turned away, and prayed earnestly herself, nor once looked again from the altar. After mass, she saw her mother comfortably established on her couch, and propped up by pillows.

"Now, mamma, I will bring M. d'Arberg to see you. We will come in by the garden-door in the next room."

"You must let me rest for an hour, dear child, and then you may come."

"Very well, dearest, then I shall take him to see the house, if he wishes it, for Father Lifford will not be in the library for some time, I know.—Yes," she said to herself, as she went slowly across the hall, " I should like to take him to every part of this old house of mine" (for the first time she complacently called it her house), "so that the perfume of pleasant memories might attach itself to every corner of it."

When she opened the door of the drawing-room—that formal square room with its heavy furniture and cheerless aspect—it seemed too like a dream to see Adrien there. But there he was, and the window where he was standing was the first of the stations which her fancy meant to cherish. "Are you well, Lady-Bird?" he asked her kindly and warmly. "You have not been walking too much in the day, or reading too late at night?"

"I shut up my book every night as the clock strikes twelve," she said. "I am trying to keep rules; it is hard work, but I hope there will be method in my madness at last."

"It is madness to waste health," he said with a smile, "at least without making a good bargain with it,—getting something more valuable in return."

"And information is not that, I suppose?"

"O no—not for its own sake. What a very peculiar place this is."

"What do you think of it?" she said, throwing open the window out of which they both leaned.

"I don't dislike it, but I cannot flatter you either by praising or abusing it. But tell me, is the chapel as old as the house?"

"Not the one that is used now, but the one upstairs under the roof, which is now out of repair. There is near it one of the hiding-places for the priests which were used in the days of persecution."

"Will you show it me, in return for the stories of the catacombs which I told you the other day?"

"Yes, I will!" she eagerly exclaimed; and leading the way through long passages and winding staircases, continued, "I had no notion till I met the other day with a little book called 'Records of Missionary Priests' of the heroic lives and deaths of these men, of whom some may have taken refuge in the very place I am going to show you. These accounts are quite sublime, although—or rather perhaps because—they are so simply given. But, M. d'Arberg, I cannot endure their loyalty to Queen Elizabeth: it may have been fine, but it provokes me to death."

"You are given to rebellion. I have perceived that before."

"But you are not surely for passive obedience?"

"You must not make me talk politics *here*. I am afraid of the ghosts of your ancestors. But I do admire from my heart the absence of party-spirit in men who died for their faith, with less of earthly stimulus and sympathy than any other martyrs were ever cheered and supported by before. It was done in the discharge of an ordinary duty, all in their day's work; and their dying prayers for the Queen and the country appear less like great efforts of Christian virtue, than an absence of bitterness more surprising still. They were strangers and pilgrims; and to be thrust aside from the world, and hurried on to eternity, was an injury which hardly excited their resentment."

"But they gave up the out-posts too readily. They stipulated for nothing but the very citadel, and defended it only by dying."

"True," he answered, "it was an error, perhaps, but a noble and not an unchristian one. Is this the place?"

"It is," she exclaimed, "and we may well call it holy ground, for martyrs here, in Mrs. Hemans' words,

'Uncheer'd by praise
Have made the offering of their days,
And silently in fearless faith
Prepared their noble souls for death.'"

Adrien gazed with emotion into the dark recess, which was usually concealed by a sliding panel, which gave no outward sign of the existence of a hiding-place within. After an instant he turned to her and said, "I had often heard of these places of refuge, but had never seen one before. Your old house may be gloomy at first sight, but it speaks more to the soul than Audley Park." They went down stairs again, and sat upon the terrace. "Will you sit on this bench while go and see if mamma is ready to receive you?"

"No; but I will walk up and down here till you come back." In five minutes she returned again, and led him through the little library into Mrs. Lifford's room.

It was long since her mother had seen a stranger; and her cheek was flushed, and her voice a little tremulous as she spoke to him in Spanish, which was familiar to him as his own tongue. His manner was gentle to every one, but to that bruised and suffering being (and who could look upon her, and not feel that such she was) it was gentleness and tenderness itself. That manner, the tones of his voice, the expression in his eyes, were inexpressibly soothing to her. She had not been so addressed for years and years. Father Lifford was very kind, but he was rough and abrupt. Gertrude had latterly been affectionate and attentive, but her high spirits and impetuous nature gave something startling to her very tenderness; while her husband's coldness and her son's formality were in another way depressing. She had been used to something so different in her childhood and early youth. There was a sound in Adrien's voice that reminded her of Assunta, the sister she had lost. She listened to him with a pleasure she could hardly account for, and he at once won her heart. "No wonder," she thought, "that Gertrude had found him charming, that he had made her long to be like him. Who would not admire that face?—who would not be fascinated by that voice, won by that perfect kindness, swayed by those speaking eyes, subdued by that matchless nobleness of countenance and manner?" Such were her thoughts as she sat listening to him, and now and then addressing to him a few earnest words. They understood each other so well He in the busy walks of life—she at her silent watch—had served the same master, and learned the same secrets. In her heart there rose a hope, a wish, at the strength of which she was alarmed; for she thought that she had learnt that great lesson—not to wish anything too intensely. But that he should like Gertrude,—that he should in time wish to marry her,—was a vision of happiness for that beloved child that rose irrepressibly before her. Such a haven of bliss and of safety, such a shelter through the storms of life, such an escape from dangers that would thicken on her path, in or out of her home!

When Adrien asked if he might come and see her again, she pressed his hand, and smiled assent. Never had he felt more sympathy for any one than for this pale suffering woman. Her eyes haunted him, and as Gertrude led the way back to the library he was silent and thoughtful. He turned to her half absently, and said something in Spanish. "I don't understand Spanish." she said, hastily. "Not your mother's tongue, Lady-Bird! Not that beautiful language which she speaks so eloquently! How is it possible that you have never learnt it." "It does seem strange to me now," she answered, colouring—and a resolution was taken at that moment. Not another day passed without her applying herself with a kind of passionate application to that study.

Father Lifford now joined them. He was not fond of Frenchmen, but he had made up his mind that Adrien was as little of one as possible, and he could not, in spite of himself, help liking him. They walked up and down the avenue discussing English politics, on which they agreed more than about those of the Continent. Gertrude slipped into her mother's room to hear her say that Adrien was charming; and then from her bed-room window she gazed on the yew-trees, as if they had suddenly been illuminated by the most radiant sunshine. She wished the day not to advance—she dreaded to hear the luncheon-bell ring—every minute seemed a whole day of enjoyment. There was not a gesture of Adrien's that she did not watch; she knew from which tree he had plucked a branch, where he had let it fall from his hand, on what bench he had sat for a moment and traced a pattern on the sand, which of the gamekeeper's dogs he had caressed as it passed him, and where he had shaded his eyes with his hand to gaze on some distant point which Father Lifford was pointing out to him. At last the bell rang, and she went down to the dining-room. That table laid for three, how often she had sat down to it with a heart that felt as hard and dull as a stone! When Father Lifford said grace, she silently returned thanks that life was no longer what it had been to her,—thanks that a ray had shone upon it, and melted away the ice that had gathered round her heart. She was amused at observing how skilfully Adrien avoided those subjects on which he and Father Lifford would have been likely to disagree, and with what "Christian art" he sought to please the old man whom he respected.

"We are going to vespers at Stonehouseleigh," Father Lifford said to her, as they left the dining-room, "will you have the gamekeeper's pony and ride there?" She had done this once or twice before, and felt very grateful to him for proposing it now. When she was lifted on the saddle, and gathering up the reins, slowly moved from the door, Adrien walking by her side and now and then laying his hand on the pony's mane, or brushing away with a branch the flies that were teasing him, she thought of the day when, with Edgar, she had left that door for another ride, and one which led to consequences that made it an epoch in her life. "Don't you go and play us tricks again, Miss Gertrude," Father Lifford said to her; "mind your reins. Who knows but this old creature may take it into its head to rush off with you somewhere or other, if you leave it entirely to its own inventions." She looked back with a smile of such sweetness that her whole countenance seemed changed, and the old man muttered to himself, "I believe the foolish mother was right after all, and that what the child wanted was a little happiness."

"I had forgotten to give you this note from Lady Clara," Adrien suddenly said, and drew it from his pocket. She read it, and turning to him her expressive eyes, she put it into his hand. "Am I to read it?" "Yes," she said, "you see she wants me to go back to Audley Park. I think mamma would let me go, but——" "But don't you wish to go?" She looked at him without answering, as if she were inwardly deliberating. She wished to guess his thoughts. she would have given anything to abide by his decision. But she did not venture to ask for his opinion. She had not yet any hope that he cared for her. The very kindness of his manner, though she felt happy in it, was discouraging. The love she felt for him—for she could not disguise from herself that she loved him—was at that stage of its progress singularly unmixed with hope or fear. Its existence alone seemed enough for her happiness. With a strange humility, she scarcely dared to look for a reciprocal affection from one whom she almost deified by the silent worship of her heart. To be something to him, to have reason to hope she should sometimes see him, that he would not altogether forget her, and that he might some day or other know how transformed she had been in thoughts, in feelings and in conduct, since she had known him, since his mind had spoken to hers, since a spark of that fire which burnt in his soul had animated hers:— this seemed enough for her; at least she thought so, but it was under a sort of infatuated belief that he would always be what he then was. The least touch of jealousy, the supposition or the report that he was turning his thoughts to marriage, that he was interested in any other woman more than in her, or that he might dedicate himself to the religious life, would all at once have opened her eyes and raised a storm in her soul.

But there is a lethargy as well as a fever in happiness, one often precedes the other, and on this day it seemed that as long as she could see him and hear his voice, the future was nothing, the present all in all. Submission to him seemed her ruling desire. In a nature so rebellious and proud, this was the result of a mastering passion. But with that artless artfulness which characterised her, she did what perhaps served her purpose better than anything else. She answered after a pause: "I should like to go, but I will ask Father Lifford's advice. He will know what mamma would really wish." Adrien looked at her more than kindly—almost tenderly—and said, with his usual simplicity of manner: "I hope she will really wish you to go." Her heart bounded with delight. How lovely the lane through which they were passing at that moment seemed to her;—how blue the sky overhead, how sweet the clematis or the branch of honey-suckle which, here and there, still remained in the hedges;—how fresh and balmy the air that caressed her cheek.

At one point of the road there was a fine view of distant country, and they stopped an instant to look at it. He said it was like one near his chateau in Normandy, and, for the first time, he spoke a little about his home. He had not been educated there, and it was more like a home to his brother who was married, and lived in it with his wife and children;—every year he spent some time with them.

"And shall you never fix yourself there?" she asked, unconsciously blushing as she did so.

"Perhaps," he said, "but I never make projects for the future—not that I think it wrong—but it does not occur to me to look beyond the work of the moment. I like that line in a little book I saw on Lady Clara's table the other day; 'I do not ask to see the distant scene, one step enough for me.'"

"And I," Gertrude said, "am always, or at least always was thinking of the distant scene, and during many years would have liked to '*sauter à pieds joints*' the steps between me and it."

"But not now?" he said inquiringly.

"Oh, not so much now," she answered hastily, "I am very willing to let time go as slowly as it pleases just at present. But it is apt to hurry when we least wish it, and to creep when we would hasten it. Like this old pony, who would not go out of a foot's pace last Sunday, when I was late, and to-day seems bent on walking fast, as if on purpose to tire you." After a pause she said, "I am almost surprised that your present existence suits you."

"And how do you know it does?"

"Because I do not understand why you should stay at Audley Park if you did not like it."

"But why should you think I do not? It is very pleasant to leave for a while one's own particular way and habits, and see people who have not looked upon things through the same glasses as one's self. They may be better or worse spectacles; but a peep through them always shows one something new or useful."

"Ay," she said eagerly, "that is the reason, I suppose, that some very good people are provoking. I suppose it is those who have never used but one pair of spectacles," and her eyes, perhaps unconsciously, glanced at those which Father Lifford was at that moment wiping.

Adrien smiled and said, "Oh, but for *use* one pair is enough, if the glasses be good."

"I should have thought that the very thing I like so much at Audley Park would have bored you,—its busy idleness."

"I think idle business worse."

"But you are neither idly busy, nor busily idle."

"I hope not always; but you know the old saying, 'All work and no play makes Jack a dull boy.'"

"Ay, but I think your *play* would be of a different kind. I can understand your liking to travel, or to——"

"Well, I am not sure that I had not rather spend a week amongst new people—if they are at all out of the common way—than see new places, though that is amusing in its way, too."

"But beautiful scenery you delight in, I am sure."

"That," he answered, "is like fine music in a church. When you get it, and your mind is in harmony, it almost amounts to ecstacy, but there are few places where a similar effect is not within your reach. I doubt whether the Alps or the Italian lakes have awakened higher feelings of enjoyment than the nearest meadow, with buttercups and daisies, near London or Manchester, and I am sure that a flower-pot in a window has given as much pleasure as the parterre at Audley Park."

"Then I suppose," she said in a very low voice, "that you think a person might be happy at Lifford Grange?"

They were just stopping at the gate of the little church-yard. He took the pony's mane in his hand and did not answer for an instant or two, and then said, with a shade of emotion in his voice, "Yes, I think so." She was startled, not by the words, but by something in his manner. Was it possible that he was not so calmly and so merely kind to her as she had fancied, or was it that he was longing to tell her something of his thoughts on happiness, such as he understood it? She knew that there was often that kind of emotion in his countenance, when the subject nearest to his heart was alluded to, and his eyes—not his lips—bore witness to his deepest feelings. It might have been one or the other of these causes, she knew not which, and now their walk was at an end, and she could not investigate this point any farther. While she knelt at church by his side, she once thought if ever she became his wife, how easy a thing it would be to be good,—how every duty would be a pleasure, and life a foretaste of Heaven; and for the first time she poured forth passionate supplications that this blessing might be vouchsafed to her, but they too much resembled in their spirit the prayer of Rachel, when she exclaimed, "Give me children or else I die!" There is something fearful in such prayers, and when they are heard, and the hand grasps what it has wildly sought, then is the time to tremble.

When they came out of the chapel, and Father Lifford was still in the sacristy, Gertrude sat down on her old favourite seat near the gate, and Adrien took leave of her; the post-chaise had been sent to meet him there. "Then I shall tell Lady Clara that you will send an answer. I hope it will be to say that you will come; but anyhow I shall see you again before I go to Ireland,—that is, if I may do next Sunday as to-day." She was looking her assent to those last words, when the organist passed them. He hurried by without speaking, but Adrien called out, "Halloa, Maurice, are you here? I might have guessed that nobody but you would have played that voluntary just now in this small place. Are you going back to Audley Park? I can give you a lift." "Thank you," said Maurice, with a singular smile. "You have given me many through life;" and then he muttered to himself, "and much good they have done me." Then passing his hand over his forehead, he approached Gertrude, who shook hands with him. The coldness of his hands struck her, and the dim look of his eyes.

"I am going to sleep at home to-night," he said, "but to-morrow I return to Lifford Grange—I mean to Audley Park.'

"Here is Mary!" Gertrude exclaimed. "M. d'Arberg, you ought to know her, and her mother, Mrs. Redmond." She went up to them, and Adrien followed her. Maurice stood at a little distance whilst they spoke together.

"Yes," he said to himself, "it must be so, and fool that I am to mind it. Did I ever think she could be mine? Would I, if I could, give up Mary? Would I be false to the dearest and holiest affections of my childhood and my youth? Did I not snatch her hand last night, and imprint a thousand kisses upon it? Did I not again speak of our marriage? What a brute I am not to feel always as I did then! Is my hand such a rich gift that I should give it her without my heart? But my heart is hers. Yes, all that deserves to be called heart! O, Lady-Bird, Lady-Bird! I could almost curse you for standing between me and duty, and happiness, and Heaven also. For but now, in church, to see her kneeling by d'Arberg's side drove devotion away, and awoke the worst feelings in my breast. Curse *her!* Do men curse what they adore? I don't know; all I know is, that if she ever speaks to me again with that smile of hers,—if she expects me to talk to her of Mary as if she were not Mary's worst enemy, I may tell her something of my sufferings, and if that is to insult her, let her complain to d'Arberg, and make him turn my enemy too. Fool—idiot—that I was to be always talking to her about him! Could I suppose she would see him, and not love him? Oh, that he may make her suffer what I suffer!"

As he mentally expressed this wish, his eyes accidentally fixed themselves on the cross, near which he was standing, and he was struck to the heart with that silent lesson. He went into the church, and burying his face in his hands, remained there a while. Perhaps, during those few moments of silence and of meditation, he had a glimpse into his own real feelings; he saw for an instant the utter selfishness, the heartless ingratitude of his conduct; a transient repentance passed over the surface of his mind, and when Mary softly went up to him and whispered: "Mother is waiting," he raised his head, and his eyes were full of tears. She saw that he had been weeping, and he was surprised at her suddenly stopping and wringing her hands, as if she could hardly struggle any longer with some intense anxiety. "Mary?" he said, with a kind of inquiring expostulation. "I cannot endure *that*," she said hurriedly, "*anything* but that, when I know ——." She stopped, and her manner changed. "Come, make haste, dear boy—we shall be late for tea, and I can endure anything but *that*," she repeated gaily. putting her arm in his, and holding out the other to her mother. They went home together, and he appeared calmer and happier that evening than he had done for a long time.

CHAPTER XV.

"He that but fears the thing he would not know
Hath by instinct knowledge from other's eyes
That what he feared is chanced."
SHAKESPEARE.

"The love that follows us sometimes is our trouble,
Which still we praise as love."
Ibid.

"Happy and worthy of esteem are those
Whose words are bonds, whose oaths are oracles,
Whose love sincere, whose thoughts immaculate;
Whose tears pure, messengers sent from the heart,
Whose heart as far from fraud as Heaven from earth."
Ibid.

IN the course of the next week, Gertrude returned to Audley Park. Her mother had readily yielded her assent to the request contained in Lady Clara's note; and although Father Lifford had growled a little about it, he did not on the whole object. He said that he supposed foolish people must please themselves, which they well knew was his way of withdrawing from active opposition. It was therefore with a light heart and a radiant countenance that Gertrude set out for Audley Park, looked again upon its brightness, and entered the drawing-room which had been the scene of so much enjoyment, and where she was now most affectionately received.

Lady Clara kissed her, Lady Roslyn smiled, and Mr. Latimer exclaimed, in the words of Maurice's song:

"Come, Lady-Bird, come rest you here,
O do not fly away."

"We caught her the first time," Lady Clara said; "now she has returned of her own accord."

"D'Arberg," said Mr. Latimer, "could not tell us whether you were coming or not. We all longed to fly to Lifford Grange yesterday in that yellow post-chaise, which bore him off at an early hour. You cannot think how we have missed you. Lady Clara has been quite depressed, Lady Roslyn cross, Mrs. Crofton melancholy, poor Mark on the point of hanging himself, and ——"

"You, Mr. Latimer?"

"O I,—I sent for arsenic yesterday, and had you not returned to-day there would have been a coroner's inquest to-morrow. I can't eat at dinner, the Miss Apleys talk to me so much."

"That is a hint."

"No, Lady-Bird, *your* warblings help digestion. By the way, Lady Clara, I hope the magnetiser is coming here again. She ought to know him."

"He said he would dine here on Wednesday."

"We had great fun the other night. He sent Miss Apley fast asleep, and put Fanny, on the contrary, in such a state of excitement that she talked the most charming nonsense. He is to tell us a great deal about clairvoyance the next time he comes."

"I have often heard Mesmerism spoken of," Gertrude said, "but have never seen it practised."

"O then, Mr. Edwards shall devote himself to you on Wednesday."

"What nonsense d'Arberg talked about it. Not safe to have any thing to do with it! I should have thought him a more sensible man. I really think he believes in witchcraft."

"O no, he does not."

"I beg your pardon—he said he could not see how one could explain away what was said in the Bible about it."

"And do you?" Gertrude asked.

"I don't know. I never tried."

"Then you disbelieve without examining," Lady Clara said; "that is hardly philosophical. M. d'Arberg was not at all dogmatical about it."

"You always stand up for him, Lady Clara."

"But I do not set down any one else—not even you, which I own would be difficult." He laughed and said: "And I own that you are the best natured person in the world;—I never heard you run down any one."

"It is so fatiguing," she said with a pretty little yawn (if such a thing can be pretty). "I have not Mrs. Crofton's energy."

"Malicious humility!" he exclaimed,—"Admirable laziness!—the merit of virtue and the charm of vice. I like to see you idly reclining in your arm-chair, letting the stitches drop from your work, with the same charming indolence with which you spare the reputations of your neighbours. And have you missed *us*, Lady-Bird?" he continued, "have you in the shades of Lifford Grange given one thought to those you left behind? I had some thoughts of disguising myself as a sailor, or a tramper, and laying wait for you in some of those dark thickets near the Leigh; but there is a story in the neighbourhood that your father keeps bulls in his park, and I was afraid of being tossed in your presence,—not by conflicting feelings alone, but by the horns of one of those domestic favourites." She laughed and denied the report, and soon after went to dress.

She found herself sitting at dinner that day between Sir William Marlow, and Mr. Egerton, Lady Clara's brother. The former did not like her at all. In the first place, he had rather an instinctive dislike of clever people; though very clever himself in some ways, he was slow at entering into anything like humour; and was provoked to death that Gertrude's pointless remarks, as he considered them, made people laugh, and turned away their attention from himself. Her other neighbour had not yet made much acquaintance with her, but this time they got on very well. It would have been difficult not to like him, he was so pleasing, intelligent, and agreeable. That day, in the course of conversation they happened to talk of emigration; and amongst other things he informed her that Adrien was deeply interested in the subject, and had organized the plan of a settlement in America, to which he had sent a great number of the poor Irish in London, and which promised to succeed very well.

"I admire him so much," he said, "and could like him better than almost anybody. But I can never get on quite satisfactorily with him, and I think he has some very overstrained notions. I like people to be as happy as possible, and I have almost as much horror of their tormenting themselves, as of their tormenting others."

"But you do not think him a self-tormentor, do you? He seems to me a particularly happy person."

"But I do not like his way of being happy. Perhaps because I could not find pleasure in it myself. I think him too indifferent to some things, and too much engrossed by others. He is not practical enough."

"That is a word I do not quite understand. Do you mean that he does not himself act up to his theories?"

"No; but that his theories are not generally reducible to practice, and are therefore unsuited to the world we live in."

"But is not the very condition of the world a struggle? Virtue will never altogether prevail in it, and yet you would not on that account cease from the contest which it carries on against vice?"

"I would act as well as I could myself, but not aim at a visionary perfection."

"No, not at a visionary one; but would you not, or at least can you not understand that a person should aim at the highest perfection possible?"

"I think that in aiming too high, people often fall lower than they would otherwise have done."

"Do you think *he* does?"

"No; I said before that I admire him very much, but I fancy he could be much more useful in his generation if he were more like other people."

"But he neither lays down the law, nor dictates to others; nor is there an assumption of superiority in his manner. I thought I heard you say the other day that his manner was singularly unpretending."

"So it is; and I know nobody who, in proportion to his talents, has so humble an opinion of himself; but what I mean is, that one is always conscious that he measures everything by a standard not adapted to the world in its present state, and thus his efforts overshoot the mark, and so he misses his aim."

"But perhaps you do not quite know what his aim is?"

Mr. Egerton smiled, and Sir William Marlow said, "I always regret to see so remarkable an intellect hemmed in by such narrow boundaries."

"Are you sure that what you take for boundaries are not roads," she said, "leading to regions you have never explored?" He looked at her in a manner that seemed to say he had explored everything. "Besides," she continued, "a fortress has boundaries, a fruitful garden has walls; it is deserts and swamps that have no defined limits."

"I prefer the Alps," he ejaculated, "to a French garden!" and then turned away with a lofty contempt—himself a little Alp in his own esteem.

"I think d'Arberg has bit you with some of his notions," Mr. Egerton said good-humouredly.

"Perhaps," she answered, and thought of Wilberforce's answer to a lady who told him that Whitfield was mad:—"In that case," he said, "I only wish he may bite us all,"—and then went on to reflect on the extraordinary manner in which persons who view certain subjects through different mediums are impressed in a totally opposite way by the actions and the conduct of others. The very same line of conduct which excites admiration in one case, inspiring only astonishment, if not aversion in another. Perhaps a short time ago the want of sympathy between herself and her two neighbours would not have struck her in the same degree, and the absence of worldliness, which she so well appreciated in d'Arberg, in Mary Grey for instance might have appeared to her unreasonable; but she did not analyse her own sentiments narrowly, and was well satisfied with the consciousness that she alone out of that numerous society understood the principles as well as shared the feelings of Adrien.

That day and the next, she had but little conversation with him, but she thought he watched her, and on one or two occasions she asked his advice about little things that she was in doubt whether to do or not: there was not the least coquetry in this. She showed him, as plainly as a woman's dignity would permit, that she had but one wish, and that was not so much to captivate him, as to make herself what he would approve. It would have been impossible for any man not to be touched by this tacit homage. This singleness of purpose and simplicity of action did not naturally belong to her character, but to the intensity of the passion which had taken possession of her heart. She was like Juliet in her love, and the contrast between her utter artlessness with respect to it and her general subtlety of intellect and reserve of character was singular and attractive. He began to ask himself if he loved her?—if he ought to marry?—if she were in reality all she seemed to him to be?—and though he talked to her less than during her first visit to Audley Park, his manner began to show an interest which he struggled not to mark too plainly. Gertrude felt it, and with a sort of instinct seemed anxious not to hurry into premature development, or draw the attention of others to that delicate blossom of happiness which she watched day by day unfolding, and on which she fearfully staked every hope for her life, for her mind—I had almost said for her soul, whose new-born virtues were only the reflection of his. She had not gone with him to the source whence he drank, she had only caught the drops as they fell from his cup: he did not see this, and in his admiration of the fruit, he saw not or could not see that the roots had not struck deep into the soil. Her rare intelligence and noble sentiments answered to his aspirations and he began to think her beauty was the least of her merits, and to find a fresh stimulus in her society towards everything great and good. It was a beautiful thing, the love of those two beings, both so handsome and so highly-gifted, and looking formed—

"He for God only; she for God in him."

Others began to take notice of this growing attachment. Mark was disappointed, but—amiable as he always was—only congratulated himself on not having proposed to Gertrude, and consoled himself with the reflection that she was, perhaps, too clever for the ordinary purposes of life, and that

"There were maidens in [England] more lovely by far"

that would gladly wed the heir to so many acres and the future possessor of Woodlands Hall. Maurice was not the last to become conscious of the interest with which Adrien had inspired her whom he watched with unremitting though hopeless anxiety; but his calm and self-collected manner of addressing her, the caution with which he avoided any appearance of exclusive devotion to one whom he had not yet resolved to marry, were so different from what Maurice's own conduct would have been in his position, that it kept up in him the hope that d'Arberg had no such intentions, and that in her undisguised admiration for him there was more enthusiasm for his character and talents than affection for his person. And yet, when he saw her eyes turned upon him with that bewitching expression which he had once described as so fearfully attractive to him, the sudden pain that shot through his heart was almost greater than he could bear. He often made resolutions to depart the next day, but when the morrow came he found some excuse for remaining, and indulging the fatal pleasure of seeing her, embittered as it was by torments of jealousy.

One day she was sitting in the conservatory drawing an American flower, and intently busy upon it, when he came in with a letter in his hand, and sat down at a little distance from her. She made some trifling remark about the weather, without raising her head, and after an instant's silence he began,

"I wish to ask your advice, Lady-Bird: I have had a letter from Mary, which disturbs me much, and I think you, better than anybody, would understand my feelings and counsel me how to act." Gertrude was struck by the hollow nervous tone of his voice, and said kindly—"I will do my best, my dear Maurice, but how should I know how to advise others, I who am hardly wise enough to guide myself?" "First read that letter," he said. She took it, and it was as follows:—

"Dearest Maurice—I have been often wishing to say what I now write, but lately courage has failed me to do so, and during the short moments we have occasionally spent together, you have looked so ill and unhappy that I did not know how to begin talking of anything that might distress you. But now my mind is made up, and writing will be easier than speaking. I think you must guess what I am about to say—you must give up the idea of marrying me. It has all been a mistake from the beginning. We have loved each other dearly—how dearly God only knows, and I love you, if possible, more than ever. But I feel now that it does not answer for two persons who have been brought up together from infancy and lived like brother and sister to fancy, when grown up, that they love each other in a different way. I believe it is the mistake we made upon this point that has caused your misery. I saw this a good while ago, but I had many reasons for not saying so, some selfish ones doubtless, but also others for your sake. I hoped to save you from giving yourself up to a feeling that will make you miserable if you indulge it. It is so dreadful to love and not to be loved. It is so bad for a man to spend his time in sighs and tears; it does not signify so much for a woman; and if you could have loved me—I mean if I could have kept you from loving that other one I was speaking of, it would have been for your happiness. With that hope I stood between you and her till my heart was ready to break, but I can see that your suffering is greater than ever, though you struggle to hide it. This is worse than anything else. If the conscience is at rest the heart can bear its burden, however heavy it may be. But if not, strength and patience fail. Now, I will make your conscience easy—I release you from your engagement to me; your love shall be as free as air, but, if it be still possible, abstain from loving her. If that is beyond your power, then love her silently, hopelessly, but without remorse, that is, till she marries another. I can fancy that you will be much happier, at least for a while after getting this letter. I am, I assure you, after writing it. Ever, dearest Maurice, your affectionate
"Mary."

Gertrude felt considerably embarrassed and annoyed as she read this letter. She had almost forgotten till then that at one moment she had amused herself with the idea that Maurice admired her, and even now—probably because she did not wish it—she would not admit to herself that Mary alluded to her. If it were so he would be acting most strangely in asking her advice, and she determined not to allow him to suppose that she thought that possible. Her manner was cold, however, as she returned the letter to him, and said: " It is a very touching letter. I am sorry for her, and still more for you, that she had occasion to write it."

" What can I do?" he said, with his eyes fixed on the ground. " I love Mary with all the strength of my will. I would die for her, but ought I to deceive her—if even I could —and when she has read my heart, try to persuade her she is wrong?"

" Is she *right*, then?" Gertrude asked still in the same cold manner.

" There is a passion in my heart," he said between his teeth, " that is killing me by inches, that leaves me no repose either by day or by night, that is merciless like revenge and tenacious as life, that robs me of Mary and gives me nothing but despair instead. Is a man guilty for suffering? Would he choose to be wretched? Is he to be broken on the wheel, and then reproached for his agonies!" His voice quivered, and she looked up. He could not meet her eyes, but hid his face in his hands. He felt as if she would never speak to him again if he gave her too clear an insight into his heart. With the courage of despair he looked at her, and murmured: " In Italy I loved her!"

" In Italy!" she exclaimed, and then thought of the verses that she had once imagined must have been addressed to herself, and now felt greatly relieved that it was otherwise. " But, Maurice, then why renew your engagement with Mary when you returned to England, if you loved another?"

" I did not know my own feelings then. Mary is right; I have struggled with my conscience till I am almost worn out, and her letter has aggravated instead of relieving my doubts. Tell me how to act—your words shall rule my destiny."

" But I do not quite understand how the case stands," she said. " This Italian whom you love——"

" Not an Italian," he abruptly interrupted.

" Well, but her whom you loved in Italy—in what position of life is she?"

"Far, far above me."

"Too much so for the possibility of a marriage between you?"

"Who can say what is possible or impossible, in that respect?"

"True," she answered thoughtfully, "but have you any reason to think that she likes you?"

"No—only the belief that there is a love so ardent and so patient as to win back love at last."

"And when you are with Mary, the image of this person haunts you, and stands like a cloud between you and her, turning what should be happiness into grief?"

"Like the form of an angel it stands between us, but like the angel that stood at the gate of Paradise with a flaming sword in his hand."

"Could you not by a strong resolution tear this passion from your heart? Could you not drive it away by an act of your will? and is not your affection for Mary—your affianced wife—strong enough to banish that dangerous vision, till, with time, in the sunshine of home and the atmosphere of duty, it shall no longer haunt you, and shall become not a dream but the mere shadow of a dream? Count the cost of such a sacrifice, and throw into the scale its reward. Have you strength for this?"

"I have strength to shut up in my heart the secret of my misery, to hide it from every eye but Mary's, which has read into its inmost recess, to look upon the face that has been 'the bane of my life, the ruin of my glory,' and not by a glance or a sigh to betray what I suffer. All this I can do, for I have done it already; and I can stand at the altar by Mary's side, and pledge my faith to her, and never, so help me God, injure or desert her, but I dare not say—I dare not hope—that in my home and in my walks, by our bed and at our table, that same vision will not stand, then no more as a stern angel shutting up the path to happiness, but as a fiend that will tempt to sin and to despair. Can you understand such a love or such madness as this? One only favour I implore,—that you will direct my course. Do not refuse it to one whose wretchedness deserves pity at your hands!"

"It is a dreadful thing, Maurice, to love as you love, and to love hopelessly. Heaven help all those who may ever love thus! I believe Mary is right; even more right than she knows. You must not marry her. You must not place the sacred barrier of duty between yourself and the passion, which, tremendous as it is, is not yet guilty. That barrier must not be rashly exposed to so powerful a torrent. Better that it should sever you from her now than sweep you both into an abyss hereafter. I ask myself what I should do in your place? Is the object of your love worthy of such a passion? Do you respect her, Maurice, as much as you adore her?"

"I do!" he fervently exclaimed, putting his hand to his heart, as if to still its beating.

"Then," she continued, with excitement.—" then continue to love her, as Mary bids you, without remorse and without fear. Practise every virtue for the love of her, exert every talent you possess for her sake, and bide your time with as much courage as you can find in yourself. Nothing is hopeless, nothing is impossible, as you said just now. There is a strange power in a noble affection; there is a mighty strength in an unselfish devotion. Never put a voluntary obstacle between yourself and her you love; and, as I said before, Heaven help all who want help and strength!—and who do not, Maurice?"

He stood silent an instant, looking very pale and nervous, then suddenly threw himself at her feet, kissed the hem of her dress with passionate fervour, and rushed out of the conservatory. He, as he stood alone under a tree in the shrubbery, where he had taken refuge in the height of his emotion, she at the place where he had left her, were both asking themselves a similar question: had they understood or misunderstood one another? "Had she believed his evasive statement?" he said to himself, "and really thought he loved a stranger?" Did she not rather read at once the secret of his heart, and had not those exciting words she had addressed to him been the only encouragement she could venture to give to his almost explicit avowal of passionate affection? And Gertrude, who, strange as it may appear, had been deceived at first by his subterfuge, could she doubt, after the strange revelation of that scene, that she was herself the object of that wild adoration which had so long been struggled with and never subdued? And if so, what encouragement her words must have seemed to give him, and yet how could she recur to the subject and retract her advice? This harassed her a little, but at the bottom of her heart she was touched at having inspired such a feeling, and thought kindly of Maurice as of one who loved not wisely but too well. She was sorry for Mary also, but it was not perhaps in her nature to sympathise with the trials of a character so different from her own. She pitied him much—the most of the two. "Adrien," she said to herself, "would never love her in that way; he never would adore her." But one kind glance of his eye, one of those calm, earnest words of his, which implied an interest in her fate, were more precious to her than the homage and devotion of all the world besides. And that he loved her she could no longer doubt; and that evening few of the people at Audley Park doubted it either.

It might have been better for Maurice had he been there also, and seen what must have opened his eyes to the miserable delusion which he was madly cherishing since he had parted from Gertrude; but he left Audley Park immediately afterwards, and carried away with him a dangerous hope, which—traversed by many a doubt, shaken by ever renewed misgivings—was to be nursed in solitude and cherished into life. His interview with Mary on the afternoon of that day was strictly characteristic of both: he was much affected, and ill with excitement and agitation; he spoke of his affection for her, of all she had been to him, of his misery at being obliged by his conscience to acquiesce in the resolution she had formed, until he would have seemed to others, and, indeed, felt himself to be the greater sufferer of the two in the parting of that day. In truth, he could not but be aware of all he was relinquishing for the sake of a passionate dream, in all human probability never to be fulfilled; and when on his way to London, with his burning head in his hands, he analysed his feelings with an indignant impatience at his own weakness, he was in reality more to be pitied than she who—with

> "Her gentle dreamings gone forever,
> Her innocent hopes and wishes gone,—all gone;
> A rainbow imaged on a crystal river,
> Was not more frail—it shines—and now *has shone*"—

turned to her household duties, and all the gentle charities of life, without one murmur or one bitter thought. The load she had to bear in those first days of sorrow was doubtless heavy, but it had none of those sharp edges which run into the heart, and fester there.

Mr. Edwards, the amateur magnetiser, who had been at Audley Park the week before, came there again on the evening after Maurice's departure. He was introduced to Gertrude, and sat by her at dinner. He was an agreeable man, and she was much interested by all he told her about Mesmerism—that mysterious subject which can no longer be treated with ridicule, but is still as far as ever from any satisfactory solution; which baffles so many theories, opens a door as it were into another kind of existence; shows glimpses of a mode of being, an agency of the senses, and a whole order of natural laws or supernatural effects which are well calculated to confound man's reason, to humble his presumption, to alarm his scruples, and to suggest the exclamation of Hamlet, "There are more things in heaven and earth than are dreamt of in our philosophy." Mr. Edwards was, like most other people, much charmed with Gertrude; and perhaps Adrien, for the first time, felt how much he cared for her by his involuntary annoyance at the interest with which she listened to him. He had a strong instinctive dislike to Mesmerism, and avoided as much as possible talking on the subject; but could not conquer his misgivings, his repugnance to its use, his horror of its abuse,—and struggled with himself not to dislike Mr. Edwards, who certainly did not practise it with any idea that it was wrong.

When the men came out of the dining-room Mr. Edwards was surrounded by the women, who eagerly listened to his accounts, and were very anxious to know which of them he thought most likely to be susceptible of magnetic influence. He said that Gertrude was the one he fancied he could most easily mesmerise, and he asked her if she would let him try. Fanny and Harriet Apley pressed her to do so; both said it was very curious and very pleasant, that they had submitted to the experiment the week before; that they were ready to do so again; and Lady Clara exclaimed, "I am sure you will fail. Gertrude will set that firm will of hers, which I often envy, against your mesmeric influence, and baffle all your efforts." "Do sit down in that arm-chair, Miss Lifford," Mr. Edwards said, "and let me try."

Half reluctant and half persuaded. she was just complying, when Adrien entered the room. He came up instantly to her side, and said in an authoritative manner, "You must not do that, Miss Lifford." She started up immediately. and stood behind Lady Clara's chair. who was surprised at Adrien's unusual impetuosity. Mr. Edwards seemed annoyed, and turning to Mrs. Crofton, asked her in a low voice if it was Miss Lifford's brother who had thus peremptorily interrupted the essay? This question made Gertrude colour; and Adrien who was generally so calm, appeared a little disturbed, and went to join a group of men in the next room. As there was some embarrassment in consequence of this abrupt little incident, Lady Clara said, " Come, Mr. Edwards, try if you can succeed in sending me to sleep better than last week. You know I consider myself proof against your passes." He placed himself before her, and began to make the usual gestures; after a few minutes she closed her eyes, and pretended to fall asleep; then suddenly starting up with a gay laugh, shook her head triumphantly. "Come, Lady-Bird," she exclaimed, " you would not go through the ordeal, and do not merit the same honours as I do. Let us go to the music-room."

She turned round as she said this, and saw Gertrude standing immovable near the chimney—her countenance fixed, and her eyes with that vacant expression which indicates a state of natural or mesmeric somnambulism. "You have mesmerised *her!*" she exclaimed, with an uneasy feeling, for she had a sort of instinctive dread of Adrien's displeasure; and felt at once that Gertrude was dearer to him than she would have supposed a few moments before. "Undo what you have done," she hastily said; " it makes me nervous to see her in that state." Mr. Edwards attempted it, but, as it seemed, in vain, and he grew anxious himself. "I did not direct the magnetic influence directly towards her," he hurriedly exclaimed, "and I do not know how to deal with her present state. Perhaps I can make her follow me;" and he walked a few steps backwards. They anxiously watched his movements and hers. She mechanically advanced, and followed him with that painful and apparently irresistible sort of movement in which the will seems unconcerned, and the soul absent. At that moment Adrien returned towards the door of the room, having felt an unaccountable uneasiness while he stayed away. He turned pale, and his eyes flashed fire when he saw what was going on. Lady Clara, who was already very nervous, actually trembled when he said to her in a voice of inexpressible indignation,

" What have you been doing with her?"

"It was all involuntary," she said, "on her part and ours."

" It was, was it?" he exclaimed with a mixture of anxiety, of anger, and of agitation, which he could hardly control. "Mr. Edwards," he said, commanding himself with a violent effort to speak calmly, "what are you doing now? What *can* you do?"

"I can draw her on, you see—I could lead her wherever I choose;" and as he moved more rapidly she precipitately followed.

"Gertrude, Gertrude!" Adrien exclaimed in a voice of such excessive vehemence that it startled the society in the next room.

Whether she was then partly awaking from the trance, or whether his voice had power to reach her even through that sleep of the soul, so it was that at its sound she turned towards him with an uncertain but different kind of step; he met her, drew her arm in his; she clung to it instinctively, and laid her face on his shoulder. He felt an inexpressible mixture of emotion, of uneasiness, and of tenderness, saw how she was unconsciously betraying her feelings—and in that instant his mind was made up. He looked proudly and fondly upon her, and made a sign to Lady Clara to join them. They left the room together, and still supporting her he led her to her room; there before leaving her, and in Lady Clara's presence, he respectfully and tenderly kissed her hand, and then left her to the care of others. She slept a few hours, and in the morning had only a dreamlike remembrance of that scene. Lady Clara went to her early to see how she was, and explained to her what had happened. Gertrude asked if she was mistaken in fancying that Adrien had objected to her being mesmerised?

"Certainly he did, Lady-Bird, and you were as docile as possible," Lady Clara answered with a smile, "and I was kind enough to assure him in the midst of our agitation that you had not disobeyed his command. Perhaps it was out of gratitude for that submission that he kissed your hand most reverently when he consigned you to my care last night."

Gertrude coloured and said, "That, too, I remember, but exactly like a dream, and only fancied that I had had an uneasy restless night. Dearest Lady Clara, I hope I did not do anything odd when I was in that strange state."

"No, dear child, I do not think you did anything *odd*," she answered, with a kind of smile that did not satisfy Gertrude, and the tears came into her eyes.

"Tears, my Lady-Bird! What vexes you, dear Gertrude?"

"Did I say, or do, or——"

"Well, my Lady-Bird, I will tell you the truth. You showed, perhaps, a little, that you cared for Adrien d'Arberg, but I think you need not torment yourself about that, for he showed quite as plainly how much he cared for you."

The embarrassment, the nervousness, and the joy of that moment quite overcame Gertrude; she turned abruptly away and burst into tears. Lady Clara sat down by her, and held her hand while her head was still averted. "I should be glad to think you liked one another. There would be such happiness in store for you both."

"It is impossible!" Gertrude exclaimed. "How foolish I have been to let you see my weakness."

"I love you all the better for it, Lady-Bird. I always told you that Adrien d'Arberg was one of my heroes, and if you had been insensible to the interest that such a man has shown you, I really think I should have loved you no more." She kissed her affectionately, and later came to fetch her down to breakfast.

Gertrude felt keenly annoyed at the looks of curiosity that were, or that she fancied were directed upon her; but Mr. Latimer relieved her embarrassment by beginning at once to joke about the alarm they had all experienced at her trance, and asked if the enchanter had not begged her pardon yet? Mr. Edwards, upon this, approached, and sitting down at her other side, expressed his regret at what had occurred, and she gradually recovered her self-possession, though not quite her usual spirits. After breakfast, Adrien spoke to her some time; and he, too, asked her to forgive him for his interference the night before.

"It was more than I could endure," he said, "to see you thus playing with edged tools. If you had held a glass of poison in your hand, I should have hardly felt more compelled to snatch it from you."

"I feel too nervous to speak much about it," she said; "but I hope you know that it was not wilfully that I disregarded your warning. By the way," she added with a smile, "our acquaintance began with a warning."

"It is not perhaps the last I shall give you, Lady-Bird, if you receive them so well."

She felt that there was more in those words than met the ear. She ceased to care for what others had thought or seen —he was not displeased with her; that was enough. All that day and the next, his manner to her was too devoted to leave any doubt in her mind, or in that of others, that he liked her; but there was in it at the same time a reserve, a diffidence, that banished all idea that he had drawn encouragement from the involuntary expression of her feelings which he and others had witnessed.

A few days later the carriage was sent to fetch her home. A letter from her father had arrived that morning, stating that Edgar had met with a serious, though not alarming accident.

His horse had stumbled, and fallen with him, as he was making an excursion in the neighbourhood of Seville. Though he was doing well, the process of recovery would be likely to prove tedious, and as he was himself obliged to return to England for unavoidable business before his son could travel, he earnestly requested Father Lifford to set off immediately for Spain, to take charge of him during his absence, and at the same time to superintend those affairs which he had put in train, but which required the presence of some member of the family to carry them on. This letter had much agitated Mrs. Lifford; her anxiety about her son overcame her regret at the Father's departure; but the absence of such a friend in her state of health, and under all the circumstances, was trying in the extreme, and she felt alarmed at the idea that her husband and her daughter would be thrown together on their own resources, without the safeguard of his rough but genuine kindness. She felt very miserable, but never doubted that he must go, and she sent for Gertrude to come and take leave of him. Some time ago it would have been little sorrow to her to part with him; but during the last year she had learned to appreciate his excellence; and her affection for him now was as great as her respect. Like her mother, she trembled at the idea of finding herself alone with her father, and she had hardly been aware how much she had looked to Father Lifford's guidance and support, in the future which was vaguely sketched out in her imagination. He had written her a short note, and she sat with it in her hand, absorbed in these thoughts, when Lady Roslyn, who was the only person in the drawing-room with her, asked her kindly if she had received bad news. She roused herself, and answered "That her brother had met with an accident in Spain, but not a dangerous one, and that, in consequence, her uncle Lifford was about to leave England to join him, and that she must instantly go home to wish him good-bye."

"But you will come back?"

"No," Gertrude answered decidedly, "no, not at present, and a long 'at present' it must be; I cannot leave my mother during Father Lifford's absence. Do you know where Lady Clara is?"

"Look for her in the morning-room. She was there just now."

Lady Roslyn knew that Lady Clara was walking in the garden gathering some roses, and that Adrien was writing a letter in the room she had pointed out, and it amused her to bring about an interview which she fancied might be a decisive one. More than any one else she had watched the course of that "true love," and it pleased her fancy just then to remove a pebble from its course. When Adrien raised his head from his writing, and saw Gertrude looking into the room, he started up and went to her. "Come in here a moment, will you?" he said to her with some emotion in his voice. She did so, and gave him Father Lifford's note. He read it twice over, and then said: "I am very glad that your father is coming back so soon."

"Are you?" she answered in a dejected manner. "You are not?" he said in a tone of inquiry. She made no answer at first, but fixed her eyes on the ground. In an instant she murmured in a low voice: "I am very sorry to part with Father Lifford." "Partings are sad things," he said, and seemed to read again the note he held, as if to gain time and prevent her moving. "Gertrude!" he began at last, and sat down by her side while she trembled visibly, "Gertrude, as soon as your father returns, I shall ask to see him, and then my fate will be in his hands and in yours." She turned as pale as death. There was at once too much joy and too much fear in her heart. It made her shudder to hear of her fate left in her father's hands,—but she did not venture to express this feeling, and made no answer. He became uneasy at her paleness and her silence.

"Gertrude," he exclaimed, "have I been wrong? Have I hoped too much?"

She raised her eyes slowly to his. Those eyes which spoke more than the most eloquent tongue.

"How could you," she faintly said, "be wrong? Oh Adrien d'Arberg, do you indeed love me?"

"Dearly—tenderly—devotedly," he murmured, and pressed her hand to his lips.

"Then," she exclaimed, with a mixture of excitement and of emotion, "then life has no greater happiness to give. Adrien. I do not deserve to be your wife. I wish I might die now. Is it not enough for me to have heard you say what you did just now? I *have* been happy. Adrien,—my soul is satisfied,—I dare not hope much for the future."

"Is this misgiving, dearest, a nervous fancy, or do you foresee obstacles to my wishes?"

"No, no,—why should there be obstacles? There ought not to be.'

"I think that in a worldly point of view they are not likely to arise. That with regard to what you and I should neither think of nor care about, I may be able to satisfy your father. Gertrude, dearest Gertrude, you do not look happy. Tell me what you feel, and what you fear."

"I don't know what I feel; I don't know what I fear, except that I feel that I love you, and that I fear to part with you—more than I ought to do or at least to *say*." she added, with a tone of such inexpressible tenderness, tinged with that nervous anxiety which she could not repress, that Adrien was deeply affected. She saw it and exclaimed, "There are tears in your eyes, Adrien! Are you sorry for me that I love you so much? Do you pity me in your heart? Well you may, if this is only to be a dream of happiness. If you were not what you are, I should be ashamed of having been so easily won; but I am not ashamed.—I am proud of loving you, proud that your eyes are looking kindly upon me, proud of being something to you, who are everything to me. Heaven forgive me if I love you too much!"

Adrien seized her hands and pressed them fervently to his lips. She did not draw them away, but turned her eyes towards the sky, and for an instant scarcely seemed to hear him, while he spoke to her of his love in words which nevertheless vibrated in her heart, but which she listened to in silence, as if "the harps of the skies had rung, and the airs of Heaven played round his tongue." Never had he thought her so beautiful, never had he felt so strong, so absorbing, so painful an interest in any human being. Perhaps in that instant a doubt, faint as the shadow of a cloud on a lake, passed through his mind, —a doubt of her being the woman whom he had once pictured to himself as the ideal of her sex, as the model of a wife; and the remembrance of Ida's calm and serene face rose for an instant before him. But it was not disenchantment, or coldness, or regret that he felt; on the contrary, having loved her enough to assume the responsibility of her destiny, touched to the heart by her tenderness, transported by her beauty, he looked upon her as from that hour his own, his treasure, his precious and fearful charge.

The very strangeness of her character endeared her to

him; and there was something of respect as well as of gentleness in his mode of addressing her. He instinctively felt that in such a nature there were great lurking virtues, and deep unknown dangers; whether he had done well and wisely for his own happiness in winning that heart of fire, and in gaining such mastery over that wayward spirit, he did not ask himself. His own happiness was always the last of his thoughts; a new duty was in his life and a new object in his hopes.

"I must go," she said, "and vanquish this foolish feeling of dread for the future."

"You must indeed," he said, "you must *trust*, my Gertrude; you must learn the full meaning of that beautiful English word."

"I trust you," she said. "If you deceived me I should never trust anything again on earth or in ———" she stopped short, and did not end her sentence.

"May I," he asked, "spend another Sunday at Lifford Grange and see your mother once more? After that I would go to Ireland, and return by the time your father arrived."

"Yes, oh yes, another Sunday. Another little life of eight hours. Now I must go; I see Lady Clara is in the garden."

When Lady Clara met her she was struck by her paleness and nervousness, but which the note she showed her sufficiently accounted for, and at that moment she did not suspect any other cause of that emotion; but after she was gone Adrien told her what had passed between them, and that he intended to propose for her when Mr. Lifford returned to England. She took the greatest interest in the subject, and made him promise to write to her to Paris, where she was going to spend the winter, to acquaint her with the result. "Not that I feel any doubt about it," she said; "a name and a fortune, such as yours, are not likely to be refused by the most fanciful father in the world. But I shall be curious to hear how you are received, when you 'beard the lion in his den, the Lifford in his hall.' I am quite jealous of your having seen Lady-Bird's mother, though now I have no right to be so. Is she like her?"

"Fancy Lady Bird—as I fervently hope you may never see her—with all the colour washed out of her cheeks, the fire extinguished in her eyes, but not the tenderness and the beauty; like the shadow of herself; like the rose after, not a shower but a storm, its bloom and its life almost fled—all but its sweetness: so she seemed to me."

"How I should like to see her! I spoke to Lady-Bird about it, but she was not encouraging."

"Dear Lady Clara, there are many drooping flowers in the world that you can revive by your presence, but this one is trembling on its stem, and even a breath might be fatal."

"But I would breathe so gently?"

"Do not try experiments, especially where you know not how sore memory may be."

"I think I might do good."

He smiled and said, "Our old dispute, more anxious to do good than afraid of doing harm."

"Yes, I adhere to my opinion.—By the way *have* I spoiled Lady-Bird as you predicted? Is she not more charming than ever?"

"Quite charming enough, Heaven knows! What is there about that girl that enchants one so much? I feel it too much to define it."

"O she is Lady-Bird, that is all I know.—she is the most high bred of untamed creatures,—the most gently wild, the most femininely bold, the most innocently mischievous of human beings. What a bird to have caught M. d'Arberg! What a prize to have found under a tree in the park——"

At that moment, Mrs. Crofton and Mr. Latimer joined them, and scolding in his usual manner, he exclaimed, "Why have you let Lady-Bird go? I can't do without her. What do you mean by letting her go?"

"It is like the story of the House that Jack built," Lady Clara answered. "She must go to her mother, whose uncle is going to Spain, whose nephew has broken his leg, whose father is coming home——"

"What, what's all that? Who has broken his leg?"

"Lady-Bird's brother, the heir of all the Liffords."

"Confound the boy! he is *always* breaking his leg."

Lady Clara and Adrien laughed, but Mr. Latimer was really cross, and walked away repeating: "It is quite true—she is always going away; they never keep a pleasant person here two days together. Those Miss Apleys, I dare say, will stay us all out." Mrs. Crofton smiled as she looked at him with her spying-glass, and cried,

> "O blest with temper whose unclouded ray
> Still makes to-morrow cheerful as to-day."

CHAPTER XVI.

> "Ours was love indeed,
> No childish day-dream, but a life intense
> Within our hearts; we spoke not of our love,
> But in our mutual silence it was felt,—
> In the intense absorbing happiness
> Of mutual long, long looks, as if our souls
> Held sweet communion through our passionate eyes."
>
> And is he gone? On sudden solitude
> How oft that fearful question will intrude!
> 'Twas but an instant passed! and here he stood,
> And now!—Without the portal's porch she rushed;
> And then her tears at length in freedom gushed,
> Big, bright, and fast, unknown to her they fell,
> But still her lips refused to say 'Farewell.'
> For in that word, that fatal word, howe'er
> We promise, hope, believe, there breathes despair."
>
> BYRON.

GERTRUDE arrived in time to take leave of Father Lifford, and had a long conversation with him before he went. In the evening she took her work, and sat down by the sofa where her mother was dozing; it had been a great emotion to her to part with her best and only friend, and as she slept Gertrude could see by her swollen eyelids that she had been weeping. She longed for her to wake, for she had that to tell her that would make her weep again, perhaps, but from a different feeling. Her own heart was fluttering with happiness; the sort of nervous misgiving which had troubled her joy, at the moment of the realisation of her hopes, had passed away. Her confidence in the future was now as great as her diffidence had been. She thought of herself as Adrien's wife. She wrote on a paper, in her work-box, the signature that would be one day hers. "Gertrude d'Arberg," and then tore up the paper hastily, as if she had been doing something wrong. Instead of going on with the lily she was embroidering, she worked Adrien's name on her canvass, and then unpicked it. She pictured to herself his chateau in Brittany; her arrival in the "plaisant pays de France;" the share she would take in all his labours of love and of genius. There were no heights of virtue, no intellectual improvement which her imagination did not aim at and compass in anticipation.

Her mother murmured in her sleep, and then awoke with a frightened look. "Gertrude, is it you, my child? I have had a painful dream, and am glad to be awake. It was only a dream. How pleasant it is to find thee there by my side. Hast thou been there long?"

"For an hour, I think, dearest, but it has seemed like a minute. My waking dreams have been sweeter than your sleeping ones. Shall I tell you, mamma, what they have been about?"

"Yes—put thyself here, close to me, with thy face near to mine, that I may look at thee while thou speakest. What hast thou been dreaming of?"

"Happiness—happiness!—immense, deep, and wide as the mind can reach to, and the heart contain. He loves me, madre mia,—he loves me! Is not that the greatest bliss that earth can give?"

Mrs. Lifford clasped her hands, and pressed them on her eyes. Gertrude saw the quivering of her mother's mouth, and threw herself into her arms. She felt her heart throb against her own; and then throwing back her head, and seating herself on the edge of the couch, she said, "Now don't weep, mamma, but smile and wish me joy."

"I am glad he loves thee—glad of that, anyhow, and I hope, O fervently I hope, that thy father will let thee marry him."

A resolute and singular expression passed over Gertrude's countenance as she said, "On that point my mind is made up. I am almost of age, and my father's will shall not stand between me and virtue, happiness, and peace of mind. Adrien possesses every one of the worldly advantages which my father cares about, and which I only value, as belonging to him, who ennobles everything that even remotely appertains to him. Should my father, without the shadow of a reason or excuse, refuse his consent, nothing on earth will ever persuade me that conscience requires the moral suicide which would be imposed upon me. I would as soon throw myself into the river at his will, as give him up to whom my soul is bound by ties which never can be severed. But it is impossible that he can refuse his consent, unless he hates me with an unnatural hatred, and that I will not and cannot believe, till I see it."

"Be calm, Gertrude. Be calm. I implore thee."

"I am perfectly calm, dearest, because my mind is made up. I am my father's daughter in one respect, and have a will that may break but which will not bend."

"But he may break it," Mrs. Lifford murmured in a tone of anguish. "He may break both will and heart."

"No, both are beyond his reach. There are no lettres-de-cachet in this age and country, thank Heaven! Mamma, do not look so frightened. I am calm and happy. The future is bright, plain and clear before me; like to the sky at this moment. See, the clouds have rolled away, and in front of us there is nothing but the pure soft blue expanse, with the first stars glimmering here and there in their beauty,—

W   'The pale stars watching to behold the might of earthly love,'

as one of my favourite poems has it."

"Did you speak about this to Father Lifford, Gertrude?"

"I did, mamma; we talked about it a long time. He would not commit himself, or seem to approve of it till he knew whether my father would consent, but I could see that he wished that it should be so,—I am sure he does. How could it be otherwise? He is good, and he admires goodness. He is kind, and he has seen me suffer. He knows me better than any one else in the world, and he must feel that everything is at stake for me at this crisis in my life. Happiness and virtue on the one side—on the other, nothing short of despair."

"Gertrude, Gertrude, did he not reason with thee?"

"Yes; and I reasoned with him. He said it would be my duty to submit to my father, whatever his will might be in this matter; and I then asked him solemnly, not as my uncle—not as Mr. Lifford—but as a priest, and in confession, whether it would be a sin, in a case like this, where not a word could be said against him I love, even by worldly wisdom, when nothing but arbitrary caprice could withhold consent,—whether it would be a sin, after patient entreaties and humble remonstrances had been tried, and tried in vain, to act as the law would permit, and marry without that consent? He said it would be undutiful; but then I pressed him again to say, if no length of time, if no circumstances of character, no peculiarities of position would ever give a sanction to such a course? He said that would be a question for consideration when the time arrived,—I saw he could not pronounce against it,—I saw that in his mind there was a doubt, and that was enough for me. I feel strong against the future,—strong in my confidence,—strong in my resolution. The waves of life may toss me yet to and fro, but my anchor is cast, and my helm is pointed."

"Gertrude, dearest, my feeble reasonings I will not urge

upon thee. Indeed I know not what I could, or ought to say. Pray for thee I will ardently, unceasingly. Thou hast compared thyself to a ship, dear child. Shall I tell thee what I think? Thou art going too fast before the wind. The sails of thy bark are too boldly unfurled."

"My anchor is cast, I cannot drift away."

"O Gertrude, my child! Chains have snapped ere now. Trust in none but God."

"I trust in Adrien, as I trust in God."

"That is what I fear. Thou hast made him an idol."

"And a noble worship it is."

"Tremble, Gertrude!—tremble at what thou sayest, or I must tremble for thee, and for him thou so much lovest."

"Yes, mother mine," Gertrude exclaimed, falling on her knees, and throwing her arms around her neck. "Yes, I tremble for myself, but I will hide me in thy bosom; on that breast which has suffered so much, which has endured so nobly, I will lay my throbbing head. Plead for me, mother, with Him whom thou hast loved and served from thy youth up. Call down His blessing on thy wayward child. Ask for her all she dares not ask for herself. I once read of a sinful woman who, when frightened by a thunder-storm, made an innocent child lie over her, to shield her from the lightning.* So mother mine, I would place you and your sufferings and your patience between me and the punishment that my undisciplined heart deserves. There is but one that it fears, to lose Adrien; and that would indeed be greater than it could bear."

The following Sunday was the happiest day that Gertrude had yet known. Adrien's presence imparted to her a sense of security in her present happiness, and of calm anticipation of the future which she had not yet experienced. He had a long interview with her mother, in which he unfolded to her his feelings, his hopes, and his projects. As much as was possible he imparted to her the conditions of fortune and of family which he would have to submit to her husband; and looked in her eyes for the approval he solicited. She held out her hand to him, and in a few words of heartfelt emotion told him that to confide Gertrude to his love and care, to see her his wife, would be the dearest of her wishes, the greatest source of joy to her during the time she might yet live, and at the moment of death.

* Madame de Montespan.

"Yes," she said, still holding his hand, "you must think of my words, if I should die without seeing you again. You must remember that a mother has trusted you, more than she ought perhaps, but not more than you deserve. I have let you come here to-day. God only knows if I have acted rightly; but I know you, and if I have done imprudently you will not make me repent of it. Never at any time, never under any circumstances, will you belie what I now read in your eyes, what the pressure of your hand confirms; her happiness, but above all her virtue, her honour will be safe in your keeping. Even to your own loss, to your own bitter grief if needs be, you will never tempt her to offend her God, or to swerve from duty. She loves you too much perhaps for her own peace of mind; but it must be safe to love you, such an affection will not mislead her. You understand all I would but cannot say. My tongue falters, but your tears reply."

"I carried her once in my arms," he answered, "pale and motionless as death, and looked upon her with respect and admiration. That day I began to love her, and I have loved her more and more ever since. To protect and to cherish her through life and till death is my hope and my prayer. If her father refuse to give her to me, I will wait, and watch, and pray for her at a distance; and if ever I tempt her to aught approaching to a sin, may the blessing you now give me turn into the curse I shall merit."

She pressed his hand, and drawing from her finger a small ring which bore the image of a cross, she put it upon his, and once more fervently blessed him.

"You will plead for me with your husband the next time I come?"

Tears came into her eyes. "I will pray to God," she answered; "*He* will hear me." Adrien sighed deeply. Mr. Lifford's character was rising before him every moment more clearly. In his wife's meekness, in his daughter's impetuosity, in his uncle's silence, it stood revealed. No one had said he was hard, but all shrunk from his name.

Adrien and Gertrude, on that October afternoon, sat together in that solemn garden by the deep still stream, opposite to the chapel where they had knelt together, and to the room where her mother had blessed him. The silence of Nature in its decaying beauty, the withered leaves falling near them, or trembling on the boughs, would have beseemed a scene of sorrow more than one of such intense happiness. It was a strange visitant in the old silent garden, that joy which filled their hearts, and which beamed in their eyes. The stone bench on which they sat, the straight alley through which they walked, the cold statues near which they stood, seemed to wonder at the sight. There was a pale, sickly-looking rose-tree near the bench where they rested; he gathered some of the flowers. and said,

"This is the same species which grows in brilliant masses in the court of our Norman château."

"Ay," she said, "flowers and people are modified when transplanted."

"You would like that old place, I think, though it is very unlike Audley Park——"

"And Lifford Grange?"

"And Lifford Grange also. Picture to yourself four grey turrets overgrown with ivy; a portal covered with wallflowers and blue larkspurs, a paved court with a well, and a seat which the moss has invaded; the rose-trees I was speaking of clustering up to the windows, and a flight of stone steps outside the wall on one side. But you must not judge it hastily."

"Do I ever judge thus, M. d'Arberg? One rash judgment I made near the grotto of Woodlands, but I have not repented of it."

"Well, only be as indulgent to the old castle as to its owner, and I shall be satisfied; live in it, and by degrees I think you will love it. Its picturesque exterior, its wild flowers in every crevice, its magnificent view over oceans of cornfields, and forests of fruit-trees, its sunny little terrace where lizards run in and out of the low grey wall, and the Norman church, half way between it and the village,—my brother, and his wife, and the old curé, who always used at every visit to exhort me to marry, how happy they will be when I take home to them my English bride. The children, too, I sent them a message in my last letter to Henri. I reminded them of a hunt we had last year for their favourite Lady-Birds, and said that if they were good I would try to bring them an English 'oiseau du bon Dieu,' more beautiful than the little living toys they were so fond of then. Gertrude, my own Gertrude, am I wrong to talk with such confidence of the future—to draw such pictures of happiness, till that happiness is actually mine? If your father were not to consent to our marriage, how I should reproach myself for having dared to speak to you of my love as I have done, at the selfish joy it has been to hear from your lips that you love me. Gertrude, I sometimes reproach myself very much for having——"

"Made me happy," she said, with one of her own smiles. "Adrien, I am afraid you are too good."

"If you have no other fear than *that*, petit oiseau du bon Dieu——"

"It is a great fear," she answered seriously, "but not my only one I think it is very likely my father will refuse his consent to our marriage."

"Gertrude, you speak with a strange calmness. You do not really mean that you expect this? on what grounds do you suppose that he will object to it?—have you any reason to imagine that he has other views for you?"

"No, not the slightest; but it has ever been his practice to oppose my wishes on every subject, and why should he act differently on this occasion? O Adrien, you do not know my father."

A cloud passed over d'Arberg's face, and he sighed deeply She waited anxiously for the next words he would utter.

"If indeed he does not love you," he exclaimed, "which I can hardly conceive, will he not the less object to your marrying a foreigner? If he does not value the treasure he possesses, will he refuse to bestow it upon me? But you are right, we cannot foresee the nature of the obstacles he may oppose to our wishes and our prayers. We cannot reckon upon the future,—I have been too sanguine. O Gertrude, how could I bear to lose you now?"

"O yes, you would bear it," she exclaimed, "you are not weak against suffering. You walk the earth with a charmed life, and despair never showed its wild visage in your path."

There was a mixture of tenderness and of irritation in her manner that he scarcely understood. She dared not speak the words that were trembling on her lips, and break through the barrier that he seemed to regard as sacred. If he had guessed her thoughts he might have soothed her feelings, not by tempting her to defy her father's authority, but by assurances of his unalterable fidelity to her, as long as she remained unshackled by other ties; but the necessity of such protestations did not occur to him, and perhaps he felt also some scruples, all the stronger since his conversation with her mother, in binding her more stringently to himself, before her father's will was ascertained. He knew she loved him, but not how fearfully strong was the passion which was lying in her heart, smoothed at present into repose by hope and by his presence. It was not feebly that he loved her, it was not coldly that he contemplated the probability of losing her. She had become to him inexpressibly dear, and to have given her up would almost have broken his heart, but he thought more of her than of himself; his own happiness was a secondary consideration: but it was that very unselfishness, that very unconsciousness of the unbounded affection he had inspired, that made him abstain from speaking the words which she was passionately anxious to hear; and deep and fervent as was his love, there was that in him which kept down with a strong hand the vehemence of the flame. His heart might break, but the breaker would be one whom he loved more than the object of an earthly passion, and at whose hands he would accept the keenest blow life could inflict.

It was but a transient cloud, however, that passed over that day's joy. Again they returned to their projects. He could not believe in tyranny or unkindness—she could not now believe in existence without him, and again they talked together of the future. Normandy would be their holiday; every year they would go there; but his large estate in one of the most distressed parts of Ireland, which he had inherited from his mother, would be their post and their work, their interest and their duty. Together they would toil—together one day reap on earth or in Heaven. Then he would take her to Paris—that city of great crimes and great virtues—that strange battle-field of life with its armies in presence; the worst of Satan's crew, and God's elect soldiers. They talked of various parts of the world which thence they might visit together. He spoke of Italy, also, but with less enthusiasm than Maurice had done. Rome he deeply loved; but the luxurious charms of the Mediterranean shores, the enervating nature of its brilliant climate, the versatile character of its people, was not to him as attractive as it had been to the young artist's somewhat congenial disposition.

They wandered together through every alley of the garden, and into the park till late that afternoon. Adrien liked the old Grange. He had been there but twice, and had been very happy in its quiet and solemn rooms, its stately formal gardens. He had gathered there the flower which had charmed his fancy. He had found there the woman who had touched his heart. It had, also, a *prestige* in his eyes from its historical associations, and Gertrude had never told him how she hated it; indeed, she did not feel to hate it then; perhaps one day she might have loved it. The hours went by, and Adrien was to go. They stood together on the stone steps of the entrance-door. "In about six weeks," he said, "I shall return from Ireland, and your father will be at home. Then, dearest Lady-Bird, I shall be here again. I shall see you; for whatever be his decision he cannot refuse me the permission to see you once more. It may be a most painful hour for us both, but meet again we must, so this is no farewell. I go with a heart full of hope in the future, full of trust in you. I might have written this very day to your father, and awaited his answer at a distance; but I think my words may plead more effectually than a letter. The chief objection he would make to our marriage would probably be the country of my birth; and when he hears me speak your language that prejudice might vanish; and then again, should he refuse his consent, he might forbid my coming here, but if I am here he cannot deny me that parting interview which would be necessary to my peace and to yours."

"You are right, you are quite right," she hurriedly exclaimed; "remember, Adrien, these *must* not be the last words that we speak to each other. There is that in my heart which must not be trifled with."—— She put her hand on her forehead, and pressed her temples tightly. He looked at her anxiously, kissed her hand, and went away.

For a fortnight Gertrude saw no one but her mother, whose strength was every day diminishing. She began to feel very uneasy about her, and nursed her now with devoted tenderness. The doctor and Mr. Irving, the priest of Stone houseleigh, who often visited them, did not reassure her. There was no immediate danger, but her state was very precarious, they said, and all agitation must be carefully avoided. Mary Grey about that time came one day to see her. This painfully recalled to her mind what she had almost forgotten, —the conversation, or rather the scene with Maurice in the conservatory at Audley Park. She looked half-anxiously, half-curiously at Mary to see if she could read in her face any expression indicating a knowledge of what had passed; but could not satisfy herself on that point. Mary looked pale and thin, but not unhappy. Gertrude inquired after Maurice, and she answered quietly that he was better in health, and had a professional engagement in London that kept him there almost entirely, and answered very well.

"He is anxious that my mother and I should establish ourselves in town, and at his age it is such an object that he should have a home, that we are thinking of doing so."

"What, leave the cottage and Stonehouseleigh!"

Mary's lips quivered, but she said cheerfully, "Yes, it will be an effort; but as my mother is willing to make it for her son, it is clearly right I should not object."

She did not usually call Maurice her mother's son; and Gertrude understood that her doing so now was meant to convey to her that this change of plans had nothing to do with any project of marriage. The recollection of her own last interview with him made her shy with Mary: she could not but feel that kind and friendly as her manner was, she must consider her as a person who had done her an injury, however involuntary that injury might have been; and her conscience did not altogether acquit her in that respect, when it brought to her recollection the many occasions in which she might have checked, instead of encouraged, the kind of romantic homage which, since his return from Italy, he had been in the habit of paying her. This consciousness gave an appearance of constraint to her manner, and she was more grave and silent than usual.

"Is it soon that you will move?" she asked.

"The time is not yet fixed," Mary replied, "but it will not be for some weeks at all events: not till the lease of the cottage is up."

"I am sure this is a great trial to you."

"A *great* trial, dear Miss Lifford! No, indeed; if any, a very little one. I should be more sorry to think that Maurice wanted us, and that we could not be with him. When he marries, we may, perhaps, return to Stonehouseleigh."

She had said this last phrase with a steady voice, but she could not help the colour rising a little in her cheek. She was afraid that Gertrude would ask for an explanation. But the latter only kissed her, and said, "Mary, would that I were as good as you. The next time I sit near the wishing-well, *that* shall be my wish."

"A niggardly one, indeed. But tell me, dear Miss Lifford, is it true that your faithful Jane leaves you. I was so sorry to hear it, for a friend of that kind who has been with you so many years, and is so very much attached to you, must be a loss."

"It is indeed a great loss; but she is going to be married, and must settle in London with her husband. Her parents will live near them also. and I hope she will be comfortable; but I shall miss her sadly. She is one of the few persons in the world who cares for me, and I think everybody is leaving me. Father Lifford is gone, and mamma——" She turned away for an instant, and then said quickly: "But I will not talk sadly. There may be great happiness in store for us all. I think I am growing very sensible, Mary. I dare say you think it is high time I should. So do I."

"Now, you are Lady-Bird again," Mary said, with a smile; "I hardly know you again when you have not your old frowns nor your old smiles."

"I have learnt and unlearnt a great deal lately—'*mais chassez le naturel il revient au galop,*' and the sight of your dear little demure face provokes me, I believe, to talk nonsense again."

They conversed together for some time in that strain, and then parted as good friends as they had ever been in their lives.

CHAPTER XVII.

> "All day within the dreamy house
>   The doors upon their hinges creaked,
> The blue fly sung i' the pane; the mouse
>   Behind the mouldering wainscoat shrieked,
> Or from the crevice peer'd about.
>   Old faces glimmer'd through the doors,
>   Old footsteps trod the upper floors,
> Old voices called her from without.
> She only said 'My life is dreary;
>   He cometh not,' she said;
> She said, 'I am aweary, aweary,
>   I would that I were dead.'"
>
> TENNYSON.

AT the end of about three weeks, Gertrude's father returned. She could not see him again without emotion; not, alas! that she felt the least affection for him, but that she connected his arrival with so much that was important to her, that the first sight of his face was a kind of signal to her of the consequences that were to follow, and her heart beat when she went to meet him on the stairs. He received her as graciously as he ever did, and that is not saying much. There was neither pleasure nor displeasure in his face. " How do you do, Gertrude; is your mother pretty well to-day?" was his salutation. And when they met at dinner, the conversation between them was as civil and as proper as possible. He looked at her once or twice more attentively than usual. It did not seem to escape him that she was more beautiful than ever; that since she had been at Audley Park, she dressed more becomingly than she used to do, and that her manner, while it was as graceful as usual, had more *aplomb*.

A day or two after his arrival, he made her for the first time a present. It was a diamond necklace in a case, on which the arms of the family were engraved. She thanked him, but neither did his manner of giving it, or the nature of the gift afford her any particular pleasure. Her mother was so feeble now that she did not venture to speak to her often of the subject nearest to her heart, for she perceived that it always called up a flush in her cheek, and a look of too much excitement in her eyes. Mrs. Lifford was agitated by the doubt whether she would be furthering or hindering the object of her most intense wishes by mentioning it to her husband. Her natural timidity inclined her to silence; but her anxiety about Gertrude made the suspense painfully trying. The time of Adrien's return was approaching. Twice she had forced herself to speak of his visits to Lifford Grange, and to say that she had seen him. The first time she did so her husband made no comment on the subject; but on the next occasion, he observed in a sneering tone, " I thought you were never well enough to receive strangers. I am glad you are so much stronger; or, perhaps your curiosity to see this French author was irresistible!"

" He is a man of very good family," the poor woman murmured faintly, with her fearfully bright eyes fixed on his countenance, or rather face; for countenance he had none, except when unusually excited.

" Indeed!" he ejaculated, lifting up his eyebrows, in a manner that implied neither assent nor dissent.

" Yes," she persisted, " your uncle says the d'Arbergs were a very old German family. His father was naturalized in France."

He got up and walked to the window. She felt that the opportunity of speaking was lost, and yet how difficult again to recur to the subject. Then she also feared that if he were averse to Adrien's proposals he would refuse to see him when he came, and she could not believe that even Mr. Lifford could be wholly insensible to the influence of his manner, and of his words. Once she said something vague about Gertrude's future destiny. He briefly answered, "When the time comes for a decision, I shall inform you of my views upon that point." Gertrude, meanwhile, passed the days by her mother's bed, for she seldom left it now; and during those silent hours of watching, one only thought incessantly occupied her. She looked alternately from that dying form to the Duke of Gandia's picture. It was so strikingly like Adrien, that she forgot it was not really his portrait. These two images filled her mind; they were connected together in her heart; fear and hope, the past and the future, were blended in those long meditations. Day followed day, Mrs. Lifford spoke less, but looked with more intense affection at her child. Six weeks had elapsed, and there was in her face each time that Gertrude entered her room a mute inquiry, to which no answer was returned but a forced and painful smile, and nothing changed around them.

It was getting late in November; and no one had been at Lifford Grange,—not a single letter had been received by Gertrude or her mother, except one or two from Father Lifford and from Edgar. They were still detained in Spain by protracted business, but Edgar was quite recovered. Once Gertrude had heard the sound of wheels in the avenue. Her mother was asleep with her hand locked in hers, after a night and day of suffering and unrest. It was towards dusk; she did not venture to disturb her, though every nerve was trembling with excitement, and she feared that the beating of her heart must awaken her, so loud did it appear to herself. After a little less than an hour the same sound was heard, and Mrs. Lifford moved, and murmured something in her sleep. Gertrude disengaged her hand, and walked softly to the window. She drew the curtain, and looked out. It was a cold clear night. The moon was shining amongst the trees; she saw a carriage passing. A faint feeling came over her, and yet she could almost have smiled at her own folly. Solitary as was the life at Lifford Grange, it was not, however, such a very unusual event that a carriage should come to its door. The doctor, the priest, the clergyman, the agent, occasionally drove up to it. At dinner, she asked her father if Dr. Redington had called upon him that afternoon.

"Why?" he asked, "has he not been to your mother to-day?"

"Yes, this morning, but as I heard a carriage in the park two hours ago, I thought he might have come a second time.

"Not that I know of," was the answer.

Jane was gone, and she had a foreign maid who had only been with her a few days; it was of no use to ask her. Late that evening, as she was going to bed, she met on the stairs an old butler who had been a long time in the family.

With a trembling voice she inquired who had come to the house in a carriage, that afternoon. "I don't know, Miss," was his answer, "I took up a card to Mr. Lifford, and I showed the gentleman up, but I did not see the name." Gertrude turned very pale, and leant against the banister.

"Did he stay long, Marston?" she asked in a faint voice.

"Some time, Miss."

With cheeks that burned like hot coals with shame and pride, she asked, "Was this gentleman tall and dark?"

The old man looked at her with surprise. "I did not observe particularly, but I think the gentleman was tall."

She darted away, and went into the library—her old haunt. She put her candlestick on the chimney-piece, and walked up and down the room with hurried steps. She could not rest; she could not enter her mother's room,—she could not breathe in this state of suspense. It was like a nightmare. She heard her father's voice on the stairs giving some orders to the servants, and then the noise of the door of his study, as he closed it. With a feverish courage she snatched her candle, and went down stairs; she paused a minute before the door, and then with a desperate effort knocked.

Her father was standing with his back to the fire, and his eyes fixed on the ground. He said "Come in," but gave a start when he saw his daughter standing before him, and looked at her with astonishment. "Forgive me," she said, "for interrupting you; and still more, forgive me for asking what it concerns my peace to know. It must seem very strange to you; but by my mother's sick bed I must be calm, and therefore forgive me if I ask who called upon you to-day?" She joined together her hands, and clasped them tightly—her eyes were fixed on the ground. She did not see that her father's face flushed in that moment. He took a card from the chimney, and threw it on the table before her. She saw a name that was not Adrien's, and all her courage vanished. She knew not exactly what she had hoped or feared. She felt at once relieved and disappointed and unable to utter another word, but murmured something unintelligible, and left the room.

The next day came, and the next, each like the last, except that both the mother's and the daughter's cheeks grew paler, though with a different paleness; that the mother's mute inquiries were accompanied with dejection, and the daughter's smiles—when she smiled—were painful to behold. Another month passed by, and Adrien had neither come nor written. That he was ill was possible; that he was *dead* was possible, too, Gertrude felt with a pang of terror,—for how would the news reach her in that living tomb where she was languishing? She sent for Mary, and asked her, in the course of conversation, if she had heard anything from Maurice of M. d'Arberg. She had not; and there the question dropped.

"Maurice," she said a moment after,—"Maurice would have been sure to tell you if anything had happened to M. d'Arberg."

Mary started. "Happened to him! Have you heard that anything has?"

Gertrude forced a smile, and said. "I dreamed the other day that he was dead. For the curiosity of the thing, write and ask Maurice if he knows anything of him."

Mary did so. The answer did not come quickly; such answers never do. but several days after, she showed Gertrude the letter she had received. It contained these words: "I have not heard from M. d'Arberg for some time; but he is certainly not dead, for a letter I had from Paris a week ago, speaks of his being there, and in such a frame of mind that I have little doubt my old prophecy will come true, and that he will end by becoming a priest." Gertrude's heart died within her; but her spirit soon rose with indignation. "God will not accept a traitor's devotion," she inwardly exclaimed, "nor the Church receive the vows of a heartless deceiver." But with that burst of passion, her fears subsided. It could not be; she had wronged him by the doubt. Forsake her without a word —it was impossible!—it was monstrous! She went home and when her mother took her hand and pressed it to her lips, she whispered, "He is at Paris; affairs may have obliged him to go there from Ireland. It is strange; but hope is strong in my heart. *Madre mia*, did you not say after seeing him, 'I would trust him, on the faith of his eyes, not with my life only, but with the child of my soul'?"

"Yes," murmured the mother "I *have* trusted him, God

knows! But too much, perhaps. Gertrude, I am very ill. I have not been much to thee, my child; but yet, what wilt thou do without me?"

"Fear not for me, my mother. There is in a deep love a strange independence. Paradise on earth with him, or without him death,—preceded by the more or less long agony, called life."

These were not soothing conversations for a sick room. To do Gertrude justice, it was seldom that such vehement expressions escaped her in her mother's presence. She generally kept down her feelings with the iron rigidity of her strong will, but these emotions and this continual constraint were wearing her out. If the society at Audley Park could have seen her they would have been astonished at the change; and Mary Grey on Sundays, when she sometimes had a glimpse of her, was startled at her appearance.

CHAPTER XVIII.

"Joy for the freed one, she might not stay
When the crown had fallen from her life away,
She might not linger, a weary thing.
A dove with no home for its broken wing,
Thrown on the harshness of alien skies
That know not its own land's melodies,
From the long heart withering early gone;
Her task is done."
MRS. HEMANS.

"There stands a spectre in your hall;
The guilt of blood is at your door;
You changed a wholesome heart to gall;
You held your course without remorse."
TENNYSON.

A DAY came on which Mrs. Lifford felt herself still weaker than usual. She sent for Mr. Erving, the priest of Stonehouseleigh, and he stayed with her some time. Afterwards she asked to see her husband. Gertrude was sitting in the dressing-room when he went in. She could hear their voices, though the door was closed. A word here and there reached her ear. Once she heard her mother exclaim, "No, it is not possible,—say you did not do so." Another time, "I tell you Henry, that you have done wrong, very wrong. You do not know what you have done." Then there was a low moaning like the cry of physical pain, or of an intense inward suffering. An instant afterwards the door was thrown open, and Mr. Lifford, with a face as pale as death, said, "Gertrude, go to your mother,—she is dying." He rang the bell with violence, and rushed down stairs.

When Gertrude saw her mother's face she felt at once it was no vain alarm. He was not likely to have been startled too soon. Mrs. Lifford was gasping for breath, and could only hold out her arms to her child. She spoke only two words during the few minutes that life was trembling on the verge of death. Once she looked up to Heaven, as she pressed Gertrude's head closer to her breast, and murmured the word " Father ; " and then in her ear she whispered " Try——" More she could not utter, but gazed into her eyes for a moment with an unutterable expression of tenderness, fear, and supplication,—and then she died. That heart which had throbbed so long ceased to beat, and the spirit returned to the God who had given, tried, and exalted it, in the fiery furnace of suffering.

When Mr. Lifford returned to that room, followed by others, he stood an instant at the door, and a cold shudder passed through his frame. His daughter turned her face for one second towards him, pointed to the form of her whom she still held in her arms, and in a tone of unnatural calmness uttered the word, " Dead." She did not add, but in that dreadful moment her eyes said, " You have killed her !" With a wild and piercing cry she turned from him, and, as he slowly approached she stretched out her arm behind her, as if to keep him away. It is possible that at such a moment even his heart might have been touched and softened ; but to be thus repulsed, and in the presence of others, awakened the bitterest and most vindictive feelings in his mind. He went away, and she remained alone with her misery—alone though others spoke to her. Alone. then, and for days afterwards. If her grief had been simple in its nature it would have been ess dreadful ; but fear, suspense, resentment against the father whom she ought to have loved, and against one whom she did love with all the strength of her soul, were mixed with her sorrow, and embittered every tear that fell in that dark room. She would not move from the foot of that bed, from that spot where her father never came again. She would not look at the picture opposite to it, on which she had so often gazed ; her eyes were fixed on the ground, and they seldom shed tears.

The priest came and prayed by the bed-side; and for her mother's soul she prayed with intense fervour, but not for herself. It seemed as if all her feelings were suspended within her till she could learn her fate, and the rigid endurance of that suspense was offered up as a sacrifice in that chamber of mourning. When the priest addressed to her words of consolation, she raised her eyes for an instant, and said, "Yes—soon, perhaps, I may feel that." And he saw that the seed did not penetrate the surface, and he spoke oftener to God of that poor child, and less for the present of God to her. Then came the day of the funeral, with all its gloomy grandeur and solemn pomp. So the pride of the living had willed it. The ruling passion strong even in the face of death. The prayers and sacrifices of the Church,— the same for the rich and for the poor,—were offered up for that humble spirit which had been indeed poor in the midst of riches, but the husband who had not loved her, and scarcely wept over her corpse, had it consigned to the grave with all the pomp and circumstance of human pride. Gertrude's soul sickened within her at the sight of banners and escutcheons by the side of the shrine which held the mortal remains of her mother. During the service for the dead (at which they both assisted), she once looked towards her father, with eyes almost blinded by tears. His were dry, and it might be accident, but they seemed complacently fixed on the shield on which were quartered her arms and his. She turned away, and hid her face in her hands. Perhaps she prayed that she might not hate him. The funeral was over, with all its soothing religious duties, with all its stately worldly pomp. Once there came into her mind lines which she used to repeat years ago—not applicable, but akin to what she felt that day:

> And they bore away the royal dead
> With requiems to his rest,
> With knightly plumes and banners,
> All waving in the wind;
> But a woman's broken heart was left
> In its lone despair behind."

The next day Gertrude went for the first time into the drawing-room. She was in deep mourning. There was not the least trace of colour in her cheeks; the stern expression of her features was unrelieved by any of those soft shades or playful lights which used to flit over her face with such indescribable charm. Whatever light there was in it now came from the excessive brightness of her eyes. She had not shed tears enough to dim their brilliancy, and there was a fire burning in them which had been fed, not quenched by sorrow. She was resolved to have an explanation with her father; she must know if Adrien had abandoned her—with or without reason. She must know if there was any hope left for her of happiness on this side the grave. She felt the most profound conviction that the scene which had been fatal to her mother had had reference to her destiny. In some way or other he had laid his cold hand upon it, and blasted it by his touch.

When the post came in, he received a letter, which seemed to pre-occupy him considerably. As he left the room he said, "I wish you would come to my study in about an hour, as I have something of importance to communicate to you." A sudden revulsion of feeling came over Gertrude at that moment; he had perhaps heard from Adrien,—her suspicions, her fears, her misery might have been groundless. She tried to be calm; she sat opposite the clock, watching the minute-hand as it went round,—too slowly as she felt at one moment,—too fast as the hour was nearly elapsed. When it struck the appointed time she slowly walked to the study.

Mr. Lifford was sitting at his table. There was a shade of embarrassment in his manner, and he cleared his throat two or three times before beginning to speak. "I have received a letter this morning," he said, "which has somewhat embarrassed me, as it may be disagreeable to you, as well as to myself, to have any exertion to make so soon after your poor mother's death; but it is inevitable, and as the circumstance I allude to is of paramount importance to you, I must at once speak on a subject which I had intended some time longer to defer. You may have heard of the family of Mirasole, with whom we have had many family affairs to discuss. I saw the Marquis de Mirasole in Spain, and came to an understanding with him on several points of great importance to your brother's fortune. Amongst others it was agreed upon between us that a marriage between you and his son would be highly desirable, and having assured myself that the young man would in every respect be a suitable husband for you, I gave my consent to the proposal, and nothing can be more satisfactory than all the conditions of fortune and position that it affords. Besides the advantages to yourself there are others, as I said before, of vast consequence to your brother, and I rejoice that the interests of both thus coincide But what I scarcely rejoice at is, that M. de Mirasole, whom I expected here but not quite so soon, has in this letter announced his arrival, and that he will be here to-morrow morning. However, as he cannot be considered henceforward as a stranger by us, it will not be thought extraordinary that we should receive him even at this early period of our mourning, and I hope that his attentions and the new duties you will enter upon before long will prevent your giving way to an excessive depression of spirits."

Mr. Lifford had said all this without once looking at his daughter, a mode of proceeding which was rather habitual to him, especially when addressing her. As he did not now receive any answer he was obliged to raise his eyes towards her.

"Will you be kind enough," she then said, fixing hers steadily upon him, "to answer me one question? Have you received no other proposal of this kind but the one you speak of?"

He seemed to hesitate for an instant, and then answered, "None that deserved consideration."

"Then you have received proposals," she said in the same calm manner, "from Adrien d'Arberg?"

"The gentleman you mention did me that honour," he answered with a sneer.

"And you refused those proposals without consulting my mother or me?"

"I did so, Miss Lifford. Pray what is the drift of these questions?"

"Bear with me a moment. How long ago did this happen?"

"It may be four or five weeks ago."

"M. d'Arberg was here then?"

"He was."

"And you denied it!" she exclaimed.

Mr. Lifford turned pale with anger and said, "If I evaded your inquiries on that occasion it was from the wish to spare your mother unnecessary agitation."

"And you refused him, then, without consulting her or me? What did you say to him?" She uttered these last words with her eyes bent on the ground, and her lips tightly compressed.

"That he did me much honour, but that I had other views and intentions."

"Did he ask to see me, or *her?*" she said, clasping a small picture of her mother, which she wore round her neck.

"These questions are unnecessary. Pray dismiss that subject from your thoughts at once."

"Dismiss it!" she slowly repeated. "Dismiss it! Has it ever occurred to you that there are thoughts which will not be dismissed?"

"I have not patience to listen to any folly of this nature. From your birth you have irritated me. Abstain from doing so now. There are points on which I cannot be thwarted with impunity."

"And you imagine that I shall accept a husband at your hands. You think that I shall submit to you in a matter, not merely of life or death, but of honour and of dishonour. That I shall smile on the stranger you have brought here to woo me over my mother's grave, and stand with him at the altar with a lie on my lips and despair in my heart? You have embittered my childhood, you have clouded my youth, you have——" Here she stopped short; even in the passion of that moment she trembled at the dreadful words she was about to utter, and clasping her throat, went on: "You have endangered the happiness, the peace, the virtue of your child, but I tell you, father, that you have not the power to break my heart. I shall be true to him on whom my mother's dying blessing rests, to him whose image at this moment stands between me and despair. If I were never to see him again—if I had not the strength of that hope I should tremble for myself——"

"You may tremble, then, for there is little prospect that you will ever behold again the presumptuous suitor who dared to thrust himself into my house in my absence, and even into your mother's presence. Her deplorable weakness——"

"O, for Heaven's sake, do not speak of her," Gertrude cried as she wrung her hands in almost intolerable emotion. "I dare not think of her, for I would forget that scene—that cry——"

"And who but you," he exclaimed, "hurried your mother to the grave?—you and this wretched man whom I forbid you ever to name again?"

She stood opposite to him, drawn up to her full height, her lips as white as a sheet and each muscle of her frame rigid.

"You were right in saying that you were not to be thwarted with impunity. The words you have uttered will haunt me continually. You are sufficiently revenged: but listen to me now. I will not marry M. de Mirasole. I will not be made a sacrifice to the furtherance of your views for Edgar. I will not break the promises I have made."

"Ah, this honourable man has prevaricated then. He told me you were bound by no promise."

"He gave me up then!" she exclaimed, in a tone of such anguish that even Mr. Lifford started at the sound. But he thought the moment favourable, and drawing a French newspaper from a heap on his table, he put it under her eyes, and pointed to a passage. She read the following words:—

"*Nous apprenons avec un vif intérêt que le Comte Adrien d'Arberg, auteur des "Essais Philosophiques sur le Christianisme," après avoir cédé, par un acte formel, ses propriétés en Bretagne au Comte Henri d'Arberg, son frère, s'est rendu au séminaire d'Orléans, décidé à suivre la vocation qui paraît depuis longtemps lui être réservée, et à entrer dans le sacerdoce dont il formera, sans aucun doute, un des plus beaux ornements.*" *

After reading these words Gertrude remained silent; her father watched her for a moment, and thought he had attained his purpose, for the vehemence of her excitement seemed at an end. She looked almost as calm and as stern as himself, and in an instant left the room. Perhaps if he had remembered at that moment what he had felt himself on the day that Lady Clara dismissed him, and while he went to the opera as usual, and sat in a box opposite to her without flinching, or betraying a symptom of what he was enduring, he might have guessed at what was passing in his daughter's heart. Her anger was calm, but it was fearful. The cup was full, and that day it had overflowed. Duty, principle, conscience were silenced by a resentment deep and strong as the nature that it swayed. She was his victim. Her will had been vain against his. He had

---

* "We have been much interested in learning that the Count Adrien d'Arberg, the author of "Philosophical Essays on Christianity," after having concluded the arrangement of his affairs by the formal surrender of his property in Brittany to his brother, the Count Henri d'Arberg, has proceeded to the seminary of Orleans, with the intention of following the vocation which has long appeared to be marked out for him, and to enter the priesthood, which will doubtless reckon him hereafter amongst its brightest ornaments."

shivered to pieces the fabric of her happiness, and had stolen away the light of her existence. And she had been feebly loved by him whom even now she adored with an idolatrous worship. He had forsaken her, and his conscience was doubtless at rest. He would toil for others, he would save other souls perhaps, but of hers he had made sad havoc. He ought never to have loved, or never to have abandoned her. She was alone, completely alone in the world. She had told him there was that in her heart which must not be trifled with. She had lately at times felt a strange incoherence in her thoughts. She felt as if her father was pursuing her, and this sensation became a waking nightmare. He might drag her to the altar, and she would have no strength to resist. He had sent Adrien away, and she had not had power to prevent him. Was she a slave? Could not she escape? She was under the influence of this strange oppression—half feverish and half real,—when the sound of a carriage startled her. "It is that man," she wildly exclaimed; "it must be that man he has sent for!"

She snatched her bonnet and her shawl, and rushed down the back-stairs into the garden without meeting any one. When she passed the stone bench near her mother's window, where she had sat with Adrien the day he went away, her steps faltered; at the chapel-door she knelt an instant; but when she tried to pray, though her lips moved, passion and anger rose like a mist between her and Heaven. Once she exclaimed: "Father Lifford, Father Lifford, would to God you were here! Why have you forsaken me too?"

There were steps on the gravel walk, and she fancied once more that she heard the sound of wheels in the distance; and without knowing what she was doing, she hurried on through the park. It was a false alarm, but she did not stop to listen. "I cannot go back to that house," she said to herself, "I cannot see that man. I cannot meet my father again. I will leave his roof. His face, his voice, stand between me and peace. My mother's death I cannot forget. Her last cry is in my ears. He hated me before, and now——O, there is an abyss between us which never can be filled up. I will go to Mary Grey, and to her mother. They will protect me; they are the only friends I ever had. Why have they not been to me in my sorrow? But I forget, I would neither see any one, nor read any letters. I will go to them now. I cannot think for myself, they will think for me. O, for a kind hand to hold mine, but for an instant now, for a drop of cold water to slake this burning thirst."

"She opened the gate of the park, and hurried on towards Stonehousleigh. It was a clear frosty night, and in the distance she saw the roof of the cottage with the icicles hanging from the straw; a light was burning in the window. She hurried on, for she felt faint and ill. Unclosing the latch with a trembling hand, she passed through the little gate and knocked at the door. It opened. "Mary," she said in a hoarse whisper. It was not Mary's voice that said, " Good Heavens, Miss Lifford!" "Maurice, where is Mary? Call Mary directly—call your mother; I am ill." She staggered, and he threw open the door of the little parlour, and closed the outer one. She sank on a chair. "Call them, Maurice," she repeated, " I want Mary." He looked at her with a mixture of fear and embarrassment. He scarcely knew what to say.—he was afraid to tell her that they were not there,—that they had gone to London that morning. He had remained behind to conclude all the arrangements. His heart was beating violently;—what could he do? She was looking fearfully pale. He left the room for some water, and held it to her lips. "Where are they? are they *not* here?" " No, my Lady-Bird, no." She fainted away; he carried her to the couch and knelt by her side, chafing her brow with cold water—he had nothing else at hand—and looking at her with eyes which would have recalled life in the dead, if eyes could ever do so.

It was some time before she opened hers, and then her marble cheek was resting on a cushion, and her hair had fallen on her shoulders. Her face was wet with the water with which he had bathed her temples, and her hands with the hot tears he had shed upon them. She started up affrighted.

"Where am I? What am I doing here, Maurice?"

"You are in the cottage, Lady-Bird, where you have often spent happy hours, where from your childhood you have been welcomed by true affection. You came to Mary,—Mary is not here."

"Nor your mother? alas!"

"No, but you are as safe as if the whole world were around you."

"I never doubted it," she coldly and proudly replied. "I must go."

"Where, *where?*" he anxiously asked.

"*Where,* indeed!" she ejaculated, and tried to rise, but fell back exhausted. " I am undone," she murmured to herself, "I may die here; but if I did—O shame! O terror!

Maurice, go for Mr. Erving this minute, go; he will help me and guide me."

"But I cannot leave you alone—I cannot, indeed."

"You must: go this instant. Go, Maurice, as you value my blessing or my curse."

"But, Lady-Bird, for God's sake listen to me; I am expecting a man here to carry these trunks away to the station. If he does not find me he will come in; if I lock the door he may call the neighbours." She made a strong effort to get up, but became giddy after a step or two, and was forced to sit down again.

"Miss Lifford, you can trust me; be calm, and listen to what I say to you. Let me get you a bit of bread and a glass of wine from the kitchen. Try and eat, and then lie down on that couch for an hour; you are exhausted with grief; you cannot walk now, that is clear."

Tears for the first time fell from her eyes in abundance, and turning to Maurice, she said, in a tone of touching helplessness, "I will do what you advise; I cannot think for myself."

He brought her the food, and she swallowed a little. He watched her as a mother does a sick child, and then said in a low voice, "You are suffering intensely. In the name of the friendship that has united you and Mary, will you not tell Mary's brother what has made your cup of sorrow overflow? We have been friends since the days of childhood. O, Lady-Bird, will you not open your heart to one who would give his life to spare you a tear? If others have been unkind to you, will you not confide in an affection that never can fail you?"

"Affection!" she bitterly answered; "there is no such thing on earth. Where I should have been loved, I have been hated; there is no happiness for me, and I must now return, for I am a little stronger now, to that detested house where my mother consumed away her life, where my youth has been saddened and my soul for ever blighted."

Maurice's eyes suddenly sparkled with excitement, and a deep colour rushed into his face. "I understand it all," he cried; "you are going to marry the Count de Mirasole. I have seen him, Gertrude, a miserable being, utterly unworthy of you. I was told in London that he was your destined husband, and shuddered at the thought. But he has rank and wealth, and pride like your father's."

"So help me Heaven, they may kill me, but I will not

marry him. And yet to dwell at Lifford Grange,—my mother's living grave——"

There was a pause; neither of them spoke, but a tumultuous rush of feelings was invading his heart as he looked upon her, bowed down with sorrow, and shuddering at the thought of the home she had left. He knelt by her side, and with those eyes which had sought to recall her to life a moment before by the impassioned tenderness of their gaze, he tried, as it were, to speak the thought which was struggling in his mind. She partly understood him, for she held out her hand to him, and murmured, " I am not ungrateful for your sympathy," and burst into tears. Then trembling with agitation, he said,

"Gertrude, listen to me. We are alone, but never were my feelings so deeply respectful; for the sake of Heaven do not start at what I am going to say. You will die if you remain at Lifford Grange; your life will waste away in that gloom and solitude. A slow persecution will establish itself against you if you refuse to marry the husband of your father's choice. My heart beats so that I can hardly speak. Gertrude, as you once told me to do, I have loved in silence,—I have adored you in hopelessness. I shall love you whether you become the wife of Mirasole, or pine away your life in the dungeon called your home. Pure, as it is ardent—humble, as it is passionate—I dare speak of my love, even here, alone with you; for you could never mistake a heart that at all times has been yours. If some have hated, I have worshipped you. If some have feebly loved, I have adored you. If others have forsaken, I have clung to you; and with my soul, and my pen, and my toil, and with what talent Heaven has given me, and with my life, I will serve you, and ask nothing in return but that you will accept that devotion,—that you will let me take you to my mother and to Mary, who will be a mother and a sister to you; and then ask yourself there, if without repugnance you can give me the right to live for you. You do not care for rank, thank God,—you have suffered from the pride and the coldness of others. O, Gertrude, will you not try the ardent love of an artist's heart,—of a spirit untrammelled by the barriers that men, and not God, have placed between loving hearts? Will you be my wife,— and fight our way through the world amidst the frowns of its votaries and the sneers of its slaves? Will you see life as it is, or will you return to the cold shadows of existence in which your youth was spent, or be the tool and the victim of your father's pride?"

"Hush, Maurice, hush!" she wildly exclaimed; "you do not know what you are saying."

"I know that I love you as woman has seldom been loved,—that is enough for me. O can it not be enough for you? My Gertrude,—my Lady-Bird, come with me to a home where none but loving eyes will look upon you, none but loving words be addressed to you. Let me rescue you from the tyranny that has embittered all your life. I do not ask you to love me as I love you Few love thus; but let me be your husband———"

"My husband!" she exclaimed. "*You!* O leave me,—leave me. What are you talking of, Maurice? Do you not know———" She got up and went towards the door; he turned so deadly pale that she thought he was about to faint. Despair was in his face. "God help me!" she said, "am I breaking his heart as mine is breaking!" He heard her, and the expression of his eyes changed,—a sudden hope shot through them; again he pleaded, again implored, and a strange conflict arose in her whom he addressed as she listened to his feverish words of tenderness—a passion which soothed her bruised and aching heart. The idea of revenge, too, arose in that proud spirit. To reward a love which had been long as time and patient as faith, to fly from scenes which seemed to wither her soul as she looked upon them, to brave the prejudices that had been fatal to her peace, and the father who had shivered to atoms her happiness, to show Adrien in his serene indifference—his virtuous abstraction—that she too could take a decisive step;—and instead of weeping in solitude over the fate to which he had left her, all this conspired at that moment to bewilder and confuse her. She felt a pining desire to be loved and protected. She felt utterly unequal to meet the struggle that awaited her at Lifford Grange; and the difficulty of returning there at that time of the night, or to account for her long absence, the chance of being obliged to explain it to her father, her horror of the husband he would force upon her,—all this threw weight into the scale in that hour of weakness, of infatuation, and of despair.

Maurice was not designedly artful; he loved her passionately, and to show it was the highest art he could employ; he pleaded with his whole soul, with his eyes, and with his words he combated the scruples of her conscience, the misgivings of her heart, with all the arguments which sophistry could furnish and eloquence employ.—blinded all the while by the delirium of passion to the fearful sin he was committing against Heaven and against her. He privately ordered the person who called for the luggage to be in readiness at four with a carriage to take him to the railway. She was fatigued, over-excited, jaded with emotions; she scarcely realised what she was about. She began to fear with a terrible fear that she would be missed at Lifford Grange, and be discovered where she was. Once she had a good inspiration; she insisted for a moment that Maurice should take her to Mr. Erving's house, should show her the way to it at least. But then he might be absent, and what would his servant think? And if she did find him, what could he do but insist on her returning to her father; and that seemed to have grown beyond her power. At moments she trembled like a leaf. Then again a fierce irritation supported her. She had been sacrificed to the cold heartless pride that had counted her happiness and her misery for nothing; she had been refused to the man she adored, and promised to a stranger, as if she had been a slave, a machine, or a piece of merchandise. But now, when the proud Spaniard would arrive and claim his bride, what would her still prouder father answer? She had fled from his house like a galley-slave from his chain. He had refused Adrien, with his title, his noble blood, and his riches; and she would marry the son of a poor fiddler and of an Italian singer! There would be a blot for ever on that hateful escutcheon, which had been her foe and her bane. A morbid gratitude, a feverish terror, a boundless resentment blinded her. She scarcely looked beyond the present moment, and was conveyed away towards the railway-station, with no definite thought but the fear of being overtaken. But no one had missed her,—her father had not asked for her. Her maid never attended her in the evening: the tea, which she had lately taken instead of dinner, was carried up to her room and left there. Those who did not see her in her apartments concluded she was in the drawing-room, and those who did not see her there, imagined she was up-stairs. It was only in the morning that the truth flashed upon the bewildered servants,—Miss Lifford had not slept in her bed that night. They were informing her father of the fact at the moment when the carriage of the Count of Mirasole was driving up to the door.

CHAPTER XIX.

> "The real hardened wicked
> That know no check but human law,
> Are to a few restricted.
> But, ah! mankind is unco weak.
> And little to be trusted;
> When self the wavering balance shakes,
> It's rarely right adjusted."
> — BURNS.

> "The frowardness of rashness is no better
> Than a wild dedication of ourselves
> To unpath'd waters, undreamt shores; most certain
> To miseries enough; no hope to 'help us,
> But as we shake off one, to take another."
> — SHAKESPEARE.

IT was eight o'clock in the morning when the sun was just beginning to make his way through the lingering darkness of a London atmosphere; when the air felt as raw and chilly as if it had not been shone upon for months; when the smell and the taste of fog were pervading every sense, and the hard, dull part of life's business was beginning to stir in the streets, that a hack-cab stopped at a house in one of the streets near Manchester Square. Maurice, who was on the box, jumped down and rang the bell. When a maid opened the door, he sprung up the narrow stairs, and found Mary in the sitting-room. Her bonnet was on, and she was just going out. His sudden appearance did not startle her much, for she expected him that day; but she said,

"So early, Maurice! I did not know you were coming by this train."

He seized both her hands, and looked at her so strangely that she felt frightened. "What has happened?—What can have happened?"

"Something so extraordinary that at this very moment I am not sure that I am not dreaming. But it is all true—true as I am here; you will hardly believe it. How it has all happened I scarcely understand myself; but Lady-Bird is with me,—she is in the carriage. She has left her home for ever, and with me!"

Mary turned very pale, and clasped her hands together. "Are you married, Maurice?"

"No, but we must be married immediately. Come, dearest Mary, and bring her up-stairs and take care of her, while I go to get a license, and speak to a priest."

Mary went down to the carriage-door, feeling bewildered. It passed through her head that Maurice had gone out of his mind, and that she should not find Gertrude in the carriage. But she was there,—pale and motionless as a marble statue,— looking more like a corpse than a bride. "Miss Lifford! dear Miss Lifford!" was all she could ejaculate, as she led her up-stairs. She made her sit down on the sofa near the fire, and then looked at Maurice with an expression that seemed to ask for an explanation. He knelt by Gertrude, and whispered in a low voice, "She is ill and cold,—she has suffered so much!" Gertrude opened her arms, and said, "Mary!" in a tone of such intense misery, that though she shed no tears Mary's streamed down her face while pressing her to her heart. Then Maurice went away, and left them together.

It was a strange interview. Neither was disposed to enter upon explanations. They seemed almost equally miserable. Gertrude, from the moment that she had entered the railway-carriage and had been relieved from the immediate fear of pursuit, had fallen into a sort of stupor that had prevented her thinking over what she had done, or what she was about to do. To draw back was impossible; and this made her impatient for the moment when all would have been gone through, and her fate irrevocably fixed. What could she say to Mary? *Nothing.* It was useless to explain. What had she to explain? Driven almost wild, and from the impulse of the moment seeking a refuge where she alone hoped to find one, step by step she had been drawn on to the point where she now was, scarcely knowing if she had injured Maurice, or he had wronged her—whether he was the betrayer or the betrayed, and herself saved or undone.

Tired to death she fell asleep on the hard couch, and Mary stood looking at her with a mixture of pity and of grief. "Then she loved him," she said to herself. "Poor Lady-Bird, she has always loved him! But how have they met? How has this been brought about? So soon after her mother's death! How will he support her, used as she has been to so many comforts? But perhaps her father may forgive her; though I am afraid he will not. Good Heavens! who would ever have thought this possible? Gertrude Lifford— Lady-Bird—Maurice's wife! She must have loved him very much to have acted thus. But how could she make up her mind to it? I hope he did not over-persuade her. Will he want me to go to church with them? Perhaps he will not like to ask me, but I will, and my mother shall go too. It will be a sad wedding."

She put some wood on the fire, and lit a candle, for the fog was getting more yellow and dense every moment. Gertrude's bonnet had fallen on the ground. She picked it up and hung it on the screen, laid her own shawl on her feet; then softly slipped out of the room to go and prepare her mother for this strange arrival. Mrs. Redmond was quite bewildered at the news, and gazed at her daughter in silent astonishment. "Bless my soul!" she ejaculated in a moment; "what odd things do happen, Mary!" This was her resource in all embarrassing moments in life, from a dropped stitch in her work to the greatest event that ever came across her quiet path—"Mary!"—a look at that kind serene face, an appeal to that invariable goodness and sense which she almost superstitiously trusted in. "Mary says it must be done," or "Mary says there is nothing to fret about," were oracles which had never found her rebellious or incredulous. "Mary!" Mary knew what that meant, and said gently,

"We feel, dearest mother, that it would have been much better that this had never happened,—that Maurice must have been wrong, and poor Lady-Bird very wrong in acting in this way. I don't know how it has come about. But though they have committed a great fault, it is no crime, mother, and God only knows what excuses they have had. She has been so unhappy at home, and her love for him must be very great to have led her to this; now she must become his wife directly."

"His wife, Mary! I had once thought you would be his wife."

A painful expression for one instant passed over her daughter's face, but it quickly disappeared, and she said: "That was a great mistake, dear mother. Maurice is coming back," she added in a moment, "with the licence. We must go to church with them, and you must give her your blessing; poor motherless Lady-Bird—no father will give her away— no mother will stand near her. O, she has done very wrong; but had I been in her place, who knows that I should have had strength to act differently?" Her voice faltered as she said the last words, but Mrs. Redmond was satisfied. Mary had said it was all a mistake her fancying that Maurice had ever loved her. Mary had said that Maurice and Gertrude had been very wrong in running away together, but that there were probably what the French tribunal would call *des circonstances atténuantes*, and that she, Mrs. Redmund, was to give them her blessing and be kind to them; and that was quite enough for her,—Mary must be right.

Poor Mary did not feel so sure of being right. She asked herself if she ought not to put more questions, to learn more of what had happened, to advise Gertrude to pause and to reflect before she irrevocably bound herself to one whose worldly position was so inferior to hers, and set at defiance her father, who, cold and heartless as he had been, was still her father. She thought of her aged uncle also, and the sorrow and indignation he would feel at the news of this strange marriage. She had an instinctive feeling that after such a flight, and such a journey, a return to her home would be impossible; but could not she pause for a while, and take advice before this rash act was completed? But again, how could *she* stand between Maurice and the happiness he was on the point of attaining? If by her advice she induced Gertrude to retrace her steps, and give time to her father to claim her,—if she and Maurice were forcibly separated, and made quite miserable,—would not she have incurred a great responsibility? She was well acquainted with Mr. Lifford's character. He would never forgive his daughter, but would move heaven and earth to prevent what he must consider a disgraceful marriage. What a destiny her interference might be preparing for Gertrude!—What misery, what despair for Maurice! And was she sure enough of her own heart, not to mistrust its motives in this hour of trial? Maurice adored Gertrude, and she also most dearly loved him. They would have to toil and to struggle, but their devotion to each other would sweeten those toils and struggles. What business had she to interfere? Faint, tired, and agitated as she was, a word might sway Gertrude, and the consequences might be important beyond what she knew. No, there was no time for advice, for anything but endurance and prayer. She would stand by that suffering, pale bride, and leave the future in the hands of God.

With that resolution she returned to the room where she had left her. Gertrude awoke and shivered a little. Then got up and walked up and down the room, and as she looked out of the window said in an absent manner, "And this is London?" Then returning to her place on the sofa, she sat silently contemplating the fire. Some tea was brought, of which she took a little, and then said to Mary, "Did you ever hear of a daughter marrying a fortnight after her mother's death?" The colour rushed into Mary's face; she knew not what to answer. "Yours is not an ordinary marriage," she hesitatingly said. Her heart was aching dreadfully. She felt much that she dare not utter. There were religious duties which both ought to have accomplished before receiving the marriage blessing. Did they know this? Had they forgotten it? She was just about to speak, when a rap at the door made them both start. "Remember," Gertrude exclaimed, with a wild expression, "that I am of age, and that no power on earth shall induce me to return to Lifford Grange."

"It is only the postman's knock," Mary said, and an instant afterwards she heard Maurice's voice in the passage. "He is come back, is he!" Gertrude ejaculated. It was some minutes before he came upstairs. He had gone into the room below. When he entered the one where Gertrude and Mary were sitting. he was as pale as death. The expression of his face—his whole manner—were changed from what they had been, when he had arrived that morning. Then, in the midst of agitation and emotion, there was joy and hope; but now his eyes had a dark and troubled expression. and he seemed in a kind of agony of irresolution. Passion and conscience were at that moment waging war in his soul. The one was fierce and the other weak, and the combat was unequal. He approached Gertrude and twice he tried to speak, but his voice failed him. She did not observe it, and it was she who said at last, "Is all ready?" perhaps with a sensation akin to that with which that question has been asked at the foot of the scaffold. He had an instinctive knowledge that at that moment the words of passion and of tenderness, which had wrought so powerfully on her feelings the day before, would be displeasing to her. Nor could he now pour them forth out of the fulness of a heart which, weak and guilty as it had been, till this hour had been true in its devotion to her. He could only seize her hand, and articulate the word "Come." Mary whispered to him, "I will call my mother; we are both going with you." When she returned with Mrs. Redmond, Gertrude turned away with her cheeks burning. and her lips quivering. The old woman went to her, took her hand in both hers and murmured, "My dear young lady—my dear child." "*My mother!*" Gertrude exclaimed, as if her heart was breaking, 'O my mother!" then suddenly became calm and said—

'Now I am ready, let us go." They all went in one carriage, and through the foggy streets to the chapel. Mary said to herself, " And this is Maurice's wedding-day ? "

And what did he feel during that time? Like the gambler, when the decisive card is about to be played,—when the winning horse is nearing the goal. In another moment Gertrude would be his, and no earthly power might put asunder those who would then have been joined together. When the ceremony was over, and they were returned to the house in King Street, she suffered from such a violent headache, and appeared so ill, that Mrs. Redmond insisted on making her rest on the sofa, and giving her some draught of her own preparation to drink; desiring Maurice and Mary not to disturb her for a while, for that her pulse was so quick and her hands so burning, that unless great care were taken of her she might be seriously ill. Maurice knelt by the sofa, kissed both her hands, and then her forehead. He could hardly realise that she was indeed his wife. It was like a feverish dream, from which he fancied every moment he must awake. She neither stirred nor spoke a word,—till hearing him sigh deeply as he rose from his knees, she opened her eyes and held out her hand to him. He passionately kissed it again and again. She said, " I will try to make a good wife to you, Maurice." " Idol of my heart ! " he exclaimed. " No, no," she murmured ; " it is wrong to have idols." Then, oppressed with fatigue and heaviness, she fell asleep. He went down to the little parlour below, where Mary was sitting with her work in her hands—hands that were never idle, however busy her thoughts.

"You, too, must be very tired, brother," she said as he came in. When they were children it had been her habit to call him so, and during the last few months she had gradually resumed it. " But I suppose you are too much agitated, too happy, to sleep. Sit down in that arm-chair, and tell me the history of this strange event. I long to know, Maurice, what I feel persuaded of beforehand—that you have been both as little to blame as possible."

" O, Mary, she came to the cottage last night, in all her beauty, and in the deepest grief. Her mother's grave was scarcely closed, and her own tears undried, when her father attempted to force upon her acceptance the hand of a total stranger, who was to arrive this very day. She had gone through a dreadful scene with him ; and distracted by his unkindness, she fled like a wounded bird to the only friends who had always loved her. She expected to find you and mother, and fainted away with fatigue and the anguish of disappointment. when I was forced to tell her you were gone. What could I do then ? I dared not leave her, nor summon any one to her assistance. We remained there together, and the time passed by. When she came to herself, her tears flowed bitterly, and I implored her to confide in me. She trembled, and spoke of her grief and loneliness, and I saw her shudder when she thought of returning to Lifford Grange ; and then it was not in man's nature to refrain from offering her a refuge. from making the confession of a love——" He hesitated; he could not but remember how often he had told Mary that he loved *her*, that he would never love any but her ; and the sense of his ingratitude, and of the angelic patience with which she had met it, almost overcame him at that moment. But she looked at him calmly, and taking up his words, she said,

"And you forgot everything but that love which you had so long struggled to repress. You forgot that you ought not to have revealed it at such a moment. You were tempted, Maurice, and you yielded to the temptation. It seemed to you, perhaps, in that moment of agitation, that it was right to offer her your heart as a refuge, and this poor home as a shelter ; and when you found that she loved you, in the joy of that discovery——"

An ashy paleness overspread Maurice's face as Mary pronounced these words, and he murmured in hesitating accents "I hope she loves me"

Like a flash of lightning the thought passed through her mind, that perhaps he was not certain of it, and had too readily taken advantage of her distress of mind, her dread of returning home,—of her sufferings, in short,—to persuade her to a step, that nothing but a strong affection on both sides could palliate or excuse. This was a dreadful moment for Mary. She started at the vision of past sin and future misery which was suggesting itself to her mind, and she exclaimed :

"But you did not over-persuade her, Maurice ? You gave her time to reflect—to pause ? O, for Heaven's sake tell me you did so ! "

"There was no time for deliberation," he rejoined with increasing vehemence, as he saw her emotion. "Do you think that at such a moment a man is in the full possession of his senses ? I described my love and my despair till she allowed me to speak of her future fate also—I told her what it would be if she remained at Lifford Grange. I argued away her scruples,—Heaven knows my own reasonings seemed just to me at the time. She had once told me to love her on, and to bide my time—and the time seemed to be come. I believe she loves me, I am sure she does."

He got up and walked about the room with impetuosity. Mary remained silent; her misgivings were not removed; but she felt it was done, it was over, it was irrevocable,—and nothing remained but the hope that God, in his infinite mercy would bring good out of evil, should her worst fears be realised; but she also knew there was such a thing as *retribution*, and her heart sunk within her. She kept her eyes fixed on the ground, scarcely venturing to look in his face.

"If I have done wrong," he began.

"If! O Maurice," she rejoined, in a tone that pierced him to the soul; for, if she condemned him already, what would she have felt and said if she had known what no other creature but himself did know,—a secret that was lodged in his breast, never to be revealed to her, or to any one; but which, like a thorn, was to dwell there, while his writhings would only serve to drive it in more deeply.

Both feared to say more about the past. Each had understood more than the other had expressed in words, and a painful silence ensued. She communed with herself; and, knowing his character, felt it necessary to encourage him to look forward with resolution to the future. "Speak to them that they go *forward*." This sentence of the Bible had fixed itself in Mary's mind when she was very young, as a sort of spell that carried her along through discouragements and trial, as if borne upon an angel's wing. It stifled regrets, self-pity, self-indulgence, and braced every nerve for the duty or the struggle of the hour; and now she felt it to be a greater duty to urge him to future efforts, and atoning virtues, than to reproach him for the past.

"You are now," she said, "Gertrude's husband, her protector, her sole support; for the world will be against her, and not much mercy will it show to either of you. I do not say this to discourage you, God knows, but to excite you to be all to her that a husband can be to a wife who has given up everything for him. Hers is not a common claim on your love. O Maurice, dearest brother, begin well this new life of yours. You will need God's blessing upon it,—seek it day by day at his feet, and then work hard for Gertrude; dear Lady-Bird must not want a single comfort which our labour can obtain." He pressed her hand, and both were again for a few minutes absorbed in thought. Then (for there are a thousand little necessary details of life which assert their claims even in the most exciting moments) she said to him, "Where shall you live, Maurice? Here, I hope; at least, just now."

"Will it be possible, Mary?"

"Quite possible. There are two rooms upstairs which you can have; and I should think, just at first, that as you know little, and Lady-Bird nothing, about housekeeping, it will be a good thing for her to have somebody to manage little arrangements, and to supply the place of her maid; I can lend her some clothes, also until——"

"O Mary, here is my purse, for Heaven's sake, buy whatever she may want."

"No indeed, my dear Maurice, you have been tolerably well off as a single man during the last two years, but as a married man you must be very prudent. It is likely, that even should Mr. Lifford cast off his daughter, he will send her what was her own until now. Then, again, there is something which I think you should carefully avoid, and that is proposing any change in your wife's habits of life. Any such alteration should come from herself alone, and not be suggested by you, or by us. Most likely she will wish to dress less expensively—indeed it will be inevitable if her father does not contribute to your support—but it would not be desirable that you should procure for her less costly things than she has been used to. If hers are not sent to her, it will be time enough then for you to explain to her candidly the amount of your resources, and to let her decide on the line she will adopt in these respects."

"Mary, you are a little Solomon," Maurice said, with a smile, but it was one which was soon followed by a deep sigh. For what would he not have given to have been able to surround his wife with all the comforts and pleasures and luxuries of life? and he looked with loathing at the narrow dull rooms, the dingy walls and comfortless furniture of that poor lodging house. If, indeed, he had been convinced that she loved him, all would have been well. On that day, at least, he would have given care to the winds, and have bade defiance to the frowns of fortune; but such love as his was too clear-sighted long to deceive itself; although he strove to persuade himself,—in spite of former jealous suspicions, and of a startling confirmation which they had received that very day—that she did love him, and that her heart had prompted the rash act she had committed: still, as he repassed in his mind the scenes of that eventful day, he could not recall one glance of real love, one word that set at rest the terrible misgivings of an awakening conscience and a torturing jealousy.

Mary, meanwhile, was as busy as a bee. She concluded with the mistress of the house the bargain for the rooms upstairs, and set about helping the maid to give them a thorough cleaning. The pale sun was beginning to conquer the fog, and she threw open the window to let in that transient ray. Every bit of furniture that could be considered ornamental was transferred from her mother's room and her own to Gertrude's. Every picture and print she possessed was hung on the walls. There were some that Maurice had brought her from Italy, and which used to be her treasures. One in particular, a pretty engraving of the Madonna di Foligno, before which she had ever since said her prayers. She hesitated an instant, but then thought that those prayers would have been poured forth to little purpose if they had not prepared her to part with everything that referred to a time she must now never remember. One fervent kiss was pressed on the sacred feet of the Virgin's child, and then the picture was placed where the light would best fall upon it. Her prettiest looking books were ranged on the shelves—several little knick-knacks were laid on the table. When the fire was lit and the flame burned brightly, she thought the room looked cheerful; and cheerfully she had worked, in spite of the aching of her heart—for it was aching, notwithstanding every effort—it was aching more than any one could have conceived. Many a woman, with such a suffering heart, would have been drowned in tears. Many another, who had loved, and did still love, like her, would have turned from Maurice with bitter resentment, and from Gertrude with cold severity: but people are very different, and there are different ways of showing feeling. Mary's was to work very hard for the runaway pair all that day, and for a few minutes in the afternoon to pray fervently for them before the altar where they had been married.

"To be left alone for ten minutes," this, it was said, was the first request of a young Queen upon coming to the throne. In the most different situations under the most different emo tions, that wish, that aspiration has been felt. It was Gertrude's passionate desire on the day after her marriage to be left alone for a while, and to reflect on all she had not ventured to think of while her fate was not yet irrevocably fixed. She had been used all her life to the vast lofty rooms of Lifford Grange, to its parks and its gardens; and whenever either sorrow or excitement oppressed her, she seemed to find relief in the space that she could range in, and in the power of rapid movement which it afforded her. She was absolutely stifled by the atmosphere of London, by the closeness of the small house in which she found herself. Even when the door of her own room was shut, she could hear voices and steps, below and above her. And if a louder sigh than usual escaped her, if after an instant's silent weeping a sob burst from her breast, Maurice rushed anxiously back to her side and asked if she was grieving at having made him happy; and she was obliged to give him her hand, and to endeavour to reassure him by a smile. She felt the scrutiny of his eyes upon her every moment, and asked herself if people had ever been driven mad by being watched? In the afternoon of that day she told him she had a task to perform which would cost her much suffering, and for which she wished to be alone. It was to write to her father, and to inform him of her marriage. She did not say she would show him her letter. He had thought they might have written it together; but this seemed never to have occurred to her. He went out to walk a little with Mary. Gertrude looked from the window, and saw them turning the corner of the street. Then, for the first time since her mother's death, she gave way to an uncontrolled and vehement burst of crying, and murmured in a choking voice, "What have I done?—what have I done? O my God! what have I done?" After a few moments she felt calmer, and sat down to write. This was her letter:—

"*King Street, Manchester Square.*

"I do not write to ask your forgiveness, for I well know you never will forgive me, nor to relieve you from any anxiety about my life, for I know you would rather hear of my death than of the marriage I have made, but only to save you the trouble of making inquiries which would give you needless trouble. That I was born to be a curse to you I cannot but feel. That you have made my life a curse to me may be no more than I deserve. I do not reproach you now. Two days ago I had, perhaps, a right to complain. Now I have none. It would be impertinent in me to say I forgive you, and yet as I do not expect you will ever choose to see or to hear from me again, I should like to say it as if on my deathbed. I forgive you for never having loved me or looked kindly upon me in my youth. I forgive you for having driven me to offend you beyond the possibility of forgiveness, for having tempted me to take my fate into my own hands, and incur the sin and misery of disobedience without the excuse of passion. Your anger will be great: I do not say it will not be just. For the sake of my mother, of her long sufferings, of her recent death, one only favour I ask of you. Do not curse me, my father, when I tell you that I am Maurice Redmond's wife."

She did not sign this letter, but hurriedly sealed and directed it. Two days after, as Mary had expected, several trunks arrived containing everything that had belonged to Gertrude at Lifford Grange. It was the only sign that her letter had been received. As Mary was unpacking her clothes and ranging them in the drawers, while she sat watching her with a kind of mechanical attention, the latter held out to her a sheet of paper which had been laid at the bottom of the trunk; as she did so, some drawings which it contained fell to the ground. She saw her copy of the Duke of Gandia's picture, with the words written under it, and gave a sort of scream which startled Mary, who on turning round saw her standing over the fire while the flame was consuming that drawing, and she was murmuring to herself the Latin words,

"*Dies iræ, dies illa,*
Solvet sæclum in favillâ."

When the last blackened remnant of the sheet of paper turned to ashes, she said in a louder voice, "That always reminds me of the hymn on the Day of Judgment,

'When shrivelling like a parched scroll,
The flaming heavens together roll.'"

Mary resumed her labours, and laid on the table a gorgeous case with an embossed crest, containing the necklace which Gertrude's father had given her. She gazed upon it for a moment in silence and then asked,

"Did you ever read a novel called 'Love and Pride,' Mary?"

"No, what made you think of it now?"

"I don't know—that diamond necklace perhaps."

"*You* had to choose between them," Mary kindly said, "and you chose love, not pride."

Gertrude turned to the window and made no answer.

CHAPTER XX.

> "O could'st thou but know,
> With what a deep devotedness of woe,
> I wept [his] absence o'er and o'er again,
> Thinking of [him], still him, till thought grew pain;
> Did'st thou but know how pale I sat at home,
> My eyes still turned the way [he] was to come,
> And all the long long nights of hope and fear,
> [His] voice and step still sounding in my ear.
> Oh God! thou would'st not wonder that at last,
> When every hope was all at once o'ercast,
> This wretched brain gave way. . . . . .
> MOORE.

> "Our God, the all just,
> Unto himself reserves this royalty;
> The secret chastening of the guilty soul,
> The fiery touch, the scourge that purifies,
> Leave it with him."
> MRS. HEMANS.

THE first time that Gertrude walked out with her husband the dreamlike feeling that had haunted her since her marriage was stronger than ever. It seemed as if a sponge had been passed over the whole of her previous life. Lifford Grange, her parents, Audley Park and Woodlands, Lady Clara, Mark Apley, Mr. Latimer, and even Adrien himself, appeared like recollections of some other state of existence, totally unconnected with what now surrounded her; exhausted by recent excitement the power of suffering seemed dulled within her. She did not feel just then any poignant regrets—Adrien was ost to her; that was not so much a regret as the destruction of one part of her being. The spring was broken, at least she fancied so, and perhaps suffered less where she was than she would have done at home or elsewhere. London appeared to her like a great hive in which millions of creatures buzzed about without disturbing her. It was better to gaze at people moving along the streets than to have nothing to look at. She sat a great deal at the window, and Mary fancied that when Maurice was out she was watching for his return. Now and then she said something in her old way—something droll that made them all laugh; but the sound of their laughter always seemed to make her grave again.

Maurice—like her—was in a strange state of mind. There were moments when he looked upon her with transport, and almost went wild with joy at knowing she was his wife. But his happiness was far from being perfect. She was not exactly cold to him; but yet there was something in her that prevented his feeling at his ease, and this was a most irritating consciousness to a husband. She never consulted him about anything—never gave or asked advice on any point. She had never evinced in her manner any sense of a disparity of rank between them at any time, but he thought her manner might have been different now from what it was. Had she been proud, or petulant, or unkind to him he would almost have felt relieved. To a man who adored her nothing was so trying as her calm self-possession. He never ventured to talk to her about affairs or business. She never made a single remark or asked a question about their future plans or the extent of his resources. Mary told him once or twice that he must leave off sending excuses to his pupils, and begin again giving lessons,—that his avocations as an organist and a composer were not sufficient to rely upon,—that he was to make hay while the sun shone, and not allow the grass to grow under his feet. Little Mary had a lurking Sancho-like love of proverbial sayings, and they often made part of her exhortations to Maurice.

"You must also go on with your opera," she said. "You must make yourself a name in the world by your talents. Lady-Bird in marrying you gave up all worldly considerations; but a day may come when even in that way she may feel proud of her husband. Depend upon it, Maurice, it will not do to cross your hands, and sit for hours looking at her beautiful eyes. Your love must be a spur—not an opiate."

"Why does not she talk to me as you do, Mary? I could do wonders if she took an interest in what I did."

"She does not know you yet as I do, nor how you require to be kept up to the mark, how fond you are of going to sleep on your oars."

"Mary, do you think she loves me?"

"I think that is a wicked question, Maurice. When a woman has given up everything for you and broken through every obstacle to become your wife, it is unpardonable to doubt that she loves you."

"Given up everything for me—for *me!* O that I could think so!"

"Maurice," Mary exclaimed, almost angrily, "if you begin self-tormenting in that way, and so soon, you will make yourself wretched and your wife also."

"Did you see how pale she turned yesterday, when somebody called her Mrs. Redmond?"

"That was perfectly natural. The sort of way in which she married cannot be always pleasant for her to think of, however she may love you."

"Do you think she looks as if she loved me? Have you ever seen a woman, married to a man she loved, so pale and so silent?"

"But, Maurice, remember her deep mourning, her mother's death, her father's anger, the thoughts she must have about her brother and Father Lifford's return. Do you think all that likely to make her gay?'"

"If she loved me as I adore her, the whole world might hate and abuse me, every human being perish around us, and I would clasp her to my heart, and be the happiest of men."

"No," Mary said in a tone in which there was a little indignation. "No, I do not think she loves you in that way."

"I think she *could* love in that way," he murmured to himself, and then muttered still more indistinctly, "*Le vent qui vient à travers la montagne me rendra fou.*"

About ten days after Gertrude's marriage, Maurice had gone to give some lessons. He had told her the day before of his intention of doing so, in a hesitating manner, fancying it might annoy her to be reminded that he must thus gain his livelihood. He was half relieved and half disappointed at the way in which she took it, as a matter of total indifference to her. At dinner she reverted to the subject, and asked some joking questions about his pupils. There was not a grain of one kind of pride in her composition. If he had told her he was going to turn shoemaker, she would not have cared much. On the morning in question she and Mary went and took a long walk in Hyde Park. Her spirits were a little better than usual, and walking fast seemed to exhilarate her. Meanwhile Mrs. Redmond was at home working at a carpet rug, and thinking of her flowers at the cottage, of her tisanes, her rose-water, and her elder wine, and wondering if the present occupant of the garden was as fond of it as she used to be, and then why everybody became so pale in London. Mary and Maurice and Gertrude all looked wan and thin since they had been in town; it was a great pity they could not live in the country. It was of no use to think of that now, and yet she made certain matter-of-fact castles or rather cottages in the air, which amused her and made the time pass quickly.

About an hour after Gertrude and Mary had left the house, and when she was beginning to expect their return, the door was thrown open, and to her amazement, Father Lifford and Edgar walked into the room. A pair of ghosts could not have startled Mrs. Redmond more. Her knitting and her spectacles fell on her knees, and she looked the very picture of consternation. Not having foreseen such a casualty, it had never occurred to her to inquire if Gertrude's marriage was a secret; she was sensible that a great fault had been committed, and that an agitating discovery was at hand; and her tender heart and illogical understanding led her to feel herself, by some means or other, implicated in the offence; and she would have been capable of accusing herself of it, and imploring Father Lifford's pardon, just as if she had not been as guiltless of the whole affair as the babe unborn, an individual whom she was often in the habit of alluding to. She remained gazing at her visitors, as if the floor and not the door had opened to introduce him. He put a chair for himself next to hers, which obliged her to sit down, while Edgar,—who always looked stiff,—placed himself opposite. They had arrived that morning from Spain by a different ship than the one they had intended to sail in, and finding no letters in town, Father Lifford had proposed to call at Maurice's lodgings, with the hope of hearing from him what were the last accounts from the Grange.

"Well, Mrs. Redmond," he began, "I hardly expected to find you in London, though we knew of your intended removal. How are you?—and how is Mary?—and Maurice, is he getting on well?"

"As well as can be expected, dear sir," she answered, not feeling certain that he was ignorant of the late event, and adopting that useful phrase, as a safe one in any case.

"You have a nice house, I see," Edgar remarked, a thing which people often say of houses where they would hate to live themselves.

"There is not quite room enough for us——" she began,

and then trembled as if they knew exactly how many rooms there were, and that it would have been large enough if Maurice had not married.

"Where is Mary?" Father Lifford asked; "I have brought her a little present from Spain."

"Oh, you are too good," Mrs. Redmond ejaculated, and was going to add, " she does not deserve it," so strong was her impression of their being all involved in Maurice's delinquency

She took to praying mentally that they might go before Gertrude and Mary returned; and, what with these mental prayers and her deafness, the conversation did not go on briskly.

Father Lifford said, "We are only just landed, and were glad enough to arrive after our wretched passage. We started several days before our appointed time, and must have missed our letters. I hope we shall find his poor mother pretty well, but I did not quite like the last accounts of her."

Now poor Mrs. Redmond's agitation increased. They did not know of Mrs Lifford's death. Then they knew nothing. Then everybody must give themselves up for lost. This was her only impression, and she looked so perturbed that Father Lifford perceived it, and a sudden fear shot through his heart. A presentiment of sorrow had haunted him during the journey; it was doubtless mercifully sent to prepare him for the evil of that day, which indeed was to be abundantly sufficient for it.

He was looking from Edgar to Mrs. Redmond, afraid of questioning her, and receiving an answer which might be too sudden a blow for the dull but affectionate boy, who had no fear or misgiving on the subject. He took snuff; he got up and examined a print on the chimney, and then said, "Edgar, is our cab waiting for us? Just open the window and see." The boy got up to do so, but before he reached it the door opened, and Gertrude, in her deep mourning, entered.

There are moments in life which no pen can describe, as there are effects of light in the heavens which no pencil can render. She came in; her eyes met the eyes of the old man who had been her mother's only friend. She neither fainted nor screamed, but a sort of convulsion passed over her face, and throwing open the door of the back room, she cried, "Here, here, and with you alone." He followed her mechanically, and sat down, for his limbs could hardly support him. She hid her face on the side of the arm-chair into which he had fallen, and murmured, "For her sake who died in my arms and who prayed for me with her last breath, do not spurn me now!" The old man tried to raise her head with his trembling hand, but not succeeding, he laid it upon her forehead, and said, "God's will be done, my child. She is dead, then, your poor mother." Surprised, she raised her head for a moment, and, in her paleness and her suffering, looked so like her whom he spoke of, that his stout heart gave way, and turning away from her, he wept, but held out his hand, which she seized and covered with kisses.

"Perhaps for the last time," she again murmured, for she felt he knew nothing; and then suddenly letting it go, she stood before him pale, resolute and stern:—"You are weeping, but there is greater suffering in store for you than you are now enduring."

"What do you mean, Gertrude? Has anything happened to your father? Good heavens! why are you here? Have you lost him too? For God's sake, speak!"

"He is alive," she said hurriedly; "he is alive; nothing has happened to him, but——"

"But what, but what, Gertrude? You terrify me!"

"I have left him for ever, and have married Maurice Redmond,——not from love, but from despair." She added the last words in a whisper that to the ears of the listener sounded fearfully distinct; and then she stood again silent and motionless, as if awaiting her sentence. He was silent, too; but the veins in his forehead were swelled to bursting, and his eyes glared from beneath his bushy eyebrows; his hands trembled; he tried to get up, but, unable to stand, fell back on the chair and groaned deeply.

"Gertrude," he hoarsely ejaculated, "did you abandon your mother? Did you kill her, unhappy child?"

"Abandon *her!* I have told you she died in my arms. Her last words were a blessing; her last embrace, her last look were mine. I have nothing left but that recollection; nothing but the memory of that hour. She was left to me— to my love, to my tears, to my solitary watchings, till she was borne to her grave; and then I was alone; and grief, passion, and despair wrought like madness in my brain. He robbed me of all earthly hope; he forced a husband upon me on the very morrow of my mother's funeral; he drove me wild, and accidentally—yes, I swear it, accidentally—I met with one who has always loved me. It is too long to tell how I was tempted—drawn on by the power of that love which had been true and constant, when every other had failed me, and which at that moment offered me a refuge. I fled with him, I married him, and I am cast off—even by *you!*" she exclaimed; for Father Lifford had risen, and seemed about to leave the room without a glance or a word.

There was a terrible struggle in his heart. His naturally proud and violent character was asserting itself at that moment. She had degraded her family and her name; she had dishonoured her mother's memory; thrown a slur on her father's character, and had been true and just to none; for he knew she had married one man while she loved another, and he was at that moment aware that the noblest and truest heart in the world was hers; he possessed the proofs of that devoted affection, and his very compassion for her miserable destiny augmented at first the bitterness of his wrath. He could have cursed her for the rash self-destruction she had wrought, and for an instant he felt it impossible to look at or to speak to her. But he was a priest; and what to him, as such, were family ties, and honour, and reputation? What was her own earthly happiness, or that of others, that it should move him thus? What concern had he with aught in comparison with her soul—her immortal soul? Would violence awaken contrition for the past? Would contempt soften a hardened heart, or awake from despondency a prostrate courage? He prayed for calmness, for patience, for meekness. He bade himself forget that it was Gertrude Lifford that was standing before him. He forced himself to look upon her as he would have done on any suffering and penitent woman whom it was his duty to exhort, advise and console. Gravely and calmly he turned towards her, and said:

"Gertrude, my child, you repent of your sin? of having forsaken your home? of having abandoned your father?"

"No, Father Lifford—no. I will speak the truth. I cannot deceive you—not even to obtain kind looks or words which I long for; more than I can express. I do repent of having married poor Maurice"—here she again dropped her voice, and spoke in that painful whispering tone—"of having married him without any sentiment but gratitude. And I do not even always feel that. He might have seen how distracted I was; he ought not to have married me without asking me if I loved him. But it is wrong and ungenerous to say this Mine has been the fault; let mine alone be the penalty, if possible. I repent of having wronged *him*, I repent of having grieved and offended you, but as to my father, he has more need of my forgiveness than I of his; *he* has broken my heart—I have only wounded his pride."

He gazed upon her, and she trembled under that silent reproach. "Poor child!" he said at last, "God deals with you in His secret way; through much sorrow He will bring you to His feet. You will not know one instant's peace, till you have forgotten, in the depths of self-abasement, that others have sinned against you. The day when you will implore from your father a pardon you perhaps never will receive, may be the turning point in your destiny—not for time but for eternity."

"Do *you* forgive me?" she said.

"There is no question of my forgiveness, my child: as your father's uncle I dare not say I forgive you, and your brother shall leave this house without speaking to one who has brought shame and sorrow upon his home. He must obtain his father's permission before he sees you, Gertrude. But, O my child, what have I to do but to call thee, not to my feet, but to my arms; to hold thee for an instant to my heart, while I implore that merciful God whom I have served from my youth up to bless thee. My life will not be long——"

"Do not die, Father Lifford, do not die," she convulsively ejaculated, while she hid her face on his arm.

"If I am never to see you again, my child —"

"O, but you will see me. You said you would not discard me. I will not let you go if you do not promise to see me again."

"As much as man can promise it, Gertrude, I do; be calm, and listen to me. I fear for you other reckless moments of what you may call despair, or a weak sinking under the weight you have chosen to carry. It is a heavy cross you have taken up, my child, but it may be a school for the highest virtues: you were rich, and you have embraced poverty; you were proud, and you have disgraced yourself for ever; you loved, and you have put an eternal barrier between yourself and——"

"*He* did, *he* did," she murmured; "I cannot think of that now. *There, there* was the feeling that maddened me. *He* did it, not I."

Father Lifford saw that she had fancied herself forsaken by

Adrien, and felt he must not at that moment undeceive her. "You have entered," he went on, "on the most thorny and difficult path that a woman can tread, but in proportion to your trials let your courage rise. From heroic virtue such a life of privation and obscurity might have been adopted. Act as if you, out of virtue, had sought it. Accept the destiny you have chosen, and devote yourself to your husband as if you loved him; and forgive him, Gertrude, all that I can scarcely forgive. Remember that *his* excuse—and in your eyes at least it should now be one—is the love which blinded him to the fearful sin he was committing. Henceforward, my child fulfil every duty with patient humility; toil with your hands and with your whole heart, and if needs be, endure hunger and fatigue. Expiate the past, and at each trial you may encounter, look down, and feel that yours is the fault, but also look upward, and believe that the lesson comes from God."

In this stern advice there was something suitable to Gertrude's present state of mind. It wanted softening on the one hand, and bracing on the other. This interview had, for a time, that double effect upon her. Once more Father Lifford blessed her, and allowed her this time to kneel to receive his blessing; then he left her, and called Edgar as he passed through the other room. He took his arm as they walked down stairs, and refused to let him speak. Mrs. Redmond had abruptly left him alone when Gertrude had drawn Father Lifford away, and the poor boy's eyes were red with weeping; for he had guessed, from her mourning, that his mother was dead. He could not conceive why he was hurried away in this manner. When he got into the carriage his forebodings were realised, and the cause of that abrupt departure explained. The grief, the horror, the amazement which succeeded one another on his usually tranquil face were remarkable. He spoke with such severity of his sister's conduct that his uncle was obliged to say, "Come, Edgar, you could not say more if she had committed a crime." And when he wept over his father's fate, and the dreadful blow which had fallen upon him, speaking of him as if he had been the kindest of parents, and in the strongest terms of his sister's ingratitude, again Father Lifford coughed and moved uneasily in his place.

"He is much to be pitied, and you must do all in your power to comfort him, and to soften him towards Gertrude. And remember, Edgar, when you marry and have children, be always kind and affectionate to them, and do not fancy that all the faults are on one side, when such sad events occur in families. Edgar, my boy, when I was teaching you the Catechism, I do not think I spoke to you enough about the dreadful sin of *pride*. If we all had been less proud, this might not have happened. Alas! when we draw near to the grave, we see things in a different light, even when we have tried to act rightly during life. Let us try never to mistake our vices for virtues."

When they arrived at home, Mr. Lifford met them with his usual manner. He embraced his son, and shook hands with his uncle; and saying a few words about his wife's death, which made Edgar weep, he gave each of them some things she had bequeathed to them. Not a single allusion did he make to Gertrude. Her picture had been removed from the drawing-room, and the old butler had taken possession of it. He silently pointed it out one day to Father Lifford, who sighed deeply, and said, "Will you lend it me for a little while?" and had it hung up in his room. He was not well, and seldom left it now. Edgar often came to sit with him, and he showed him much affection, but the old man's heart was sad and heavy. The patient suffering mother, where was she? In Heaven, he trusted, and felt consoled. The reckless and beautiful child, where was she? Tossed by the roughest waves of life; drifting along on the world's wide sea. But she was breasting the billows and might yet reach the haven, and that thought gave him comfort. But where was the man whom he had loved in his youth,—the son of his brother, whom he had nursed on his knees? He was near him, but on what road? A traitor to his God, for he was called a Catholic, and was one only in name,—the destroyer of his wife, for he had blighted her life, and embittered her death,—the author of his daughter's misery, for he had driven her to despair, and goaded her to sin. On what road was he then? The road to destruction. The old man prayed for him; for the faith that sleeps may yet live again, and the love that is cold may yet warm again, and the heart that is hard may soften or break.

He prayed a great deal in the chapel and elsewhere. He sometimes went to sit alone in the room which had been Mrs Lifford's. Once he raised his eyes to a picture, which reminded him of something in the past, and groaning in spirit, he exclaimed, "O child, child! if thou hadst known ——," and then stopped short. He missed her at meals; he missed her in the drawing-room, in the chapel, in the gardens. Her voice, her smile, her faults, her follies—he missed them all. He grew very ill, and knew that he was dying. Then he sent for his nephew, and talked to him a long time; and when Mr. Lifford left the room, he was paler than when his wife expired—paler than when his daughter fled. The old priest died, and his grave was made near to Mrs. Lifford's. He bequeathed the little he possessed to Gertrude, and sent her his blessing, through Mr. Erving, who had attended him in his last moments. Soon after his death, the establishment at the Grange was broken up, and Mr. Lifford and his son went to travel abroad.

When Gertrude received the news of her uncle's death, she experienced a sensation of such utter desolation that it prostrated for a while all her powers of exertion. But the resolutions she had made after her last interview with him were confirmed; and when she recovered from the indisposition which had followed that severe shock, all the listlessness of her manner had disappeared, and an expression of stern endurance and energetic self-reliance had taken its place.

CHAPTER XXI.

"No wounds like those a wounded spirit feels;
No cure for such, till God, who makes them, heals.
And thou, sad sufferer, under nameless ill,
That yields not to the touch of human skill,
To thee the dayspring, and the blaze of noon,
The purple evening, and resplendent moon,
Shine not; or undesired, or hated, shine,
Seen through the medium of a cloud like thine.
Yet seek *Him*, in His favour life is found;
All bliss beside a shadow or a cloud;
Then Heaven eclipsed so long, and this dull earth,
Shall seem to start into a second birth."
COWPER.

"Never did thine eye
Look on me but in glistening tenderness;
Never did thy voice
But in affection's deepest music speak;
Never was thine heart
Aught but the kindliest sheltering home to mine."
MRS. HEMANS.

WHAT is called the *season* was beginning again; and spring was showing its sickly and premature verdure in the squares and the gardens of London. On a warm April day—a rare thing and a beautiful—when a few soft showers had washed off the houses and the trees some of the accumulated dust of March, Maurice was slowly walking back from the railway station, where he had accompanied his step-mother and Mary, who were returning to the country. Mrs. Redmond's health had suffered so much from the winter spent in London, that the change had been considered absolutely necessary for her; and now that Maurice was married, there seemed no reason for their remaining in town. Gertrude had applied herself with unwearied patience to learn the details of their simple housekeeping. She worked indefatigably from morning to night. Never once since the day of her last interview with Father Lifford, had she complained of anything, or omitted any one of the duties of an active and devoted wife. She worked at her needle for several hours in the day; she went into the kitchen, and with that rare intelligence which characterized her, she mastered all the details of domestic economy, and spent less money, and made her husband as comfortable as the most experienced housewife could have done. She never had spoken harshly or unkindly to him. Her submission was implicit. She obeyed him as a nun obeys her superior, or a soldier his captain. Without him she never went out, except early in the morning to church or on business. With him she went wherever he asked her—into Hyde Park, by the side of the Serpentine, when the full tide of society was swarming along its shore,—still in her mourning, with her majestic beauty—for it was majestic from grace and dignity—however slight her form and delicate her features. Some have walked on hot ploughshares, and not winced as they did so, weak women as they were, when their honour was at stake. Perhaps even they did not suffer more than she did during these summer walks by the cool river, under the old trees that have shaded so much misery and joy. Numberless eyes were turned upon her in curiosity and admiration; never once did they obtain a glance from those dark orbs, which, veiled by their thick lashes, seemed turned inward, as it were, so little notice did they bestow on any outward object. She toiled all day long. She copied out music for him till her head throbbed, and he snatched the pen from her aching fingers; but she never asked him to play.

Once he began the first notes of the Lady-Bird song. She turned pale, and he saw it. He then sang the "Fou de Tolède," and her lips became white. He snatched his hat, and rushed out of the room with a feeling of rage in his heart. What could he do, and what more could she do? She fulfilled her duty to the uttermost; did not even show depression, or give way to lowness of spirits. What had he to complain of?—That she did not love him. Do women devote themselves so patiently and unweariedly to husbands they do not love? Mary, still the only person to whom he opened his heart, had reproached him almost severely for his misgivings. She had become enthusiastic about Gertrude. She called her an angel.—thought her conduct most touching and admirable. No one pitied him, and yet his heart was breaking. At that time he suffered probably more than she did. Her strong will and independent judgment had adopted a line on which every energy of her soul was bent. She had taken hold of those words of Father Lifford in their last interview, "Devote yourself to your husband as though you loved him," and acted upon them to the letter, but not in the spirit—for that devotion hardened instead of softening her heart. She joined to that recollection one of her old and inveterate errors,—that the will can influence actions, but not feelings. She found a sort of stern pleasure in making every sacrifice, and even that of her own will, on a thousand occasions, because it was her will to give up everything but the one proud sense of having paid her debt of duty to the uttermost farthing, in a coin which the debtor could not question, but which was worthless to his aching soul. She did not wrong him even in thought—she never wilfully directed her thoughts to Adrien. Not one of the many little objects associated with the memory of her happier days did she preserve. She never opened his books, or dwelt upon the past, but the heart from which she shut him out was henceforward to remain a desert. Maurice had not ventured to read it before he availed himself of her distracted state of mind to hurry her into marrying him, and he had no right to insist on reading it now.

It was a subtle error under which she was acting. She never tried to love or prayed for the power of loving her husband; and who could have supposed this to be the case that had seen her anticipating his slightest wish—bearing his irritability (for he was becoming very irritable) with a patience which he was sometimes tempted in moments of exasperation to curse, while to all others, and even to herself, it must have seemed the highest virtue. When he was ill she sat up with him all night; she wrote his notes of excuse to his pupils.

She went herself to his patrons to apologise for his absence from their concerts. She seemed to have quelled her pride, mastered her temper, and shaken off her indolence. But to have looked at him in a manner that he might have mistaken for love, to have used a single word of endearment that might have implied more tenderness than she felt, *that* she was firmly resolved never to do; and with the characteristic peculiarity of her race, was all the time, as Father Lifford had said, mistaking a vice for a virtue. He was supported in his trials neither by the proud consciousness nor the illusion of virtue. He knew well that he had not the courage or the justice to test her feelings previous to the decisive hour, by the fulfilment of a solemn duty, the accomplishment of a sacred trust; the sin had been great, but it had not been deliberate. The atonement was long and severe. Through the stern calmness of her face he was continually striving to discern what its serenity concealed. It was like the veil on the face of the Prophet of Khorassan; he dreaded and he wished to tear away that smooth impenetrable barrier between himself and the object of his continual misgivings, his still passionate affection, and his perpetual scrutiny. He tried every means to pierce through it. He proposed to read out loud to her, and she agreed to it as to everything else he suggested. This was perhaps the hardest trial to her equanimity. He chose whatever was most likely to move her feelings, and by awakening emotion to bring to light the secret sufferings of her soul. He was ingenious in the art of tormenting himself and her. He knew how to select the poem, the tragedy, or the novel that would probe deepest the wound which she concealed with such stoical courage. He used suddenly to raise his eyes from the book when affecting or startling passages occurred in these experimental readings, and see with mingled sensations of pity and of rage the tear gathering on the eyelid, but forbidden to flow; the deepening flush of the cheek, the momentary abstraction, the upward gaze, or the trembling of the hand when each muscle of the face was compelled to be motionless.

Who that had taken a cursory survey of that little room on such evenings as these would have guessed the misery that was dwelling in those two young hearts? The beautiful wife, in all her stately loveliness, sitting by the round table with her work before her, diligently employed in mending the clothes, or sewing the linen required in the house, never relaxing one instant from her toil, and listening in silence to the accents of love or sorrow, of passion or regret, by the ablest readers, masters, and spokesmen of the human heart; and he, the artist, the husband, the lover, the gainer of the treasure which has turned to stone in his grasp, pale with suspense, with eyes that flash fire through gathering tears, and a voice that trembles with emotion, reading what feeds perhaps the flame which burns under that ice without thawing the suface that hardens as he gazes,—how like happiness was the outward aspect of that home, how deep a current of suffering was flowing underneath!

While she every day grew more proudly and harshly virtuous, he became more waywardly and deeply miserable. Fits of ill-humour succeeded one another, bursts of anger immediately repented of, but recurring again at frequent intervals; days of dejection, in which all labour was irksome, and constraint insupportable. His talents were paralyzed in that mental conflict. He lost all energy for study and composition, and gradually most of his pupils discontinued taking lessons. Then he felt an intense wish for any change, and he pressed her to go into such society as was open to them, and to accept any invitations that were sent her. At first they were few, and from persons of obscure station. She did not seem much to care where she went, and dressed and talked and sat up as long as he chose, and listened to those who spoke to her, as if she were neither more nor less unhappy in one place than in another. She could hardly fail to be agreeable, when she exerted herself at all: her conversation was irresistibly interesting to those who surrounded her, attracted by her singular beauty and the circumstances of her marriage. She never wore anything but a black velvet gown: one day he asked her why she did not put on her diamond necklace, when they were going to some concert where he was to play. She did so immediately: and no hair shirt ever felt so irksome to its wearer; but she bore these little trials, like the great ones, with unflinching fortitude.

At a party one night at the house of a painter of eminence, who had been many years a friend of Maurice's, she met Mr. Egerton. He did not know her again at first;—but after a moment's hesitation he felt sure he was not mistaken, and claimed acquaintance with her. With the extraordinary self-control she possessed, she did not betray the least agitation but conversed with him for a long time—not playfully, as of old, but with more cleverness still than in former days—talked about politics, and literature, and a variety of subjects, as if her heart were not aching to a degree which would have made her groan aloud had she, for an instant, given way. He told her Lady Clara Audley was still abroad, and was, he knew, anxious to learn her direction that she might write to her. In her last letter she had said: "Mind you find out something about my Lady-Bird? I will not lose sight of her." A name, a phrase, the tone of voice in which a word i uttered, how sharp is the pang they can inflict! but after a long dull aching pain there is sometimes a sensation of relief in a change of suffering, and she went on talking of Lady Clara, and asking questions about her.

"How does she like Paris? How does Paris like her?"

"The liking is mutual. She is excessively admired, and she amuses herself from morning to night with every gay and serious thing that comes in her way. She has friends of all sorts and kinds, and they take her to the most different places. She sees people of the most opposite politics, and there are curious meetings in her drawing-room. During the short time that I was with her, she gave me a specimen of the various interests to be found in this new page of her life. It was high time that she should go abroad; she had exhausted novelty in England, and wanted some new canvas to work upon. It would amuse you to hear all the different things that she does in succession. How she goes from a crèche, or an hospice, to the morning rehearsal of an opera; from a sermon at St. Roch to a dinner at a café; how she begins the day with a messe en musique at the Madeleine, and ends with the theatre of the Palais-Royal. Her Paris Sundays are curious: she rushes from one church to another, from the discourses of an Unitarian preacher to the conferences of Father Lacordaire; from the Swedenborgian meeting, or perhaps from the synagogue, to Notre-Dame-des-Victoires, where she braves the heat and pushes through the crowd, for the sake of the thousand voices that strike up at once their enthusiastic cantiques. I was nearly dead after following her through her successive religious amusements last Sunday."

"She must be very good not to be afraid of thus playing with the most tremendous subjects on earth and beyond it."

"Why, never having hurt a fly in her life, or spoken an unkind word—though she may have uttered many thoughtless ones—I suppose her conscience has no need to give her uneasiness. Time has as little ruffled her soul as wrinkled her face;—she is nearly as pretty as ever."

"At that moment Mr. Egerton was struck with the expression of Gertrude's face, on which twenty-two years of life had left traces which nearly forty had failed to impress on his sister's. It was not age, it was not even sorrow that had marked it thus. It was something that he could not understand, something that made him write to Lady Clara the next day: "Your Lady-Bird is, if possible, more beautiful than ever; but, if I am not much mistaken, the iron has entered into her soul. I never quite understood that expression before, but it came spontaneously into my head as I looked at her last night."

Whether from curiosity to see the effect which would be produced upon her by the mention of the name of a person whom, at one time, she had been supposed to like, or from thoughtlessness, he went on to tell her that he had seen Adrien at Paris, and related on what occasion. How he had gone one day with his sister to the subterranean chapel of St. Sulpice, where what is called the Associations of the Sainte Famille hold their assemblies. Six or eight hundred workmen, with their wives and children, attend conferences, which create a singular bond of union between them and those who devote themselves to their instruction; the humanising effect of this intercourse, and the strange interest which is attached to a great school for men, makes it one of the most exciting and touching scenes imaginable. Laymen in great numbers, and some of them eminent in various ways, second the clergy, and often address familiar discourses to those rough children of St. Francis Xavier; for it is under that wonder-working name that these men in blouses enroll themselves. Mr. Egerton had briefly described this curious scene to Gertrude, and then said, "We were taken by surprise, when after a few words full of liveliness and fun from Father Milleriot, another person came up to the table in the centre, and began talking to that singular audience. Guess who it was? Clara gave such a start that it made our neighbours look round."

"I suppose it was Monsieur d'Arberg," Gertrude calmly said. It was the first time she had pronounced his name since she had done so in her father's study a year ago. "Did you see him only that once?"

"Only that once," he answered. "Clara had a long visit from him afterwards. He never goes out anywhere, I believe

People cannot understand why he does not become a priest, for he lives a strange life for a man of the world, and seems to have lost all interest in politics and literature, or anything but hard work amongst the poorest people."

"Is he *not* going to be a priest?" she asked, fastening on that idea, but as if afraid to grasp it.

"There does not seem to have ever been any question of it, Clara told me. I never saw any one so altered. He is handsomer than ever—but looks very ill. You are not going yet, Mrs. Redmond, are you? Malibran is just about to sing."

She sat down again, simply because she could not stand. Thoughts and feelings were rushing too violently upon her. With all her might she was shutting out of her soul that desolating torrent. People go through a great deal sometimes; and in that moment the singer and the song brought before her the past in bitter contrast with the present. "To the dregs," she said to herself. "To the dregs," and sat resolutely draining the sufferings of that hour.

When she went home something seemed altered in the part she had assigned to herself. She was not so calm or so stern as before. Maurice was startled at the expression of her countenance. He felt an imperative desire to question her, to probe her feelings more directly than he had ever yet done. He felt as if for a time he would suffer less, if he had something definite to complain of. He longed to be able to reproach her or himself. A terrible temptation beset him that night. He had remained alone in the sitting-room after his wife had left it; and he went to his desk and took out of it a sealed letter, which he gazed on for some time in silence, as if he would have pierced with his eyes through the folded paper,—as if the seal was the barrier between him and something which he at once feared and longed to look into.

The letter was not directed to him, "If I were to leave it in her way," he said to himself, "and could watch her while she read it, I should see by her eyes, by her colour, by her attitude, what interest it excited, what emotion it awakened. But to give it to her without knowing its contents—I cannot do it. O that this detested letter had never reached me! One quarter of an hour later, and my conscience would have been free from the horrid self-reproach that comes between me and peace every moment of the day. Nothing but this seal to break, and I should learn all. Has not a husband the right to know his wife's secrets? Yet in this way, entrusted to me, and by him too who never knew what it was to suspect or to betray. 'I know you to be an honourable man.' Why did he say that in his accursed note? I ought to have destroyed or returned this letter the day of my marriage. It haunts me as if it was a living thing. I think of it the last thing at night, and the first thing in the morning, when I walk about the streets; I see it there in its place in my desk, as if it was defying me to read or to destroy it. I *will* destroy it." He started up from his chair and went towards the fire, and held the letter over it, but could not unclose his fingers to drop it. "Never to know what that man had to say to her; never to ascertain if the phantom that pursues me, and stands between her and me, is a delusion or a reality! What an absurd weakness, not to break this seal!' It was to the honour of one who had no claim upon her that he trusted—not to mine, who am her husband, and who ought to have her love."

He put down on the chimney the letter that was causing him such a terrible struggle. It was a strange inconsistency, perhaps, that a man who had not fulfilled a trust by delivering it, when he ought, to her to whom it was directed, should now so hesitate to make himself master of its contents—should tremble at this sin, when he had committed a greater one. His head was buried in his hands, and he was sunk in deep thought. In an instant he felt, more than perceived, that there was some one standing by his side, and he turned as pale as death when he saw that it was Gertrude. Mechanically he put out his hand to snatch up the letter, but she had seen it, and said in her calm stern manner, "That letter is for me—my name is upon it." His hand trembled; for one second he thought again of destroying it, but felt giddy and did not do so. She took it from him, and he did not resist: she looked at it again, and recognised the handwriting. A slight trembling came over her, and she turned towards the door.

"No, read it here," he abruptly ejaculated. She had used herself to obey him, and sat down at the table. He remained leaning at the chimney. There was a profound silence in the room. He heard the sound of the breaking of the seal, and the unfolding of the paper. She read it through, and he watched her. He had often watched her before, but never as then. The hectic spot rose on her marble cheek, and deepened into intensity, till it grew into a burning flush: the blue veins on her forehead swelled, and swelled, till they seemed unnaturally distended; her mouth quivered, and she began again to tremble. It was dreadful to see her thus motionless, except for that trembling; it was like the silence of nature before a storm—the rustle of the leaves before the crash of thunder. Then came the cry of despair, the burst of grief, which nothing could repress. Long held down, it broke forth in that hour. All was forgotten for an instant; and with her hands on her temples, and torrents of tears streaming down her face, she murmured Adrien's name, and groaned in spirit.

The fiery element, which from his Italian mother had passed into the veins of Maurice, inflamed his soul at that instant, and he sprang from the place where he was standing with a fierce impetuosity that would have frightened any but a profoundly miserable woman. It was nothing to her at that moment that he looked as if he could kill her, but it was dreadful to him that he felt it. The reaction was so strong that he staggered and would have fallen, if he had not caught hold of the handle of the door. She saw his deadly paleness, and her heart smote her. "Maurice! poor Maurice!" she said, and held out both her hands to him. He had sat down, and murmured, "Give it me." She obeyed, put it into his hands; and now in her turn sorrowfully, silently, with something between compassion and reproach, she watched him read this letter that had remained so long unread, and which, earlier seen, would have changed the fate of three persons. It had been enclosed in one to Maurice, and had reached him only the very morning of his marriage, when at the point of gaining that end he had so recklessly pursued. Adrien had simply requested him to take an opportunity of giving it to Gertrude, either himself or through Mary, or in any way that would ensure her receiving it. He had added, that he could trust him, knowing he had to deal with an honourable man, and one who knew him (Adrien) well enough to rely on the integrity of his motives in desiring such secrecy.

If Maurice had known that an engagement had previously existed between Adrien and Gertrude, he would not in all probability have kept back that letter, even at that moment of distraction; but he supposed it contained his first avowal of affection, and a proposal of marriage, which his misgivings whispered to him might endanger her peace if she married him, or overthrow the whole fabric of his happiness, if it induced her to change her mind. She would then appeal to his generosity; and no alternative would remain to him, but the almost insupportable misery of losing her. To steel his conscience against the voice of duty, to drown the sense of right by specious and rapid reasonings, to say to himself that whatever that letter contained it came too late to give it to her, that it would not even be fair to Adrien, who was ignorant of the strange circumstances under which it would be received, and of the position in which she stood with regard to himself —was the work of a moment. This miserable sophistry was like laudanum taken in raging pain, which stills without drowning the sense of suffering; and the fatal letter was thrust into his breast, and lay next his heart while he pronounced the marriage vow. Great was his sin, but great also was the penalty that followed it; for this was the letter he had seen her read, and which she now placed in his hands :—

"Dearest Gertrude. We were to have met again—we had reckoned upon it, in that hour of sorrow and of joy, when we parted for a while with hope in our hearts, and a strong trust in each other. You know, or alas! you may not know, that I have been refused by your father. I was denied that short interview for which I pleaded with an earnestness that could have scarcely been withstood, if arguments had not been used which struck me dumb in that moment of suffering and of agitation. I was charged not to disturb your mother's peace, and thrust myself into your presence while you were watching her dying bed. I prayed to be allowed to write to you, even though my letter should be read by your father, and offered to pledge myself not to write again, if thus far he would condescend to my prayer. He refused even this; he told me that you were promised in marriage to another person, and that all attempts to correspond with you would be useless, as he would take measures to prevent any letter reaching you, and literally drove me from his house. Gertrude, I knew you would suffer, but I knew also you would trust me—that no false appearances, no calumnies, no assertions of friends or of enemies, if we have any, would make you doubt me, and this alone enabled me to be calm at first.

"I have written to Father Lifford, and implored him to convey to you the assurance, not of anything that could offend your father, but only of what it might concern your peace to know—that one whom you had trusted had not deceived you; but I feel compelled, by a vague and increasing anxiety, to seek some more direct way of conveying to you an assurance, without which I feel it myself every day more difficult to bear without flinching the burthen of the hour.

"I do not ask anything of you, Gertrude. You are free: no promise, no duty binds you. But, O remember not to be weak; whatever is right, that do. God forbid I should ever stand between you and your father; but it cannot be right to love one man and to marry another: and you *have* loved me, you do love me; deep in my heart's core I feel it, and never, in the days we were together, never, during the brief sunshine of our love, have I felt for you what I do now. This is all I can—all I will say. I am bound to you by a tie as strong as if you were already my wife; not the less strong because I hold you to be free, and have no right to reproach you if you obey your father.

"I am going about the work of life again. The dangerous illness of one of my oldest and dearest friends, at the seminary of Orleans, calls me to his side, and afterwards matters of business, to my brother, in Brittany; but there, and here, and everywhere, one only effort, and one only prayer shall be mine —to become worthier of possessing you one day, or to prepare myself to resign you; and, in so doing, every hope of earthly happiness, if such should be God's will.

"I shall not write again, my beloved Gertrude, but when I once know that you have received this letter I shall have no fears for you or for myself.

"Your most affectionate
"ADRIEN."

The letter dropped from Maurice's hands, and he hid his face with them. She knelt by the side of his chair; she felt very sorry for him, more than she had ever done before. "Forgive me," she said, gently, "forgive me, that I married you." He turned suddenly round, and his eyes flashed fire through their tears. "Forgive you, while you love that man! No, by all I have suffered, no! I do not forgive you. Burn that letter before me, I cannot touch it again.—Burn it this instant." She stooped to pick it up, and looked so pale, so unspeakably wretched, as she dropped it into the fire, and watched the flames consuming it, that a sudden reaction occurred in his feelings; he threw himself at her feet, and with startling vehemence exclaimed.

"I received that letter, Gertrude on the morning of our marriage, and *I* was trusted with it. I might have given it to you before you had sealed your misery. O, can you not hate and despise me?"

"*You* had it!" she said. "That letter was in *your* hands! It would have saved me, and you did not give it me! Did you do this, Maurice? O then you deserve the fate you have found. God help us both; we are doomed to a life of sorrow."

"You never told me you had loved that man; you never told me that you had been engaged to him."

"You saw my heart was breaking. Did you ever ask me if I loved you?"

"O, cannot you love me? At the altar you swore to love me. Have you no pity, no conscience?"

"What do you care for my pity? What have you to do with my conscience? I am your wife; you would have it so. Adrien trusted you. O fool that he was to trust you or me!"

The deep flush of resentment overcame, at that instant, the ashy paleness in Maurice's cheek, and he left the room without uttering another word. For the second time in her life it seemed to Gertrude as if the fair edifice of virtue, which she had been so sternly and sedulously raising, had crumbled to the ground. Once again it had been built on the sand; though it had looked firmer than the first, it had given way under this new blast of agitating grief. She was deeply disturbed in spirit by this scene with her husband. She felt as if she could not now forgive him, or resume that life of practical devotion to him which had been her support during the last year.

When Maurice returned to his home, a look of settled gloom had fixed itself on his face. There was something reckless and wild in his manner. He no longer asked her to walk with him, or to go into society. He never read, and talked to her but little. She was alone for hours; and now the barrier which she had called virtue, but which was partly made up of pride and resentment, was too feeble to keep back, at all times, the torrent of regrets, of unmastered passion, and intense feelings which were overflowing her soul like a desolating flood. She ceased to deny herself the fatal indulgence of her old habits of dreaming, and no longer banished Adrien's image from her mind. It pursued her everywhere. To confession she dared not go, for she would not renounce the sin of that thought; to mass she still went, but it hardened her heart, for she would not have it softened, but only dared not stay away. She had a wild strange feeling of resentment, that not even in prayer could she meet Adrien in spirit; she was without that region where his soul doubtless found peace; and yet she would not break the chain with which passion bound hers. Once more she read his works, secretly as an act of guilt is performed; it was his voice once more in her ears; it was his mind once again speaking to hers; and her cheek burned, and her heart throbbed, but not with the bright enthusiasm of former days—not with the spirit which then roused her to the knowledge and to the love of virtue. The more fervid was his eloquence, the more noble his sentiments, the more she writhed with the anguish of their irrevocable separation. His earnest words brought back to her memory the voice she was never to hear again; and when he spoke of God, of Heaven, and of goodness, it seemed but the echoes of a music which once had been familiar, but to which her blighted but unsubdued heart no longer responded.

It was a great relief to her now that Maurice stayed so much away from home, that he no longer seemed to require her society; and she did not observe how haggard was the expression of his face at times, or how moody were his long fits of abstraction at others. He was enduring at once the double pangs of jealousy and remorse. There were moments when anger and resentment prevailed; but others again, when he pitied Gertrude, and would have intensely longed to replace her in peace and in freedom, unscathed by the misery he had so recklessly drawn her into. Trials of every kind were staring him in the face; poverty was becoming every day more imminent, and its prospects more galling. His want of power to strive with his own sufferings deprived him gradually of all the resources from whence he had drawn an income. They were soon reduced to live on the small amount of fortune which Father Lifford had bequeathed to Gertrude. It was a perpetual torment to him thus to owe his support to her, and he made imprudent and desperate efforts to ameliorate the state of his affairs.

Mary had been right. He could not steer alone his bark through a rough sea; the burthen on his heart and that on his conscience were too much for his strength. Gertrude's coldness, which had now deepened into unkindness, paralysed every nerve, and checked every effort. Before that terrible day when both had read Adrien's letter he had had the stimulus of hope and of fear; now he neither feared nor hoped, and his mental energies seemed to die away within him. He used to absent himself as much as possible; and unable to pursue his former occupations, all his anxiety was to spend nothing upon himself that he could possibly avoid, and to devise schemes for improving his worldly position. Their solitary meals were generally silent. She was the least depressed of the two; but there was a gloomy abyss between them and an image ever present before the mental sight of both. Once or twice during that time old friends sought them out—he got out of the way to avoid them. He shrank from the eyes of others with a morbid sensitiveness. He felt as if Gertrude hated him, and to be hated by one whom he passionately loved, seemed to stamp upon him a brand which made everything odious to him.

And he never had loved her more than now. Sometimes when he came in late in the evening after wandering through the streets for hours he would find her asleep in her chair, worn out with a long day's toil (for work she would with a feverish assiduity); and he would gaze at her with a tenderness which matured for a while both jealousy and resentment; and by degrees the bitter trial he was going through was breaking up the soil where once good seed had been sown. It was as if scales had fallen from his eyes, as if he had perceived for the first time, almost, the extent of his guilt,—the reckless selfishness of his course,—the miserable amount of his offences in God's sight,—the dreadful injury he had inflicted on the woman he so passionately loved, and the man whom his lower nature hated, while his better self recalled his virtues and the long arrears of gratitude he owed him. Things that Mary used to say to him, now often came to his mind again. He began to look upon the future in a different way from heretofore; to feel that he might never be, nor deserved ever to be happy again. At moments he struggled against that conviction—he felt to want "*du bonheur à tout prix.*" He tried to persuade himself that his punishment was greater than his sin; but once awakened, the conscience of a man who is not wholly perverted is too strong for him, and its logic too powerful. Every succeeding day he reproached himself more and others less; and saw in a clearer light his treachery to Mary, his ingratitude to Adrien, and his cruelty to Gertrude. A deep discouragement took possession of him, and his useless passionate efforts to redeem the past, to procure her happiness of some sort, to change something in a fate which appeared to him more and more hopeless, only enhanced the misery of his life.

He vainly tried to compose as he used to do. His genius seemed to have forsaken him. Once only a faint gleam of it returned. He was walking one day in a meadow some way out of London, and as he was strolling listlessly along he saw a troop of children pursuing with eager delight a richly-painted butterfly. Still it eluded their grasp, and flew from flower to flower, its purple and gold wings shining in the sunlight; but one eager hand caught it at last, and the curious children pressed around the fortunate possessor. He opened his hand, and there lay the crushed insect, with the bright colours rubbed off its light wings, with its life nearly extinct, and its form almost motionless. Maurice turned away, and he murmured as he went, "O my Lady-Bird—my Lady-Bird—thus have I dealt with thee!" When he went home that evening he told her the story; but without any comment. She looked up from her work and said, "Poor butterfly." He wrote a song that night, and called it "The Child and the Butterfly." It was the only good thing he had composed since his marriage. If he had been always able like that day to turn his sufferings into music, he might have marched rapidly towards fame, for he had an ample store to draw from.

There came a day when Gertrude was struck with the perturbed expression of his countenance,—and it would have been strange if she had not, for in addition to the usual care-worn look which his features had lately worn, there was something quite new in their aspect. He was suffering the keenest anxiety regarding money matters. The mania for speculation was then at its height; and tempted by the ardent desire to improve, not so much his own as Gertrude's destiny, he had embarked in an undertaking which promised fairly, and the risks of which he had not sufficiently considered. The result was unfortunate, and his liabilities surpassed by far his slender means of meeting them. He had only one intimate friend, the young painter, Dee, who in former years had introduced him to Adrien d'Arberg. He was one of the few persons who was often with him and with Gertrude, for whom he had a great admiration; he admired her beauty, but still more her conduct. He saw they were not happy, and wondered why they were not so; but her patience, and her indefatigable industry astonished and charmed him. One day, the same on which Gertrude had been struck by the extreme misery that she saw in his face, Maurice went to William Dee, and disclosed to him the desperate position in which he found him self He knew the young painter could not assist him, and in the midst of his distress there was a calmness that perplexed his friend. He offered to persuade others to go security for him,—he endeavoured to find some remedy for the evil, but Maurice stopped him, and said,

"I have no means of retrieving myself; I have been imprudent, and must bear the penalty. My folly has been immense; I have risked more than I shall ever be able to pay. If I had not been deceived my conduct would have been dishonourable. But I had no notion that I was committed to such an extent. There is one thing I am deeply thankful for; Gertrude has a small income settled on herself, which will keep her from absolute destitution. I am liable to be any day arrested, and I care not now how soon it happens. Anything is better than the state of miserable suspense in which I live: I would not have troubled you about this, dear William, but for one reason,—you will, I know, be kind to her when the blow falls on me. She will want advice, perhaps——"

"And comfort," the other ejaculated, with glistening eyes.

"None, that you or any one in this wide world can ever give her," Maurice exclaimed, as if suddenly unable to control his feelings.

He hastily moved to a different part of the room, and struggled with himself for a moment; then wringing his friend's hand, he left him.

A few days after this Gertrude was sitting by the fire, at the usual dinner hour, wondering that Maurice did not come home. The hours went by, and he did not return. All sorts of thoughts came into her mind, of a most contradictory nature; a nervousness, an anxiety to see him return—not very consistent, perhaps, with her habitual indifference; and then a vague idea that perhaps he might never return passed through her mind. The night wore on, and he did not come; she did not go to bed, nor close her eyes; but sat on by the fire, gazing into herself as it were, and pondering over her strange feelings. She longed to hear his footstep on the stairs, but it was more because her anxiety was irksome than because her heart was softened towards him. If he should desert her entirely she would not care, she said to herself, and then she thought of her utter loneliness, and of his melancholy impassioned eyes, and wondered if it would make her sad never to see them again.

The daylight came, and her restlessness increased. Towards nine o'clock William Dee arrived, and when they told her he wished to speak to her, she had a faint sensation at her heart. "Something has happened," that vague sentence which embodies so much vague apprehension! He broke to her, with more caution than was necessary, the fact that Maurice had been arrested; for the instant she heard the nature of the event which had detained him, she was perfectly calm and very cold. He was provoked at her apparent insensibility, and owned his fears that Maurice was plunged into inextricable difficulties, but that he bore them with resignation, supported by the knowledge that she was not reduced to poverty by his imprudence; that he was anxious to know if she would come and see him in——prison; and then that he hoped that she would send for his mother and Mary, and try to arrange living somewhere with them for a while. He supposed she would not like to go to Stonehouseleigh.

"O no," she said with a shudder, "*there* I never can go. But what does Maurice mean by these plans? To what extent is he involved—what are his liabilities?"

"It would be useless to explain them to you, Mrs. Redmond. They are greater than he can meet."

"But not than *I* can meet."

"That he would not hear of. His only comfort is, that your small fortune is safe from his creditors."

"Not safe from them for one hour longer than I can help. Mr. Dee, if you will not assist me about this, I will instantly apply to some one who will do for money what you might out of friendship."

"I must implore you for Maurice's sake not to think of this,"—(her lip curled)—"it would make him miserable."

"It is not a matter of feeling," she said sternly. "More or less misery to either of us signifies but little. His debts must be paid immediately. He *must* be free this very night. I would rather *not* go to see him where he is, but I will if you think he wishes it, even though he should return here to-night."

"But, Mrs. Redmond, you will not do this without his consent?"

"I will, and in a way that may ruin me and not serve him, if you do not help me. Come with me instantly to a lawyer's. I have a *will*, Mr. Dee, that has often asserted itself where it ought to have given way. It will *not* give way now. Be sure of it. Maurice has done nothing dishonourable, has he?"

"Not in the least—he has been imprudent, but more sinned against than sinning."

"Ay, he has indeed," she exclaimed; and, weak with the long sleepless night and the agitation she had undergone, she burst into tears, but in an instant conquered her emotion.

She acted all that day with an intelligence and an energy that astonished her companion. In spite of his remonstrances, which grew more feeble as he witnessed her firm resolve, her perfect consciousness of the sacrifices she was making, with at the same time her calm indifference about them, she achieved all the necessary arrangements; and by parting with all but one thousand pounds of Father Lifford's legacy, she met all Maurice's difficulties, and placed him again in an honourable position in the eyes of the world. His friend went to communicate to him what had been done, and was quite alarmed at his grief and indignation when he heard of it. William Dee was good-hearted and very simple-minded. He did not set much value upon money. It came into his hands and went out of them in a way that did not make him rate as highly as many other people would have done Gertrude's sacrifice of her fortune, and not acquainted with the secret of his friend's heart and destiny, it seemed to him natural enough that his young wife, who had already given up so much for him, should act in this manner. He was not prepared to witness the burst of bitter sorrow mixed with anger against him, with which Maurice received the intelligence, and he kept urging him to go home, as if there he was likely to find consolation and repose.

When Maurice did return, Gertrude received him with more of her old manner than she had ever shown since their marriage. She smiled a smile he had not seen for many a long day. It went through his heart like a dagger. She made a playful remark upon his absence. His lip quivered:

"I cannot thank you, Gertrude, for what you have done t has been no kindness to me."

"No, and I did not mean it as such," she answered. "I have pleased myself, and I like our present prospects better than I have done anything for a long time."

"What do you mean?" he said.

"I mean that of course we must emigrate now. J'ai brûlé mes vaisseaux. The world is a wide one, and a new one will suit you and me, Maurice. Let us go,—let us leave everything behind, and see if the Yankees will not give you work in your profession; and if not, we will to the backwoods, and lead a savage life. I yearn for the forests and the falls of the New World. What do you say to a log cabin? Shall we not breathe there more freely than here?"

His heart beat as she spoke, and he tried to catch her eyes to read their expression, but they were fixed on the fire, which she was stirring while she spoke.

"Thank God," he ejaculated, "that you *have* a wish. I can say no more."

"Say nothing, and see to-morrow about a passage," she answered.

He thought of Mary and her mother, but did not speak of them. The next day, and the next, Gertrude was kinder to him than usual, and she talked with pleasure of the plan of emigrating. But when it was really settled, she could hardly speak of it in the same tone. The past rose again before her. This was indeed cutting the cable, and going adrift. Never to hear again of Adrien,—never, even by chance in the course of long years, once to see his face; for she had thought of that chance, till it had grown into an expectation, and her heart sank within her at the very thought of new scenes which she had for an instant imagined would relieve the restless pain of an incessant looking back without peace, and forward without hope. Her fits of abstraction were longer and deeper than ever, till the work of preparation began. Then she worked as if a slave-driver had been near her. He sold the copyright of his opera for a trifling sum, and bought a travelling case for her. He put it in her way, but did not give it her as a present. He wanted no thanks—not even a smile.

He went into the country to take leave of Mary and Mrs. Redmond. Once more he sat in the little garden under the thorn-tree, and looked on the familiar scenes amidst which his childhood had passed, and he had a great deal of conversation with Mary. He confided to her the story of his sin, his sorrow, and his remorse. They strolled together to the bridge over the Leigh, and sat under the shade of the dark alders, they visited the graves of Mrs. Lifford and of the old priest they had loved, and the church where Maurice used to play the organ. He spent an hour with Mr. Erving at Stonehouseleigh, and Mary waited for him, kneeling before the altar, with her face buried in her hands, and walked with him afterwards to the station. Up and down the platform they paced for a few minutes, and then the train came in sight, and they stood still. "Now, good-bye, Mary; I will never forget what you have done for me to-day. The way may yet be long and difficult, but the crushing weight is removed." She could not speak, but wrung his hand, and he bent down to kiss her. The train was soon out of sight. She stood where he had left her till it disappeared, and then walked home; and her mother thought her very pale, but there was a deep thankfulness in her heart, a gratitude in the midst of her grief, which gave a heavenly expression to her face.

Maurice had gathered a nosegay of flowers in the cottage garden. When he arrived in London he laid them in a corner of the room without speaking. Gertrude saw them when she came in, and began to arrange and tie them up. Everything in their room was packed up. There was nothing else to do that evening. She seemed to like those flowers,—she gazed on each of them and smelt at them repeatedly, but they did not trust themselves to speak of the visit he had made. It was their last evening in England. William Dee called upon them, and they all tried to talk cheerfully. The next day they embarked.

CHAPTER XXII.

"Déjà ma barque fugitive
S'éloigne à regret de la rive.
J'affronte de nouveaux orages;
Sans doute à de nouveaux naufrages
Mon frêle esquif est dévoué;
Et pourtant à la fleur de l'âge
Sur quels écueils, sur quel rivage,
Déjà n'ai-je pas échoué?"
LAMARTINE.

"Oh vista inaspettata! oh vista
Cara non men che dolorosa!"
ALFIERI.

ONE of those vast receptacles of human beings, one of those floating worlds, those temporary homes, which carry away from our old worn out time-honoured country—our old England—which we all love with a love that some of us can hardly understand, but which asserts itself in ways at times, and in hearts where it would be least expected, compelling them to exclaim, " England, dear England!" something in the same spirit which made James II cry out, when from the coast he saw his French allies dispersed by the British fleet, " Ah, my brave English!"—the patriot's, not the politician's cry. One of those great refuge-houses of the poor and of the homeless, —one of those ocean caravans that bear away so many youthful energies, and so much life, and spirit, and hope, and sorrow from our shores to those of the New World, was lying at anchor at Blackwall. The part of the vessel allotted to the steerage passengers had been gradually filling with persons, who seemed almost more numerous than the huge ship could contain: but still they came, and found their places, and looked about them with excitement or with listlessness, with pleasure or with pain, with hope or with fear, according to their ages, their characters, or their prospects. Some were leaving their hearts' treasures behind them; some were going to find them again on the other side of the Atlantic; some few, perhaps, had laid up theirs in Heaven, and ceased to care for anything but the interests of the Kingdom which is not of this world; to others, again, the past was a dream, and the future a blank. Some came well provided with comforts for the passage; others had nothing but the scanty outfit of an emigrant. Some wept because one they loved had hung about their neck, and had given them a last kiss that day; others wept because no hand had pressed theirs, and no kind voice had said " farewell," or " God bless you."

What an epitome of life, with its various griefs, its gradations of outward prosperity, its inward and unsuspected trials! One poor Irish woman was crying because six little children were crowding around her.

" And what will I do with them, the craturs?" she ejaculated, as they began to shiver and complain.

" And what will I do without my baby?" murmured another younger woman, who had buried her only child the day before. " Nobody shall comfort me now, and it's myself will die of grief." But one there was who did comfort her, and she died not of grief; for He put it into her heart to nurse the baby of the woman who had too many little ones to care for, and she learnt during that voyage that it was " more blessed to give than to receive."

It was a strange subject for study and for thought—that crowded deck. The thrifty, neat, and well-dressed group,—

the squalid, dirty, poverty-stricken families,—side by side; the vicious degraded countenances of some poor wretches, who were escaping perhaps from detection and punishment; the daring impudence of one, the stolid stupidity of another; the mischievous quickness of a third; the contrast between the few English and the numerous Irish passengers,—none amongst the first so degraded in men's eyes; but not any of them perhaps so near to Heaven as some of the last,—famine-stricken creatures who had patiently borne an incredible amount of suffering, and had passed spotless through the ordeal of London, that fearful abyss in which so much purity and virtue sink to rise no more. It is a strange and a moving sight, that great assemblage of human creatures, about to seek a new existence in that strange country, which has all the hope, the freshness, and the faults of childhood; which opens its wide arms to the wanderers of the earth, its boundless soil to every hand that will plough it—its deep vitality to every mind that will stir it.

The cabin passengers had also arrived. They were seeking their berths, and stowing away their luggage. In one very small cabin, Gertrude was sitting, feeling at that moment more bewildered than unhappy. She had been for some hours on board, and hardly having slept for the last two or three nights, had dozed a little that morning, in spite of the strangeness of the scene. Maurice came to ask her if she wished for anything. "Yes," she said, "to go awhile on deck, and fix in my memory the last impression of the country we are leaving." How she had once longed to leave it, she thought to herself, as she mounted the narrow stairs up to the deck. How, as a girl, she had often repeated to herself the lines that begin—

"O'er the glad waters of the deep blue sea;"

and longed to fly away, not to be at rest, but in the very midst of the strife and excitement of life.

It is so singular to go calmly and coldly through times and scenes which would once have made our hearts bound, and our eyes sparkle with delight. She stood on deck, and gazed more curiously than sadly on the shore, on the forests of masts, on the boats going to and fro, on the mass of human beings on the other end of the deck, and on the numerous passengers on theirs. Maurice stood by her side, and was surprised and glad that she did not see a more deeply moved as the moment of departure approached. He felt it very much—far more than she did, in one sense; but he seemed hardly to care for anything now, but the varying expression of her face. She said in a low voice, "There lies that great city which we shall never perhaps see again, that country which we are probably leaving for ever. I suppose that to some people, death is very like such a departure as this." Whether they went down to the bottom or landed in America, the change could hardly be greater.

"Are you afraid of the sea, Gertrude?"

"Afraid? O no. I am afraid of nothing." He sighed.

"It is very cold," she said, and drew her shawl round her.

"Will you go down again? It will be long yet before we move."

"No. I would rather stay here. It amuses me to watch the boats going to and fro, to look at this busy scene, and fancy it some great human ants' nest; and wonder what the angels think of us when we trouble our heads about the grain of sand that falls upon our heads, and deem it a mountain, and strive and struggle to free ourselves. How strange it is to see that immense concourse of human beings, and feel that amongst them there is probably not one that we have ever seen before, or ever will see again. I cannot go down to the cabin, but it is very cold. Will you fetch me my cloak?"

Maurice went to look for it, and she remained gazing on the water with a kind of vague and vacant interest. A boat had put off from the shore, and was nearing the steamer. It was full of ladies, and one or two men also, besides the rowers. Gertrude was short-sighted, and did not discern their faces. They came alongside the ship, on the other side from that where she was sitting. In a few minutes she heard a person who was standing near her say to another, "There is a party of smart folks arrived to see the ship before she starts, and stare at the emigrants. They are walking about with the captain. I suppose we shan't be off for another hour, at soonest." A moment afterwards, Maurice came with the cloak, and said to her hurriedly,

"Had you not better come downstairs again, Gertrude?"

"Why?" she said. "Let me look upon land as long as I may. I shall have enough of the close cabin soon."

"There are people on board whom you used to know."

"Who—who do you mean?"

"The Audleys, and some others."

"Lady Clara! O is she here?" Gertrude ejaculated, and pressed her hand on her forehead. One moment she remained silent, and seemed to be communing with herself, and to be agitated by conflicting impulses.

"I will go down to the cabin," she said hurriedly, "and there, if possible, I should wish to see Lady Clara for one instant. Will you have this note conveyed to her?"

She hastily wrote a few lines in pencil, and drawing down her veil, hastened across the deck, and down through the labyrinth below to the hiding-place she sought. "Dying people," she said to herself, as she sat down on the edge of the narrow couch—"dying people may often do what would be wrong in others; and is not an eternal absence a kind of death? If I can speak to her, perhaps this throbbing heart will beat more calmly, through its remaining years. O how strange, that out of that great city I was gazing upon, should have come at this time one of the very few I have known, who has ever shed a brightness over my path, and never looked upon me but with kindness! Perhaps she will not come; she may be afraid of a scene. O, if she knew how calm misery can be when it reaches its height!" She waited some time, and then the cabin-door opened. "How do you do, Lady Clara?" she said with that coldness which suppressed emotion gives. "How are you? Well, I hope? I am so sorry to have given you this trouble."

Lady Clara had an anxious perturbed look. She pressed Gertrude to her heart, and struggled not to shed tears. They sat down side by side, each scarcely venturing to look at the other; but Gertrude was infinitely the more composed of the two, and able to keep down her agitation, and to speak in her usual tone of voice, while the other could hardly command herself.

"How little I could have thought to see you again here," she falteringly said; "I dare not ask you all I wish to know. What are your plans—your intentions? If it is as well with you, as with all my heart I wish it to be, I hope, dearest Gertrude, that you are only leaving England for a short time."

"I am leaving it for ever, and therefore I have wished to see you, to thank you for the kind interest you have always shown me."

"Does your father know? has he suffered that you——"

"There is a deeper gulf between us than the ocean. I do not complain of him. O no! It is better that I should go far from him—from you—from every one. I wished to go. It is my own will, my own doing. But I have asked to see you, not only once more to look upon a face that I loved in other days——" She fixed her eyes steadily on Lady Clara, and saw that she was striving to master her emotion, and went on in the same calm manner—"but also that I must ask you to do for me what you only can. If I were not going away for ever, I could not do this; but as I shall never see M. d'Arberg again——" A strange expression passed over Lady Clara's face, but Gertrude did not see it, and went on, "As I never shall see him again, I think I may ask you to tell him or to write to him, that I never heard from him before my marriage; that I have been reckless, rash, and much to blame, but not false; that I was deceived into believing he had forsaken me, and, till a short while ago, never knew that he had not. I wish him to know this, and I hope he will remember me in his prayers. Will you tell him so, Lady Clara? Kind friend of my happy days, you only know what I had gained, and what I have lost. Will you do what I have asked you?"

Lady Clara was looking painfully embarrassed, her colour went and came. "When I can do this, dearest Gertrude, I do not exactly know, for M. d'Arberg is going— I suppose I had better tell you— It is so strange, so extraordinary! Did you indeed never expect to see him again?" Gertrude's eyes were fixed on hers but she did not speak. "He too is going to America—I—I have just seen him." She turned very pale and murmured, "*Where?*" "I had better prepare you for it; I don't know how much or how little you will mind meeting him again, but at all events you ought to know that at any moment— In short, the fact is, he is on board this very vessel—"

Gertrude stood up and put her hand on Lady Clara's arm "Then," she said, "take me with you. Take me to see him once more—and then all will be over. He will go away with you, but once before my death I shall have seen his face again. I have longed for it till I almost expected it, up to the last few weeks. That moment is now come. Take me where I can see him, Lady Clara. If I wait much longer I shall not have strength to go through it calmly. Now I can. Do not be afraid. Let us go."

Lady Clara was much agitated: she did not know how to act—she had never been in any difficulty—had never encountered a trying scene before: she was nervous, and afraid to speak or to explain. But she felt it was necessary, and taking both Gertrude's hands in hers, she said, "Dear unhappy child, you will have, I fear, but too many opportunities of seeing him. It is a sad position for you and for him; at least I fear from your looks, from your words, that it will be a trial to you, as it must be a great one to him, but he is going in this very steamer,—going with a party of emigrants. It was to see him off that we came here——'

Gertrude leant an instant against the door of the cabin, and hid her face in her hands. When she raised it again, it would have been difficult for any one to read its expression. There was a tumultuous sensation in her brain and in her heart. She could not speak. At that moment some one knocked, and she heard Mr. Audley's voice calling Lady Clara. "We must go, my love. They want us away—the boat is ready." One long kiss Lady Clara gave Gertrude, and burst into tears. "Come, make haste," her husband said, as she came out. She looked at him through her tears, and said, "Say good-bye to her." He looked into the room, but Gertrude had turned away, and he followed his wife upstairs.

It had been a false alarm that the vessel had been about to start. There was yet a further delay. "I have seen her husband," he whispered, as they stood again on the deck. "We met face to face, and shook hands. Does d'Arberg know they are on board?"

"No, I am sure he does not; where is he?"

"Looking after some of his people, I believe—stowing them away under proper protection, and comforting those who take on, as they call it, at bidding farewell to this old land of workhouses and parochial relief. Well, well, this 'Amor patriæ' is a funny sort of thing, and lurks in strange corners of the human heart. Let us look for him amongst the steerage passengers. Do you mean to tell him that that Lady-Bird of yours is here?"

"I don't know what to do. It will be kinder, I think. In such cases nothing is so bad as meeting unprepared."

They joined some of the other people who had come on board to see the emigrants off, and looked for Adrien in every direction. They could not find him, till just when the last bell rang, and they were hurrying into their boat, he joined them for an instant; but there was only time for her to shake hands with him, and she looked upon that ship with a strange interest, as they rowed away from it. She thought of all that it contained, wondered over the extraordinary coincidence that had brought together two persons who had been everything to each other once, who had been so abruptly, so irrevocably parted as it had seemed until this day, and now he was near her, and he did not know it, and she was near him, and she knew it. How soon would chance bring them together? What would their meeting be? What would their parting be? What a strange episode of life to both that Atlantic passage might prove. Would it be the end of the romance of their existence, or the beginning of sin and of sorrow? Lady Clara was thoughtful; she felt glad that her path had never led through briars and precipices,—that it had been so smooth and so straight. Perhaps she did not thank God enough, for it is a great blessing not to have been exposed to temptation: it is a greater one, however, to have passed through the furnace unscathed.

The voyage has begun. The vessel is gliding along the yet smooth waters, but the wind is whistling, and the rain is beginning to fall. Gertrude is lying on her narrow couch, and with closed eyes listening to the beating of her own heart; he is near her—he whom she has loved as few women love; he is near her, here, where for awhile nothing can part them. They may avoid each other, but far apart they cannot be. The same ship holds them,—the same waves carry them,—the same wind drives them on, and they breathe the same air. She opened the little window of her cabin, and gazed upon the water so near to her head. It gave her a dizzy vague feeling of trust and of fear. She was carried on she knew not whither. She was safe, and yet very near destruction. There was a plank between her and the deep sea. What was there between her and sin; not even in that hour a good resolution. She was very tired of suffering—that was all she knew. O how busy the tempter was in that hour with that weary spirit, how he whispered in that watching ear, how he hung over that silent form. No thought of guilt did he send to pass before those closed eyes. He only said, "Rest a little. Do not fight so incessantly with what no human strength can conquer,—the might of a love, which is a part of yourself. Look once more upon that face, which you had thought never to see again. It will calm, not disturb you,—it will strengthen, not weaken you. Was it not from him you once learned what since you have forgotten? Go and learn again from him to be good, to be strong."

Thus spoke the tempter, and she listened, but he was only sowing seed; she did not act upon those thoughts,—not one step would she have stirred to advance the moment on which her soul was set, but at the approach of which, at the very idea of which, she trembled like a leaf. Maurice came and sat by her some time. He thought she was asleep. A bell rang, and he—as he fancied—awoke her, and asked if she would come to dinner; she refused, and begged him to go without her. She could not bear that together they should see Adrien for the first time. She felt they would now meet, and the hour that he was absent appeared to her a whole day. When he returned she looked at him, and drew a deep, quick sigh, but there was no agitation or difference in his manner. He began talking of insignificant things, and giving her some account of their fellow-passengers. Was he dissembling, was it possible he did not feel all it was to her to see Adrien again? Had he forgotten the letter, the scene? It was impossible he could have seen him, or he would not be so unmoved. Was it a mistake or a dream?—Was Adrien *not* on board? Then, by the cold, heavy feeling at her heart, she almost thought she must have been happy during the last few hours.

Towards evening her head was aching intensely, and she longed to breathe the fresh air. She went to the deck, and sat some time watching the waves and the sunset clouds, or gazing on the persons who were passing and repassing before her. He was not amongst them. She began to think that she had dreamt that Lady Clara had ever told her he was on board. She went into the principal cabin, and still he was not there; she became almost convinced that her ears, her fancy, her senses, had deceived her. Thus did the next day also pass, and the next also—till towards night she overheard two persons, who were sitting near her, talking of something that arrested her attention.

"Did you say he was a Frenchman?" one said to the other.

"So I was told; it's queer, isn't it? Lives with them entirely; eats, and sleeps, and sits where they do;—talks to them at nights too, and in English, which is curious. Those Irish crowd about him, as if he were St. Patrick himself. I went on the deck on purpose to hear him last evening. It is amusing enough; he tells them stories, and they groan, and laugh, and ejaculate, and cross themselves all in one time. They're a strange set, those Irish."

" But what does this French count do it for?"

" He is half English, they say, and has property in Ireland, and some of that set are his own people, and he has come out with them to set them going on the other side, and he lives with them to learn how they are treated, and give the government an acccount of their hardships, which are many, I fear, poor souls. It's a Quixotic sort of thing. Might have learned it all, I dare say, without so much to do about it."

" The wind's getting up; we shall have a rough night of it, I expect."

" It's cold sitting here. Let's walk."

That night Gertrude laid her head on the pillow, and the noise of the wind and the waves seemed again, as on the first day, to speak of one who was lying not far off on a hard and narrow couch, whose thoughtful eyes were raised to Heaven in prayer, as the ship bounded along, and who little weened that she whose image still haunted him, amidst his days' long labours and his nights' short rest, was also watching and listening to the same melodies, and gazing at the same stormy sky.

" Mrs. Redmond, ain't you bored to death?" said to Gertrude a pretty little woman whom she had sat by at meals, and who had been civil and kind to her during the last three days.

" No," she answered quickly, "*that* is one of the sufferings I have ceased to experience. I am never bored. I envy those who are," she added in a low voice.

" Well, I think you are a very happy person. When I am at home and have plenty of things to attend to, it does very well, but I am too sick to read or work, and my husband likes to be on deck all day, and I don't know really what to do with myself. If it is not very rough this evening, would you mind coming with me to look at the steerage people, and listen to what that strange gentleman that's always with them reads and says to them? Somebody told me it was very curious."

" I should like it," Gertrude answered in a low voice, " if we do not go too near them."

" O you don't fancy going amongst those low people, neither do I; but we need not be close to them, you know "

That was little in Gertrude's thoughts. Would she have shrunk from the poorest and the roughest of those creatures amongst whom Adrien sat?—of whom he took such careful heed? Did she not envy the child who sat at his feet—the poor orphan girl who told him her tale of sorrow, and heard words of comfort from his lips—the old man whom he supported up the narrow stairs, and placed by his side when they all gathered together after their evening meal, to forget awhile the common hardships of their lot? And the sufferings of the steerage were, for passengers in an emigrant vessel, greater then than they are now. The ordinary comforts of life were scarce; age and infancy had much to endure; and even those who had been used to the wild roughness of their Irish homes, or the wretched dens of their London abodes, had trouble to bear up against the varied annoyances of this passage in their poor lives, this, in a twofold sense, their passage to the New World.

The two women whom chance had thrown together that day sat down in a corner of the ship, sheltered by some bales of goods, with their cloaks on, and their veils down. They came there, the one to seek amusement, the other——What! O what are you going to do there, Gertrude? What business have you to look on that face again? What right have you to listen to that voice which thrills to your very heart?—Yes, hide yourself from his sight; pull the veil closer round your head. The wind is blowing about you, but there is something wilder than the wind in your heart and in your brain. He speaks, and you tremble. Are you sure it is he? For one instant look up—there he is opposite to you—not very far from you; he is looking pale and very thin, but the light in his eyes is not dimmed. The soul shines out of them as brightly as ever, and the smile that illumines that face was never more beautiful than now. All those expressive countenances are turned to him; they crowd about him, his poor emigrants; most of them he personally knows, and if they were his children, his manner—when he speaks to them—could not be more gentle. What if in that instant his eye should fix itself upon you, Gertrude—would it be gentle or stern? You know not, but one thing you feel; once before you leave that ship you must speak to him, you must carry away with you the remembrance of one kind word from his lips.

Now the groups of listeners are hushed into silence, for he

is reading to them. It was the account of the shipwreck of St. Paul. When he came to the verse "For an angel of God, whose I am, and whom I serve, stood by me this night," there was one in that audience who forgot that he was not speaking of himself. She felt as if God's angel were indeed standing by him: she felt as if God's claim upon him had been too strong for an earthly love to dispute it, and she hung on each word that fell from his lips as if it contained a message from Heaven. Then he spoke to those Irish hearts, as one who knew them well—their strength and their weakness,—their childlike faith, mighty in life and in death, and fervent as their passions. He set before them vivid pictures of vice and of virtue, of Heaven and of hell, clothed in familiar words and illustrated by fanciful similes. It was strange to observe how his genius and his eloquence, which had often commanded the applause of listening assemblies, knew how to assume a form that captivated the attention of that restless group. How their eyes glared and flashed when he bade them fight with the devil, and snatch from him his victims; how they laughed a wild laugh of delight when he told them how to cheat him of the souls he had made sure of, by turning their back upon him when he least expected it, and beginning, even the very worst among them, to serve God that night. He drew pictures of good and bad Irishmen; all good servants, however,—all zealous of their work, and intelligent at their business—sure of high wages at last and a high place somewhere; they would do nothing by halves. When they served Almighty God it was with all their hearts; when they bound themselves to Satan they were clever at his work and very like him in his ways, for they never ceased believing while they blasphemed, and trembling while they cursed.

Once in the midst of his discourse, he pointed to the sky, to a bright star that shone amidst the clouds, and asked them who it was like, and simultaneously there rose from the whole group the "Ave Maris Stella," that hymn which has cheered so many mariners through the surges of life, as well as on the billows of the ocean. When the singing died away he told them tales of other times, or gave them descriptions of the land they were going to, or set before them some high example of patient suffering, or heroic exertion. Before parting they all knelt together and said the night prayers, which most of them had been used to. In the course of them there is a short and impressive pause for the examination of conscience.

When many are joined together in this, there is something solemn and touching in the sudden hush of many voices—the profound silence of those few moments during which each separate heart is questioning itself and laying before God its various and widely different amount of guilt and of temptation. It was so in this case, and deep to her heart's core did Gertrude feel it. It seemed as if Adrien must be reading there the sin that she had ceased to struggle with; perhaps she then felt also that we are sure of God's mercy, but never of man's, for she shuddered at the thought of Adrien's knowing how she, the wife of another, gave way to a guilty though secret affection, even though he himself were its object.

When the prayers were ended, and her companion who was somewhat weary rose to go, she followed her, and found Maurice waiting for her in their cabin. He was sitting at the small table against the wall with his head leaning on his hands. She put hers on his shoulder, and asked him if he were asleep.

"Where have you been?" he said, without turning towards her.

"On deck," she answered, while a sudden flush suffused her cheek. He looked at her attentively, as if to scan the expression of her face. She turned away, and he murmured,

"Well, everything must come to an end, I suppose."

"Are you already weary of the voyage?" she said.

"I am weary of my life."

He went away, and came back again. He moved impatiently about the narrow little slip of a room, and then stopping opposite to her, said with bitterness, "It is a pity that we are not steerage passengers. It would have made you happier, I suppose." The colour left her cheek, and she bit her pale lips almost through. "I do not mean to be unkind to you, Gertrude, but you know, oh you must know that a man's heart can be tried almost beyond endurance." Neither of them mentioned the name of Adrien; and the next few days passed like the preceding ones.

M. d'Arberg never left the part of the vessel where he had cast his lot; the cabin passengers often spoke of him. Some thought he must be a little deranged; some admired his conduct, and wondered at his self-devotion; many went of an evening to listen when he read or conversed with his people Gertrude always sought that same place where she had sat the first night. There, with her face concealed by her veil, she remained in all weathers. Her little companion grew tired of sitting with her. It amused her well enough at first, but she became weary of Gertrude's abstraction, who was too much absorbed in the scene to converse with her. She did not seem to hear when she whispered remarks about the queer faces that appeared amongst the listeners. Mrs. Darton, for that was her name, came to the conclusion that Mrs. Redmond was after all very stupid, and she left off going to the same seat, and nobody else found their way to it. That one figure in black was always there. Adrien's eye now and then rested upon it. There was something in its attitude which he fancied was familiar to him, though he did not discern what it was that it recalled to his mind.

One evening, when he came as usual to his post, he looked worn and fatigued. Disease was beginning to spread on the lower deck. The sleeping rooms were dreadfully close—the food was bad—the weather had been heavy and disagreeable during the last few days—the winds contrary. The passage promised to be long and tedious; murmurs and complaints had been loud in the passengers' cabin that day on the subject. Maurice had said nothing; but his heart had sunk within him as he heard it. He loathed that ship with inexpressible disgust. He looked sometimes at the waves with an expression that would have pierced through Mary's soul, had she seen it. But what did Gertrude feel? She felt like a criminal reprieved—like one respited on the very verge of the grave. On the evening we are speaking of, Adrien had seen much sorrow and suffering amongst the emigrants, especially amongst those who were not his own people. For them he had managed before starting to ensure a certain degree of comfort. But he was no longer the rich man that he used to be. He had taken some time ago the gospel advice, the evangelical counsel, and had sold all or almost all, had given to the poor, and was now following his Lord's footsteps, but with a thorn in his heart which he endured without wincing, but which was sharper than toil, or abstinence, or bodily pain.

He felt on this day that it was difficult to meet the usual exertion of that hour. He was anxious about a poor child below who had sickened with the fever. He was not contented with the care that the surgeon on board bestowed upon it—he had seen the mother's wistful countenance, and it haunted him. But he roused himself, and perhaps more than ever reached the hearts of his audience, when after reading to them a while, he began talking to them out of the depths of his own. He compared the voyage they were making to the great voyage of life, and the illustration came home to them with strange power. He spoke of sorrow, of trials, of those which God sends to us as if straight from his own will, of those in which men and their misdeeds are the agents; of palpable and of nameless suffering, of disappointment and of hopelessness; of remorse and of confession, of sin and of contrition; of faith and its triumphs, of light in darkness, and hope against hope. Once he alluded to himself; he said it was not a theory with him, that deep sense of the value of suffering which he wished to impart to them. No, those who had never gone through a severe affliction knew, as a point of faith, that it was precious as expiation, and weighed in the balance of eternal justice; but they could not know what it did for the soul, till they had themselves become familiar with it, and received it as a bosom friend. When every earthly hope of happiness is departed, when a man stands alone with his God and his suffering, then he could tell them by experience (and his voice trembled) how that God reveals himself, how that grief, like the burning couch on which martyrs have smiled, becomes dear and sacred to his soul, and wins for him peace at first and joy at last.

"I know," he continued, "that some of you have sad thoughts to struggle with; I know some of your sorrows; I know some of your tears: would that I could tell you how one short year ago I felt as if my cross were heavier than I could bear, how the sudden blasting of the dearest hopes I had cherished——" He paused, and turned as white as a sheet. What had he seen just then? That face—those eyes with their deep, shadowy, heart-rending expression. Those eyes that had met his and darted into his very soul, not the memory, but the actual living presence of an unforgotten reality. O was it a vision,—an instant's delusion? Again that motionless form, that bent down head, that shadowy figure was shrouded as before, as night after night he had seen it. Was it a dream that mocked him for an instant,—a phantom that had been raised, and had looked at him with the eyes he was ever trying to forget? He spoke again of peace, but it was with a more tremulous voice. His own had a sure foundation, but its surface had been disturbed. The rock was unshaken, but the waves had washed over it.

And she who had listened, and had looked upon him that night—what strange impulse had made her raise her veil at that moment? What fear had made her cover her face with her hands when his eyes had met hers? There she remained long after he had ceased to speak. She had not stirred or looked round. Once a heavy sigh had been breathed close to her ear. But her soul was absorbed, and she thought not of it again. Adrien's words had reached many hearts that night, but had sunk deeper into one than into all the rest.

"I always thought there was a likeness between him and Mary," Maurice said to himself, and almost felt as if she had been speaking to him through the lips of the man whom he had once so much loved, and for a while so much hated. "Well, we are all miserable enough," he ejaculated, as he left the deck and slowly sought his cabin; and at that moment the words of the Bible came into his head, "And we indeed justly, but this man has done no evil." And from that hour his feelings changed, and he ceased to hate Adrien

---

CHAPTER XXIII.

> "Most dangerous is that temptation which does goad us on
> To sin in loving virtue."
> SHAKESPEARE.
>
> "'Tis one thing to be tempted,
> Another thing to fall."
> *Ibid.*

THE following day several of the emigrants were ill with the fever, and Adrien then found that the task he had undertaken was no light one. There was more suffering and inconvenience in the mere fact of living amongst them than most men would have encountered; but when illness was added to privation and discontent, the hardships became almost intolerable. but then, in proportion, increased the opportunities of usefulness, both to the bodies and the souls of these sufferers. As far as his power went, he ministered to them assiduously. He had passed a restless night; for having ascertained the previous evening from the list of passengers that Maurice and Gertrude were indeed amongst them. he remained awake, reflecting on that strange meeting that chance had effected; or if he slumbered awhile, he was haunted by those eyes which for a moment had been fixed upon him, disturbed by dreams in which that face was ever present, and would start up under the impression that she was near him—she whom he had never expected to see again.

Sleep fled from his eyelids; he mused on her fate,—he wondered whether she had preferred Maurice to him, or if not, what had induced her to marry him? Against his will his thoughts recurred to the period of their love and their parting. Emotions which he had mastered, regrets he had, as it were, trodden down, seemed to rise again; and it was only in hard work the next day, in practical devotion to the objects of his interest, that he recovered that inward, as well as outward self-possession which he had long struggled for, and lately had attained. When the evening hour of converse with his people approached, he had some trouble to preserve that composure; and while preparing his subjects of reading and discourse, he felt as if each word that night had a double meaning, and might convey to Gertrude a reproach, an appeal, or a regret. He intended to seek her and Maurice that evening. *He* had not injured them, though they had injured him; and both might be happier for his forgiveness. It was not in his nature to stand coldly aloof. He could understand their shrinking from his presence, but why should he turn away from them? Perhaps it was poverty that was driving them from England. There was a world of misery in that one glance, that one rapid vision of her face he had had the previous night. He longed to see it once more, and drive away the memory of that look that had given a mute but too expressive answer to the allusion he had made to his own subdued sufferings,—his own mastered grief. He talked to his people of the patient endurance of bodily pain; he could not trust himself to speak of the trials of the soul. He told them stories of the first discovery of America, the land they were bound to. Some might have thought that the tone of his mind was more cheerful than the day before. Much that he said was in rather a gay strain, and there was more laughing amongst his hearers than usual. He steered clear of any of those topics that move men deeply.

After the assemblage broke up, he stood irresolute for an instant. One by one they disappeared, and he was left alone, or nearly so. But he felt he must speak to her; she had hastily risen from her usual seat, and was going away in another direction. He overtook her, and said in a low voice, "Will you not shake hands with me?" She stopped; the moment so longed for, so dreaded, was come, and she had to meet it as best she might. With eyes averted, she placed her trembling hand in his, and then stood still, as if unable to move or to speak.

"Will you not sit down one instant," he said, "and tell me something about yourself, and about Maurice? Believe me, I care for your happiness as much as ever. I have prayed for it every day of my life."

"Then you have prayed in vain," she passionately exclaimed. "Cease to weary Heaven with such prayers,—they are a mockery."

He was silent. This answer struck a chill into his heart, and a sort of cloud passed before his eyes. "It had been better that we had never met again," she said, in a low voice, as if speaking more to herself than to him; "better for you, at least, if indeed you had supposed I was happy, for I believe you wish me so, and I cannot deceive you. It would have been right, I know, to shake hands with you kindly, and then talk of our respective plans and projects, and speak, and look, and seem as if we had never spoken, or looked, or felt differently. This would have been right, perhaps, but there are things that some people *can* do, and that others cannot."

There was something reproachful in her manner of saying this; and greatly moved, he exclaimed, "God help me! Gertrude, do you imagine *I* have not suffered?"

She looked at him, and in his pale, calm face she saw an expression of such deep and painful anxiety, as he gazed into hers, that she knew at once that he felt for her even more than she felt for herself.

"It is of no use," she hurriedly continued. "Why should we talk together? Why have we met again? I have nothing to reproach you with, and you will not, I know, reproach me; though you might, and perhaps you ought."

"You have said too much already thus to leave me, Gertrude. It will be better for both of us now to clear up the mystery of the past, and understand how it came to pass that we, who parted as we did, should meet again as we do now. Did you receive a letter from me before you married?"

"No," she answered, with her eyes fixed on the ground. "But I have seen it *since*."

"It arrived, then, too late!" he exclaimed.

"Too late for me," she was about to say, but the words died on her lips, and she left him in his error; but when he said, with emotion, "*I* would have trusted *you* through years of silence and suspense," she exclaimed, "O do not speak to me in that way, Adrien, remember, there are sufferings that lie dormant, there are thoughts that sleep and must not be awakened. There is a calmness that lasts as long as memory can be kept at bay. O that I should be thus speaking to you!"

"Gertrude, there can be no peace in ——"

"Who spoke of peace? Did I not say calmness? Do you think I ever dream of peace?"

"O, my God!" Adrien ejaculated, in a tone of the deepest feeling. "This is worse than I feared. Gertrude, now we must speak the whole truth to each other, I must know how you came to marry as you did." In a low but firm voice, she answered. "Despairing of ever seeing you again, believing that you had abandoned me, bewildered by the fear of a marriage I abhorred, grateful for a love which on that very day was revealed to me—when my mind was almost distracted—I was wrought upon—persuaded——" Adrien turned pale; and clenching his hand, uttered a word which did not reach her ears, and she continued, "I have suffered not more, perhaps, than I deserve, but more than you can understand. I should not have dared to speak the truth, I should not have shown you the real state of my mind, and of my heart, if I had not felt that in you, and in myself—in our past history—in our present strange meeting, there was that which would forbid us from seeking, in this brief intercourse, anything but the consolation of knowing that we have not wilfully been untrue to each other. That I have been false to myself, unjust to one whose great sin it has been to love me too much, God knows I confess; but you I have not injured. O no. Each day I live I feel more deeply, perhaps, that 'He whose you are, and whom you serve,'—ay, I heard you say those words not long ago,—He has dealt mercifully with you, and broken to pieces, for your sake, the worthless object of your ill-directed love."

"Gertrude, you must not say, you must not feel this. With both of us He has dealt with the severe kindness of a father; our hearts may break, but we must submit and adore."

"Teach me, then, to submit; teach me to adore: you have been the angel with the drawn sword in my path; sheath it if you can, and show me the way. Once before you pointed to it; it lay then in a smooth and flowery road; now it must be through a narrow and thorny one; but perhaps a light may rise upon it. You toil enough amongst the poor outcasts of this world's making, and may have a more arduous task to perform now."

Adrien's eyes flashed with a bright expression of love and of hope. " Gertrude, I have felt, ever since I first set eyes on you—O do not be afraid of looking back, dearest; do not shudder at the thoughts of what might have been, but which now can never be. There, in that first meeting, in our love, in our parting, with misgivings but with hope, in our irrevocable separation,—ay, I can speak of it without faltering, though God only knows how hard a struggle it has been to submit,— in this our strange reunion, I see, I feel, I bless His guiding hand. O Gertrude, we shall not have met, we shall not have loved, we shall not have suffered in vain; and not in vain have gone through this trying hour, if He deigns to use me as His instrument to re-awaken in you, in your strong will and ardent spirit, the deep enthusiasm of a real vocation, the one resolution which masters every passion, and treads under its feet every sorrow, every anguish, every discouragement. He had a purpose for both of us; I know it, I feel it. Never let us say, even when we suffer most acutely, ' Would we had never met.' *I* have never done so, Gertrude !"

"Nor I," she faintly murmured.

"My dearest—I may call you so, for nothing on earth is so dear to me as you—my dearest, let us so live, let us so die, that to all eternity we may say, 'Thank God that we met.' Thank God that we understood the meaning of our love, the meaning of our sufferings, and recognised in them the source of higher fruits of virtue and of love than happiness could ever have yielded. Since the first day I saw you something impelled me to watch you, to pray for you, to feel that I was to influence your destiny. Once, for a while ——" he paused, there was a swelling in his heart which he could hardly subdue, but mastering his emotion he went on, "That dream passed away; I saw not that I had mistaken God's purpose, but the way in which it was to work, and I hoped that in the end we should not have met in vain. Now I am sure of it. Now a light has flashed through the gloom; now you too will draw courage and strength from past and from present sorrow. Oh, Gertrude, our two hearts are bruised in the fierce trial we have past and are now passing through. Let each pang that we endure prove a blessing to others. Let innumerable good deeds and earnest efforts be the fruit of our sufferings; and then on the day when every tear, every sigh, every cup of cold water is counted, shall we not say, if by His infinite mercy we both stand on His right hand, 'Thank God that we met!'"

Both were silent,—both were overcome. Their hands were joined in silence, and they withdrew. Another had been near them, and every word of that conversation had been heard. "It is easy for them to be resigned," Maurice said to himself, as he tossed to and fro on his narrow couch that night; "but for me, for me, who stand between them and happiness, it is too hard a task,—too dreadful a fate. Well, it may be simplified one of these days,—my life may be cut short."

The pain in his head and in his heart seldom left him now; but still it is wonderful how people suffer and live on. He saw Adrien the next day, and they spoke kindly to each other. Both subdued the feelings which would have led them to turn away from the other; for Maurice could not look calmly upon the man whom Gertrude not only had, but still, loved, nor Adrien on him who had betrayed his confidence, and hurried her into a sinful and miserable marriage. It had been an act of heroic virtue on his part to forbear from expressing to Gertrude his indignation at her husband's conduct; and the friendly though grave manner with which he addressed him was one of the greatest conquests over himself which he had ever achieved.

At the hour when the emigrants met on the deck, Maurice said to Gertrude, "You had better not stay in this close cabin, Lady-Bird. It is a beautiful day, I believe. The sea is quite calm; there are not many more evenings to come before we reach New York. Go and breathe the fresh sea air."

"Will *you* come?" she said timidly.

"No; I do not feel inclined to move. Leave me that book you were reading this morning." She did so, and arranged the cushions of the couch for him. He took her hand and kissed it. She lingered a moment near the door; he opened the book and read; she went away, and he closed it. Deep and sad were his musings that night, and once or twice he murmured Mary's name; and the stillness of the sea was irksome, and he now dreaded as much as he had wished that this hated passage should end. His manner to Gertrude was very kind now; those bursts of irritability which used to recur so frequently ceased altogether. He wrapped her tenderly in his own cloak when the wind was cold; he borrowed books for her; and if she was not well, he thought of a variety of little things to relieve her; but he could not bear now a smile from her. Truly her smiles were very unlike what they used to be. Perhaps he felt this. He had ceased to be jealous; he knew everything now, and he feared nothing more. Hatred and resentment had all given way to self-reproach and profound dejection.

One night, at that time, he composed the following rambling lines, and set them as it were in his own mind to the murmur of the waves:

> I knew a noble goodly tree that lent my youth its shade,
> To blight it with insidious art was the return I made.
> I knew an Ivy branch that clung with shelt'ring love to me,
> I little thought that faithful bough would once forsaken be.
> I knew a bright, a blooming flower, and gazed on it too long,
> I snatched it rudely from its stem and did it grievous wrong.
> I loved them all, I wronged them all; I bear a heavy load,
> I see no gleam of light to cheer my sad and lonely road.
> If I could die! but death comes not to those who want it most,
> I snatched a moment's joy,—alas! I counted not the cost.
> The waves are whisp'ring Mary's name—once, once, I loved her well.
> O Lady-Bird! my broken flower——

There the pencil fell from his hand, and the unfinished verses on the floor near the couch.

That night and the following ones, Adrien spoke to his poor people, and Gertrude listened, and for a while afterwards they talked together. As once before, the fire that burned in his fervent soul kindled a spark in hers. When he spoke of a life of effort and of virtue she felt capable of anything; as long as he stood by her side she understood how short was this life, how worthless was everything but the prospect of another. She learnt more and more of the meaning of those high spiritual truths which he sought to impart to her; but to learn is not to feel, and knowledge and grace are as distinct as the shadow and the substance, as a dream and an action. She could not acquiesce in the sacrifice of a final separation. She struggled against the acknowledgment of its necessity. Her tongue never uttered a word, but the deep impassioned language of her eyes protested against it. when with faltering accents he spoke of it. Yes, with faltering accents, for in his heart also a fearful combat had arisen.

There is no height of virtue, no strength of faith, no length of time spent in continual advances in holiness and in good ness, that secure a man against temptation, that place him beyond the reach of startling impulses to evil. Adrion was in danger during those days, in which everything seemed to combine against him. In danger of self-deceit, in danger of mistaking the cause of that deep interest which would have made him ready to lay down his life for the sake of her virtue and her happiness,—he saw, he felt his influence over her; a long, if not a final separation awaited them. He feared to lose time—he returned too often to her side. Every moment that could be snatched from duties of religion and of charity. which he never neglected, he devoted to her; but did it make him less eloquent that the subjects which he spoke of were those which lend the deepest pathos, and inspire the most ardent enthusiasm in those who have ever felt their influence and understood their scope? Did it make his pale face less beautiful in her eyes that it had gained that paleness in long nightwatches by the bed of poverty and of suffering? Did the blessings that were poured upon him every day and every hour by the poor creatures that surrounded him make her admire or love him less?

They stood on the brink of a precipice and knew it not; perhaps while he was lending her his aid to scale the rocks, and mount to the heights where he longed to lead her, he was unconsciously losing his own footing. Perhaps she knew more of the secret perils of her own heart—she had had more cause to mistrust it—but perhaps also she feared less the first approaches of evil. She had but one care, but one thought, but one object, and she knew what it was. There was no self-deception in her; she gave way to the unresisted influence of feelings that seemed too powerful to be withstood, that made her cling to his presence as to a safeguard against the long anguish she had endured, and shrank from enduring again.

They had sat together in the same spot where they first had met. on a calm and lovely evening which had succeeded a stormy day; the wind had been violently contrary till then, now it seemed to second man's wonderful agent, and to impel them along the ocean with a rapidity that carried joy to the hearts of many weary and worn-out passengers. Glad voices had said that day, " Now we shall soon arrive; a very few days more, and we shall be at the end of this tedious voyage." " The end of this voyage!" Gertrude had said to herself, and it was like the announcement of the sentence of death to the condemned criminal. They had sat together a long time; the sky was pure and bright with its thousand stars, and the moon made its road of light on the waves, which were gently rising and falling after their recent agitation, like the sobs of a child whose passion is subsiding. They had spoken of their arrival; she had asked if she should see him again when he returned from the settlement he was to visit. She asked it with a look that thrilled through his heart; she had turned pale when he hesitated; when he had assented there was a flash of joy in her eyes which carried him back to the day when he first promised to go to Lifford Grange. All the past rushed upon him at that moment, with a startling power. He felt she loved him *as* then, *more* than then; a wild involuntary joy, mingled with a sensation of terror and remorse, shot through his heart. He had meant never to see her again after these days of constrained intercourse—now he had agreed to do so. He had done *wrong*.

Few people know what is the awakening of that consciousness in those who have in earnest lived a life of continual self-discipline, who have walked under the Almighty eye, till they have learned to shudder at the first approaches of sin. In that instant he was called to the bedside of one of the emigrants who was dying, and to that scene he carried his wounded conscience, and his intense agitation; but there is that great blessing attending a course such as his had been, that in the first instance no agitation interferes with practical duty, so habitual has self-control become; and secondly, that agitation never can last long, even though grief and fear, or self-reproach, may prevail. He soothed the mental agony of his poor patient, even as if he had not been suffering himself. He suggested to him every thought that could awaken contrition, and supply in a case of absolute impossibility those spiritual supports which were far out of his reach. He saw him grow calm, and sink by degrees into a kind of sleep, and he remained by his side, praying ardently.

How strange it is, how marvellous it seems sometimes, that there are human beings who *never* pray, who do not know what it is to send up those cries for strength, for guidance, for rescue,—which burst from other hearts with such vehemence, that they never wield an instrument which effects so much in this world, and beyond it!—which, like the trumpets that overthrew the walls of Jericho, can break down with its feeble strength the might of every obstacle, and the arms of every foe. He knew, he now saw the extent of the abyss he had neared; there was that which *he* could lay hold of.—there was a staff he could grasp, and which has never yet failed under the heaviest weight that has been trusted to it. Strong in Him who is mighty to save, all his fears were for her,—her to whom he had once hoped to be a guide and a blessing. She, in whom he had first awakened the energy of an hitherto dormant faith; she whom he had loved and prayed for so long, so unceasingly—was she to be abandoned to a sullen despair, an aimless life, and a hopeless heart? He prayed it might not be so. He accepted everything, offered up everything; but asked that, if possible, although he saw no way to it, they might part, not as they had parted that day,—not as they would part, unless she learnt what he could not, and what none but God could teach her.

It did not seem at that moment as if the prayer were heard. She was musing on that last hour they had spent together, with no misgivings then, nor with any self-reproach. She felt that she could struggle no longer, that it was in vain to strive with destiny. She impiously murmured, " O, if I must not love him, why did Heaven thus bring us together!" and then a sudden intense wish for freedom rushed like a hurricane over her soul. It seemed to suggest thoughts which she dared not frame in words. Why was she bound by an irrevocable chain? Why *must* she be miserable? Why had one rash act, one fatal impulse, sealed her doom for ever? " Until death us do part," floated in her ears. Death—death alone could break that chain. Then for an instant, then as once before, a vision of freedom passed before her, not as a deliberate thought,—far, far less a hope. But she could not escape the consciousness that this dreadful idea had shot through her mind like a dark phantom.—" If *he* were to die, I should be free." It found no verbal utterance; but the rapid mental protest against it attested its existence.

She remained on the deck that night, and then slowly sought the cabin, where her husband was asleep. She sat down with a book in her hand, the same book out of which he had been reading by the lamp he had left burning. His sleep was disturbed; he spoke incoherent words, and moved restlessly about. It was late before she lay down in her berth. Every now and then she woke up, as he moaned and murmured, and once she asked him if he was suffering? He was asleep again, and she closed her eyes and the ship went on its way, and the hours elapsed, and the morning dawned, and every one was stirring within those wooden walls. Who knows what a day may bring forth? The sun shines on the evil and on the good, and the morning of one day is like the morning of another; but the days themselves! O, they are as different sometimes from those that precede and that follow them, as Earth is from Purgatory and Purgatory from Heaven.

CHAPTER XXIV.

"Forgive me that thou couldst not love! it may be that a tone
Yet from my burning heart may pierce through thine when I am gone,
And thou perchance mayst weep for him, on whom thou ne'er hast smiled."
                                                    MRS. HEMANS.

"In her chastened soul,
The passion-coloured images of life,
Which with their sudden startling flush awoke
So oft those burning tears, have passed away."
                                                    Ibid.

"Yet I was calm; I knew the time
My breast would thrill before thy look,
But now to tremble were a crime;
We met, and not a nerve was shook."
                                                    BYRON.

WHEN Maurice awoke from a troubled sleep the next day, the pain in his head which had been more or less troubling him since he had embarked was more violent than ever; his limbs ached, and a feverish thirst parched his lips. He called Gertrude and asked for some water. In taking back the glass from him she felt that his hand was burning; and laying her cold one on his forehead started almost at the scorching heat it found there. "Maurice," she gently said, "do you feel ill? I am sure you are not well." He raised his eyes slowly to hers and shook his head. She made some little arrangements for his comfort, and went to get him some tea. When she brought it back he tried to eat a piece of biscuit, but could not.

"Maurice," she again repeated, with a kind of nervous anxiety, "I am *sure* you are ill. You must see the doctor."

"The doctor! No; he will do me no good, and his rough, disagreeable manner will drive me wild. I will not see him; open the window, and let me breathe the fresh air, and then come and sit by me."

She did so. There was something peculiar in his manner; he had not looked at her in that way for a long time, perhaps never before, with a sort of calm tenderness. "Will you read something to me, Gertrude, out of this book?" He drew from his bosom a little book of poetry which Mary had written out for him. "I should like to hear you read what *she* wrote." The book opened at a passage out of Longfellow's " Psalm of Life." Her voice trembled as it uttered the words—

> " And our hearts, though stout and brave,
> Still like muffled drums are beating
> Funeral marches to the grave."

Looking up she saw that his hand was pressed on his heart as if it counted its pulsations.

"Why do you make me read to you these things?" she hastily exclaimed, and rapidly turned over the pages of the manuscript.

"Your voice does me good; read on, Gertrude, read on. It is the only music I can hear now. It sounds like an echo of the strains I once heard. Last night I dreamed that I was broken on the wheel, and that you were singing to me all the time in a low, soft voice that hushed my groans into silence. Read on; you do not know what your reading of these verses is to me. 'Whose touch upon the lute chords low, had stilled his heart so oft.' Were not those lines in a poem that you used to repeat years ago, in the Chase—something about the might of earthly love. Have you forgotten them?"

"No; but I will not repeat them now; they are too exciting, and you must try to sleep, you are feverish." "Feverish!" he re-echoed, and a strange smile flitted over his lips. There was a burning fever in his veins. She read in a low voice some time, and then she stopped, thinking he was asleep. She remembered, at that moment, how from a boy he had loved her. She thought how changed he was, since the time that with a cloudless brow, and a glowing cheek, and a sparkling eye, he used to make plans for the future, and speak of art and fame with so much feeling and fire. She looked at his sunken cheek, his thin hand, the grey hairs that were visible here and there amongst his dark locks, and yet he was scarcely twenty-five years old. What had blighted his youth? What had checked his promising career? What had drawn him away from the tender and watchful love that had been given to him in childhood, and confirmed in youth?—what, but that fatal passion which had outweighed even conscience and duty, and survived even jealousy and despair?

He opened his eyes, and looked uneasily about him. "Lady-Bird," he whispered, "you will not hate me when I am dead?" She started, and laying her hand upon his mouth, answered in a hurried manner: "O, for God's sake, do not talk in that way, Maurice!"

"Why not? If you know what a comfort it is to me to think that I shall not always stand between you and happiness." The colour left her cheek. What could she say? Did she not deserve that he should say this? but it was dreadful. There are ideas that pass through the mind calmly, but which appear too shocking when suggested by another.

"You make me very miserable, Maurice, speaking to me thus." He raised himself in his bed, and leaning upon his arm, with his other hand he clasped hers, and looked into her eyes with those eyes which she had once wondered if she could wish never to see again.

"Do I make you miserable, Lady-Bird? Yes, I know I do—I know I have done so. The consciousness of it has been my long agony. I wish you could sympathise with me for once before I die—that once you could hear without turning away the outpouring of my heart. That is why I spoke, just now, of what gives me consolation."

"Not to me, not to me! This is dreadful. O Maurice! Maurice!" She hid her head in the bed-clothes, and he fell back exhausted. In a moment he said, "I have not been trying to work on your feelings, Gertrude. I believe what I say, or I should not have said it. I know too well all your kindness, your pity, and what must be your——" The word was unuttered; it was hope he was going to say, but he felt it conveyed a too cruel reproach to himself and to her; but he continued with agitation: "Your kindness, I accept. I thank you for these tears; but, O keep your pity—you should have pitied me before, but not now."

"Maurice!" she exclaimed impetuously, raising her head, "you must not—you shall not feel thus. I am sure you are not as ill as you think; if you were you ought to have seen the doctor long ago. You must see him instantly."

A wretched recollection crossed her mind then how she had heard from Adrien, that this man was unskilful and negligent, but there was no help for it now, and she sent for him. It was a long while before he came. There was a great deal of illness in the ship, and Adrien was accompanying him through the infirmary of the lower deck, compelling his attention to every case in succession, and refusing to let him leave the most wretched amongst them, to go and attend the sick passenger who had sent for him. He little thought who it was that was counting the minutes, and watching every sound. When he came there was little comfort to be found in his presence. He was one of the worst specimens of that class of men that used to be, and still sometimes are sent out in emigrant ships— men who accept the insufficient and miserable pittance thus afforded them, because they have neither the skill nor character with which to succeed elsewhere. He shook his head, and said that Maurice was very ill, but not dangerously so, as far as he could see. He had a great deal of fever, and there had been evidently previous depression of the nervous system which aggravated the case. There was acute pain in the limbs, and continual thirst. He sent some medicine, and promised, if possible, to see him again in the evening. His abrupt and familiar manner had been painful to them both. He joked by the bed-side. If a sick-room is sometimes a fitting place for jests, it certainly was not so in this case. When he closed the door, Gertrude bent over the bed and said, "You see, dear Maurice, you are not so very ill." She had never, since their marriage, called him "dear Maurice." He knew it, and the blood rushed with violence to his very temples.

At the time when she usually went upon the deck he showed her the watch, and pointed to the hour. "No, no, not to-night," she said, "I would not on any account leave you, Maurice. I won't," she added, with one of her old smiles, as he murmured that he wished her to go. "Well, I will let you stay—you are right, I think, not to leave me. I feel very strangely at times, and I fancy the fever is increasing. There, sit down opposite to me, and put the lamp on that side, so that the light may fall upon you. Is the sea very rough to-night?"

"No; it is quite calm. I see from here the moon shining on the waves."

"Full many a fathom deep."

"What are you saying?"

"I don't know; I was thinking of a funeral at sea which I once saw a long time ago. But there was a priest on board. I am glad I went to see Mary before I came away. You will be always kind to Mary, won't you, Gertrude?" His eyes closed, and she felt a great difficulty in sitting quietly on, listening to the broken sentences that dropped from his lips.

He was in that state between waking and dreaming in which the thoughts seem more busy with the past than with the present. There is always something awful in the ramblings of the mind, even when no secret sufferings are disclosed; but when there are, and when the listener is and has been the cause or the sharer of such griefs, those long and silent watches are hard to bear. Gertrude tried to read, tried not to think. She sought to stifle memory, to look neither backward nor forward, to banish from her mind all thought but of the present moment; the relief that could be given, the kind word that could be spoken. But it would not do. Back came upon her the recollections of her mother's death, of all that had accompanied and followed it. Her dying form seemed stretched before her on that bed where Maurice was lying, and she gazed on his pale face with mingled sensations of grief and fear.

The hours went by, and still the doctor came not. It grew very late, and he became gradually worse. He was not light-headed now; but the pain was increasing, and his breathing was oppressed. She felt alarmed, but was afraid of leaving him to call for assistance. Hurrying out for an instant she caught sight of one of the stewards and begged he would find the doctor, and entreat him to come directly. When she returned, Maurice called her in a low voice and made her sit down close to his pillow. "Now listen to me, Lady-Bird, for I can speak now, and perhaps for the last time I call you by that name. Forgive me all I have ever made you suffer. It would have been better for you that I had never been born; but if I die now, then my life will not have done you much harm: will it, Gertrude? You are very young still, and you may be happy a long time. You will forgive me, when you *are* happy, for having loved too much during my short life,— and that my love made me selfish, and wicked, and mad. Do not weep, Lady-Bird—do not hide your face from me. Will you kiss me once?" She passed her arm round his neck, and pressed upon his fevered lips a kiss such as he had dreamt of, but never felt before. A sudden faintness came over him, he gasped for breath—" One of the draughts—give it me quick —I am choking." Her eyes blinded with tears, a mist before her sight, she poured out the medicine into a glass, and gave it him. He swallowed it, and exclaimed, " How strangely it tastes!"

What horrible vision has passed before her? What sudden terror has made her cheek livid, as she kneels by the lamp and reads the label on that empty bottle, "Laudanum, Poison." There is a miraculous strength in fear and in anguish, for she neither staggered nor fainted, but rushing wildly to the door, she called out in a tone of such agony for the doctor, that two or three persons started up at once out of their beds and ran for him. It was at the dead of night, and some awoke in their cabins and heard that scream, and thought it was the cry of a drowning wretch. She sat by the narrow bed, and put his head on her breast, and gazed upon it, as if her eyes had turned to stone and her brain to fire. "If he were to die I should be free." Is there a fiend in hell cruel enough to remind her in that hour of those words, which she had trembled at yesterday, and which to-day resemble the despairing cry of the condemned when their sentence is pronounced. It was an appalling sight, that visage of hers bent over his, but so placed that he could not see it. He complains of strange sensations, and her heart dies within her, but she speaks calmly, for she possesses a power of endurance which has never yet been called forth. She feels that if he should die, the ceaseless anguish of remorse on earth at least will be her portion; but while there is life there is hope, and God's mercy is immense, as boundless as her despair.

The doctor came, disturbed, angry; many are ill and dying at once in that miserable ship, and they have been clamouring for him all night. "Mr. Redmond can't be much worse than when he saw him last." She has taken the bottle and placed herself between him and the bed, and she whispers in his ear, "I gave him *that*." He starts back and mutters an oath, "Then, by G——, it's all over with him." She does not faint, but wrings her hands and says, "Try, try to save him, do what you can;" and then she stands by his side while he employs all the means common in such cases, all the expedients which can be resorted to at such a moment, and in breathless silence watches his every movement with agonizing anxiety. "I can do no more," he said at last. "and I cannot stay any longer; I am wanted elsewhere. You must keep him awake if you can, it all depends upon that: any way you can, talk to him, rouse him. I must go." She seized his arm, and with a look that startled even his stolid nature, she said,

"Tell Adrien d'Arberg to come here this instant. Tell him Maurice Redmond is dying, and that it is his wife that has killed him." She knelt before her husband, she did not now hide her face from him, she spoke to him with a voice, she looked at him with eyes, which seemed to rouse him from the growing stupor that was invading his senses. She called to him aloud, and raised his hands in hers and convulsively pressed them.

The door opened, and Adrien was by her side, pale, firm, and composed. She murmured without looking towards him, "What will become of me, if he dies!" Maurice's eyes closed, and he no longer seemed to hear or to feel. She turned then and gave Adrien a look of such dreadful despair, that he turned still paler than before. He laid his hand on her shoulder, and said, "Gertrude, pray, pray with all the strength of your despair, and let me watch by his side. This night we shall spend together, and then whatever God ordains. Whatever happens——"

"We part forever," she slowly uttered, and he said, "Amen."

"This is a vow," she exclaimed.

"As solemn as this hour," he replied. "Now go and pray, that God may have mercy on you and on me."

Then, Adrien strove with all his strength, with all his skill, with all the resources of intelligence and experience. He supplied the doctor's place, and with all the energy of his calm but intense volition sought to recall animation in that sinking frame, to struggle with the fatal sleep that was invading it. He felt strong with an almost supernatural strength; he felt that the safety of an immortal soul might be, that the future peace or the unspeakable misery of another *was* at stake; and he wrestled there with the mortal enemy, as Jacob wrestled with the Angel in the mysterious hour of mystical strife and dearly won victory. He offered up his whole existence on that day, in exchange for the boon he passionately implored. Life for him, grace for her, was the cry of his deep soul; for himself, the cross, the desert's scorching air, the missionary's path, or the martyr's grave.

Human efforts, at times, are extraordinarily blessed. There is a force in prayer,—there is a strength in sacrifice, —there are mysteries in grace,—there are strange dealings with men's souls,—marvellous changes in destinies, and wonderful triumphs of faith. Maurice's life hung on a thread that night and all the while Gertrude prayed some of those wordless prayers,—those cries of the heart which none but God can hear; confessed her sins with agonizing contrition, and, when her brain grew sick with terror and her soul waxed faint within her, convulsively called upon her who prays for us to Jesus, when we can no longer pray for ourselves. He who had ever been in his father's house, and she who was returning to it in that hour, both knelt by that bedside. Each made a promise, each recorded a vow, and in the fiery trial of that night a new heart was given her. O, if in His mercy God would cancel the sentence of death which was writing upon that face its unmistakeable character,—if He would give back to her keeping that loving heart which had well nigh ceased to beat, and open again those eyes which else would haunt her to the grave,—would not life be too short for gratitude, and earth not wide enough for her zeal? What were now past sufferings in her sight? *Nothing* to the pangs she was now enduring,—like the tears of childhood by the anguish of manhood! She vowed to love her husband. O, she loved him already. A single hair of his head had grown precious to her heart, and her burning lips were pressed to his cold hands with feelings that hope and joy could never give. Truly as Adrien was striving and watching by her side that livelong night, sharing and mastering its terrors and its anguish, she felt that an angel had come to her aid; but earthly passion passed away, even then, from her soul, and never from that day forth did she think of him but as one of those ministering spirits who lead the way to Heaven, but are not destined to walk the common paths of life by our side. Maurice opened his eyes and saw them both kneeling by him. His brain was dizzy, and he gazed strangely upon them. Nothing perhaps could have roused him from that deadly stupor so powerfully as their presence, and they spoke to him in words that recalled his soul from the confines of death. She threw her arms round his neck, she pressed him to her heart, she called him her husband, and told him she loved him. He sat up in his bed and pointed to Adrien. "Once, but not now," she said in a low voice. "Believe me, dear Maurice, by all I have endured this night, —by all we have suffered since our marriage, you may believe me now. My love is yours henceforward—yours alone. I gave it you, Maurice, in an awful hour, and one of the most dreadful trials that ever was sent to crush a stubborn spirit has not been sent in vain." He read in her eyes the truth of those words and the rush of conflicting feelings they awakened was almost too much for his enfeebled frame. There were still alternations of hope and of fear with regard to his health, but from that hour he rallied. The fever had been subdued through the very means which had brought him to the verge of death, but from which he had so miraculously recovered.

When he became strong enough to converse he sent for Adrien, and wished to see him alone. He told him all that he had only suspected before. He spoke with detestation of his own conduct, and implored his forgiveness for the breach of trust he had been guilty of in his regard; and he whom he had so much injured heard that humble confession, and soothed the bitterness of self-accusation with all the tender charity of one who had ceased to feel anything as keenly as the offence which that sin had been against the majesty of the Most High. Maurice was soon able to rise from the bed of suffering, of death, and of deliverance. The day before the vessel reached New York, he earnestly entreated to be carried on deck, and pointed to the place where he had once suffered so much, and he asked Gertrude to sit there with him. She came, looking pale and worn, but serene as a summer evening after a violent storm. The brightness of her eyes was not quenched; but it was a different light shining through them than had ever beamed in them before. An unspeakable peace was reigning in her soul, and hovering over her every moment. She looked like one who " Had been she knew not where, and seen what she could not declare." She *had* verily gazed into the abyss, and stood on the brink of an awful chasm, and now her feet were on the rock. She looked up to Heaven with unutterable thankfulness, and the eyes that were raised in adoring gratitude fell tenderly on him who from the very jaws of death had been won back " by the force of prayer."

She had not much to learn in the way she was now beginning to tread. She had seen it, that way, from her childhood up. The seed had been sown long ago, but it had withered away for lack of moisture. No gentle showers could have pierced the hard surface, no light wind could bow down that indomitable will; therefore it was that God, who had marked her for his own, had made all his waves pass over her; and not in vain had this last and tremendous storm well nigh overwhelmed her. She knew it—she felt it; her past life now rose before her as a miracle of mercy, a prodigy of love. She remembered her kind and stern old instructor's words—" If light sufferings are not enough to bring you to His feet, God will in His mercy send you some of those strange trials which break what would not bend, and crush what would not yield." But He had not crushed her—no; He had bowed her down under His Almighty hand, and showed her in one horrible hour what His wrath can do; and then His saving hand was stretched out, and she stood on the shore, strong and erect with the strength He had given her, with the energy He had implanted in her.

When the hour approached for the last meeting of the emigrants on deck, for the last words that Adrien was to address to them, Maurice turned to her and said with emotion,

"Will you stay or go?"

"Stay, if you like it," she answered, with perfect serenity.

"He saved my life, Gertrude, that night, did he not?"

"And more, far more than my life," she answered, and drew closer to his side; but he murmured as she did so, "Would to God I had died."

Steadily Gertrude gazed on Adrien, as he advanced to his accustomed place. She breathed an inward thanksgiving that her heart did not throb wildly as it used to do at his approach. She felt astonished at what is granted to those who surrender themselves wholly into His care who can rule the waves and subdue the storm. She pressed her husband's hand in hers and said, "May God bless and reward him, Maurice," and he fervently uttered, "Amen." That Amen recalled to her the solemn one pronounced not long ago by those lips on which she had once hung with all but idolatrous worship. He spoke, and she listened calmly. He gave a few plain practical instructions, a few kind words of advice to his poor fellow-passengers—to those especially whom he was to lose sight of the next day, perhaps never to meet on earth again. But his voice did not falter, nor did her cheek blanch. When the words "Farewell, and God Almighty be with you, and bless you, and guide you wherever you go, and send his angels to bring you on your way," were pronounced, she bent her head as if to receive his blessing. When he said, "Pray for me, my friends; pray for one to whom great mercy has been shown; pray that his long delays in the upward path may be forgiven, and that while striving for other men's souls he may save his own," she joined her hands and prayed that in Heaven they might meet; and the few tears she shed, and which fell on Maurice's hand, were as pure as the source from which they flowed. There was no passion in that grief, no bitterness in that parting.

When the crowd dispersed, Adrien came up to them and held out a hand to each. Maurice was dreadfully overcome. She wept softly and silently. "I leave in a boat early to-morrow," he said. "So now we part, and I know I carry away with me your kind wishes; I reckon on your prayers."

"O Adrien! Adrien!" Maurice exclaimed. "Would you had ever reproached me."

"Hush, hush, dear Maurice," he rejoined; "we have all three learned a deep lesson—the one lesson of life; henceforward we have to practise it. By Heaven's immense and undeserved mercy we have done no fatal injury to each other, though we have all more or less sinned and been near to great dangers; we have not any of us ruined or perverted a human soul, and that is a priceless blessing—we feel it in this parting hour: we have all suffered, and it has wrought good in us all; has it not, dear friend? You, who have been on the brink of the grave, and you,"—his voice faltered a little as he addressed himself to Gertrude—"who won back his life by your prayers, are bound by a double tie; and God's claims upon you both are twofold since that day."

"Do not take leave of us thus, dear, dear Adrien," Maurice exclaimed. "Do not speak as if we were not to meet again for years."

"God bless you both for ever!" he answered, and hastily moved away.

Gertrude hid her face on her husband's shoulder, and both for a few minutes wept together. She was the first to dry her tears, and when he raised his eyes to hers there was not a cloud on her brow.

CHAPTER XXV.

> "Be it enough
> At once to gladden and to solemnise
> My lonely life, if for thine altar here,
> In the dread temple of the wilderness,
> By prayer and toil and watching I may win
> The offering of one heart, one human heart—
> Bleeding, repenting, loving."
>
> MRS. HEMANS.

> "I stand upon the threshold stone
>   Of my ancestral hall;
> I hear my native river moan,
>   I see the night o'er my old forest fall.
> I look round on the darkening vale
>   That saw my childhood's plays;
> The lone wind in its rising wail
>   Has a strange tone; a voice of other days—
> But I must rule my swelling breath."
>
> *Ibid.*

THE shades of evening had fallen, and there was silence in the ship; Maurice and Gertrude had retired into their cabin. Adrien was, for the last time, sleeping alongside those towards whom his labour of love was now accomplished. The moon was just rising in a cloudless sky, and the vessel was steadily and rapidly advancing on its course. Most of the passengers had been rejoicing that on the morrow they were to land, and begin a new existence in the New World they had sought. There had been much merriment at the evening meal, where, for the last time, the same company had met. They were looking forward to the future with eagerness; but some few of them felt a regret at leaving the semblance of a home which that huge ship had presented. Many kind words had been spoken, and farewells exchanged. Land would soon be in sight; by the time of sunrise next day their eyes would behold it. This was probably the last thought of those who went to sleep on board the brave ship that night.

It glided along, and the wind was in its favour. The watchers saw the lights gleaming along the coast. The sleepers dreamt of the past—the sleepless of the future. No unwonted sounds stirred the silent air—no presentiment of evil disturbed that repose. But suddenly through the vast ship there ran a word, at which the watchers started as one man, the sleepers awoke, the boldest trembled, and the reckless shuddered. "At midnight a cry arose—" "The ship is on fire!" and from each one that heard it there came a cry, a groan, or a sigh, such as the hearts of men send forth when death is at their door. Then it was that they showed of what metal they were made. There was no time for thought, or for prayer, save a short, hurried one for mercy and aid. The word of command was given, the boats lowered, the passengers marshalled; the sea was calm, and the heavens serene. The sailors were brave, and the captain firm; but from the upper and lower decks there arose a sound more awful than the raging of the waves, more appalling than the crash of thunder; the confusion, the strife, the rushing to and fro, the shouts and the prayers, the curses and the groans, grew with the advancing flames, and rose with the clouds of enveloping smoke.

There was one in that moment whose only thought was his wife, who, pale and motionless, was standing by his side, in silence preparing her soul to meet its Judge. But that hour was not come; for their turn is arrived, and she is placed in the first boat, and her husband is in it too. The land is near, and will soon be gained. There is a mist before her sight; but her eyes are fixed in one direction, her hands clasped together, and her lips moving in prayer. They stand on the shore, and a crowd gathers round them. The boats are putting out again; women and children are weeping and wailing, and there are breathless supplications and loud cries from some, and a silence deeper than death in others, as they watch the blazing vessel, and by the lurid light it throws on the water are striving to discern the forms which the boats are conveying.

Gertrude is leaning on the edge of a narrow pier, and Maurice is by her side. They do not speak to each other, but their eyes and their thoughts and their fears are in unison; for they know that Adrien will be the last to leave that burning wreck while one human soul is in danger of perishing there. Once more the boats are gone back for those who tarried behind, and there runs a murmur through the crowd, as they rush forward to the brink of the waves—"This is the last time they can approach it; they cannot save them all." Gertrude shuddered, and ceased to look. She laid her head upon the stone wall on which she was leaning, and a trembling came over her; for the hands were few, and the ship burning now with uncontrollable rapidity, the flames were mounting to the sky, and a faint distant shout of despair—the dying cry of expiring hope—was wafted by the wind to those listening straining ears. She turned round and looked wildly around her, as if to ask for help, where no help could be given. Maurice was gone. He could brook it no longer. Adrien must not die, and he live to see it.

There was a small shattered boat, which had been left aside until then, as too unsafe for use. He has commended himself to God, and called upon Mary; and in that little bark he makes for the scene of danger and death. He rows for the life of his friend; he nears the vessel; he reaches it at last. He pushes alongside the last boat that is leaving it, and with his whole remaining strength he calls on Adrien. He is there; his tall form conspicuous in the light that illumines the terrific scene,—a child in his arms, and another in his hand. The mother had been thrust into the boat that was departing, and with wild gestures was imploring him, whom in her distraction she fancied was an angel, to restore them to her arms. In an instant he perceived the little bark beneath; and springing into it at once, with the children he had saved from the flames, he took the oars from Maurice, who fell back exhausted. The boat was leaking, the surge was dangerous, the children scared; not a word was spoken; there was no sound but the stroke of the oars, now wielded by a powerful arm.

The sun was just rising on that scene of horror and of mercy. When Gertrude at the edge of the waves met that bark as it landed, Maurice stept on to the shore, went towards her, and murmured, " He is saved;" then leaning upon her arm, he fainted. She uttered a short cry, and in an instant Adrien was by her side, and both saw at once what had happened. Maurice had broken a blood-vessel.

In the small inn of an American village Gertrude sat by the bedside of one who had greatly sinned and deeply suffered,—her dying and repenting husband. A priest from a neighbouring mission has been with him, received his confession, and administered the last sacraments of the Church. Adrien was watching in the next room. There was a calm and beautiful expression on Maurice's face; he was not merely resigned, but willing to die. That God should have granted him such a blessing as to give his life for the friend he had injured, and at one time hated, struck him with a sense of grateful astonishment. Gertrude's kindness, the tenderness of her voice and of her looks, which were inexpressibly soothing to him now, would not have been sufficient to allay the torments of self-reproach under different circumstances. They might even have awakened it more keenly than indifference. During the last few days he had reviewed the past with the most intense contrition, and, though he had resigned himself to live as a just expiation and a continual atonement, death was to him the highest boon that could have been granted to his weary and repentant spirit. He distrusted his own strength for the long journey of life, and blessed the merciful God that was withdrawing him from its snares and its perils.

He was capable of an heroic action, and it had been given to him to perform it. In deep humility he felt, " Lord, now let thy servant depart in peace," for the peace of the absolved, of the pardoned, was his. The faith which had never been effaced from his soul was now again as bright and fervent as ever. His mind—long stored with images of beauty and dreams of harmony—readily turned to the vision of Heaven. He sent for Adrien, and gazed upon him with an unutterable expression, which was answered by these words, " But for you, dear friend, my earthly task would be over; you leave me to labour, and are going home early." A change came over his face, and detaining him by the hand he called Gertrude, who had withdrawn when Adrien came in. They never stayed with him together, but while one was watching him the other knelt in the next room. But now, he wished them both to remain. He made her stand on one side of the bed, and him on the other, and gave a hand to each. Then he fixed his eyes upon her and said,

" Once more say that you forgive me, Gertrude."

She bent over him and answered, " Rather forgive *me*, my husband. O Maurice, God once gave you back to my prayers ——"

" Ay," he exclaimed, " and priceless was the boon *then* of the life restored, and lent for a few days. To die *then*, my beloved, would have been a deserved but a sad fate; whereas *now, here, thus*, my wife, my friend, it is a blessing as great as his mercy —— Hush, do not interrupt me now. The time is short, and I have something to say to you both. First, dearest Gertrude, tell her whom I loved before, and only less than you, that in my dying hour I have blessed her. That here, round my neck, I have always worn the little medal which she placed there the first time that we parted. Tell her that through all my sins and my sufferings, I have never omitted to say every day the short prayer she then gave me Take it, Gertrude, and let Mary have it. And now listen both of you, to my last words, my last wish, my last request There is a thought that would give me inexpressible consola tion in these my last moments. Adrien! Gertrude! I have stood between you and happiness during my life. O let it not be so after my death. Give me your hands—let me join them together—let me feel that you will both be happy when I am dead, that the memory of all I have made you suffer will only unite you more closely to each other, and that thoughts of tenderness and pity for one who sinned against you so deeply will be mixed with every recollection of the past."

"Do you think I could ever feel anything but love and gratitude for you, Maurice?" she murmured almost inaudibly, and Adrien grasped more tightly the hand he was holding.

Maurice made a faint attempt to unite theirs, and articulated with effort, but with an imploring expression, "Promise me that you will marry." She shook her head, and passed her arm round his neck. "For my peace, for my sake," he ejaculated; simultaneously she and Adrien joined their hands for one instant, and then bent over him in speechless emotion, for life was ebbing fast, and death approaching. A look of repose settled on his face, a faint smile played on his lips, and his spirit passed away. Adrien and Gertrude repeated the "De Profundis" before they rose from their knees, and then separated, only once to meet again,—by the side of Maurice's grave in the cemetery of New York. There they parted, with silent blessings and a mute farewell, their tears falling less in sorrow for the dead or their own parting, than in memory of the past, with its buried affections and its chastened griefs. From that spot where for the last time they knelt together each went on his way,

"With heart subdued, but courage high."

On her arrival at New York Gertrude had sought an abode in a convent, where for a short time she remained, and from thence wrote to Mary Grey, sending her Maurice's medal, and briefly stating the circumstances of his death, and her own intention to devote the rest of her life to the service of God, in whatever way it would seem His will to lead her.

In the first days of her widowhood she had entertained the hope that the religious life might be the lot that He had appointed her, but another duty, another consolation, a great and unexpected blessing was granted to one who felt alone in the world, and to whom it seemed as a token of forgiveness, and a direct gift from Heaven. A few months elapsed and Gertrude had a child. She loved it with all the tenderness which she had so long refused to its father; and when in her infant's face she saw again the eyes that had been so often bent upon her with unrequited affection, its tears fell fast on the little cheek that was closely pressed to her own.

She did not write to her own family, but Edgar Lifford, as soon as the news of her husband's death and afterwards of her son's birth had reach him, sent letters which, although couched in his usual formal style, were full of kindness and good feeling. He inquired after her worldly circumstances, and made her offers of assistance: she wanted but little, and that only for her child; poverty was her choice, and labour her happiness. Amongst the poor Irish who are continually landing in America she found every kind of suffering to alleviate, of sorrow to console. It was her delight to watch for the arrival of the emigrant ships, and to give a welcome to the lonely heart, a helping hand to the helpless. Children who had lost their parents during the passage, widows who had seen their husbands die in their arms, the girl who had sinned and longed to repent, the father who had babes, and no wife to care for them,—found a friend in the pale woman in deep mourning who never turned away from their tale of woe, —and who with her child in her arms, and later in her hand, knew the road to their poor homes, and the way to their warm hearts. She was known in that foreign land by her old familiar name, and it became a byword of love in the mouths of the poor.

It was little Maurice that had taught it them. One day that he had brought in childish glee a "Lady-bird" home, he wondered at the tears that started in her eyes, even though she smiled at the same time. But she whispered, "That was mother's name once," and he lisped it often afterwards, and others learnt it of him. The sufferers in the hospitals asked for her. The poor in their hovels welcomed her. The children hung on the skirts of her black faded dress, and all who knew her face with its beauty, and her voice with its melody, and her smile with its sweetness, would murmur as she passed along the crowded streets on her errands of mercy. "Heaven bless that fair Lady-Bird, who goes about doing good."

Some years elapsed, and then one day Gertrude received from her brother the following letter:

"My dear Gertrude,—At last, after our long travels, we have returned to Lifford Grange, and I grieve to tell you that my father's health is in a very unsatisfactory state. He is much altered in every way.—both in body and mind. His memory is much impaired; at least it is so in many respects, though in one instance alone it seems more lively than it was. I had imagined, my dear sister, that he had entirely forgotten you, for until quite lately he never made any allusion to you, or seemed to recollect your existence. But since we have returned to this place he has often spoken of you. He does not know that I am writing, but I have been consulting with Mr. Erving, and we both think that if you could come to England, he would see you, and that it might work in him a favourable change.

"Indeed, my dear sister, he is in a very sad state. The extraordinary part of it is, that he seems to think himself—somehow or other—to blame about our poor mother's death. It is a nervous fancy, but it preys much on his mind. He has chosen now to occupy the apartment in which she lived, and can seldom be persuaded to leave it, and when he does go out it is not beyond the park. I hear from Mary Grey that you have no intention of becoming a nun, though you lead the life of a Sister of Charity. There are good works to be done everywhere, and a very good one here, I am convinced. I wish I could write to you a persuasive letter, but it is not in my line. You would hardly know your father again,—his hair is quite white,—no one would think he was only fifty years old.

"I am afraid you will not understand from this letter how much I wish you to come. I cannot be quite certain that my father will receive you, or that he will be willing to see your little boy, but Mrs. Redmond can give you a room at the cottage, if he does not invite you to remain here. I think very differently about many things from what I used to do. Perhaps it is the same with you, and that we may be surprised to find how much better we agree than formerly. I often go to Mrs. Redmond's cottage, and talk about you with Mary Grey. Pray write soon at all events, and believe me, your affectionate brother,

"Edgar."

Gertrude sat an instant absorbed in thought. It was a great emotion that was stirring her heart. Old thoughts, old places, the faint shadows of long departed dreams, the names of her father, her brother, Mary, Lifford Grange, and Stonehouseleigh, the living and the dead all rose before her, and for an instant her bosom heaved, and the old troubled look passed through the depths of her eyes. She could not be glad to go home. For her the familiar scenes which exiles have sighed for, as a thirsty man longs for a cup of cold water, had no soothing charm. Hers were not griefs which could enter into the feeling of tenderness, "*pour ce bon vieux temps où j'étais si malheureuse.*" Old things had passed away.—new and blessed ones had arisen; and she loved the New World, where her child was born, where she had begun a life of virtue and of peace; but there hung too deep shadows on the path she had trodden—there was something too awful in her recollections of what she had once felt and had been—to allow of the fond and softening enjoyments of sympathetic association. But she was not the less grateful that her brother had sent for her; she did not the less readily prepare to go to that father, whose character she understood better than formerly, perhaps through the continual and deep examination she had made of her own.

* * * * * * * * *

The room which for so many years his wife had occupied, Mr. Lifford now inhabited. There was not a single thing removed, or altered in it, since the day of her death. He was an old man in appearance, though not in reality,—not more amiable in manner, but yet very different from what he used to be. There is a great power in the words of a dying person; the heart must be hopelessly hardened that can withstand *truth* when uttered at such a time.

Mr. Lifford had been a self-deceiver from his youth upwards. He had shut out the voice of conscience with the same strength of volition with which he had resisted every will but his own. Father Lifford had spoken to him on his death-bed some of those words that *cannot* be shut out. He kept them at bay for a long while; but in a dangerous illness he had had abroad, and in the protracted weakness that followed it, they pursued him incessantly, and obliged him to hearken. But it was terror not repentance, remorse not penitence that overcame him; his wife's last gasping sigh,—his daughter's look when he approached her that day, were ever present before him. Did Gertrude think he had killed her mother by that scene which had been fatal to her? This was the question he was perpetually asking himself; and his memory became confused, and he felt as if that stern and beautiful face which he had never looked on with pleasure, and which he now longed to behold again, was haunting him continually, and would haunt him to all eternity with its silent reproaches.

When he returned to Lifford Grange, the impression became stronger than ever. He shut himself up in what had been his wife's apartment, and refused to see any one. Once Mr. Erving was admitted to him, and probed the wounds which had so long been concealed by an icy surface. He did not measure their depth, but guessed they were profound. Mr. Lifford had long neglected all religious duties, and he now apparently gave himself up to a settled despair. Nothing roused him from this sullen dejection and silent apathy, except accidentally awakened recollections of the death-bed of his wife. He seemed to have forgotten everything about Gertrude's marriage, her widowhood, and the birth of her child; or at least he never alluded to these facts; but, as Edgar had said, named her sometimes, but as if he was speaking of somebody who was dead. Why he chose to live in his wife's rooms, nobody could understand, except those who know that remorse has sometimes the same instincts as affection. It was then that his son wrote to Gertrude, and counted the days till he received her answer.

She came on a summer evening back to the home of her youth, after years of absence. She came to it as people in a dream arrive in well-known places, and without surprise find everything different and yet nothing altered. Edgar had met her at the station, and in his heavy and calm features an appearance of emotion was perceptible. He took her child in his arms and kissed him. There was another person also waiting at the station, whose long-disciplined heart was beating less calmly than usual, as she caught sight of Gertrude and her child; and, falling on her knees, threw her arms round the boy. "O Maurice!" was all she said; but when he asked in childish surprise, "Are you another mother?" she whispered "No, I am only Mary;" but she felt, and he seemed also to feel that his own mother did not love him more than Mary. He was consigned to her care, while the long-parted brother and sister drove away together along the well-known lanes, towards that house she had hated and fled from.

They spoke but little till they reached its gate. The womar at the lodge courtesied to her, and the rooks made their accustomed noise in the branches over-head, as they drove through the avenue. "Gertrude," he suddenly said, "his mind is not right; he talks very strangely at times about you and my mother. We think you had better go to him at once. Have you the courage to do so?—He might be angry."

"I braved his anger too often in my wilfulness," she replied, "to shrink from it now, when I would give my life to comfort him."

For one moment she looked about her with a bewildered feeling as she entered the house. There was the same look, the same sound of the great clock, the same indefinable smell, the same sensation she knew so well. Was she dreaming of being Gertrude Lifford returning to Lifford Grange, or had the last years been a long dream compressed in the second of time between sleeping and waking? The old butler came up to her; she seized his hand, and then the floodgates were let loose for a moment. She gave a kind of cry, but soon was quite calm again. "Now," she said to Edgar, "now at once; let me go to him, but be near us in case he should be too much agitated."

She walked through the narrow passage out of the hall, and up to the door of the room where he was,—that room with the pictures, the crucifix, and the couch! She knocked, and then went in. He looked up—what would she have done if he had not opened his arms, and cried "Gertrude!" she knew not, but he did so; and for the first time in their lives the father's and the daughter's lips met in one long embrace. "Gertrude," he whispered tremulously without letting her go —"Gertrude, I wanted you." He did not ask any questions; he spoke not of the past; perhaps he felt sufficiently absolved by that embrace from his worst fears. He did not show her any tenderness; it was not in his nature; but both felt that henceforward she was to be the only possible comfort of that cold and silent man, who sighed when she went away, but did not ask her to remain. He hated the thought of the marriage she had made as much as ever, and could not bring himself to speak of her child; but he was restless the next day till she returned, and her daily visits became to him what music is to the blind, or repose to the weary.

She took up her residence in Mrs. Redmond's cottage, and occupied what used to be Maurice's room. Every day she left that little cheerful abode, which was as full as ever of flowers and of sunshine, and where her boy played with her under the old tree, or sat on Mary's knee, listening to nursery tales; and through that same path which she had once trod in misery and despair, she walked to the gate of the Grange, and up the long avenue of yews, to the well known room where her father always sat, and spent some hours with him. She used to bring her work, and sit opposite to him while he wrote; and sometimes she read out loud, or walked with him on the terrace. He never appeared so tranquil as when she was present.

This strange mode of life was a trial to one whose character, although disciplined and exalted, was eager and enthusiastic still, and had been used to spend its fervour in toils and pursuits which were less hardships than enjoyments; but she had now but one object, one guiding principle, and duty had become the passion of her soul. The forms which memory recalled, the images of the dead and of the past which haunted those scenes, only strengthened her resolutions and confirmed her patience. It had its reward, though it seemed long deferred.

One day that she was reading to him the French newspaper, which he had taken in for years, and the sight of which had turned her pale the first time it met her sight, she came to an account of the martyrdom of some of the Jesuit missionaries in China, and of the hair-breadth escape of others, who were still labouring in the same regions. Her eye glanced down the page, and faltered a little. "Why do you stop?" her father asked, and, subduing her emotion, she went on to read the following sentence:—

"*L'un de ces généreux apôtres, qui ont échappé presque par miracle à une mort effroyable, portait autrefois dans le monde un nom assez célèbre. Le Comte, maintenant le Père d'Arberg, dont les écrits ont si puissamment contribué au réveil religieux de la France, brave le trépas dans les contrées où son zèle l'a conduit, et la voix que jadis nous avons connue et admirée, annonce l'Évangile aux enfants de l'Asie.*"*

Mr. Lifford looked at his daughter, and her eyes met his.

---

* Amongst the generous missionaries who thus narrowly escaped the horrors of a lingering death was the Father, once the Count, d'Arberg, whose works so powerfully contributed to the religious reaction in France. He is braving the danger of martyrdom in the remote countries where his zeal has led him; and the voice we knew so well and admired so much is preaching the Gospel to the children of Asia.

Another father and daughter might perhaps have spoken then, and a reciprocal pardon been sought and obtained; but this was not in their characters. She glanced once at the picture that hung near the couch, then at the crucifix that stood at its foot, and proceeded to read the " Foreign Intelligence," a literary review, and whatever else the newspaper contained. Yet in that short instant much had passed in the minds of both, and a tacit understanding arrived at between them. They knew from that day forward that not one shade of resentment existed in either, and that the silence they maintained was not that of indifference.

A short time afterwards Mr. Lifford sent for his grandson, and Gertrude soon removed to his house not to leave it again. The sight of that child was doubtless a trial to the repentant but not yet altered man. Men's prejudices may be overcome to a certain degree, but, especially at that age, not altogether removed. The boy had the run of that large house and those wide solemn gardens, and filled them with childish glee and laughter. He was a great favourite with his uncle, who instructed him in languages and natural history, and had visions of a change of name for him hereafter, which honour his mother never meant to consent to; but into the terrace-rooms, as they were called, he seldom went, but used now and then, from the corner of the walk, to peep at his grandfather's stately form and melancholy face—wondering in his childish cogitations if he were doing penance in that room; and he guessed rightly.

It was a long and bitter penance, and it bore fruit in the end. That room and his daughter,—its aspect and her presence—wrought a final change in him, and grace found its way to his soul. The sources of past and recent sufferings became, as it were, sacraments of reconciliation and symbols of pardon. He made his peace with God, and returned to his religious duties. He atoned for past neglect by many kind and charitable actions; and the curse of a hardened heart and an unforgiving spirit passed away from him for ever.

With duties showered on her path; with a father to console, a child to cherish, and a brother to love; with the *poor* (that inexhaustible mine of bliss to those who have once worked it) to serve, Gertrude was happy with a subdued and quiet happiness. In repentance, in affection, in admiration, they all gathered around her and called her blessed. Those who, like Lady Clara Audley, knew the history of her life, wondered at her cheerfulness, and others, who did not, sometimes thought they saw

"A story in her face,"

especially on the day when Mary Grey accomplished the desire of her heart and became a Sister of Mercy, giving henceforward to Jesus, in his suffering ones, that deep store of love which had once been lavished on one only of his creatures. In the words of the American poet,

"Other hope had she none, nor wish in life but to follow,
Meekly, with reverent steps, the sacred feet of her Saviour;
Patience and abnegation of self, and devotion to others,
This was the lesson a life of trial and sorrow had taught her."

She in her holy vocation, and Adrien d'Arberg—in the first instance in a foreign land, and then in his own country—labouring with one end, living but for one object, expending all the best powers of intellect, all the rich treasures of the heart with which Heaven had endowed him in the furtherance of God's kingdom upon earth, were both happy indeed, with the happiness of angels—happier than earth's most happy children. Who could doubt it? Who would pity them, who do not pity Elias in his exile, John the Baptist in the desert, or the widow of fourscore, who departed not from the temple day or night?

"O there are various paths and ways, the rough ones and the sweet,
Through which God's guiding hand conducts his children's wandering feet.
Thorns are in all, but some have few to tread down as they go,
And every tree and bush they pass its blossoms o'er them throw;
The bleeding feet, the aching brow, the desert's scorching air,
The tempter's voice, the inward strife, of others are the share.
Which are most blest? We dare not say; He has a work for each,
An aim, a purpose, and an end, that to his feet will reach."

Lady Clara Audley and Mr. Lifford met again. The wound, which had so long remained open, was closed at last, and to forgive *her*—the first and the only person he had really loved—was one of the results of the change which sorrow, remorse, and the influence of his children had gradually wrought upon him. It was not without agitation, however, that he beheld her again the first time she drove up to that house where he had once hoped to bring her as a bride; and it was with a strange mixture of pain and emotion that he looked at her, as she stood on the terrace by the side of his daughter, and that he heard the sound of that laugh which had once awoke in his breast such alternations of joy and despair.

As he gazed on her still radiant beauty, he could hardly believe that they had indeed been young together, that not many more years had passed over his head than over hers. Time, which had laid so heavy a hand upon him, had dealt very mercifully with her; and he could now reflect without bitterness, and even acknowledge with gratitude, that it had been better for both of them to part as they had done, than to have lived, she to suffer at his hands, and he to see her beautiful face shaded by sorrow or hardening into indifference. He knew himself now well enough to rejoice that she at least had escaped the blighting influence of his remorseless tyranny, that at least that fair flower had been spared the withering touch of his hand.

Lady Clara did not muse so pensively, or meditate so deeply upon the past, on her first visit to Lifford Grange; but, weary as she was growing of the same round of amusements, the same society, however agreeable, and the endless source of varied and yet monotonous amusements in which her days were spent, she found it pleasant to add a new interest to those which were beginning to pall upon her, and soon became as fond of Lady-Bird as at the time of their first acquaintance. She learnt from her some valuable secrets about killing time in a better manner than she had hitherto practised, of turning her love of giving pleasure into that of promoting happiness, and expanding her taste for the beautiful into a higher development of the same faculty in more exalted directions. Their intercourse was productive of mutual improvements. At Lady Clara's suggestion, new beds of flowers ornamented the gardens of the Grange; clear water flowed through its ruined fountains; clematis adorned the porch of its schools, and China roses clustered on the walls of its almshouses; but, on the other hand, in her home and in the neighbourhood, amidst the profusion of ornament and the luxury of refinement, seeds of usefulness were sown that produced blossoms in time, and fruit in the end.

Two years after Gertrude's arrival at Lifford Grange, Edgar met at Audley Park a young girl for whom he conceived an attachment, and who reciprocated his affection. She was of a good but not an ancient family; he feared to ask his fa ther's consent to their marriage, and Gertrude felt that to be ground on which she did not venture to tread. But Lady Clara asked for an interview with the man who had once so much loved her, and pleaded the cause of the young people. She tried to smile as she did so, but there was something in his face and manner that checked that smile. She thought he was about abruptly to refuse his consent, but he looked at her steadily, and pointing to his wife's picture and to his daughter's, which had been restored to its place, he said in a slow impressive manner—

"You speak to one whose *Pride* was *their misery*. Send Edgar to me at once: does he think I still worship the idol that destroyed them?"

When Gertrude threw her arms round his neck and thanked him for the consent he had given to her brother's marriage, he held her at a distance from him for an instant, and gazed at her with an indescribable expression. "Do you think I am *not* happy?" she asked with one of those smiles which leave no doubt as to the source from whence they spring,—a heart full of the peace and joy which the world cannot give nor the world take away. Then he pressed her to his heart, and gave her one of those blessings which, though uttered by human lips, seem to descend straight from Heaven; and since that time there have been flowers in the gardens, and happiness within the walls of the old house of Lifford Grange.

THE END.

God our Father, Notices of the Press.

"GOD OUR FATHER is an interesting work, written in a simple but forcible style, setting forth the infinite mercy of God, and calming the souls of all those who morbidly dwell upon the severity of His justice in the punishment of unrepentant sinners. It also teaches how peace of conscience can be obtained, and how bodily suffering can be endured with patience. The practical illustrations are very happy, and the essay may be read with profit by persons of all denominations." *Philadelphia Public Ledger.*

"It is in particular adapted to those pious souls in whom, from a wrong view of God, spite all their wishes, fear of Him takes the place of love." *N. Y. Tablet.*

"Rarely have we taken up a book of devotion which gave us so much pleasure. There are in the world many persons, pious and moral withal, whose souls are continually overspread with gloom and despondency — whom doubts and anxieties as to their spiritual condition forever perplex and harass — and with whom the fear and not the love of God is the incentive to piety. It was to bring peace and solace to such souls, to remove their dread forebodings, to enforce the great and consoling truth that God is our Redeemer and Father, and to beget confidence in His infinite mercy and compassion, that this beautiful and useful book was written." *Wilmington (Del.) Gazette.*

"The aim of the author in this work has been the amplification of the Divine attribute of mercy, by giving prominence to the consideration of the Deity in the paternal relation to mankind. God, the Father, ready to receive and forgive sinners, is one of the most beautiful ideas of the Christian faith, and our author has been fully impressed with the beauty of his subject, and nothing can more tenderly appeal to the religious element of our natures than the impressive and loving manner in which he has presented this view of the Almighty Power. No more practical and available means of awakening the mind to the importance of religion can be suggested than in thus appealing to the finer qualities of our nature, and the pleasing manner in which this idea is carried out by the author renders the book one of great value to the anxious seeker after religious truths." *Philadelphia Inquirer.*

"The book is adapted to every class of readers, and of every creed, there being nothing sectarian about it. The Presbyterian, the Episcopalian, the Methodist, and the Catholic, can read it with equal appreciation and benefit. The same qualities of style which gave such grace and unction to the 'Happiness of Heaven' appear in this little volume. The scholar will be delighted with its perusal, while the unlettered can draw comfort and consolation from its pages — so cultured and, at the same time, so simple and luminous is the character of the language used. The author is particularly fertile and felicitous in his illustrations. They are always pertinent, explanatory and convincing." *Every Evening (Wilmington, Del.).*

"We bid GOD OUR FATHER a hearty welcome, and wish we could introduce it to every Catholic family. There are too many Christians, who, though they may be constantly living in the state of grace, still do not find any relish in their religious practices, because they take a wrong view of God. This book, if read by them, will pour a new light upon their path; it will be to them like the sunny spring, chasing away past chill and gloom, and not only cheering life, but also invigorating spiritual growth." *Sunday-School Messenger (Chicago).*

Murphy & Co., Publishers and Booksellers, Baltimore.

Moral and Instructive Tales.

HENDRIK CONSCIENCE'S SHORT TALES,
CHEAP AND UNIFORM EDITION,

In 12 vols. demi 8o. cloth, $1; cloth, gilt sides and edges, $1.25. The complete set, in boxes, 12 vols., cloth, $12; cloth, gilt sides and edges, $15.

The Publishers desire to invite especial attention to this NEW, CHEAP and UNIFORM EDITION of the SHORT TALES of M. HENDRIK CONSCIENCE, the distinguished Flemish Novelist. PONTMARTIN, the acute French Critic and Reviewer, has likened the Stories of Conscience, to "pearls set in Flemish gold," and in point of delicacy of treatment and high moral value, they richly justify the comparison.

There is a pure morality throughout the works of this author, happily blending Entertainment with Instruction, and *unmarred by Controversy*, which makes them peculiarly fitted for the perusal of the young.

1. *The Poor Gentleman.*
2. *The Conscript and Blind Rosa,*
   Two Tales in one volume.
3. *Happiness of Being Rich.*
4. *The Miser.*
5. *Ricketicketack and Wooden Clara,*
   Two Tales in one volume.
6. *Count Hugo of Craenhove.*
7. *The Curse of the Village.*
8. *The Village Innkeeper.*
   (Published in 1874.)
9. *The Fisherman's Daughter.*
10. *The Amulet.*
    (Just Published.)
11. *The Young Doctor.*
12. *Ludovic and Gertrude.*

MURPHY & Co. *Publishers & Booksellers, Baltimore.*

Happiness of Heaven, Notices of the Press.

"The book is certainly written by a man of learning, who instructs by the force of his reasoning, and charms by the elegance of his style; but its value is enhanced by the tender, genuine kindness that speaks from every page. The author feels what he says, and the words of consolation, sympathy and encouragement that fall so naturally from his pen, come from a heart filled with a sincere and earnest love for his fellow men." *Philadelphia Age.*

"We might, perhaps, appropriately designate this work as the Popular Theology of Heaven.' *Theology*, because it is strictly accurate in its dogmatic teaching; *Popular*, because the subject, without being lowered, is brought within the sphere of the popular mind. We might call it also the 'Spiritual Geography of Heaven,' since it gives us such a knowledge as we can have at this distance of the promised land, which we must hope one day to inhabit." *Catholic World.*

"This is a good Catholic book. The style is easy, graceful and flowing..... Isaac Taylor's 'Physical Theory of another Life' is a more ambitious book, and deals in more gorgeous speculations, but we doubt if, on the whole, it produces a more salutary impression on the heart of the Christian reader." *Southern Review, St. Louis, Mo.*

"There is not a single dull and uninteresting page in the book, and the logical reasoning and theological accuracy that pervade it, are rendered clear and distinct to the comprehension of every reader by the simplicity and force of the comparisons and illustrations interspersed throughout." *Philadelphia Telegraph.*

"This is a strictly religious book, and one that will be read with thrills of joy by devotional people. Probably it ought to be read by everybody, for, in picturing the happiness of heaven, the learned author has endeavored to contribute to the happiness of earth." *Missouri Republican.*

"In the chapter on the 'Social Joys of Heaven,' the author reveals a knowledge of, and sympathy with, the tenderest and truest chords of our nature; the doctrine of the recognition and enjoyment of our loved ones in heaven is accepted the more gratefully, as it accords with the natural instincts of the heart." *N. Y. Irish American.*

"The HAPPINESS OF HEAVEN is an excellent book, and its perusal cannot fail detaching our souls from the affections of this world, making us patient in trials, and impatient to reach heaven." *Boston Pilot.*

"The style is pure and graceful, reminding one, by its easy flow, of Irving or Goldsmith. * * * The book should be a *vade mecum* with every Protestant as well as Catholic. No doctrinal points are touched upon. It is not controversial, but appeals to the piously disposed of every creed and denomination." *Wilmington (Del.) Gazette.*

"The chapters on the Beatific Vision, the Beauty and Glory of the Risen Body, Social Joys in Heaven, the Special Glory awarded to different kinds of sanctity, are particularly fine." *Catholic Record.*

"It is one of the most charming books we have ever read, and though religious in its character, and severe in its logic and theology, yet so interspersed is it throughout with beautiful, simple and effective parables and illustrations, and so easy and flowing in its style, that even the reader who has seldom or never dipped before into literature of this kind, will be delighted with its perusal." *Wilmington (Del.) Advertiser.*

Murphy & Co., Publishers and Booksellers, Baltimore.

Murphy & Co's New and Recent Publications.

GOD OUR FATHER.

By the Author of Happiness of Heaven.

SECOND REVISED EDITION.

GOD OUR FATHER comes from a pen which is now regarded as one of the most interesting, as well as the most learned among modern Catholic writers; and the delight with which the Author's former volume was received by readers of all classes, is a sufficient warrant for the confidence we feel, that GOD OUR FATHER will be welcomed with equal favor. It is intended as a companion volume to its predecessor, and is uniform with it in every respect.

Extracts from Notices of the Press.

"After reading this little book, we felt an ardent desire to tell everybody we had found a treasure. Its title, a rather unusual thing now-a-days, is the true exponent of its contents. That God is our Father — our kind, indulgent, beneficent, merciful, loving Father — it proves as we have never seen proved before. We do think if Voltaire had seen this little treatise, he would not have called God a 'tyrant, and the father of tyrants,' and he, Voltaire, would not have been a fool, and the father of a generation of fools. Some Christians, other than Calvinists, are accustomed to regard God as a stern judge, or an exacting master, ignoring altogether his parental relationship. This way of regarding God not unfrequently produces a morbid spirituality, if not worse. Under its baneful influence, the soul is parched up and rendered incapable of any other sentiment than that of fear. It is true that 'fear is the beginning of wisdom;' but it is no less true that 'love is the fulfilment of the law,' and the sublime summary of the new dispensation. And who can love a being whom he sees only in the light of a stern judge, an exacting master? God, as he is represented in this work, is a being whom you cannot but love. In very truth, the author himself must love much, or he could never write so eloquently of divine love.

"To all Catholics, who look with a filial confidence to God, and love him as their Father, we recommend this book as a means of strengthening their confidence, and increasing their love. To those Catholics, happily few, who see in God only a rigid master, we prescribe the perusal of this work as the best remedy for their dangerous disease. To our separated brethren, who want to get a Christian idea of our common Father, we would respectfully suggest the careful study of this treatise; they will find it sufficiently scriptural, and sufficiently simple for their tastes.

"We cannot, perhaps, pay the publishers a higher compliment than by saying that the setting is in every way worthy of the gem."
Catholic World.

"GOD OUR FATHER is especially suited to the generation of young Catholics which is now growing up. It is written in an easy and graceful style." *Catholic Guardian (California).*

Murphy & Co., Publishers and Booksellers, Baltimore.

Murphy & Co's New and Recent Publications.

Books for the Devotion to the Sacred Heart of Jesus, and the Apostleship of Prayer.

New and Seasonable Books on the Sacred Heart of Jesus.

THE PARADISE OF GOD, or, The Virtues of the Sacred Heart of Jesus. By A Father of the Society of Jesus. Cloth, $1; cl. gt., $1.50.

Uniform with *God Our Father*, and *Happiness of Heaven*.

Just at this time, when so many of our Most Reverend and Right Reverend Prelates are consecrating their Dioceses to the Sacred Heart, and urging upon the faithful the importance and advantages of the beautiful and consoling devotion, which seems to have been given to the Church in our day, as a most powerful weapon of defence against the dangers which beset her; the publication of this work cannot but be most welcome to Catholic readers. They will find in these pages a fervor and an unction which will remind them, more than once, of good Father Faber; and they will draw from them the most solid, as well as the plainest and most practical lessons of devotion to the Sacred Heart. The work was printed by chapters, in the "Messenger of the Sacred Heart," and the praises bestowed on it by readers of every class, have induced us to hope that its publication in a more permanent form will be gratifying to the Catholic Public, and make the book more generally beneficial.

DEVOTION TO THE SACRED HEART OF JESUS. By S. Franco, S. J. Cloth, $1; cl. gt. $1.50.

This is the Second and much Improved Edition of an excellent and complete treatise on the subject; at once doctrinal and practical, and full of unction. Uniform with "Paradise of God," &c.

THE APOSTLESHIP OF PRAYER. By Rev. H. Ramiere, S. J. From the French. Cloth, $1.50.

This is a Work of unusual merit, on the excellence and power of prayer; it gives a very full and clear explanation of the Apostleship, and shows how it can be practically introduced and carried on in Parishes, Communities, Seminaries, Colleges, &c.

THE MANUAL OF THE APOSTLESHIP OF PRAYER. An abridgment of the above. 35 cents.

The Apostleship of Prayer Association. Explanation and Practical Instruction by Fr. Ramiere, S.J. Per 100, $3 net.

Tickets of Admission to the Apostleship of Prayer. Per 100, 50 cts.; in lots of 500, $1.50; 1000, $2.50 net.

The Messenger of the Sacred Heart of Jesus. A Bulletin of the Apostleship of Prayer, is published Monthly for the Proprietors. Subscription price, $2 per annum, in advance.

Rosary of the Apostleship, changed monthly. Price, per dozen, 45 cts.; per 100, $3 net.

Scapular Prints of the Sacred Heart. Per 100, 30 cents net.

Murphy & Co., Publishers and Booksellers, Baltimore.

MURPHY & CO'S New and Recent Publications.

THE HAPPINESS OF HEAVEN.

By a Father of the Society of Jesus.

Fifth Revised Edition, cap 8o. *tinted paper*, $1; *cloth, gilt*, $1.50.

☞ The sale of nearly 10,000 copies in two years, and the constantly increasing demand, the praises bestowed by the Press — both Catholic and non-Catholic — are gratifying evidences of the real merits of this charming volume.

That the reader may judge of the character of this charming volume, we submit the TABLE OF CONTENTS:

1. The Beatific Vision. — 2. In the Beatific Vision, "We shall be like Him, because we shall see Him as He is." — 3. In the Beatific Vision, our Intellect is glorified, and our Thirst for Knowledge completely gratified. — 4. In the Beatific Vision, our Will is also to be glorified, and then we shall be happy in loving and being loved. — 5. The Beauty and Glory of the Risen Body. — 6. The Spirituality of the Risen Body. — 7. The Impassibility and Immortality of the Risen Body. — 8. Several Errors to be avoided in our Meditations on Heaven. — 9. The Life of the Blessed in Heaven. — 10. Pleasures of the Glorified Senses. — 11. Social joys of Heaven. — 12. Will the knowledge that some of our own are lost, mar our happiness in Heaven? — 13. The Light of Glory. — 14. Degrees of Happiness in Heaven. — 15. Degrees of Enjoyment through the Glorified Senses. — 16. The Glory of Jesus and Mary. — 17. The Glory of the Martyrs. — 18. The Glory of the Doctors and Confessors. — 19. The Glory of Virgins and Religious. — 20. Glory of Penitents and Pious People. — 21. Eternity of Heaven's Happiness.

Extracts from Notices of the Press.

"This volume will please the pious and the learned. It will satisfy, at the same time, the exactions of literary critics and the wishes of the most fastidious theologians; the former by its accurate and flowing style, and the latter by the solidity of its theological foundations — continually underlying the treatise, though rarely set forward. This is one of the volumes that can be unqualifiedly commended."
N. Y. Freeman's Journal.

"It draws out, in successive chapters, what can be known about the Beatific Vision, the perfection of the intellect and will, the properties of glorified bodies, and social joys of heaven. The book deserves all praise."
London Monthly.

"Many will, perhaps, be astonished to learn that the happiness of the Saints does not consist in being eternally on their knees before the throne of God, and in profound adoration of the Divine Majesty, or in being so overpowered by the vision of God as to be changed into motionless statues for eternity. This is the whole idea of heaven in many a pious mind. The author does away with all these incorrect and vague notions which float in the popular mind. He maintains that the sight of God, far from interfering with the activities of our nature, perfects every one of them, and that all, without exception, have suitable or appropriate objects to act upon, and that it is, moreover, precisely in such action that the happiness of heaven consists."
Philadelphia Catholic Standard.

Murphy & Co., Publishers and Booksellers, Baltimore.

www.ingramcontent.com/pod-product-compliance
Lightning Source LLC
Chambersburg PA
CBHW021150230426
43667CB00006B/338